The United States and the Japanese Student Movement, 1948–1973

The United States and the Japanese Student Movement, 1948–1973

Managing a Free World

Naoko Koda

LEXINGTON BOOKS
Lanham • Boulder • New York • London

Published by Lexington Books
An imprint of The Rowman & Littlefield Publishing Group, Inc.
4501 Forbes Boulevard, Suite 200, Lanham, Maryland 20706
www.rowman.com

6 Tinworth Street, London SE11 5AL, United Kingdom

Copyright © 2020 The Rowman & Littlefield Publishing Group, Inc.

All rights reserved. No part of this book may be reproduced in any form or by any electronic or mechanical means, including information storage and retrieval systems, without written permission from the publisher, except by a reviewer who may quote passages in a review.

British Library Cataloguing in Publication Information Available

Library of Congress Cataloging-in-Publication Data

Names: Koda, Naoko, 1983– author.
Title: The United States and the Japanese student movement, 1948–1973 : managing a free world / Naoko Koda.
Description: Lanham, Maryland : Lexington Books, [2020] | Includes bibliographical references and index. | Summary: "The author argues that interactions between the movement and US Cold Warriors had a profound and lasting impact on Japanese society and Japan-US relations" —Provided by publisher.
Identifiers: LCCN 2020025905 (print) | LCCN 2020025906 (ebook) | ISBN 9781498583411 (cloth ; alk. paper) | ISBN 9781498583428 (epub) ISBN 9781498583435 (pbk ; alk. paper)
Subjects: LCSH: Student movements—Japan—History—20th century. | United States—Foreign relations—Japan. | Japan—Foreign relations—United States. | Zen Nihon Gakusei Jichikai Sōrengō—History. | College students—Political activity—Japan. | Radicalism—Japan—History—20th century. | Protest movements—Japan—History—20th century. | Anti-communist movements—United States—History—20th century. | Anti-communist movements—Japan—History—20th century. | Cold War—Political aspects—Japan.
Classification: LCC LA1318.7 K63 2020 (print) | LCC LA1318.7 (ebook) | DDC 371.8/1—dc23
LC record available at https://lccn.loc.gov/2020025905

Contents

Acknowledgments	vii
Abbreviations	ix
Note on Text	xiii
Introduction	1
1 The Occupation of Japan and the Unfinished Revolution	13
2 Defenders of Democracies	33
3 Clashing Concepts of National Security and the Beginning of the *Anpo* Struggle	65
4 The *Anpo*	101
5 The Reischauer Offensive: Promoting a Different Kind of Past	139
6 Robert Kennedy and Zengakuren: Seeking a Newer World	165
7 Protesting across Borders: The Vietnam War and the Global 1968	187
Conclusion	231
Appendix	239
Bibliography	241
Index	251
About the Author	259

Acknowledgments

Over the years, mentors, colleagues, friends, and family have encouraged me through this project. First, I want to thank my adviser, the late Professor Marilyn B. Young, for her continuous encouragement, support, and advice in all aspects of this project. She passed away in February 2017 before this book was completed. It is impossible to convey how much I have learned from her throughout my graduate program at New York University. When I think of her, what comes to my mind first are the many conversations we had on a bench in Washington Square Park, at her favorite table in La Lanterna cafe, and at her living room in the faculty housing. These were very precious moments for me. I am grateful to her for the privilege of granting me regular conversation sessions and for sharing her expertise and personal experiences during these enlightening discussions.

I am also deeply indebted to my dissertation committee, the late Michael Nash, Moss Roberts, George Solt, and Shinoda Toru, for their invaluable guidance, support, and intellectual encouragement. My appreciation especially goes to Robert Cohen, who has been extremely generous in taking time to help me transform my dissertation into a manuscript worthy of submission to a publisher. He and his wife, Becky Hyman, warmly welcomed me whenever I returned to NYC. I have been fortunate to receive additional encouragement, advice, and support from colleagues. I have particularly benefited from the expertise of Fanon Che Wilkins, Ryoko Kosugi, Sabu Kohso, Go Oyagi, Chelsea Szendi Schieder, Naoyuki Umemori, and the members of *Senzen-Sengo Nihon Kenkyūkai* (The Prewar-Wartime Japan Study Group), including Kuniaki Makino, Satoshi Shirai, and Kentaro Tsuneki. Comments I received from Martin Klimke, Maria Höhn, and Quinn Slobodian at the "Revisiting 1968 and the Global Sixties" conference in 2016 and Heonik Kwon and Masuda Hajimu at the Millennium–NUS Symposium, "The Cold War in Asia," in 2018 helped me considerably improve this work. I thank all my friends and cohorts, especially Roslynn Ang, Jeong Min Kim, Joel Matthews, and Norihiko and Yuko Tsuneishi. I would not have gotten through graduate school without them. At Kindai University, I have been fortunate to be associated with Virgil Craig, Yudai Fukuda, Ryoichi Horiguchi, Megumi Kuwana, Mio Murata, Aya Murayama, Carlos Ramirez, and Noriyuki Segawa. I thank them for their support and friendship.

I extend my appreciation to the following institutions and libraries. NYU's Elmer Holmes Bobst Library provided me with a working space and library privileges. I would also like to express my gratitude towards the staff at the NYU Berlin campus. This dissertation would not have been possible without valuable research materials from the following archives and libraries: the Bancroft Library, University of California, Berkeley, the Harvard University Archives, the Hoover Institution Library & Archives, John F. Kennedy Presidential Library, Lyndon Baines Johnson Presidential Library, the National Archives and Records Administration, National Archives at College Park, Princeton University Library, the Tamiment Library and Robert F. Wagner Archives at New York University in the United States, the Doshisha University library, Hokkaido University Archives, Kyoto University Archives, the National Diet Library, and the Ohara Institute for Social Research in Japan. The research and completion of my dissertation was facilitated by the travel and research grants and institutional support that I have received from the Department of History at NYU: MacCracken Fellowship, The Pennfield Fellowship Award, Margaret Brown Fellowship Award for Scholars of Women's History, Mellon Workshop and Summer Research Grant. I also thank the Japan Society for the Promotion of Science Research Funding and the Kindai University Research Fund for assisting me with additional research to complete this book.

Last, but not least, I would like to thank my family. I will be forever grateful to my parents; Hitoshi and Keiko Koda receive my deepest gratitude for their dedication and many years of support. I also thank my late grandparents Kazuyoshi and Kimie Koda, and of course Nao Seoka. Their support was crucial at every stage of this project. Completing this book was joyfully delayed by the birth of my twin daughters, Uta and Koto, who were born on April 30, 2019, the last day of the Heisei era. I dedicate this book to them.

Abbreviations

Anpo	Japanese abbreviation of the US-Japan Security Treaty
ANZUS	Australia, New Zealand and United States Security Treaty
CINCFE	Commander in Chief of the Far East Command
CNVA	Committee for Non-Violent Action
Cominform	Communist Information Bureau
DPJ	Democratic Party of Japan
FBI	Federal Bureau of Investigation
FECOM	Far Eastern Command
FTA	Free the Army
GHQ	General Headquarters
GS	Government Section (GHQ)
HUAC	House Committee on Un-American Activities
IAYC	Interagency Youth Committee
IUS	International Union of Students
JCP	Japan Communist Party
JSP	Japan Socialist Party
LDP	Liberal Democratic Party
NATO	The North Atlantic Treaty Organization
NSC	National Security Council
OECD	Economic Cooperation and Development
PPS	Policy Planning Staff
PSIA	Public Safety Investigation Agency (Japan)
RUSA	Ryukyu University Students' Association
SANE	Committee for a SANE Nuclear Policy
SCAP	Supreme Commander for the Allied Powers
SCAPIN	Supreme Commander for the Allied Powers Directives to the Japanese Government

SDS (Germany)   Socialist German Student Union
SDS (US)   Students for a Democratic Society
SEATO   Southeast Asia Treaty Organization
SIB   Special Investigation Bureau (Tokubetsu Shinsakyoku)
SNCC   Student Nonviolent Coordinating Committee
SPU   Student Peace Union
USARYIS   United States Army Ryukyu Islands
USCAR   United States Civil Administration of the Ryukyu Islands
VDC   Vietnam Day Committee
VVAW/WSO   The Vietnam Veterans Against the War/Winter Soldier Organization
WRL   War Resisters League

Japanese	Common Abbreviation in Japanese	English Translation
Akahata		Red Flag
Anpo Hantai, Heiwa to Minshu Shugi o Mamoru Zenkoku Gakusei Jichikai Rengō	Heimin Gakuren	The National Student Federation of Student Self-Governing Associations against *Anpo*, Defend Peace and Democracy
Anpo Jyōyaku Kaitei Soshi Kokumin Kaigi		People's Council to Stop the Revised Security Treaty
Anpo Mondai Kenkyū Kai		The Study Group of the US-Japan Security Treaty Problems
Betonamu ni Heiwa wo! Shimin Rengo	Beheiren	Peace for Vietnam! Committee
Bunto		Bund
Chūkaku-ha	Chūkaku-ha	The Central Core Faction
Dassōhei Tsūshin		Deserter Correspondence
Gakusei Hyōron		Student Review
gakusei jichikai		self-governing student association
Gensuibaku Kinshi Nihon Kyoōgikai	Gensuikyō	Japan Council against Atomic and Hydrogen Weapons
Hansen Dassoō Beihei Sien Nihon Gijutsu Iinkai	JATEC	Japan Technical Committee to Aid US Anti-War Deserters
Hansen Gakusei Dōmei		Antiwar Student League
Hokkaido Gakusei Jichikai Renmei	Dōgakuren	Hokkaido Federation of Students' Self-Governing Associations
Kakumeiteki Kyōsan Shugisha Dōmei Zenkoku Iinkai	Kakukyōdō	National Committee Faction of the Revolutionary Communist League

Japanese	Common Abbreviation in Japanese	English Translation
Kakumeiteki Marukusu Shugisha	Kakumaru-ha	Revolutionary Marxist Faction
Kichi Kakuchō Hantai Dōmei (Sunagawa)		Alliance against the Extension of the Air Base
Kichi Kakuchō Taisaku Renmei (Sunagawa)		Federation for Measures for the Extension of the Air Base
Kikyō Undō		Homecoming Movement
Kōan Chōsachō		Public Security Intelligence Agency
Koenaki Koe no Kai		The Voiceless Voices
Kokuristu Daigaku Gakusei Jichikai Renmei	Kokugakuren	The Federation of National University Students' Self-Governing Associations
Kokusai-ha		Internationalists
Kokutetsu Rōdō Kumiai		National Railway Workers' Union
Kōzō Kaikaku-ha		Structural Reform Faction
Kyōsan Shugisha Dōmei	Kyōsandō	Communist League
Kyushu Gakusei Jichikai Renmei	Kyushu Gakuren	Kyushu Federation of Students' Self-Governing Associations
Minnade Minshu Shugi o Mamorukai		Association to Defend Democracy with Everyone
Minshu Shugi o Mamoru Zenkoku Gakusha Kenkyōsha no Kai		The National Association of Scholars and Researchers to Defend Democracy
Nichibei Anzen Hoshō Jōyaku	Anpo	The US-Japan Security Treaty
Nihon Gakusei Kyōkai		Japan National Student Association
Nihon Kyoōsantō Dai-6-kai Zenkoku Kyōgikai	Rokuzenkyō	Japan Communist Party Sixth National Party Congress
Nihon Rōdō Kumiai Kaigi	Nichirō Kaigi	Japan Congress of Labor Unions
Nihon Rōdō Kumiai Sōdōmei	Sōdōmei	Japan Federation of Labor
Nihon Rōdō Kumiai Sōhyōgikai	Sōhyō	General Council of Japanese Trade Unions
Nihon Shakai Shugi Seinen Dō mei	Shaseidō	The League of Socialist Youth of Japan
Nippon Marukusu Shugi Gakusei Dōmei	Marugakudō	Japan Marxist Student League
Rengo Sekigun		United Red Army
Sanpa Zengakuren		Triple Alliance Zengakuren
Shakai Shugi Gakusei Dōmei	Shagakudō	Socialist Student League
Shokan-ha		Centralists
Tokyo-to Gakusei Jichikai Rengō	Togakuren	Tokyo Metropolitan Federation of Students' Self-Governing Associations

(continued)

Japanese	Common Abbreviation in Japanese	English Translation
Zai-Nihon Chōsen Minshu Seinen Dōmei		Korean Democratic Youth League in Japan
Zen Nihon Sangyōbetsu Rōdō Kumiai Kaigi	Sanbetsu	The Congress of Industrial Unions of Japan
Zen-Nihon Gakusei Jichikai Sōrengō	Zengakuren	All-Japan Federation of Students' Self-Governing Associations
Zen-Nihon Kyōshokuin Kumiai Kyōgikail	Nikkyōso	Japan Teachers' Union (JTU)
Zengakuren Chūō Iinkai		Zengakuren Central Committee
Zengakuren Chūō Shikkō Iinkai		Zengakuren Central Executive Committee
Zengakuren Fukuiinchō		Zengakuren Vice Chairman
Zengakuren Iinchō		Zengakuren Chairman
Zengakuren Jyōhō		Zengakuren Information
Zengakuren Shoki Kyoku		Zengakuren Secretariat
Zengakuren Taikai		Zengakuren National Convention
Zengakuren Tūshin		Zengakuren Correspondence
Zenkoku Gakusei Renraku Kaigi		National Students Liaison Council
Zenkoku Gunji Kichi Hantai Renraku Kaigi		National Liaison Council Against the Military Bases
Zenkoku Kankōritsu Daigaku Kōsen Gakusei Jichukai Rengōkai		Federation of the National Public University and Technical College Self-Governing Associations
Zenkoku Kyōin Kumiai Kyōgikai		National Teachers Council
Zenkoku Shiritu Daigaku Gakusei Jichikai Rengō	Shigakuren	the National Federation of Private University Students Self-Government Associations
Zenshin (newspaper)		Moving Forward

Note on the Text

Japanese names are written according to the Hepburn transliteration system except in direct quotations. In the Hepburn system of Romanization, "*n*" and "*m*" are used to represent ん. "*N*" is used for all cases, except where "*m*" is used in official English names or in direct quotations. "*M*" is used for all names of Japanese newspapers because conventional use of the *m* is firmly established (e.g. *Yomiuri Shimbun* instead of *Yomiuri Shinbun*). In the Hepburn system, macrons are places over long vowels, yet place-names in Japan and personal names are written without macrons in the text and bibliographical references, as used more often in the present transliteration (e.g. Tokyo instead of Tōkyō, Taro instead of Tarō).

Japanese names are written with the family name first, with no comma between the family name and the given name in the main text, except in direct quotations. Please note, however, in endnote references and bibliography, Japanese names are written given name first to be consistent with the citations of Western authors' names.

All bibliographical information is given in the original language. English translations of endnote references when necessary are provided by the author within square brackets to make the book accessible for readers who are not familiar with the Japanese language.

Introduction

The US was intensely involved in Asia from 1948 through 1973, years that spanned from the US occupation of Japan to Vietnamization of the Indochina War. During this period, a diverse range of American officials and policymakers, from General Douglas MacArthur to Cold War liberals John and Robert Kennedy, found themselves forced to deal with the powerful leftist student movement in Japan led by Zengakuren, formally named *Zen-Nihon Gakusei Jichikai Sōrengō* (All-Japan Federation of Students' Self-Governing Associations). In Japan, which the Central Intelligence Agency (CIA) viewed as America's "strongest anti-Communist center in Asia," the Zengakuren student movement appeared to threaten the political stability and ideological alliance with the US that had been the promise of the post-war occupation of Japan.[1] Indeed, beginning with the US occupation of Japan from 1945 to 1951, up through the Vietnam War's final stages in the 1970s, the interactions between American Cold Warriors and the Japanese student movement forced each side to reassess and revise strategies that had a profound and lasting impact on Japanese society and US-Japan relations. The United States and the Japanese Student Movement, 1948–1973: *Managing a Free World* offers a comprehensive history of the Japanese student movement and uses that movement and its interaction with the US government as a lens to assess US-Japan relations from the US occupation era through the Vietnam War era.

While the United States assumed the mantle of leadership in the post–World War II world, Japan became a crucial defender of American ideology and capitalism. The war had left Japan with a ruined economy and pervasive starvation, and Americans came to occupy this economically poor and politically unstable country. "Before us, as far as we could see lay miles of rubble. The people looked ragged and distraught. . . . They pushed and dragged carts piled high with brick and lumber," described an American journalist upon his arrival in Japan in December, 1945.[2] Japan was, in his words, "all a man-made desert, ugly and desolate and hazy in the dust that rose from the crushed brick and mortar."[3] In the first few years after the war, Americans occupying Japan witnessed unprecedented popular enthusiasm to build a new egalitarian and democratic nation, which the General Headquarters (GHQ) promised to promote. Yet, the deteriorating relationship with the Soviet Union prompted the GHQ under the Supreme Commander for the Allied Powers (SCAP), General Douglas MacArthur, to shift its focus from democratization and demilitarization to anti-Communism around 1947. This transition of the occupation policy became known as the "reverse course," which signaled, for many, the end of the GHQ's democratic revolution.

Japan was one of the first places to face postwar American anti-Communist interference. Odd Arne Westad has argued that the US experiences during the occupation of Japan "formed the main model for future American initiatives" in the Third World.[4] The assumption that empty stomachs and political instability were the open door to Communism stimulated America's fear of Communist penetration into Japan during the early phrase of the Cold War. As the "loss" of China became inevitable, the US-Japan alliance grew more important as a counterweight to the Soviet-China Communist alliance in Asia. Believing that Japan would serve as a principle ally of the US in the Cold War for its industrial potential and geographic location, Americans made sustained efforts for the future of the Japanese economy and security. Diplomatic historian Michael Schaller has further argued that these American postwar plans for Japan even shaped subsequent American actions in Asia, including Korea and Vietnam.[5] Through the alliance system radiating from Washington, the United States exercised significant political power, able to employ both coercive tactics and moral and intellectual leadership. The combination allowed the US to shape an allied state's course towards the political, economic, and social ends the US thought desirable.

By the 1950s, the Cold War had become "a battle of global alliances and of political ideas."[6] Forming new alliances, especially in the Third World, was one thing, but sustaining existing ties was equally important and required considerable effort. Historian Simon Bromley observed, "During the Cold War, two different objectives of the United States—first, 'making the world safe' for capitalism, and second, ensuring its hegemony within the capitalist world—reinforced one another."[7] The pursuit of these two objectives required Washington to interact with indigenous political groups in Japan, including those that challenged America's Cold War policies. Yet, the ways in which the United States dealt with such opposition groups within the so-called First World countries, especially outside Western Europe, have received little attention so far. A close examination of Washington's approach to the leftist student movement that challenged Japan's Cold War alliance with the United States reveals that the interactions between Cold War America and the leftist student movement in Japan initially intensified the polarization of Japanese society and played a large role in crafting a social consensus that made the security alliance with Washington sacrosanct in Japan.

Recently historians have expanded our understanding of the Cold War through their exploration of local and non-state histories, which for too long had been overshadowed by the exclusive focus on the superpower politics and state actors. Supporting their efforts to diversify the history of the Cold War, The United States and the Japanese Student Movement, 1948–1973: *Managing a Free World* argues that the Cold War was not only about the rivalry between the United States and Soviet Union, or two inherently opposing ideologies, but also that it was a complex multilayered, multisided conflict that intermingled with various international, regional, and local tensions, involving a large cast of state and non-state actors. The most obvious was the Sunagawa case in which the United States confronted a wide range of local actors, including local farmers, labor unions, and university students, who opposed the official plan to extend the US military base into Sunagawa, a small town in Tokyo, which the US thought was necessary to fight against Communism. While the US officials saw the local opposition to the extension plan as Communist-inspired, a close examination of this so-called Sunagawa struggle revealed that it was not such a monolithic Cold War ideological struggle but one that involved local memories of the wartime bombings and the gap in understanding of "national security" between the Cold War policymakers and the protestors in Japan.

Relations between the US and Japan in the postwar period have been the subject of numerous books and articles. Historians such as Walter LaFeber and Michael Schaller have provided valuable historical analyses of the close postwar interstate relationship between the United States and Japan. Yet most of these works that narrowly focused on the political processes at the top have overwhelmingly produced narratives filled with ideological collusion and Japanese cooperation with the United States. In such studies, the Japanese public becomes void and counter-hegemonic movements are represented as the diversion from a "real" political process.

In contrast, this book focuses on the historical actors operating on different levels within the structure of postwar US-Japan relations during the Cold War. It links the diplomatic history of the US-Japan Cold War alliance with the Japanese student movement that appeared, threatening the political stability and ideological affinity that the US sought to maintain in Japan during the Cold War. An analysis of the US Cold War strategy in relation to the student movement in Japan offers an alternative to more top-down approaches for understanding the US Cold War battle. The close interstate relationship between the United States and Japan arguably provided one of the most crucial dynamics of the postwar Japanese student movement led by Zengakuren.

A close examination of the US-Japan Cold War alliance and student turmoil in Japan enhances understanding of America's power that contributed to the consolidation of its hegemony in the Pacific. By the end of the Cold War, the majority of Japanese had come to accept the identification of Japan's interests with those of the United States. The anti-US military base demonstrations that occupied the core of the student movement since the Sunagawa struggle in the late 1950s are nonexistent today except in Okinawa, the southernmost remote island prefecture that currently hosts about seventy-five percent of all the US military facilities in Japan. The decline in protests against US bases outside Okinawa has so far been widely regarded as the result of downsizing and consolidation of the US military bases and facilities in mainland Japan, yet it is not enough to explain why Japanese support of US bases in Japan grew. During the Cold War, the US successfully built public consensus on its universalistic principles, ideology, and understanding of its global role that legitimated its actions and position in the world. The Americanization of conceptions of security, democracy, and modern history proved particularly influential in shaping postwar Japan. And this process of Americanization was neither unidirectional nor a simple American imposition; it was shaped by local situations as much as governmental efforts and policies.

It is also important to illuminate the complexity of the relations between the Japanese student movement and Cold War Asia—Japan's former colonies that include China, South Korea and Vietnam. The literature on the Cold War in Asia has thus far provided ample studies of Japan's political and economic roles in supporting America's war against Communism. In *Creating People of Plenty: The United States and Japan's Economic Alternatives, 1950–1960*, Sayuri Guthrie-Shimizu provided a critical historical analysis of postwar economic relations in Asia, which she argued offered a subtle realization of the imperial rhetoric of the Greater East Asia Co-Prosperity Sphere. Building upon previous studies, my study examines the impact of Asia's Cold War on the Japanese student movement. The US-Japan Cold War alliance that allowed Japanese economic expansion and America's wars in Asia provided a context for student activists to mobilize against what they called "the US-Japan imperialism." The violent decolonization struggles exacerbated by the Cold War in Asia shaped the perspectives of the Japanese student left and their self-conceived location in global structures of oppression, which I argue provides a partial explanation for the rapid growth of transnational networks between the Japanese student movement and protest movements in Western capitalist countries, especially in the United States.

In addition to providing a new lens through which to understand the Cold War, my book details the history of the Japanese student movement. It challenges some of the conventions that dominate studies of the global sixties, particularly those which draw exclusively on Euro-American perspectives. After observing similar tactics and rhetoric of American protest movements found abroad, some scholars reached the mistaken conclusion that the international student movement originated in the United States. Mark Kurlansky, for example, located the origin of the global 1968 student revolt in the lunch counters sit-in protests ignited by four African American students in Greensboro, North Carolina on February 1, 1960. He argued, "By 1968, all over the world, people with causes wanted to copy the civil rights movement. Its anthem, Pete Seeger's 'We Shall Overcome'—a folk song turned labor song that Seeger had turned into a civil rights song when sit-ins began in 1960—was sung in English from Japan to South Africa to Mexico."[8] This portrait of the global revolt of 1960s fails to account for global historical diversities and local contrasts—in nations such as Japan that witnessed mass student protests long before 1960—and even more problematically confines its database to the Western New Left, as if Asia's tradition of militant student insurgency did not exist.

Yet, this is not to gainsay the New Left's influence on the Japanese radical movements. In the late 1960s, "America" became no longer a monolithic epitome of the capitalist modernity for the youth in capitalist counties. The Japanese young activists began embracing certain perspectives, values, and ideas expressed by American dissident movements. The radicalization of the civil rights and student movements drew the attention of the Japanese young radicals. This resulted in increasingly transnational communication and growing networks between American and Japanese dissidents, especially after the escalation of the direct US military intervention in Vietnam in 1964.

Within the field of the global sixties, a few innovative scholars have recently begun to probe US government reaction to the groundswell of the international student protest movements, most notably in Europe. Karen M. Paget's *Patriotic Betrayal* revealed the CIA's covert operations that targeted the National Student Association and its international youth conferences to enlist American students in Washington's fight against Communism.[9] Martin Klimke, in his groundbreaking monograph, *The Other Alliance*—the title indicating the transnational solidarity between American and West German protest movements—explored Washington's reaction to the intensifying European student radicalism.[10] By the mid-1960s, as Klimke has shown, US government agencies, including the State Department, began regarding the global student movement as a crucial factor in shaping international relations. Though Klimke's influential book and other studies of the US response to student protests outside the US broke much new grounds, they do leave readers with the mistaken impression that the student protests abroad became a major concern for US government only in the mid-1960s. Close examination of the situation in Japan, however, demonstrates that serious US concern with student radicalism existed *as early as 1948* in Japan.

While adding an Asian component to our understanding of the global sixties, it is also important to break the chronological barrier of the Japanese sixties that is prevalent in previous studies of the student movements of the 1960s in Japan. Conventional narratives of the Japanese student movement start with the mass demonstrations against the revision of the US-Japan Security Treaty of 1960 and end with the factionalism of the student movement and the violent crimes of small extremist groups. Wesley Sasaki-Uemura's *Organizing the Spontaneous* provided a historical analysis of the Japanese protest movement against the US-Japan Security Treaty of 1960 and argued that the *Anpo* struggle gave rise to the New Left in Japan. Yet, this commonly used chronological frame inadvertently fails to take into account the multilayered complexities of the history of the Japanese student movement. It also assimilated the Japanese student movement to Western notions and chronological frames of a New Left. Although the Japanese student movement shared important characteristics of the Western New Left, it was an anti-imperialist movement that had far deeper chronological roots, extending back to the late 1940s, and was far more influenced by an anti-fascist sensibility born of memories of World War II and the democratic ethos of the US in that war, which Japanese citizens absorbed via the US occupation than was its American New Left counterpart.

It is an appropriate time to write about the history of the Japanese student movement and engage in scholarly and public debates about Japan's long sixties. The Japanese public still seeks to reconcile with its history of student radicalism. The bitter public memories of violent student factionalism and ongoing controversies over the history of Zengakuren have discouraged objective historical assessments of the Japanese student movement, leaving stories exclusively narrated by former student leaders and activists in their memoirs as the only available historical analysis.

The book is neither exclusively Japanese nor American national history. *Managing a "Free World"* focuses on the US Cold War and the Japanese student movement during the period between 1948 and 1973. It hopes to deepen our understanding of US power within a specific local context and the complex social and political processes in Japan which were shaped by America's Cold War. Although important works on US-Japan relations during the Cold War have been published, the lack of studies that examine various dimensions of US power and its interactions with Japanese society has blinded us to the fact that the intra-governmental cooperation and shared national interests and enemies were not enough to build and sustain the bilateral relations. In regard to the study of the global 1960s, this book provides a unique case that fits into neither the "West" nor the "Third World"—two distinctive categories often used in the literature on the global sixties. It hopes to construct a comprehensive picture of the "global 1960s" or "1968"—a spatial and temporal historical conjuncture that has been widely adopted in the analyses of the protest movements of the 1960s.

The first chapter examines the US postwar vision for Japan and the beginning of the Cold War in Asia. By the late 1940s, the growing Russo-American tensions forced Washington to constrict its vision of democracy and moderate its stance on demilitarization it had advocated during the war. In US-occupied Japan, the powerful popular democratic upsurge, inspired by the US occupation's democratization and demilitarization programs, continued without losing its intensity even after the US objectives of the occupation shifted its priority to combating Communism and establishing an economically self-sufficient center of anti-Communism in Asia. The leftist student movement took up the cause of democratization and demilitarization, organizing itself into a nationwide organization named Zengakuren, whose goal was to complete the unfinished revolution initiated by the US occupation of Japan. After the shift in the occupation policy, students led powerful protests rejecting Cold War America's exclusive anti-Communist democracy and call for Japanese rearmament. They relentlessly demanded that Washington be true to its World War II era democratic and anti-militarist ideals embodied in the Potsdam Declaration—the statement that defined terms for the Japanese surrender in 1945. This chapter deals with the period of the US occupation from 1945 to 1951 wherein the Cold War began with the shift in the US occupation policy and sets the stage for the discussion in the following chapters.

In the second chapter, I explore the beginning of the anti-imperialist Japanese student movement by focusing on the Eells Incident. From 1949 to 1951, the Adviser on Higher Education to the SCAP, Walter Crosby Eells launched successive anti-Communist campaigns in Japanese universities, trying to convince Japanese students of the incompatibility of communism and democracy. This sparked vehement opposition from the Japanese leftist students who, like Eells himself, saw themselves as fighting for democracy—but the students had a more inclusive democratic vision that would not ban Communists from academic and political life. This struggle for "democratic" education resulted in the radicalization of the leftist student movement and mounting criticism of "American imperialism." The examination of the conflict over the meaning of "democracy" after the occupation shifted its focus to combating Communism in Japan also contributes to a broader discussion of American promotion of "democracy" during the Cold War.[11]

The third chapter examines the Sunagawa case in which the student protestors, joining the local farmers and labor unions, resisted the official plan to extend the runway of US-occupied Tachikawa Air Base in Tokyo. With the outbreak of the Korean War, the geostrategic importance of the US military bases in Japan grew as its commitment to Pacific security increased. In 1955, the US and Japanese governments agreed to extend the runway of Tachikawa Air Base into the small town of Sunagawa to accommodate modern US jets. Many residents feared that stationing these new jets would make the town a target in case of a destructive, possibly nuclear, war between the superpowers, and so they resisted the plan. As Zengakuren students, as well as labor unions and progressive and leftist political parties, joined the local opposition, it gradually swelled into a broader national movement against the US-Japan security treaty. The public debate moved towards a discussion of the constitutionality of the presence of the US military force in Japan. The protestors argued that it violated Article 9—the pacifist clause of the Japanese postwar constitution. Here, I call attention to the contested conceptualizations of "security" between the student activists and the American and Japanese governments. While the US and Japanese governments believed that the rearming of Japan and playing a larger role in the US-centered collective security systems would ensure peace for Japan, the student protestors still firmly believed in demilitarization as the best way to achieve peace. This chapter is particularly crucial since the outcome of this case had a lasting impact on public debates on security and the US-Japan Security Treaty in Japan—even up to the present. In this chapter, I also argue that the Sunagawa struggle allowed Zengakuren to recover and reunite after the years of internal confusion and dormancy of the mid-1950s, triggering the debate over the meaning of "security." The Sunagawa struggle set the stage for the *Anpo* crisis of 1960, which is the focus of the next chapter.

In 1960, mass demonstrations erupted against the revision of the US-Japan Security Treaty (abbreviated as *Anpo* in Japanese). Scholars have paid considerable attention to these anti-*Anpo* treaty demonstrations of 1960 as one of the most crucial postwar events in Japan. Yet these protests have been discussed too narrowly as national history—viewed only in terms of Japanese history, obscuring their international implications. This book places the anti-*Anpo* demonstrations of 1960 within specific historical conjunctures of the Cold War in the 1950s and 1960s by analyzing primary and secondary sources housed in Japan and the United States. I conclude that the *Anpo* demonstrations of 1960 marked a critical point from which the debate on the US-Japan Security Treaty developed into a discussion of postwar democracy in

Japan. This "Tokyo riot" brought a shock to America's post-war confidence, suggesting that the US role as the leader of the free world was not welcomed everywhere, not even in Japan, a key Cold War ally. For Japanese student activists, the outcome of the *Anpo* demonstrations resulted in mixed feelings—confidence gained from the large-scale public demonstrations that ultimately forced the Prime Minister Kishi Nobusuke to resign, but also despair over the movement's failure to stop the passage of the revised treaty.

The next two chapters examine the "Kennedy-Reischauer Offensive," an American liberal effort led by President John F. Kennedy and his brother Robert to isolate the Communist Party from the general population including university students. To pursue this effort, President Kennedy appointed Edwin O. Reischauer as the American Ambassador to Japan. Kennedy believed that Reischauer, who was born in Japan and was an eminent professor of Japanese Studies at Harvard University, would understand the Japanese mind and develop better relations between the US and Japanese society. Like the Kennedys' Reischauer's goal was to deal with Japan's persistent problems with Communism, which he saw as the driving force behind the protests against the US-Japan Security Treaty revision of 1960. In Chapter Five, I argue that Reischauer's ostensibly intellectual attack on the Left proved effective and indeed had a profound psychological effect on the general Japanese public.

Attorney General Robert F. Kennedy's visit to Tokyo and Osaka in February 1962 was a key moment in this new liberal offensive against general Japanese acceptance of the Communist ideology. Challenging Marxist disdain for America's version of bourgeois liberal capitalism, Robert Kennedy launched a campaign appealing to the ordinary citizens of Japan. This effective campaign made Zengakuren appear powerless in the midst of the Kennedy "*bumu* (boom)." In this chapter, I also argue that his experience with Zengakuren students contributed to Kennedy's optimism about America's ability to counter the Communist diplomacy, and it eventually led him to propose the creation of the Interagency Youth Committee (IAYC), which played a central role in fostering direct contacts with young people abroad in the sixties.

The final chapter examines the anti-Vietnam War movement in the context of the global sixties. This chapter provides a comprehensive look at the connections between the Japanese student movement and its overseas counterparts. The youth/student world, which the Kennedys had sought to co-opt, was revolting against US "imperialist" policy by the mid-1960s. In opposition to the war, local, national and international protest movements converged and transformed student radicals into the global players of 1968. In a world engulfed in a wave of new radicalism, the engagement in local struggles with US power deepened the global consciousness of the student radicals in Japan and impelled them to build transnational alliances with their counterparts in Europe and the United States. During the anti-Vietnam War movement, the Japanese student radicals began increasingly to engage in active importation of ideas and tactics, especially from the protest movements in the United States. The black liberation movement in particular became a powerful source of inspiration for young radicals in Japan.

While focusing on the bourgeoning transnational networks of the student activists, I pay attention to the US government's reaction to them. Some scholars have examined the US government's growing concern with foreign youth and student upheavals, which reached its zenith in 1968. These studies rely, in the main, on State Department documents. My discovery of the "Agitator Study" produced by the US military in Okinawa in 1968 in Army records housed in the US National Archives and Records Administration has enabled me to add a new dimension to the history of the United States in the global sixties. My study reveals that the areas that hosted US military bases and facilities in Japan exhibited special vulnerability to protests, and this made the US take a more defensive posture—which included the drafting of elaborate contingency plans to resist these protestors.

The book ends with the year 1973, when the Japanese anti-imperial student movement of the long sixties seemed to collapse. The revision of the US-Japan Security Treaty, the subject of huge protests in 1960, was automatically ratified in 1970 without so much as a murmur from the general public. The US occupation of Okinawa, one of the focal points of resistance against "US imperialism," officially ended in May 1972. The Japanese national consensus proved strongly in favor of the US-Japan alliance and maintaining US military bases, which were in any case predominantly in Okinawa. These two major diplomatic events resulted in spreading a sense that the struggles of the student left were finally at an end. The radical shift in US policy toward China, or what the Japanese termed "Nixon Shock," ended Chinese opposition to the US-Japan Security Treaty. The North Vietnamese capture of Saigon in 1975 and the end of the anti-Vietnam War movement further deepened the feeling of an end to the tumultuous revolutionary period among the young radicals in Japan.

The history of the student movement in Japan is crucial for understanding America's Cold War in Asia and its relations to Japanese society. My study of the Japanese long sixties demonstrates how the US managed a fragile Cold War alliance by employing various tactics, which I conclude, ultimately proved by and large successful in Japan. By the end of the Cold War, most Japanese people had come to accept the identification of Japan's interests with those of the United States. The US-Japan Security Treaty and the presence of US military bases in Japan, which were vigorously protested between the 1950s and early 70s, became fait accompli by the end of the Cold War.

Yet the visions of postwar democracy and peace expressed by the student left during the period between 1948 and 1973 left a lasting impact on the public discourse of US-Japan relations and Japan's postwar democracy and commitment to peace.

NOTES

1. Central Intelligence Agency (CIA), Intelligence Memorandum No. 197, July 25, 1949. Papers of Harry S. Truman: Records of the National Security Council in Documentary History of the Truman Presidency, vol. 5: Creating a Pluralistic Democracy in Japan: The Occupation Government 1945-1952, ed. Dennis Merrill (Bethesda, MD: University Publications of America, 1995), 348.

2. Mark Gayn, *Japan Diary* (New York: William Sloane Associates, 1948; Rutland, VT and Tokyo: Charles E. Tuttle Company, 1981), 1; Citations refer to the Charles E. Tuttle Compnay edition.

3. Ibid., 2.

4. Odd Arne Westad, *The Global Cold War: Third World Interventions and the Making of Our Times* (New York: Cambridge University Press, 2007), 24.

5. Michael Schaller, *The American Occupation of Japan: The Origins of the Cold War in Asia* (New York: Oxford University Press, 1985), viii.

6. Westad, "Cold War and the International History of the Twentieth Century," in *The Cambridge History of the Cold War, Vol. 1: Origins*, ed. Melvyn P. Leffler and Odd Arne Westad (New York: Cambridge University Press, 2010), 4.

7. Simon Bromley, "The Logic of American Power in the International Capitalist Order," in *The War on Terrorism and the American Empire after the Cold War*, ed. Alejandro Coles and Richard Saull (New York: Routledge, 2006), 49.

8. Mark Kurlansky, *1968: The Year That Rocked the World* (New York: Ballantine Books, 2004), 84.

9. Karen M. Paget, *Patriotic Betrayal: The Inside Story of the CIA's Secret Campaign to Enroll American Students in the Crusade against Communism* (New Haven: Yale University Press, 2015).

10. Martin Klimke, *The Other Alliance: Student Protest in West Germany and the United States in the Global Sixties* (Princeton: Princeton University Press, 2009).

11. For example, Jooyoung Lee pointed out that South Korean intellectuals and student protestors responded differently to American promotion of democracy than the Japanese students discussed in this text; Jooyoung Lee, "Forming a Democratic Society: South Korean Responses to US Democracy Promotion, 1953-1960," *Diplomatic History* 39, no. 5 (2015).

Chapter One

The Occupation of Japan and the Unfinished Revolution

By the end of 1946, the containment doctrine articulated by the Soviet specialist George Kennan gained prominence and the pressure grew for Washington to play a more active role in Asia, where the political instability and economic situation seemed the opening door to Moscow-directed Communism. Because of the occupation, the changes in the US foreign policy were soon felt in Japan. In August 1947, Senator Elbert D. Thomas delivered an address at University of Michigan saying, "First of all, few have noticed that the Truman Doctrine and the Marshall Plan, in reality, have their origin in what we have done in the Far East. . . . Japan is now looked upon as the very center of American activity and policy of that phrase of the Truman Doctrine which stands for the support of peoples attempting to remain free of economic controls and political dominations."[1] Yet the problem was, as Owen Lattimore described in 1949, that Japan was "a workshop without raw materials, and a bulwark manned by defenders who may in their own good time decide to deal with the other side."[2] As the economic resurrection and political stability of Japan became the priority of the occupation, the GHQ singlehandedly extinguished the flames of the top-down democratic revolution, although Japanese popular enthusiasm for democratization remained high.

Indeed, the powerful popular democratic upsurge, which caught fire from the GHQ's democratization and demilitarization programs, continued without losing its intensity even after the US objectives of the occupation had shifted. The prominence of the role played by the recently liberated political left and labor unions as well as the magnitude of the public demonstrations gradually became intolerable for General Douglas MacArthur, Supreme Commander for the Allied Powers. In 1947, MacArthur took direct action against the mass demonstration by prohibiting the general strike set for February 1, which marked America's first open direct anti-Communist interference in Japan.

COMMUNIST THREAT IN JAPAN

By the end of 1946, suspicion about the Communist influence over Japan was rising among Americans involved in the occupation. The debates on the occupation policy increasingly came to reflect America's bipolarized worldview. In his report to the State Department on August 10, 1946, John Davies, the First Secretary of Embassy in the Soviet Union, called attention to the situation in Asia since, he argued, "the American and Soviet frontiers meet in the Japan Sea."[3] Davies warned, "Current Soviet policy toward Japan is designed to disrupt to the greatest possible degree the development of a healthy Japan oriented toward the United States. To this end, the USSR seeks to hamstring by all possible means the American program for the rehabilitation of Japan."[4] In his report, Davies recommended two policy decisions: to monitor the connection between Russia and Japanese Communists and to create an environment favorable to growth of democracy and capitalism in Japan so that it would not be "captured by the Soviet Union" after the US withdrawal.[5] John K. Emmerson, who was one of few prewar State Department Japan hands remaining in Japan, objected to Davies' analysis. Emmerson argued that American acts in Japan "should not be conditioned by a fear of Communism so strong that we lean toward the very elements we have set out to destroy."[6] Moreover, he pointed out American misconceptions of the Communists in Japan and argued that Japanese Marxists were a democratizing force, rather than representatives of Moscow, referring to their record of wartime resistance against fascism and his talk with Nosaka Sanzo, a founder of the Communist Party in Japan whom he met in China during the war.[7] Few, if any, agreed with Emerson in the late 1940s when the bipolarized worldview became increasingly dominant as events in China and Europe stimulated fears of Communist expansionism.

At the same time, few believed that the Soviets would directly attack Japan. Yet, there was no consensus among American planners as to Soviet intentions regarding Japan. MacArthur believed that the Soviet Union would utilize Japanese Communists as its foot soldiers to exercise its influence and pursue its interests in Japan.[8] Even those who were skeptical of Soviet expansionism in Asia argued that the end of American unilateral occupation of Japan would expose the fragile country to Moscow's influence. The Ambassador to the Soviet Union, Walter Bedell Smith, reported: "Kremlin, fully comprehending Japan's strategic importance, must see continuation [of] strong American influence there as exasperating obstacle [to] Communist expansion."[9] He urged that the United States should be aware that the Kremlin would revise its emphasis on Japan's importance; therefore, the United States should carefully plan a peace treaty that would allow the US to maintain its influence.[10]

In contrast, the former US Ambassador to the Soviet Union Averell Harriman thought that the Soviet's priority was to win international recognition of its great power status to be equal to the United States, rather than to pursue expansionist policy.[11] Whether the Soviet Union intended to expand or not, the crucial problem for the United States seemed to be the political and economic vulnerability of Japan that could be exploited by the Soviets.

Not only the perceptions of Soviet threat but also American's self-perceived role in the postwar world affected its attitude toward Japan. The prevailing assumption was that "what is America today will be the world tomorrow" and its mission was to teach the liberty and freedom desired by the rest of the world.[12] MacArthur believed that the Japanese were thirsty for America's guidance, and his mission was to bring them democracy and Christianity, which would embed Western democratic and cultural values in Japan.[13] Furthermore, he believed that the future of Asia depended on the US handling of Japan since "the Japanese were the most advanced of the Oriental peoples, and in that capacity they were bound to exercise in the long run the greatest influence over the others," concluding that the US occupation of Japan was a great opportunity to "plant the seeds of the appreciation of Christianity and democracy" not only in Japan but throughout Asia.[14] In the address delivered at University of Michigan, Senator Thomas expressed a similar conviction that Japan would be able to fulfill its expected role as the leader of Asia, but at the same time, "she needs the association of an honest mind and teacher."[15] In his view, Japan was "a nation that definitely wants to be led in the world affairs" and had been an ardent student of the West since Admiral Perry's "opening" of Japan in 1853 except the time when its aggressive expansionism put an end to the respected tradition of learning from the West.[16] Thus, Thomas argued that the US and Japan must resume a healthy "teacher-student attitude," otherwise, Japan would seek friendship in "less helpful centers."[17]

Yet, it was not American-style capitalism and democracy that became popular among the intellectuals and students in postwar Japan. The ideologies and political discourses that had stimulated the struggle against fascism before the war attracted many Japanese people in the aftermath of war. Marxist-Leninism in particular gained a wide support among the Japanese intellectuals and students. They ardently studied the theories of capitalist imperialism provided by such figures as Vladimir Lenin and Nikolai Bukharin. The idea that the imperial rivalry had been generated by the dynamic of capitalism which then exploded into the total war that had brought Japan to its current state of destitution was taken seriously in immediate postwar Japan. Marxist theories were cherished as the main antagonist of fascism.

The popularity of Marxist theories also reflected a popular tendency to look for wartime cultural heroes. Kurosawa Akira's 1946 film, *No Regrets for Our Youth* (*Waga Seishun ni Kuinashi*), which was based on a symbolic wartime struggle for academic freedom, the Takigawa Incident of 1933, exemplified this popular cultural attitude.[18] The high status afforded to Marxist-Leninism among the Japanese intellectuals and university students after the war explained why many student leaders, including the first chairman of Zengakuren Takei Teruo, initially joined the Japan Communist Party (JCP) cells on their campuses. Marxism seemed to offer student activists a plausible theoretical explanation of the past and future of Japan, and it became a strong ideological motivation behind the student movement.

Many ordinary people joined protests, demanding the fair distribution of basic necessities, especially rice, and expressed democratic consciousness by calling for the application of democratic rights and equality.[19] A large number of ordinary citizens joined public demonstrations and strikes initiated by the political left and labor movement. In 1946, the traditional May Day rally was resumed, and a number of demonstrations followed, gathering large crowds of people including children, housewives, students, and teachers. The nationwide May Day demonstrations on May 1, 1946, gathered somewhere between 1.25 and 2.5 million people.[20] The rise of the nationwide democratic movement after the war reflected the Japanese desire to change the nation's political culture.

The progressive and leftist forces tried to resume the task of building a wide political coalition out of the wartime anti-fascist popular front. On October 4, 1945, the SCAP issued the directive to release political prisoners in Japan. The JCP celebrated the end of the long dark valley for Japanese Marxists. JCP leaders Tokuda Kyuichi and Shiga Yoshio, who had spent eighteen years as political prisoners, expressed their "deep appreciation for the occupation of the Allied Force that finally opened Japan for a democratic revolution" in the JCP organ, *Akahata* (Red Flag), which resumed its publication in October 1945.[21] The Communists' support for American democratic reforms came from their conviction that the completion of the bourgeois-democratic revolution was the next necessary stage en route to the final stage of a socialist revolution in Japan. J. Victor Koschmann explained, "During this phrase, the JCP would attempt to combine the tactics of revolutionary organization 'from below' within a broad, temporary strategy of cooperation with SCAP and other democratic forces 'from above'."[22] The JCP tried to appeal to a great mass of people by making the party "lovable" in order to build a broad popular coalition and support the US occupation's democratization. The labor movement also tried to build a democratic front as well despite the continuing historical rivalry among the major labor federations established after the war: the Congress of Industrial Unions of Japan (*Zen Nihon Sangyōbetsu Rōdō Kumiai Kaigi*, abbreviated as *Sanbetsu*), Japan Federation of Labor (*Nihon Rōdō Kumiai Sōdōmei*, abbreviated as *Sōdōmei*), and Japan Congress of Labor Unions (*Nihon Rōdō Kumiai Kaigi*, abbreviated as *Nichirō Kaigi*).[23] These organized left and labor federations assumed a central role in the democratic revolution from below in the immediate aftermath of World War II.

ZENGAKUREN AND THE POSTWAR DEMOCRATIC REVOLUTION

Students took actions to achieve the twin objectives to democratize education and improve student lives, keeping up with the occupation's reform policy. The first postwar student strike occurred at the Mito High School (today's Ibaragi University) when students demanded the dismissal of the conservative president and his allies and the return of the progressive professors who had been expelled under wartime fascist repression.[24] Another strike occurred at the Ueno Girls' High School on October 8, 1945, when 150 students called for fair distribution of crops produced by their school farm and reinstatement of teachers who had been purged during the war.[25] A student in Ueno Girls' High School said, "We devoted ourselves to the country during the war and worked at mints, sacrificing our studies, and only thing that we looked forward to in an insufferable defeat was going back to school and study, but the school we returned to was full of injustice, which was intolerable for us, young people burning for justice. We found ourselves forced to work on the same school farm and provide labor service."[26] Students demanded the elimination of fascist tendencies at schools and alleviation of the economic hardship of students characterized by pervasive starvation, physical destruction of the country, and lack of resources. Demands for better handling of postwar distribution of food, eradication of remaining fascism and militarism, and democratization of school were all intertwined issues that students raised in strikes and protests throughout Japan after the war.

At universities, self-governing student associations (*gakusei jichikai*) became the basis of student activities in carrying out their perceived tasks in support of the GHQ's top-down democratic revolution. By the end of 1945, the self-governing student associations began establishing regional collective bodies. On November 20, 1945, student representatives from self-governing associations in Kyoto gathered to create the All-Kyoto Student Federation (*Zen-Kyoto Gakusei Renmei*), and those in Tokyo formed the Federation of Students' Self-Governing Associations (*Gakusei Rengōkai*) next day.[27] These organizations were established to coordinate and expand their actions and activities beyond their own school campuses. In November 1946, for instance, when 5,000 student self-governing association of Waseda University waged a demonstration calling for the reconstruction of war-torn campus and protested against lack of financial support for private universities, 200 members of the self-governing association of a neighboring private university, Hosei University, came to support Waseda students.[28] Within the next few years, a number of students' collective organizations grew, and they moved toward the unification of student self-governing associations throughout the nation, ultimately leading to the creation of the All-Japan Federation of Students' Self-Governing Associations (*Zen-Nihon Gakusei Jichikai Sōrengō*, abbreviated as *Zengakuren*) in 1948.

These demonstrations and the emergence of new student autonomous bodies in universities reflected the generation's indignation against the political repression, fascism, and militarism that had brought Japan into war. In postwar Japan, students exhibited strong determination to fulfill their role as the vanguard of new democratizing movement. In October 1945, an editorial of the *Daigaku Shimbun* (University Newspaper), astudent newspaper published at the University of Tokyo, announced that the social base of democracy could be achieved when "individuals who understand subjectivity, therefore, the true meaning of 'individuality' join together in collective social activity and find social space to take action."[29] The *Waseda Daigaku Shimbun* (Waseda University Newspaper), the student newspaper at Waseda University, also expressed the coming of a new era by stating, "Now the student autonomous association is moving from the era of theorizing and conceptualization toward the era of realization and action."[30] The student movement was rapidly growing beyond the campuses and began to play a crucial role in the social and political movements of postwar Japan.

THE REVERSE COURSE AND THE "CRANK UP PROGRAM" OF JAPAN

Despite the complex and diverse political groupings, the mantle of anticommunist, anti-labor was taken up by the conservative group Yoshida Shigeru which played a dominant role in shaping the nature of the US-Japan alliance between 1946 and 1954. When the GHQ purge of Hatoyama Ichiro created a power vacuum, Yoshida inherited the position of Prime Minister in 1946. From that time on, Yoshida intermittently headed five cabinets between May 1946 and December 1954. In March 1947, the declaration of the Truman Doctrine unleashed conservatives like Yoshida, who had a traditional aversion to mass politics, to take up the mantle of anticommunism in Japan. Yoshida always believed that Communism was a destructive force and hoped to maintain the wartime Peace Preservation Law, a notorious weapon for political repression, and to keep the Communist Party out of the Japanese political establishment.[31] He thought that idealistic Americans initially made a mistake by giving too much freedom to Japanese leftwing elements without knowing their true destructive nature.[32]

After the spring of 1946, the GHQ and Yoshida government tried to control the wave of mass demonstrations. On May 20, over 250,000 participants marched, demanding food and better handling of the postwar poverty in the Food May Day.[33] Alarmed by the demonstration, MacArthur warned that he would have to act against demonstrators for the purpose of the occupation and security of Japan if the "undisciplined elements" continued "mass violence and the physical processes of intimidation."[34] In June, the Japanese government passed a series of measures, including Edict Number 311 on June 12, 1946, that prohibited acts against the occupation and regulated illegal activities associated with the labor conflicts, and this edict soon became a powerful weapon against Communists in Japan.

The common anxiety about possible Communist control of the labor movement drew the GHQ and Japanese conservatives even closer. In July 1946, the union workers of the *Yomiuri Shimbun*, a major national newspaper, launched a protest against the punitive discharge of six union leaders. According to the report penned by Major Daniel C. Imboden, Press, Pictorial and Broadcasting (PPB) Chief, "Recommendation is made [by representative of *Yomiuri* Baba Tsunego] that we request General MacArthur to order the Japanese government to instruct its police to give proper legal protection to the workers on the *Yomiuri* who desire to work."[35] Although the effect of the recommendation remains unclear, the Japanese police was mobilized for the first time after the war and arrested fifty-six *Yomiuri* workers, including four out of the six discharged union leaders for "violence and intimidation."[36] During the *Yomiuri* strike, Mark Gayn, an American newspaper correspondent, wrote that the GHQ had been "sharpening its axe for use on the *Yomiuri*" in his book *Japan Diary*, a first-hand account of the US occupation of Japan between December 1945 and May 1948.[37] He wrote, "While most of the other newspapers have been induced to toe the line [with the reverse course], the *Yomiuri* remained militant. . . . It has backed the demonstrations as a democratic instrument of dissent."[38]

By the summer of 1946, the situation had become unfavorable for such a liberal press and progressive labor unions. The chief of the G2 (intelligence) section of the GHQ, General Charles Willoughby, who showed little tolerance toward New Deal liberalism, had replaced PPB Chief Robert Berkov with Major Daniel C. Imboden, who "hated the Reds."[39] The *Yomiuri* case that resulted in the discharge of six editors and thirty-one union activists became the first major red purge collaboratively carried out by the Japanese government and the GHQ, which was growing more openly antagonistic towards Communism.[40] While encouraging the red purge in Japan, MacArthur tried to preserve the occupation's reputation as a democratizing force in Japan. He tried to avoid provoking public criticism on his policy toward Japan at home by refraining from any direct action against the labor unrests in Japan, which, for instance, could turn the US labor movement against him.[41]

At the end of 1946, the anti-Yoshida coalition of political left and labor unions was gathering a massive force, and large-scale confrontation between the workers and the cabinet seemed to be in the wind. In the fall, there were two major successfully organized labor strikes: the "September Struggle" of the National Railway Workers' Union (*Kokutetsu Rōdō Kumiai*) workers and the "October Offensive" of the Congress of Industrial Unions of Japan.[42] On November 26, public workers' unions including the *Kokutetsu* union and the National Teachers' Council (*Zenkoku Kyōin Kumiai Kyōgikai*) formed a large coalition called the Joint Struggle Committee of All Public Workers (*Zen-Kankōchō Kyōdō Tōsō Iinkai*), based on their common demands, including a minimum wage increase and ban on discrimination at work, which was to play a central role in the general strike.[43] On December 17, some hundreds of thousands of workers gathered in front of the Imperial Palace in Tokyo under the banner of "Defending Rights to Live: Anti-Yoshida Cabinet," a rally initiated by Socialists.[44] To counter such challenges from the left, Prime Minister Yoshida condemned the working class strikers as "lawless renegades" in his New Year's address, and this became a direct cause that triggered the general strike of February 2.[45] On January 15, 1947, an ad hoc coalition, the Joint Struggle Committee of National Labor Unions (*Zenkoku Rōdō Kumiai Kyōdō Tōsō Iinkai*) was formed to organize a mass general strike. The workers threatened the suspension of all the public service and transportations as well as schools and mail delivery with about twenty-six million public workers and six million industrial workers out on the strike line.[46] "Students were caught up in this enthusiasm [of the political left and union workers]," and three thousand students gathered to discuss their part in this great democratic moment.[47]

On January 15, the head of the GHQ's Labor Division Theodore Cohen recommended that a major social and economic disaster could be avoided if the GHQ preempted the general strike.[48] On December 6, 1946, the 36th meeting of the Far Eastern Commission had adopted the sixteen-point Principles for Japanese Trade Unions (FEC-045/5).[49] The Japanese workers' right of free assembly, speech, and press was enshrined in the principles, but at the same time, it imposed restraints by prohibiting activities that would "interfere with the interests of the occupation" or "directly prejudice the objectives or needs of the occupation."[50] Cohen suggested evoking the principle and declaring the planned general strike would violate the cause that prohibits organized activities against the occupation.[51] MacArthur agreed with Cohen overall but still hesitated to call off the strike through the GHQ's order.[52] Thus, it was not until the morning of January 31 that the official order to ban the general strike was issued. The GHQ invited leaders of major labor organizations to give the order to publicly announce the cancellation of the planned strike and drove the chairman of the Joint Struggle Committee, Ii Yoshihiro, to the NHK (Japan's public broadcasting network) building, where he called off the general strike on the radio at 9:20pm.[53] The United States Cavalry Division in Tokyo had been mobilized to respond to any disruption that might ensure as the result of the general's order.[54] To the Japanese, the event showed that the enemy of the occupation had shifted from the fascists to the Left.

The Supreme Commander defended his action by claiming his unchanging support for democratic rights of the Japanese workers and justifying the forced cancellation of the strike as a necessary action to prevent "dreadful consequences."[55] MacArthur emphasized that the order was a result of the GHQ acting in the interest of the majority of the Japanese and the Allied forces. A year later, MacArthur wrote that his action prevented Moscow from taking advantage of the Japanese situation. He assumed that the Japanese would not readily accept orders from Russia because of their bitter experience with totalitarianism; at the same time, he feared that the Japanese were "by nature an obedient people and used to authority and would, of course, immediately shift back to the old ways in such a situation."[56]

In McCarthyite America, newspapers gave mostly supportive assessments of MacArthur's decision to call off the general strike. The *Los Angeles Times* carried one of the most alarmist articles on the event. It pointed out a "remarkable identity of views between the Russian government and Japanese trade unions."[57] The paper asserted, "It looks as if the long undercover ideological battle in Japan, in an attempt to squeeze the Americans in the middle has at last come out in the open. It could be intentional, but it is possible that somebody's red slip is showing."[58] *The New York Times* agreed with the Supreme Commander's statement that the strike would have "thrown [the country] into economic paralysis, political turmoil, and actual starvation."[59] The *Times* editorialized that the general strike was "the first sign that Japan is not entirely submissive to our rule. The elected government is cooperative."[60] MacArthur's decision to suppress "subversive manifestations" of an "unruly minority" was, in the *Times*'s judgment, logical and wise.[61] In such mainstream newspapers, the planned general strike was characterized as an undemocratic, if not Moscow-directed, challenge to the occupation.

The escalation of the GHQ's anti-Communist crusade in Japan reflected political climates in Washington, where anti-Communism was increasing accepted as a justification for economic sanctions and coercive measures. In June 23, 1947, the Republican-dominated Congress passed the Taft-Hartely Act in response to the wave of postwar labor strikes. Historian Nelson Lichtenstein describes, "Taft-Hartley's most overly ideological, best-remembered consequence was the purge of the Communists from official union posts. The law required that all trade unions sign an affidavit asserting they were not Communists, by organizational affiliation or belief."[62] The Taft-Hartley Act resulted from the most commonly perceived fear that the possibly foreign-directed Communist Party would "capture the labor movement" and "cripple the industrial potential of the United States."[63] Anti-Communism in the United States provided the GHQ a useful reference. The chief of the Civil Information and Education Section (CIE) of the GHQ, Lieutenant-Colonel Donald Nugent, advised the Japanese courts to deal with cases against the red purge in Japan by consulting the opinion written by the Supreme Court Justice Robert Jackson in support of the constitutional validity of the Taft-Hartley Act.[64]

Furthermore, Truman's Executive Order 9835, the loyalty-security program put into effect in March 1947, had reinforced the link between national security and domestic Communism by mandating the removal of Communist persons from their posts in the government since "the presence within the Government service of any disloyal or subversive person constitutes a threat to our democratic processes."[65] In Japan, a similar measure was taken to prevent Communist infiltration into governmental institutions. On July 22, 1948, the Supreme Commander sent a letter to initiate the revision of the National Public Service Law to prohibit labor strikes and agitation by government employees.[66] Despite powerful opposition from the Communists and public workers' unions, in particular the National Railway Workers' Union, which responded with strikes and walkouts, the proposal to amend the National Public Service Law was introduced in the Diet on November 11, and the conservative force secured the passage of the revision. The American political adviser in Japan, William J. Sebald, reported to the Secretary of the State that the revision of the National Public Service Law would serve as "a powerful weapon to combat the Communists."[67] Indeed, the general's bold move at the cost of possible accusation of violation of democratic principles and subsequent affirmative responses of Americans carved out spaces for them to maneuver the geopolitically and strategically important nation in the Pacific out of possible neutrality in the Cold War.

Washington's document entitled *American Policy Toward Japan: Summary* reflected the growing fear of Communist infiltration and the sense of urgency to control Communistic movements in Japan, which it claimed resulted from too much freedom given after the war. The blame was placed on the New Dealers, who had dominated the earlier occupational policymaking, for feeding Communism in Japan. In particular, the policy document criticized individuals such as Owen Lattimore, John Carter Vincent, and Lauchlin Currie, the group that "infiltrated the State Department" and advocated the abolition of the Emperor system and purge of the business classes in Japan.[68] The document concluded, "Whatever the intent of the group, either individually or collectively, their policy served Russia so well that the Soviet Union only occasionally and recently complained about American actions in Japan."[69] It further argued that the earlier occupational policy alienated the conservatives and business classes who saw themselves as supporters of the US occupation and even drove them toward Communism, and it was time to win them back.

While seeking to control mass demonstrations, US policymakers sought Japan's structural transformation and carried out plans to revive the Japanese economy. The basic assumption was that "alternatively, desperate nations might be attracted by Soviet economic blandishments or fall victim to economic chaos and subversion."[70] In October 1947, the State Department's Policy Planning Staff (PPS), headed by George Kennan, concluded that politically unstable and economically poor Japan would not be capable of preventing Communist penetration on its own after the end of the American occupation. Thus, they insisted that the United States should not relinquish its control over Japan until its political stability and economic conditions were proven capable of resisting Communist penetration.[71] Their report read that internal stability of Japan depended on "the extent to which the Japanese political psychology is adjusted to them and finds normal expression in them [the political institutions inherited by the occupational regime]."[72] In terms of economic recovery, they concluded that a critical problem facing Japan was the loss of markets and raw material source in Asia, but no matter what, it eventually had to stand on its own feet after the "tiding-over" period of the US occupation.[73]

Washington was convinced by then that Japan was a future economic power that could lead the development of Asia. Thus, it became imperative that America prevent the Soviet Union from exploiting the future economic center in Asia and revive the Japanese economy for its own use. In June 1947, US Political Adviser in Japan George Atcheson had written to President Truman, urging the necessity of the development of the peacetime Japanese economy and US assistance in financing the import of raw materials necessary for manufacture.[74] Atcheson argued that the Japanese economy, cut off from its former colonies in Asia, desperately needed raw materials to pay for imports.[75] In other words, the reconstruction of Japan's Greater East-Asian

Co-Prosperity, this time led by private businessmen, would best serve the US objectives: to alleviate Japan's economic dependency on the United States and to keep the country within the capitalist world.[76] In addition, the Chinese situation further justified the US plan for Japanese economic revival. Robert W. Barnett, who represented the State Department in Japan at that time, recalled that what State Department officials called the "crank up program" to rebuild Japan was "justified by a Washington notion that we needed a friend, an associate, for balancing purposes, vis-à-vis the Russians, and it would have been *just marvelous* if that could have turned out to be the Chinese, but Chian[g] Kai-Shek was goofing it up."[77]

The "crank up program" of Japan reflected a part of a larger vision that American Cold War architects, including Dean Acheson, James Forrestal, and George Kennan, had by 1948.[78] The creation of the interdependent economic zones—the US led Western Hemisphere, the European zone of major industrial powers, centered on restored Germany, and the renewed Japanese co-prosperity zone in Asia—would assure an alliance of great industrial powers against the Communist bloc.[79] Kennan believed that US policy should concentrate on the "five centers of industrial and military power in the world" that were the US, Britain, Germany and Central Europe, the Soviet Union, and Japan.[80] By safeguarding and recovering four zones out of the five, Kennan insisted, the US would successfully foil the Communist expansionism while the failure of the occupation of Japan would "jeopardize the United States program for world wide economic recovery and political stabilization."[81] These American policy planners formed the basic ideas for what become known as the Marshall Plan for Japan, the Japan recovery program initiated by the Truman administration in 1948. Truman hoped that Japan would be self-sufficient soon and prove itself as "a profitable ally, not only to us but to the whole world."[82] The new postwar alliance depended on the economic might of the United States and its effort to get the war-torn industrial powers back to work.

The creation of such an interdependent economic international system would also pave the way for American business to resume its Wilsonian peaceful expansionism that had been halted by the Great Depression and World War II. Before the war, Germany's economic control and bilateralism and Japan's imperial drive to Manchuria had frustrated America's vision for the global liberal economic system. Lloyd C. Gardner argued that America's prewar struggle and the goal of the New Deal diplomacy was to pressure the Axis powers accept the international trade policies championed by the United States.[83] "The Open Door Policy was," William Appleman Williams wrote, "America's version of the liberal policy of informal empire or free-trade imperialism."[84] After the war, with the Axis powers defeated, the US gained the opportunity to construct a new stage of capitalism in the world. The principles of Wilsonian liberalism and the Open Door policy remained paramount to United States foreign policy. Williams argued that the Open Door Policy assumptions continued to dominate the thinking of the Cold War architects in Washington such as George Kennan and Dean Acheson, as well as American business community.[85] In March 1947, Atcheson assured the Secretary of the State, "American commercial firms, notably those who previously have had interests in this part of the world, are prepared to assist in practical and mutually beneficial ways in the development of the peace time economy in Japan and in international trade."[86] In the aftermath of the war, the United States gained the opportunity to get the former Axis returned to liberalism and cooperation with the United States in efforts to manage the postwar international trade system.

Japanese conservative elites and industrialists celebrated "the coming of a new industrialists era" when they learned that the main occupying country would be the US after the war.[87] David Harvey points out that the Cold War united the capitalist class of the world beyond national borders against socialist internationalism. Yoshida had long believed in the importance of cooperation with the Western countries for Japan's prosperity and security. John Dower describes, "Before the war, in his idealized view, Japan could only find security and breathing space as an imperialist power by operating under the aegis of the *Pax Britannica*. After the war, he sought and obtained similar security and room to maneuver within the embrace of the *Pax Americana*."[88] The crank up program for Japanese economic revival affected the power configuration within Japan and bourgeoisie hegemony was not only preserved but also empowered through the process of incorporation into the US-led world economy and anti-Communist political bloc. As SCAP's anti-Communism became more and more blatant and consequently the political power of Yoshida's enemies dwindled, the anti-Communist conservative elites came to dominate the Japanese political scene.

The US military protection and economic assistance allowed Yoshida to single-mindedly pursue the policy of economic development. Harvey argued, "The US provided economic and military protection for propertied classes and elites wherever they happened to be. In return, these propertied classes and elites typically centered a pro-American person in politics whatever country they happened to be."[89] The Cold War was not a zero-sum game; rather, it was designed to mutually serve the economic interests of elites and capitalists of both countries whose future depended on the free world and foreign markets secured and policed by the United States. The Japanese colonial yen block was going to be revived under America's liberal economic policy, and Japan's colonial relationship with Asia was to be transformed into the articulation of new postwar global economic divisions.

A peace treaty was prerequisite for such a plan for the economic recovery of Japan; otherwise, nondiscriminatory access to foreign markets, especially in its former colonies in Asia, was impossible. Max Waldo Bishop of Division of Northeast Asian Affairs had written to the Deputy Director of the Office of Far Eastern Affairs, James K. Penfield, in August 1947 that economies of Asia and more importantly that of Japan could not be achieved without war settlement. He argued in the memorandum, which was forwarded to George Kennan on the same day, that the delay in the peace settlement would "impair effective utilization of Japan's ability promptly to contribute to economic revival and political stability [of Far East]" and "seriously diminish the immediate usefulness of Japan for our purposes."[90] A peace treaty was necessary for Japanese economic recovery, but American officials, most notably Kennan, feared that the end of US control of Japan would expose the vulnerable country that the US had invested in since 1945 to the advance of Moscow-controlled Communism.

Kennan thought that Japan, which had had been completely disarmed after the war, would be standing defenseless "semisurrounded by the military positions of the Soviet Union" in an area of high Communist activity if a peace treaty was concluded and the US occupation was ended.[91] The Policy Planning Staff's report in October 1947 suggested a solution to defense problems that would result from the end of the American occupation in Japan. First, it recommended the US permit the creation of the Japanese civil police force. Second, and more urgently, it affirmed the need to place the US military force close enough to provide defense of Japan and the Pacific against Communist expansion. The report read, "It [PPS] feels that in the coming period Japanese military security must rest primarily on the proximity (or in extreme event, the presence in Japan) of adequate US forces, and that it should be accepted as a principle of American defense policy to retain in the Pacific areas sufficient armed strength to make plain our will and determination to prevent any other military power from establishing itself in the Japanese home islands."[92] This would work toward the future of both Japanese and American defenses in the Pacific. In addition, the United States would occupy the Ryukyu archipelago for defense purposes. The PPS assured, "The Staff notes that the Emperor of Japan has been represented as suggesting that the US should continue military occupation of Okinawa and such other islands as may be required on the basis of a long-term lease—25 to 50 years or more—with sovereignty retained by Japan."[93] Thus, if this plan worked, the restoration of the Japanese sovereignty would not erode the position of the United States in Pacific.

By then, emphasis on military preparation for the possible war with Russia had grown in Washington. In his long review of the US foreign policy of February 1948, Kennan insisted, "We should stop putting ourselves in the position of being our brothers' keeper and refrain from offering moral and ideological advice . . . We should recognize that our influence in the Far Eastern area in the coming period is going to be primarily military and economic."[94] Japan was not only to serve as a center of its economic zone but also a hub of American defense system against the Communist threat in the Pacific. Japan and Philippines were considered as the "cornerstones" of the Washington-radiated Pacific security system, wrote Kennan in 1948.[95] Thus, his argument was that the US should delay concluding a peace, especially formulating arrangements for Japan's security, until it set up American tactical forces and Japanese police establishment that would guarantee the defense of Japan and the Pacific from Communism. His arguments were quickly accepted by the National Security Council (NSC) and President Truman. Kennan recalled that this policy recommendation was "the most significant constructive contribution I was ever able to make in government."[96]

To conclude, the late 1940s marked a formative period that set up the aims of the US Cold War policy in Japan. By 1948, America's Cold War battle was already in place in the war-torn country where a large part of the population was still struggling with poverty and starvation. While the United States began putting efforts to establish an economically self-sufficient center of anti-Communism in Asia, the student democratization movement began consolidating its power and established a nationwide organization, Zengakuren, to finish the democratic revolution. The differences in their objectives and priorities became apparent as they approached the 1950s.

NOTES

1. Elbert D. Thomas, "Leadership in Asia under New Japan," August 5, 1947. Papers of Harry S. Truman: White House Central Files—Official File, *Documentary History of the Truman Presidency*, vol.5, 199; Elbert D. Thomas lived in Japan as a Mormon missionary between 1907 and 1912.

2. Owen Lattimore, *The Situation in Asia* (Boston: Little, Brown and Company, 1949; New York: Greenwood Press, 1969), 7. Citations refer to the Greenwood Press edition.

3. Memorandum by the First Secretary of Embassy in the Soviet Union (Davies), August 10, 1946 in *Foreign Relations of the United States* (hereafter cited as *FRUS)*, 1946, vol. VIII, The Far East, 285.

4. Ibid.

5. Ibid.

6. Memorandum by the Assistance Chief of the Division of Japanese Affairs (Emmerson), October 9, 1946 in *FRUS*, 1946, vol. VIII, The Far East, 338.

7. Henry Oinas-Kukkonen, *Tolerance, Suspicion, and Hostility: Changing US Attitudes toward the Japanese Communist Movement, 1944-1947* (Westport, CT: Greenwood Press, 2003), 3.

8. Schaller, *The American Occupation of Japan*, 59-60.

9. The Ambassador in the Soviet Union (Smith) to the Secretary of State, December 27, 1947 in *FRUS*, 1947, vol. VI, The Far East (Washington, DC: United States Government Printing Office, 1972).

10. Ibid.

11. Schaller, *The American Occupation of Japan*, 59-60.

12. Westad, *The Global Cold War*, 9.

13. Schaller, *The American Occupation of Japan*, 70.

14. Memoranda of Conversations with General of the Army Douglas MacArthur, General MacArthur's Remarks at Lunch, March 1, 1948 in *FRUS*, 1948, vol. VI, The Far East and Australasia (Washington, DC: United States Government Printing Office, 1974), 698.

15. Elbert D. Thomas, "Leadership in Asia under New Japan," August 5, 1947, 210.

16. Ibid.

17. Ibid.

18. The Takigawa Incident of 1933 began when the Education Minister Ichiro Hatoyama ordered Kyoto Imperial University to expel the liberal professor Yukitoki Takigawa, accusing him for advocating a Marxist ideology. Despite fierce protests from students and professors, Takigawa was forced to resign from the university.

19. John W. Dower, *Embracing Defeat: Japan in the Wake of World War II* (New York: W.W. Norton & Co., 1999).

20. Ibid., 261.

21. Tokuda Kyuichi and Shiga Yoshio, "*Jinmin ni Tou* [An appeal to the people]," *Akahata*, October 20, 1945. The National Diet Library, Tokyo.

22. J. Victor Koschmann, *Revolution and Subjectivity in Postwar Japan* (Chicago: University of Chicago Press, 1996), 30.

23. Ōhara Shakai Mondai Kenkyūjo [Ohara Institute for Social Research], *Nihon Rōdō Nenkan* [The labor year book of Japan], 1949, vol. 22 (Tokyo: Daiichi Shuppansha, 1949), 222 (hereafter cited as OISR, *The Labor Year Book of Japan* with year and volume); the Congress of Industrial Unions of Japan and Japan Federation of Labor were established in 1946 and Japan Congress of Labor Unions in 1949.

24. Michihiro Matsunami, "Origins of Zengakuren," in *Zengakuren: Japan's Revolutionary Students*, ed. Stuart J. Dowsey (Berkeley: Ishi Press, 1970), 43.

25. *Asahi Shimbun*, October 9, 1945.

26. Ibid.

27. "Gakusei Rengōkai Hossoku [The inauguration of the student federation]," *Daigaku Shimbun*, December 1, 1945. Document no. 16 in *Shiryō Sengo Gakusei Undō: Zengakuren Documents* (hereafter cited as *Zengakuren Documents*), vol. 1, 1945-1949 (Tokyo: San-Ichi Shobō, 1968), 24; "Kyoto Gakusei Rengō Kessei, Kyōdai ni Shaken mo Tanjyō [The inauguration of a student federation in Kyoto,

a new social study group is also founded at Kyoto University]," *Daigaku Shimbun*, November 21, 1945. Document no. 17 in ibid., 25.

28. *Asahi Shimbun*, December 14, 1946.

29. "Shasetsu: Gakusei Undō no Hossokuten [Editorial: the beginning of the student movement]," *Daigaku Shimbun*, October 11, 1945. Document no. 2 in *Zengakuren Documents*, vol. 1, 1945-1949, 12.

30. "Sōdai Zengaku Gakusei Taikai [An all-student rally at Waseda University]," *Waseda Daigaku Shimbun*, December 11, 1946. Document no. 78 in *Zengakuren Documents*, vol. 1, 1945-1949, 126.

31. John W. Dower, *Empire and Aftermath: Yoshida Shigeru and the Japanese Experience, 1878-1954* (Cambridge, MA: Harvard University Press, 1988), 361.

32. Shigeru Yoshida, *The Yoshida Memoirs: The Story of Japan in Crisis* (Westport, CT: Greenwood Press, 1977), 38-40.

33. *Yomiuri Shimbun*, May 20, 1946.

34. *Chicago Daily Tribune*, May 20, 1946.

35. Daniel C. Imboden, Press, Pictorial & Broadcasting, CIE section, "Yomiuri Newspaper Situation," July 20, 1946. G49. Takemae Eiji File. Ohara Institute for Social Research Archive, Tokyo (hereafter cited as OISR Archive).

36. OISR, *The Labor Year Book of Japan*, 1949, vol. 22, 57-58; The Department of State, Division of Research for Far East, Office of Intelligence research, "Yomiuri Shimbun Case: A Singnificant Development in the Post-Surreder Japanese Press," March 10, 1947. G49. Takemae Eiji File. OISR Archive.

37. Gayn, *Japan Diary*, 253.

38. Ibid.

39. Eiji Takemae, *Inside GHQ: The Allied Occupation of Japan and Its Legacy*, trans. Robert Ricketts and Sebastian Swann (New York: Continuum, 2002); Kiyoshi Yamamoto, *Yomiuri Sōgi: 1945-1946* [The Yomiuri dispute: 1945-1946] (Tokyo: Ochanomizu Shobō, 1978), 147.

40. Takemae, *Sengo Rōdō Kaikaku: GHQ Rōdō Seisakushi* [Postwar labor reform in Japan: a history of the GHQ labor policy] (Tokyo: Tokyo Daigaku Shuppankai, 1982), 345.

41. Minoru Omori, *Sengo Hishi*, vol. 4: *Akahata to GHQ* [Postwar hidden history, vol. 4: red flags and the GHQ] (Tokyo: Kodansha, 1975), 277.

42. Ichiro Suzuki, *Shōgen: 2.1 Zenesuto* [Testimony: The February 1st general strike] (Tokyo: Aki Shobō, 1979), 34.

43. OISR, *The Labor Year Book of Japan*, 1949, vol. 22, 79; the National Teachers' Council (*Zenkoku Kyōin Kumiai Kyōgikai*) served as a national labor union before Japan Teachers' Union (*Zen-Nihon Kyōshokuin Kumiai Kyōgikail*; JTU) was established in June 1947.

44. OISR, *The Labor Year Book of Japan*, 1949, vol. 22, 81.

45. Ibid.

46. *Chicago Tribune*, February 1, 1947.

47. Matsunami, "Origins of Zengakuren," 45.

48. Cohen worked closely with Irving Brown who was in charge of AFL's anticommunist campaigns in Europe; see Lonny E. Carlile, *Divisions of Labor: Global-*

ity, Ideology, and War in the Shaping of the Japanese Labor Movement (Honolulu: University of Hawaii Press, 2004), 95.

49. Memorandum by the Assistant Secretary of State (Hilldring) to SWNCC (The State-War-Navy Coordinating Committee), December 10, 1946 in *FRUS*, 1946, vol. VIII, The Far East, 369.

50. Draft Directive for General of the Army Douglas MacArthur regarding Principles for Japanese Trade Unions, attached to Memorandum by the Assistant Secretary of State (Hilldring) to SWNCC, December 10, 1946 in ibid., 370.

51. Takemae, *Sengo Rōdō Kaikaku*, 161.

52. Ibid., 162.

53. Omori, *Sengo Hishi*, 245, 344.

54. *The New York Times*, February 1, 1947.

55. Ibid.

56. Memoranda of Conversations with General of the Army Douglas MacArthur: General MacArthur's Remarks at Lunch, March 1, 1948 in *FRUS*, 1948, vol. VI, The Far East and Australasia, 697.

57. *Los Angeles Times*, February 3, 1947.

58. Ibid.

59. *The New York Times*, February 2, 1947.

60. Ibid.

61. Ibid.

62. Nelson Lichtenstein, *State of the Union: A Century of American Labor* (Princeton: Princeton University Press, 2002), 115.

63. Ellen Schrecker, "McCarthyism: Political Repression and the Fear of Communism," *Social Research* 71, no. 4 (2004): 1054.

64. Takemae, *Sengo Rōdō Kaikaku*, 346.

65. Harry S. Truman, Executive Order 9835, March 21, 1947, Harry S. Truman Library. http://trumanlibrary.org/executiveorders/index.php?pid=502 (accessed on December 11, 2012).

66. The Acting Political Adviser in Japan (Sebald) to the Secretary of State, December 9, 1948 in *FRUS*, 1948, vol. VI, The Far East and Australasia, 916-17.

67. Ibid., 921.

68. *American Policy Toward Japan: Summary,* 1949. Record Group (RG) 84, Box 48, National Archives and Records Administration, National Archives at College Park, College Park, MD (hereafter cited as NARA II).

69. Ibid.

70. Schaller, *The American Occupation of Japan*, 80.

71. "Results of Planning Staff Study of Questions Involved in the Japanese Peace Settlement (PPS/10)," in *The State Department Policy Planning Staff Papers*, vol. 1, ed. United States Department of State Policy Planning Staff (New York: Garland Publishing, Inc., 1983), 109.

72. Ibid., 112.

73. Ibid., 113.

74. The Political Adviser in Japan (Atcheson) to President Truman, June 19, 1947 in *FRUS*, 1947, vol. VI, The Far East, 231-22.

75. Ibid.

76. Marilyn B. Young, *The Vietnam Wars, 1945-1990* (New York: Harper Collins, 1991), 25.

77. "Oral History Interview with Robert W. Barnett," Harry S. Truman Library. http://www.trumanlibrary.org/oralhist/barnettr.htm#transcript (accessed on October 21, 2012).

78. Schaller, *The American Occupation of Japan*, 83. (emphasis in original).

79. Ibid.

80. Ibid., 88.

81. Ibid., 91.

82. Thomas, "Leadership in Asia under New Japan," August 5, 1947, 210.

83. Lloyd C. Gardner, "New Deal Diplomacy: A View from the Seventies," in *Watershed of Empire: Essays on New Deal Foreign Policy*, ed. Leonard P. Liggio and James Joseph Martin (Colorado Springs: R. Myles, 1976).

84. William Appleman Williams, *The Tragedy of American Diplomacy* (Cleveland: World Publishing Company, 1959; New York: W.W. Norton & Co., 2009), 97. Citations refer to the W.W. Norton & Co. edition.

85. Ibid., 267-68.

86. US Political Adviser in Japan, George Atcheson to the Secretary of State, March 14, 1947 in *FRUS*, 1947, vol. VI, The Far East, 186-87.

87. Schaller, *The American Occupation of Japan*, 4.

88. Dower, *Empire and Aftermath: Yoshida Shigeru and the Japanese Experience, 1878-1954*, xii-xiii.

89. David Harvey, *The New Imperialism* (New York: Oxford University Press, 2005), 52.

90. Memorandum by Mr. Max W. Bishop of the Division of Northeast Asian Affairs to the Deputy Director of the Office of Far Eastern Affairs, August 14, 1947 in *FRUS*, 1947, vol. VI, The Far East,493.

91. George F. Kennan, *Memoirs* (Boston: Little, Brown, 1967), 376.

92. "Results of Planning Staff Study of Questions Involved in the Japanese Peace Settlement (PPS/10)," 112.

93. "Special Recommendation Ultimate Disposition of the Ryukyus (PPS/10/1)" in *The State Department Policy Planning Staff Papers*, 117.

94. "Review of Current Trends: US Foreign Policy," in ibid., 122-23.

95. Ibid.

96. Kennan, *Memoirs*, 393.

Chapter Two

Defenders of Democracies

Since the beginning of the occupation, Japan was considered America's "laboratory in which western ideas, institutions, and methods were tested within the context of an Asian society" as described by Hans H. Baerwald, a former GHQ officer who was in charge of the purge program in Japan.[1] After the war, the US attempted to inject its ideological and moral preferences into societies across the Pacific, urging that policies supportive of capitalist economic development and free trade should be adopted in the best interests of those countries themselves. Japan was expected to transform itself ideologically within the context provided by the occupation. With the reverse course, the initial democratization programs of the occupation shifted to the Cold War anti-Communist crusade. In order to achieve such a goal, the occupation collaborated with the Japanese government to initiate a large-scale red purge program, targeting individuals and groups both in public and private sectors, which met fierce opposition from Zengakuren students. The direct confrontation with the GHQ's red purge radicalized the student activists and led to open criticism of "American imperialism." By the end of the struggle against the red purge initiated by the Civil Information and Education (CIE) officer, Walter Crosby Eells, the leftist students came to lead Japan's first postwar anti-imperial movement.

From the late 1940s to the early 1950s, the changing political atmosphere provided strong impetus for the student activists to mobilize in defense of academic freedom. The CIE's "war of ideas" in education began to pose a serious threat to academic freedom for student activists in Japan. Originally established on September 21, 1945, to eliminate militarism and ultra-nationalism from education and cultural life and help ensure the healthy development of a democratic educational system in Japan, the CIE had closely worked with Japanese Ministry of Education to fulfill the occupation's objectives.[2] In

1946, the discharge of New Dealers from major posts of the GHQ brought about significant personnel changes within the CIE. In May, the first chief of the CIE, General Kermit ('Ken') R. Dyke, who had been labeled as "that damned pink" by the conservatives in SCAP, was replaced by Lieutenant Colonel Donald R. Nugent who was a "dyed-in-the-wool conservative," and he soon escalated anti-Communist campaigns against the labor movement in Japan.[3] Major Daniel C. Imboden, who had become the head of the PPB Division, began to apply more strict censorship to the Japanese newspapers and pressured them to weaken their labor unions.[4] After the reverse course, the CIE's tasks explicitly shifted to the combat of Communism in education. It began playing an important role as a main agent for carrying out Washington's Cold War policy in Japan.

In January 1949, the State Department reported that it had been "informed that Communism is especially strong in university and intellectual quarters in Japan."[5] Within a month, the CIE announced its formal decision to focus on combating Communism in education and cultural affairs of Japan and set up the Committee to Study Methods to Combat Communism.[6] Many of CIE officials did not perceive of their anti-Communist campaigns as a drastic shift in their overall objective; rather, they considered it an extension of their ongoing efforts to democratize Japan. Communist totalitarianism, in their view, was as inimical to democracy as Japanese fascism had been. From 1949 to 1951, the GHQ's anti-Communist campaign began targeting Communists and their sympathizers in Japanese universities.

In March, the US Advisory Commission on Educational Exchange published a report entitled *Trading Ideas with the World*, which called for strengthening cultural programs in order to foster better understanding of the United States in the rest of the world. "Our national history has proved," the report read, "the value of community cooperation in exchanging knowledge and ideas. The American conquest of the frontier was a cooperative undertaking by a people of many religions, races, and national origins who exchanged knowledge and ideas freely and voluntarily."[7] The cultural and educational programs, the report claimed, should be expanded and strengthened since "antifreedom forces, advocating censorship, suppression, coercion of men's minds, are attacking the United States' motives, principles, and way of life."[8] The report reflected the growing emphasis on more aggressive responses to the Soviets who were seen as exercising a great power of attraction throughout the world.

Walter C. Eells, who was to lead the campaign against Communist influence on education in Japan, shared Washington's view. Eells was Professor of Education at Standard University and a leading advocate and expert in junior college education.[9] After the war, he had served as the director of the

Division of Foreign Education of the Veterans Administration and oversaw the study abroad programs of veterans. In 1947, Eells was appointed the Adviser on Higher Education to SCAP to work with MacArthur's staff in Tokyo and participate in the GHQ's "reorientation" program to "instruct and guide 90 million [Japanese] people in the ways of democracy."[10] Recalling his experience in Tokyo, Eells said that he "unintentionally became the storm center of violent Communist-led student demonstrations" by the end of the occupation.[11] Yet, the student uprising against Eells, like Eells himself, was also calling for democratic education rather than acting as agents of Moscow or Peking.

ZENGAKUREN'S "DEFENSE OF EDUCATION"

Between 1948 and 1949, the students' democratization movement had experienced an enormous increase in strength, initially through their struggle against the plans of the Ministry of Education to reform university education. The Ministry's plan to increase student tuition threefold, which was announced during the time of raising the rates for student commuter passes, became a catalyst for nationwide student revolts.[12] Zengakuren's first chairman Takei Teruo recalled that students vigorously condemned the government's lack of sympathy for students and their families impoverished by the war.[13] On June 1, the Federation of National University Students' Self-Governing Associations (*Kokuristu Daigaku Gakusei Jichikai Renmei*, abbreviated as *Kokugakuren*) organized a rally at the Hibiya Park in Tokyo, and roughly ten thousand people participated.[14] About three hundred Korean students living in Japan joined the Japanese students at the rally held at the Hibiya Park against "the governmental oppression of education."[15] In July, the Korean youth organization in Japan gave formal endorsement for the university student movement, recognizing it as a great democratizing force against the conservative "imperialistic" Ashida Hitoshi's government. They accused Ashida of using a classic colonial "divide and rule" tactic by imposing different educational reforms and regulations for Japanese as opposed to Korean schools.[16] Progressive labor unions announced their endorsement of the students' plan for the nationwide strike.[17] The National Railway Workers' Union advocated that the workers and students should "unite against those in power that oppress the mass and attempt to destroy peace and democracy."[18] From the Hibiya Park, the protestors marched towards the Diet building and the Prime Minister's official residence building, returning to the park after passing the Ministry of Education building.[19] After the march, student representatives submitted a resolution adopted at the rally to the Diet, the Prime

Minister's office, the Ministry of Education, and other ministries, expressing their opposition to forcible implementation of reform plans.

The student strikes against the education reforms, which simultaneously took place throughout Japan, led to the rapid development of a nationwide student movement. Having failed to persuade the Ministry of Education to accept their demands on June 22, *Kokugakuren* students organized a large-scale nationwide general strike.[20] On June 26, the strike reached its climax. A total of 300,000 students from 116 universities went on strikes.[21] After the summer break, the student leaders moved to establish an independent national student organization called Zengakuren, formally named All-Japan Federation of Students' Self-Governing Associations (*Zen-Nihon Gakusei Jichikai Sōrengō*) on September 18, 1948.[22] Four hundred student representatives and participants from 148 schools attended its inaugural meeting held for three days in Tokyo.[23] Zengakuren organized 166 national, 32 public and 57 private universities—a total of 266 schools as its members.[24] Since all the individual members of the self-governing associations that joined Zengakuren automatically became its members, Zengakuren membership totaled 222,582.[25] This meant more than half of all the university students in Japan belonged to Zengakuren.[26]

The resolutions adopted by Zengakuren's inaugural convention announced their determination to struggle against the "*Fassho-teki Shokuminchi-teki* (fascist-like, colonial-like)" reorganization of education system that threatened academic freedom.[27] Suspecting Communist manipulation of the student movement, an CIE officer reported to Eells, "The meeting was not one in which students took part, but outsiders—Communists—who denounced directly and indirectly the aims and methods of the occupation."[28] Yet, it was not so much Communist ideology as the collective memory of the wartime repression and determination to defend democracy that provided the basis of Zengakuren's democratization activism. The massive wartime crack down of the leftists symbolized by the March 15 incident of 1928 and the Kyoto University Takigawa Incident of 1933 remained fresh in the memory of many Japanese people.[29] In addition, Zengakuren representatives attacked Japan's "reactionary" government for exclusively serving interests of a small capitalist class while ignoring the rest of the people as in the fascist time.[30] They expressed an uncompromising determination to "combat the last remaining fascism on the earth."[31]

When SCAP proposed a new university law aiming to restructure Japanese school system to match the decentralized American model, it further urged the student activists to rise up against the top-down education reforms. The proposal's call for the creation of a Board of Trustees or Regents, which would be composed of not only members of the university but also "men of experience and knowledge," including those from local banks or private companies in particular raised a serious concern. The opposing students perceived that the creation of the Board Trustees or Regents would lead to the erosion of university autonomy, which was believed to be the cornerstone of democratic education. During the war, the absence of school autonomy and the eventual governmental takeover of education made schools a tool of aggressive imperialism. Quoting Hubert Park Beck's *Men who Control our University* published in 1947 that criticized the concentration of business leaders in university boards in the United States, Takei condemned the plan as an effort to establish the "bourgeoisie control" of Board of Trustees and argued that it would undermine the autonomy and freedom of Japanese universities.[32] Student protesters also opposed the blind importation of the American system, believing it would not make Japan a democratic country and called instead for educational reform from the bottom-up based on the full participation of the Japanese people and serving their interests.[33] Through the struggles against the official university reform plans, Japanese students' skepticism over democracy promoted by Cold War America grew. Takei recalled, "The decisive factor that eventually united national and private university student self-governing associations was the occupying force, the GHQ that imposed self-righteous university reform plans and the Japanese government and Ministry of Education that blindly followed the GHQ and enforced educational and social plans that made confrontation with students inevitable."[34] The students demanded the GHQ keep the promises spelled out in the Potsdam Declaration: to remove undemocratic tendencies and respect freedom and fundamental human rights of the people.

In response to intensifying organized student strikes and protests, the Ministry of Education issued the directive prohibiting the political activities of students on October 8.[35] The directive gave university authorities a powerful weapon to crack down on Communist cells in universities.[36] Within a month, schools such as Nagano Normal School and Mito High School moved to forcibly expel student activists based on the ministerial directive.[37] Yet, such measures failed to serve their intended purpose, and on the contrary, students responded with more vigorous strikes, condemning such governmental acts as "*Fassho-teki* (fascist-like) repression." Confrontational situations continued the following year between the students and Yoshida's government that replaced Ashida on October 19. In May 1949, the student protest against the reform plan reached a crescendo as the Zengakuren Central Committee (*Chūō Iinkai*) announced the nationwide general strike against a revised university reform plan.[38] Each regional federation (*gakuren*) of Zengakuren went on strike one after another, and a total of over 200,000 students from 139 schools erupted in "the defense of education."[39] By May 24, the government was forced to abandon the bill altogether. The "defense of education" struggle had lasted more than a year and proved to many students that the defense of democratic education required constant struggle; mere institutional reforms would not guarantee a complete transition from fascism to democracy.

THE ANTI-COMMUNIST CRUSADE AND RED PURGE IN JAPAN

By then, it appeared to many Americans and Japanese conservatives that Communism in Japan was a serious threat to the growth of a stable democracy in Japan. The GHQ's purge had begun almost exclusively targeting Communists and their sympathizers, or simply those it referred as "troublemakers."[40] Between 1949 and 1951, the total of over 27,300 people in Japan were purged from their jobs and positions in both public and private institutions including schools.[41] The GHQ and Japanese authorities accelerated the red purge on the pretext of preempting the Communist aggression that had been demonstrated in Korea. The "troublemakers" included not only Communists but also the groups such as the labor union activists, the Korean minorities living in Japan, and many Zengakuren activists. Even though the occupation publicly maintained a "hands-off" policy, denying any direct involvement in anti-Communist purges in Japan, SCAP's "suggestion" of ways the Japanese government should handle the leftists in schools "went far beyond this and implicitly authorize[d] the discharge of teachers and students who engage in political activity" of certain kinds.[42]

The red purge reflected America's effort to enfeeble the "enemies from within." In March 1950, Political Adviser William J. Sebald urged SCAP to encourage "a widespread crack down" on the Communists in Japan who, he charged, were serving the Soviet objective of "undermining the position of the United States and directing all Asiatic grievances into channels of open hostility toward us."[43] Sebald argued that the Japanese Communist activities and its party organ *Akahata* had an anti-occupation character and violated democratic principles.[44] The sense of urgency provided by the Cold War with the Soviet Union in Asia led the US to adopt more virulently anti-Communist tones. As the crisis in the Korean peninsula worsened, MacArthur ordered Prime Minister Yoshida to remove twenty-four Communist Party members from the public office.[45] Following the order, Yoshida convened the Cabinet and took an immediate action to purge the JCP members listed by MacArthur.[46] On July 18, MacArthur wrote to Yoshida again, "I direct that your government vigorously continue the measures being taken in the implementation of my aforesaid letter, and maintain indefinitely the suspensions heretofore imposed upon publication of *Akahata* and its successors and affiliates employed in the dissemination in Japan of inflammatory Communist propaganda."[47]

The occupation's authorization of anti-Communist measures reactivated traditional anti-Communists in Japan. Akao Bin, who had been purged after the war for his wartime ultranationalist activities, was one of them. Representing an organization called the Christian Volunteers, Akao wrote a letter to SCAP asking Americans to "crush Communist aggression in Japan by force as an effective cold war measure" and expressed his desire to build a "unified anti-Communist movement."[48] Taking advantage of this new anti-Communist atmosphere, he resumed his anti-Communist crusade and organized the Society That Tells America the Truth, pledging his support for the US occupation against Communism.[49] Besides such independent anti-Communists, the occupation's anti-Communist campaign also energized those in the political establishment. A network of various American and Japanese public offices linked for the common purpose effectively sustained collaborative efforts to combat Communism. The anti-Communist network formed in Japan was of vital importance for the US occupation, which officially maintained a hands-off policy, claiming that the Japanese would never learn to self-rule, and denied any direct involvement in the red purge in education.

One of the Japanese institutions that played a crucial role in the purge program was the Special Investigation Bureau (SIB) that belonged to Attorney General's Office in the Ministry of Justice.[50] The bureau was directly connected to the Government Section (GS) of the GHQ, which was in charge of the purge program formally named "The Removal and Exclusion of Undesirable Personnel from Public Office."[51] SIB's Director, Yoshikawa Mitsusada, was a former member of wartime thought police. The bureau in practice inherited some of the tasks that had belonged to the dissolved Home Ministry that was known for its inhumane political repression before the end of the war. As the Director of SIB, Yoshikawa aimed to make the bureau modeled on J. Edgar Hoover's "highly efficient and strictly disciplined" Federal Bureau of Investigation (FBI).[52] Unlike the FBI, however, SIB only had two strictly designated missions: to enforce the Organization Reformation Order (Cabinet Order No. 64 of 1949) and the Purge Directive in order to control "anti-occupation" activities.

SIB's importance grew as the Cold War intensified. According to Baerwald, SIB's duties consisted of "helping counterintelligence agents of the occupation and keeping track of Japanese Communists."[53] SIB and the Government Section of the occupation routinely shared intelligence reports and opinions. Despite their close collaborative relationships, however, the institutional link was kept secret from the public.[54] After the outbreak of the Korean War, the bureau expanded from a staff of 537 to 1,199, and this increase was a part of the accelerated US effort to strengthen the security of Japan, in accordance with MacArthur's directive of July 8 ordering the expansion of the national police reserve.[55] The bureau made significant efforts to investigate activities of those considered politically undesirable, including Zengakuren students, and their "anti-occupation" activities.

In the summer of 1949, when the anti-Communist crusade began extending its purge program to universities, it triggered a large-scale student opposition on various campuses. Eells' speech, delivered at the opening ceremony of Niigata University on July 19, became a catalyst for the rapid mobilization of student protests against the red purge, viewing the official anti-Communist campaign in schools as the potential threat to academic freedom and democratic education. Observing the student protests against the proposed education reforms in the previous year, Eells had been convinced of the existence of effective Communist infiltration of Japanese universities. At Niigata University, Eells told the audience that the recent student protests were instigated by the Zengakuren Central Committee, which was "not interested in real student welfare or in the development of democracy in Japan."[56] He accused the student movement of being fully controlled by Zengakuren's small leadership circle in Tokyo, which itself received and followed orders from the JCP and other Communist organizations directed by Moscow. For this reason, Eells saw the Japanese students as the victims of Communism who were deprived of freedom of thought. He believed that it was his task to rescue them.

With this firm conviction, Eells called for the discharge of Communist professors and the expulsion of student strikers from universities so that universities could safeguard democratic education and academic freedom on campuses. In the speech, Eells indignantly argued that the presence of Communist professors would erode academic freedom because "they are *not free*. Their thoughts, their beliefs, their teachings are controlled from outside. Communists are told from headquarters *what to think and what to teach*."[57] He further added that the protection of democratic freedom should not be confused with allowing Communism in schools since it was "a dangerous and destructive doctrine" that seeks "the overthrow of established democratic governments by force."[58] He called for a purge of Communist professors, insisting, "the University not only has the right, it has the duty in order to preserve true academic freedom, to refuse to allow members of the Communist Party on its faculty."[59] His speech was not only a justification of a politically motivated purge of red professors but also an expression of his conviction that Communism, given its ideological dogmatism, was incompatible with a democratic system. The Eells speech portended the coming of a large-scale purge of Communists in schools.[60] His speech at Niigata University became known as the "Eells Statement (Īruzu *Seimei*)."

The Eells Statement caused tremendous repercussions and bipolarized Japanese academia.[61] President of Kyoto University Torigai Risaburo, for instance, agreed with Eells, believing that Japanese democracy was vulnerable, still being in the state of developing which required restricting movements toward extreme right or left.[62] Torigai identified Communism with wartime ultranationalists who had carried out the orders of the government on campuses, depriving the university of academic freedom and autonomy. He wrote, "Resisting any external intervention and control of university is the upmost importance for school autonomy. . . . Everyone deserves to receive equal and free education. No one must be allowed to exploit education to advance his or her interests."[63] On the other hand, the president of the University of Tokyo, Nanbara Shigeru, insisted that academic freedom meant freedom to study any ideology for the purpose of pursuing the truth.[64] His opposition was not so much to defend Communists as to prevent repeating the fascist past that had violently forced ideological coherence throughout the country during the war. Nanbara believed, "Politically, we are not yet quite 'out of the woods' in Japan, unlike America, political democracy is still almost non-existent and a sudden upsurge of reactionary forces cannot be dismissed as an utter impossibility."[65] For that reason, he thought the red purge on campuses would revitalize former fascists and eventually result in "victimizing again too many of our liberal colleagues."[66] On September 22, the members of the National Association of University Professors, except Torigai, shared Nanbara's view and voted against the Eells Statement and proclaimed their opposition to discharging professors on the basis of their affiliation with a particular political party.

Despite such public opposition, the occupation authority and the Japanese government moved to forcibly remove Communist influence from universities. On August 13, the Ministry of Justice announced its decision to apply the Organization Reformation Order (Cabinet Order No. 64) of 1949 to Zengakuren and required its members to register with the government.[67] By September, the red purge had reached the schools, extending its targets to communist professors and students. It resulted in the discharge of approximately 1,150 professors in all prefectures except Kochi.[68] Within a month, a part of the Ordinance for Enforcement of the School Education Act was revised to add a legal basis to enforce the expulsion of student leaders of campus political activism.[69] When the new semester began in September, some universities, including Niigata, Akita, Toyama, Kumamoto, and Kyushu Universities, initiated a "reorganization" of faculty members by sending notifications of discharge to alleged Communist professors, and Niigata University went further and prohibited political activities on campus as a means to weaken Communist influence.[70] On September 23, Zengakuren warned against the coming of mass purges of Communists and others who were sympathetic to their causes.[71]

EELLS'S DEMOCRATIZATION CAMPAIGN AND ZENGAKUREN'S DEFENSE OF DEMOCRACY

The red purge authorized by the occupation raised serious doubt about American democracy. In December, a progressive student-run journal, *Gakusei Hyōron* (Student Review) published a lengthy article on the red purge in American schools, providing a critical analysis of democracy exercised in the United States. The magazine said that the American anti-Communist "witch hunt" was the "tragedy of the American people."[72] In particular, activities of the House Committee on Un-American Activities (HUAC)'s attack on anti-fascists deepened the Japanese students' suspicious about American democracy in practice. In December 1945, HUAC had investigated the Joint Anti-Fascist Refugee Committee of New York and other organizations that had participated in a mass meeting at Madison Square Garden against Francisco Franco's rule in Spain, suspecting their "Communist connections."[73] In March, the HUAC decided to press joint contempt charges against seventeen members of the Joint Anti-Fascist Refugee Committee of New York City.[74] Referring to these events in the United States, the student writer in the *Gakusei Hyōron* insisted that the fact that opposition to Franco and fascism was denigrated as "un-American" raised a serious question about American democracy.

The red purge in universities that had begun with the Eells Statement provided a new direction for the student movement. After the summer vacation, Zengakuren formally declared its war against the Eells Statement and the red purge in universities. At the third Zengakuren national convention held on November 2 and 3 at Waseda University, student representatives proclaimed to end the student movement's dormancy, calling for more active resistance by a united student front against intensifying "*Fassho-teki* (fascist-like) repression," which they condemned as a product of America's aggressive ideological battle.[75] Baerwald recalled that the reverse course and subsequent red purge "coincided with the depurge of militarists and ultranationalists."[76] This coincidence of timing had the effect of giving the impression that the occupation was no longer concerned about the democratization process in Japan, but thought only of the international cold war.[77] It seemed to many student activists that the United States could not promote true democracy while fighting the Cold War at the same time.

During the years before the Hungarian revolt that prompted a wave of anti-Stalinism, the Chinese revolution and the Eastern bloc's "people's democracy" seemed the only viable alternative to the anti-Communist democracy of the United States. The resolution adopted at the third national convention of Zengakuren stated:

The intensifying intra-capitalist oppression as shown by the devaluation of British pound and French franc (September 19) and the consolidation and expansion of democratic forces demonstrated by the creation of People's Republic of China (September 21), the Truman statement announcing the first Soviet atomic bomb (September 23), and the establishment of the German Democratic Republic (October 7), and if we understand these two kind of situations as the factors that intensifying fascification of policies of our current government, we have an unprecedentedly important duty.[78]

Inspired by the ideal of "people's democracy," the Zengakuren representatives called for more active opposition to the GHQ's effort to suppress Communists in Japan and the Japanese government's resort to fascist-style repression.

Meanwhile, Eells developed some doubts on the effectiveness of coercive measures to free Japanese education from Communism. He began to think that such forcible suppression of student Communists would not lead to a desirable outcome since "they are more likely to thrive on such attempted suppression, being driven into greater secrecy only."[79] He reported that the Communist penetration of Japanese universities could be best combatted through a positive program that would, for instance, encourage non-political student organizations, such as athletic, social, or dramatic activities.[80] Lamenting the strength of "Communist" students in Japan, he hoped "the non-Communist students would exhibit one-half the zeal and passionate devotion of the Communists" in Zengakuren.[81] Motivated by the conviction that Communism had successfully filled the ideological vacuum left by the end of the war and the need to counter such Bolshevik influence in Japanese education, Eells sought to foster non-Communist democratic consciousness among Japanese students. In September, Eells and another CIE officer Donald Marsh Typer drafted a "Program for Activities in Universities" to initiate a nationwide anti-Communist tour, which would begin at Tokushima University on Shikoku island on November 7 and finish at Iwate University in the northeast region on May 19.[82]

The students responded by resisting the arrival of Eells, which they interpreted as that of mass red purge at their schools. Eells recalled that students often interrupted him on campuses by calling him "liar," "enemy of democracy," and "warmonger."[83] The largest protests occurred at Tohoku University on May 2. Students had prepared flyers that read: "No More Hiroshima! No More Eells! Japanese Education for the Japanese, by the Japanese!" and posted them on the campus walls overnight.[84] In the eyes of the Japanese students, Eells's anti-Communist campaign resembled Japan's prewar political repression that had served the purposes of Japanese militarism and aggressive war abroad. In the morning, Eells and two CIE officers Typer and William Neufeld arrived at Tohoku University campus in Sendai. Eells had prepared a lecture titled, "Academic Freedom and Communism" to deliver at Tohoku University. The lecture was going to be followed by Typer's talk on student activities and Neufeld's on physical education in universities.[85] When Eells was about to start the lecture, students demanded that he answer whether he was on official GHQ mission or making a private visit.[86] The distinction was important for the students since challenging official GHQ acts was illegal under the Imperial Ordinance 311 that prohibited anti-occupation activities. In front of the hostile audience of over eight hundred people, Eells ambiguously answered that his lecture was both official and personal and tried to proceed with his talk, but students' dissenting voices incessantly interrupted, forcing him to give up delivering the lecture and step down from the podium.[87] The students celebrated as Eells resigned himself and left the auditorium saying, "*sayonara* (good-bye in Japanese)."[88] They felt that they had successfully defended academic freedom by preventing Eells from giving the talk. The police arrived in the afternoon armed with an arrest warrant written in English and arrested four students.[89]

On May 4, students at Tohoku University held a school-wide meeting to discuss tactics to resist Eells and formed an ad hoc Tohoku University Joint Struggle Committee on the campus. This group of students proclaimed, "Having been enslaved by and used as the bullets of Japanese imperialism led by *zaibatsu* (industrial and financial conglomerates) and military cliques, the Japanese citizens, who were not yet fully enjoying the joys of liberation after the war, now face the danger of being drawn into another war."[90] Next day,

Tohoku University, May 2, 1950. Eells trying to deliver a lecture. *Tohoku University Archive.*

Tohoku University, May 2, 1950. The signs posted by students at the Katahira campus of Tohoku Uiversity. They read: "No More Hiroshima / Eals[sic.]," "Back home! Eals[sic.]," "Academic Freedom is in Danger," and "Education for the Japanese by the hands of Japanese." *Tohoku University Archive.*

the protest committee issued an "Appeal to the Citizens" that demanded the revocation of the Eells Statement and the end of red purge.[91]

Zengakuren students simultaneously went onto the streets in solidarity with Tohoku University comrades, collecting funds and picketing to send their message to the public.[92] About 5,000 students participated in the demonstration held in Tokyo, expressing their support for Tohoku University's struggle against Eells.[93] One May 4, the Secretariat of the Central Committee of Zengakuren issued an open demand to the Far Eastern Commission of the Allied Powers to deal with Eells, who had violated the democratic principles promised in the Potsdam Declaration.[94] On May 8, the Kyushu Federation of Zengakuren (*Kyushu Gakusei Jichikai Renmei*, abbreviated as *Kyushu Gakuren*) held a rally, which was participated in by sixty representatives from thirty schools, in solidarity with "Tohoku University's heroic struggle."[95] At the same time, the Central Executive Committee (*Chūō Shikkō Iinkai*) of Zengakuren in Tokyo seemed to be taken aback by the rise of powerful student protests in Tohoku. Zengakuren leaders had assumed that Tohoku, the "political insensible" and "backward" region with a relatively poor agricultural economy dominated by a small land-owing bourgeoisie class would be least likely to be the vanguard of a progressive revolution.[96] To find out what was going on and to support students protesting against Eells, Zengakuren in Tokyo dispatched a team to Tohoku University.

Eells assumed that similar student protests against him that were simultaneously being organized throughout Japan were strong evidence of Communist control over them. Eells condemned them by saying that the whole incident "follows the Soviet pattern of violence, subjecting a bulk of the nation to the power of a minority comprising three per cent of the people."[97] Yet, historical evidence suggests that the Zengakuren central office in Tokyo was in fact not able to exercise total control over Zengakuren protests in places like Hokkaido. On the eve of the anti-Eells struggle at Hokkaido University, the chairman of the Hokkaido Federation of Students' Self-Governing Associations (*Hokkaido Gakusei Jichikai Renmei*, abbreviated as *Dōgakuren*), Yanada Masataka proclaimed, "We oppose the Zengakuren Central Committee's top-down imposition of a strategy," and insisted on the importance of taking an action that corresponds with students' sincere desire to achieve the best possible education.[98]

On May 15 and 16, Eells and his team arrived at Hokkaido University. By the time of their arrival, students had filled the path toward the auditorium with flyers and placards, written in both Japanese and English, protesting the arrival of Eells and red purge in defense of academic freedom. Eells found some messages among them were also criticizing American foreign policy as being inimical to international peace and democracy.[99] As in Tohoku University, students at Hokkaido University posted "No more Hiroshima, No More Eells" flyers near the entrance to the auditorium, which irritated Eells as he walked through it.[100] After reaching the podium, Eells began with a joke, "My name is pronounced the same as 'eels,' which the Japanese people love to eat, so I was afraid of coming here today."[101] He then started a lecture on Communism and education to stress the undemocratic nature of Communism.

After the lecture, an open round table discussion was held in the afternoon. One of the professors at the table, Professor of Mathematics Moriya Mikao, challenged Eells by asking how Communist ideology could influence academic fields such as mathematics that did not relate to political, ideological, or philosophical debates. Moriya said that he was a devoted Catholic but Catholicism had no influence upon his study of mathematics, and the same could be said of Marxists.[102] Eells responded by arguing that even numbers would be distorted and students would be forced to learn that 2 plus 2 equaled 5 under the Soviet totalitarian system, referring to the dystopian novel *1984* written by George Orwell in 1949.[103] Professor of Physics Miyahara Shohei sarcastically told Eells that if that was the Soviet mathematics, then the United States should not be concerned with the defense against the Soviet Union since the Soviets could not possibly make anything, including nuclear weapons.[104]

The audience applauded Miyahara.[105] This so-called "eel roundtable" resulted in highlighting the absurdity of America's anti-Communism, and Eells failed to convince students of the incompatibility of Communism with democracy.

The roundtable was scheduled to resume next day, but Eells singlehandedly decided to deliver another lecture instead and allowed no questions from the audience during his lecture. The students vigorously protested and demanded Eells to explain why he made the schedule change, but Eells told them that students were not allowed to ask question during his talk.[106] The moderator asked Eells to allow the audience to ask questions, but Eells refused and told the students to "go back."[107] Eells's "undemocratic" way of handling the unfavorable situation led the students to rapidly mobilize against "colonial-like" forceful top-down imposition of education policy. The moderator soon announced the cancellation of Eells's talk that was scheduled for the afternoon.[108] The military police arrived with armed soldiers next day. They arrested five students and took them to the Counter Intelligence Corps (CIC) office.[109] In June, Hokkaido University announced that it would expel four students and suspend six students for disrupting Eells's lecture, and President Ito Seiya resigned in August, taking responsibility for the Eells Incident.

During the struggle against Eells, student protestors grew less hesitant to openly attack "American" imperialism. Although criticism of capitalist imperialism had been pervasive among the circles of Zengakuren, student activists had consciously avoided overtly attacking "American" imperialism since it would violate the Imperial Ordinance 311. Yanada, who played a leading role in the anti-Eells strike at Hokkaido University, recalled that even most radical students had hesitated to publicly attack American imperialism in the face of the absolute power of the occupation.[110] Yet, as the students began emphasizing their current struggle as not merely opposition against red purge, but as the resistance to the "colonial-course," the Eells struggle gradually developed into the first open anti-imperial struggle against the occupation.[111] The chairman of Zengakuren, Takei, recalled that the anti-imperial struggle ignited by the anti-Eells protests was students' resistance to America's attempts to make Japanese universities "factories of warmongering ideology" for the sake of the capitalist world.[112] In *Gakusei Hyōron*, Takei wrote that the anti-Eells struggle manifested the real enemies of democracy: American imperialism that was trying to "colonize" Japanese education, collaborating with the Japanese government.[113] Takei emphasized the importance of engaging in direct confrontation with the United States, rather than trivial political battles with the submissive Japanese conservatives.[114]

Zengakuren's vocal anti-imperialism invited international attention.[115] On May 26, a letter arrived to the Hokkaido Federation of Students' Self-Governing Associations from the International Union of Students (IUS) in Prague.

The IUS central office expressed their support for the Japanese students' anti-Eells protest and wrote that 3.6 million students of sixty different countries in the world supported their struggle to defend freedom and self-determination.[116] On May 18, a radio station from Moscow applauded the Japanese students for initiating "Japan's first demonstrations against American imperialism."[117]

ZENGAKUREN'S SECOND FRONT

The mainstream newspapers in Japan and the US expressed their concerns with the radicalizing Japanese student movement after the student protests. The *Nippon Times* condemned "unruly mob actions" by the Communist students and their sympathizers in the editorial on May 18. It stated that the student protests "proved Dr. Eells' views on the Communist reliance upon force and violence to work their will upon those who disagree with them," which seemed inevitable to conclude that the student protestors were "professional agitators with nothing better to do than to perform the dirty work for the Communist Party."[118] The *Mainichi Shimbun* wrote, "The opposition to the Eells statement today has gone beyond the limit of a genuine students' movement to safeguard the freedom of learning."[119] In the United States, *The New York Times* wrote that the Japanese student movement had adopted Communist rhetoric and turned anti-occupation, anti-America in its coverage of the student protests against Eells.[120] Despite such prevailing accusation of having been guided by adult Communists, the Japanese students movement in fact was troubling the JCP as well.

The amplification of "anti-imperialism" by Zengakuren exacerbated its relations with the JCP. One newspaper reported, "The radical movement of the Zengakuren following the obstruction of the lectures by Dr. Walter C. Eells, SCAP adviser on education, at Tohoku and Hokkaido universities in May went to such extremes that even the Communist Party headquarters criticized it as deviating from the party line."[121] JCP leaders were afraid that the growing power of the student movement had made them more assertive and more independent from JCP guidance. Yet, it was not so much the changes in the student movement as the JCP's declining popularity and influence that made the student left "deviate" from the party.

By then, the JCP's popular "lovable" approach and its democratizing movement under the occupation had proven ill-suited to the new realities of the Cold War, and the pressure to conform to the Soviet-led international Communist movement mounted. After being liberated by the US occupation, the JCP attempted to become a "lovable Communist party" that could appeal to a great number of the ordinary citizens and supported the occupation's "peaceful democratic revolution." Such JCP policy line began inviting criticism from the Communist Information Bureau (Cominform) that had condemned the occupation as the US imperialists' means to enslave Japan to its capitalist monopoly.[122] On January 6, 1950, the official organ of the Cominform, *For a Lasting Peace, for a People's Democracy!* condemned the JCP secretariat Nosaka Sanzo, who was considered having provided the theoretical foundation of the "lovable" party policy, and demanded that the JCP undertake a fundamental policy change. Following the Cominform criticism, Stalinist members of JCP singlehandedly ended the brief period of the "honeymoon with the occupation" and focused on following theoretical and political directions provided by the Cominform.[123] Nosaka accepted the criticism and admitted his theoretical fallacy, and his self-criticism was officially accepted by the JCP on January 18. The Cominform criticism led the JCP to abandon its "lovable" course.[124]

This so-called "Cominform criticism" brought instability to the internal politics of the JCP and became a catalyst for a factional split between the Centralists (*Shokan-ha*) and the Internationalists (*Kokusai-ha*). While the Centralists advocated the "Yoshida-first" strategy and an indirect attack on capitalist imperialism, the Internationalists called for a direct struggle against US imperialism. Unable to reconcile the factional conflict, the Centralists that dominated the party's leadership expelled the Internationalists from the Executive Committee. The changes within the JCP affected its relationship with Zengakuren. Zengakuren's move against American imperialism contradicted with the Yoshida-first strategy of the Centralists who now dominated the JCP leadership. The Centralists shifted their criticism toward Zengakuren, disdainfully calling them "Trotskyist internationalists." In response, Zengakuren leaders issued a lengthy statement, "Current Student Movement: Zengakuren Written Opinion," which marked the student left's first open official challenge to the JCP. In the paper, they criticized the party leadership's dogmatic bureaucratism and conservative "opportunism," which resulted in their failure to lead an effective anti-imperial movement.[125] When the statement was made public, the JCP initiated its counterattack on the student movement. Immediately after the anti-Eells protest at Tohoku University erupted, the JCP ordered the dissolution of leading Communist student cells in the University of Tokyo and Waseda University, which had been playing a central role in the Zengakuren leadership. The JCP explained that the dissolution was aimed to "maintain the iron discipline and unity of the party under the tense circumstances of the present day."[126] Yet such actions pushed the student movement further to claim more organizational independence from the JCP. The struggles against Eells and red purge, moreover, had given the student left a sense of power to act on its own.

Without being disheartened by the JCP criticism, the students continued attacking "American capitalist warmongering imperialism" and its failure to live up to democratic principles.[127] Their self-identification as the former victims of Japanese imperialism and current struggles with the US power made Japanese leftist students exhibit a peculiar blend of Marxist internationalism and nationalism. In their study on the history of the Japanese student movements, Sumiya Etsuji, Takakuwa Suehide and Ogura Jyoji pointed out, "The struggle [against Eells] made students more conscious about the international solidarity."[128] At the fourth national convention held between May 20 and 23, 1950 the Zengakuren students proclaimed their solidarity with the oppressed classes of workers, students, and farmers struggling against Western capitalist imperialism, particularly those fighting for independence in China and Vietnam.[129]

THE RADICALIZATION OF THE "COMMUNIST-ORIENTED" STUDENT MOVEMENT AS A SECURITY CONCERN

In June, the governmental authorities began acting against the student left on the grounds of violation of Imperial Ordinance 311. Education Minister Amano Teiyu declared that they would take strong measures against the Communist-oriented "radical student movement."[130] On June 11, sixty Japanese police forces entered Waseda University with search warrants and found copies of the "Communist-inspired" open letter to General MacArthur that demanded such things as the release of the protestors who were arrested for assaulting American soldiers.[131] No student was arrested on that day. Deploring the police action, the Vice Chairman of Zengakuren Eshima Yuichi lamented, "This is worse than the pre-war peace perversion measures."[132] On June 30, the police found the copies of "Real State of Military Bases," which listed the locations and descriptions of American military bases in Japan and Japanese factories that supplied the US military.[133] The copies were allegedly distributed among students of other universities. Alarmed by this incident, William G. Fritz of the GHQ Public Safety Division advised the Japanese National Rural Police Headquarters to "investigate strictly."[134] Following the advice the National Rural Police Headquarters ordered the Police Troop Commander of every prefecture to carry out an investigation of local Zengakuren offices in their regions.[135] At 6 am on July 13, the police raided Zengakuren's central office in Tokyo and regional offices and conducted a nationwide investigation of their activities with SIB's assistance.[136] The *Mainichi Shimbun* published a special issue covering these unprecedented nationwide raids of Zengakuren offices. On July 18, the Japanese police reported to the GHQ that it had successfully apprehended Zengakuren members for their anti-American activities. The police also raided homes and dormitory rooms of Zengakuren leaders, including Takei, and arrested six of them for violating Imperial Ordinance 311.[137] It reported that the 350 copies of "Real State of Military Bases," which were identified as illegal documents, had been distributed from the Zengakuren central office in Tokyo to its regional offices.[138] To their dismay, such direct attacks against Zengakuren did not solve the fundamental issue of communism in education. Still in November 1950, Yoshikawa was reporting to Major Jack P. Napier of GS that the "powerful" movement of Zengakuren "colored with politics" had grown more prominent on university campuses after the Eells incident.[139]

By 1951, the "war of ideas" had moved into high gear in Washington as well. In December 1951, the Educational Policies Commission and the American Council on Education, consisting of prominent members such as President Dwight D. Eisenhower of Columbia University and President James B. Conant of Harvard University, jointly published a manuscript titled

Photo of the police raid on the office of the student self-governing association of the University of Tokyo, Zengakuren's central office, on July 13, 1950. On the wall, it reads, "Against imperial wars." © *Kyodo News Agency*

Photo of the police officers guarding the entrance to Zengakuren's central office on the University of Tokyo campus during the raid on July 13, 1950. © *Kyodo News Agency*

Education and National Security for the purpose of making policy evaluations and recommendations in an area of education.[140] The authors argued that the period between 1945 and 1951 was marked by "Kremlin successes," as demonstrated by the consolidation of the Eastern bloc and China's fall to Communism. Now, they argued, the West had become ever more powerful economically and militarily with the signings of the North Atlantic Treaty of 1949 and the Security Treaty with Japan at San Francisco, which provided the United States with a favorable condition for rolling back Communist power that had successfully exploited the political vacuum even in the field of education in the world.[141] Yet, they also warned, "It would be quite possible, surely, for the West to build up an impregnable military alliance and yet lose the world to Communism. It would be equally possible to defeat Moscow by force of arms and yet lose the world to Communism."[142] Emphasis on wining hearts and minds was important not only to prevent "the totalitarian delusion" from entering the free world but also to foster "understanding of interdependence" to preserve the alliance.[143] This had a direct link with security of the free world. The authors concluded, "The peace of reconciliation we have just achieved with Japan is a moral and realistic victory. But we need to make clear that our retention of military bases in Asia is to help in the enforcement of collective security, not to serve as outposts of empire. This illustrates the potential misunderstanding we must constantly work to avoid."[144]

The maintenance of internal security of post-occupation Japan was another concern for Washington. Between 1949 and 1950, labor activists were making desperate efforts to resist the anti-inflation policy package known as the Dodge Line that mandated a large-scale firing of public employees in the name of rationalization. The student movement was evermore radicalizing and openly attacking capitalist imperialism. Observing such situations in Japan, General Carter Magruder, who was one of the US delegate to the negotiation of the peace treaty with Japan, expressed his concern with proposed Article 8 of the treaty, which read, "The forces furnished by the United States or other Treaty Powers shall not have any responsibility or authority to intervene in the internal affairs of Japan."[145] Magruder recommended that the US maintain the right to intervene in the internal security of Japan, especially in case of "large-scale internal Communist riots."[146] Magruder's view was widely accepted in both State and Defense Departments, and Secretary of State Acheson wrote to Truman, "There should be nothing in the Treaty which prohibits the United States garrison forces' acting at the request of the Japanese Government to put down large-scale internal riots and disturbances."[147] This was approved by President Truman on September 8 and included in the US-Japan Security Treaty signed at the end of the occupation in September. Dean Rusk further called for strengthening the Japanese police force "for internal security and to provide at least a minimum of protection to Japan, in view of the fact that virtually all American occupation troops are now fighting the war in Korea."[148] Korean Ambassador John M. Chang expressed uneasiness about rearming the former aggressor of Asia, but Rusk told him that America's objective in providing Japan necessary protection and other kinds of assistance was to protect "the rear of our operations in Korea."[149]

After the end of occupation, the student radicalism and Communist influence in education remained as a major concern in Japan for Cold War America. American traveler Ralph J. Watkins reported to President Truman in August 1952 after his trip to Japan:

> The disquieting note pertained to Japanese university faculties and student bodies. I was informed by numerous people, FECOM [the United States Army's Far Eastern Command] experts, Japanese civilians and ex-military personnel, and American personnel generally, that the Communist influence was confined to a tiny minority of the Japanese people—with the significant exception of university faculties and student bodies. And it was pointed out that an alarmingly high percentage of faculty members and Japanese students had become infected with the virus of Communism. . . . In my judgment it is highly important that

specialized teams be sent to Japan to try to influence thinking among their university faculties and student bodies.[150]

There was little sign indicating the decline of Communist influence in Japanese universities, and it continued to concern the United States. Indeed, it seemed that neither the post-Korean War economic recovery nor the purge of Communist professors failed to eliminate Communism on campuses and it required anti-Communists to rethink their strategies.

In 1952 and 1953, American officers serving at the US Consulate in Kobe conducted field research by directly approaching student activists. On July 31, 1952, American Consul General Ralph J. Blake met a student of Kyoto University who belonged to the International Student Association of Japan, a non-leftist organization that was aimed to promote international exchanges among the students.[151] Blake tried to gain insider accounts and information on the Japanese student movement. During their conversation, the student told Blake that the Communist students constitute only five percent of the student body in both Kyoto University and the University of Tokyo; however, he warned against "underestimating the power of the student Communists simply because of their numerical inferiority."[152] Blake compiled his knowledge and information he gathered in Japan and sent his report entitled "Communism in Japanese Universities" to the State Department. In the report, he warned that the United States should not underestimate the organizational strength of the Communists and their power to attract and provide "external aids" to the students in Japan.[153]

In 1953, Glen Bruner, another consular officer, produced a detailed report on student radicalism entitled "An Example of the Failure of Material Success to Eliminate Student Leftism" based on information he had gathered from former student activists. It reflected his growing doubt about the idea that economic hardship made Communism attractive. Bruner wrote that a Japanese student told him that the Japanese leftist students believed that Marxism "answers to all the stubborn political and economic problems confronting present-day Japan" and the McCarran Act, which was aimed to control un-American and other subversive activities, "must be a stupid law since an internationally recognized artist of the stature of Charles Chaplin is denied admission."[154] Bruner became convinced that Americans should "correct" the Japanese students' understanding of the United States, rather than simply filling their stomachs, in order to fight Communism in Japanese universities. A student named "Mr. Oguri [first name unknown]" seemed to interest Bruner the most.[155] Mr. Oguri, according to Bruner, showed "a certain hostility, a certain indefinable air of anti-Americanism" and confronted him by pointing out American hypocrisies; for instance, he said that African Americans "were held down socially and economically" in the United States.¹⁵⁶ Bruner told Mr. Oguri that progress was being made and the racial problem would disappear in the future, and this, according to Bruner, seemed to make Mr. Oguri "genuinely convinced by the arguments presented and admitted that he had an entirely incorrect conception of our racial problem."¹⁵⁷ Bruner concluded from this experience that the lack of contacts with Americans and the language barrier created a "distorted and biased picture of the United States."¹⁵⁸

Samuel D. Berger, an US Embassy officer in Tokyo, emphasized in his report to State Department in June 1954 that the United States "should not underestimate the degree to which communist influence in the 'intellectual front' contributed to current confusions, or the long-range threat this poses to American policy vis-à-vis Japan...."¹⁵⁹ The best way to combat Communism in Japan was, Berger suggested, for the United States to develop an effective anti-Communist front with the Japanese anti-Communist conservatives, and in order to do so, he argued that the US had to aid the Japanese conservatives both "financially and in other ways."¹⁶⁰ It would help the United States avoid directly intervening in the internal affairs of Japan without harming its "vital interest in seeing that something is done to deal with it [the problem of Communism in Japan]."¹⁶¹ Berger concluded, "The plain fact of experience shows that improving economic conditions and raising standards of living accomplish little or nothing, unless they are accompanied by a variety of measures to reduce and eliminate communist power and influence."¹⁶² By the mid-1950s, persistent popular agitations and the popularity of Marxism among the intellectual community in Japan challenged the idea that economic hardship was not the only reason why Communism attracted the Japanese. For Japanese and American authorities, it also seemed to have proven that repressive measures did not yield desirable outcomes.

To conclude, the GHQ, which had assumed almost sacrosanct authority since 1945, faced its first direct challenge by the Japanese. It came from neither the JCP nor union workers, the traditional suspects of Communist agitations, but university students who took an uncompromising stance to expunge fascism in Japan. With the reverse course, the students grew hostile to the United States as they became convinced that the US had abandoned its earlier promises of democratization and demilitarization in order to fight an ideological battle against Communism. In 1950, Eells's call for a red purge in education and his subsequent anti-Communist campus tour triggered a wave of vehement student protests. This so-called "Eells incident," or "Eells whirlwind" had a profound impact on nascent Zengakuren and Japan's postwar student movement. It led Zengakuren to openly attack *American* imperialism for the first time.

Through the Eells struggle, at the same time, the relationship between Zengakuren and the JCP deteriorated, but the JCP continued to have a powerful influence over Zengakuren. Alarmed by the growing independence of the Zengakuren movement and its capacity to organize direct actions without the help of the party, the JCP tightened its control of the student Communist activities. As the result of the Internationalists' defeat in the JCP factional dispute, the small group of the Zengakuren members who sided with the Centralist faction took advantage of the defeat of the Internationalists within the JCP and forcibly took over the Zengakuren leadership, bringing a major shift in the organizational line after 1951.[163] Under the Centralist student leadership, the Zengakuren movement lost its energy and appeal, and the Japanese student movement suffered from confusion during the period between 1951 and 1955. The Centralist-dominated JCP shifted their line and now advocated a direct struggle with the US imperialism, following the Cominform directive, and even employed violent tactics from the rural villages, modeling on Maoist armed struggles, until 1955 when it finally admitted its tactical failure at the Sixth National Party Congress (*Dai-6-kai Zenkoku Kyōgikai*, commonly called *Rokuzenkyō*). Between 1951 and 1955, Centralist-dominated Zengakuren was left with a small group of Centralist students, employing violent "revolutionary" tactics and engaging in mountain village guerrilla warfare, following the JCP directive.[164]

Despite of the period of dormancy that followed the Eells struggle, Zengakuren's democratization movement during the occupation had paved the way for the coming age of the student movement. The anti-JCP faction of the Zengakuren, including Takei, continued their efforts to build an independent student movement behind the scene. In November 1951, the anti-Centralist students formed the Antiwar Student League (*Hansen Gakusei Dōmei*) to fight for "peace and independence" and acted independent from the Centralist-dominated Zengakuren. This small group of the communist students established the basis of the *Bunto* faction of the Zengakuren that was to lead the historic movement in 1960 against the US-Japan Security Treaty.[165] Koyama Kenichi, Morita Minoru, and Shima Shigeo were among the few who still kept their membership in the Communist cell at the University of Tokyo, although they remained critical of the JCP leadership. Morita recalled, "By the fall of 1952, the student movement had become powerless. . . . [When Koyama became the chairman of Zengakuren after the *Rokuzenkyō* in 1956], it was only three of us left at the University of Tokyo's Komaba campus to rebuild Zengakuren."[166] In 1956, the struggle against the plan to extend the runways of the US owned Tachikawa Air Base in the small town of Sunagawa played a crucial role in reuniting Zengakuren.

NOTES

1. Hans H. Baerwald, *The Purge of Japanese Leaders under the Occupation* (Berkeley: University of California Press, 1959; Westport, CT: Greenwood Press, 1977), 1; Citations refer to the Greenwood Press edition.
2. Mark T. Orr, "Educational Reform in Occupied Japan, 1945–1950: A Study of Acceptance of and Resistance to Institutional Change" (Ph.D. dissertation, University of Chicago, 1952), 48–51.
3. Takemae, *Inside GHQ*, 180–81; Dyke was a business man from New York who had worked as a PR for Colgate and NBC. Nugent had studied Asian History at Stanford University.
4. Oinas-Kukkonen, *Tolerance, Suspicion, and Hostility*, 79–80.
5. From Department of State to the Acting United States Political Adviser for Japan (William J. Sebald), Tokyo, January 4, 1949. RG 84. Box 49. NARA II.
6. Isao Myojin, "Red Purge in Universities in Occupied Japan (2): A Study on Eells's Address in Niigata University," *Journal of Hokkaido University of Education* 47, no. 1 (1966): 46.
7. *Trading Ideas with the World: International Educational and Technical Exchange*, Report of the United States Advisory Commission on Educational Exchange, March 31, 1949 (Washington, DC: Department of State, 1949). File: CIE Administrative Branch. RG 331. Box 5388. NARA II.
8. Ibid.
9. Eells was the author of *The Junior College*, published in 1931, which encouraged the growth of junior college programs in the United States. His reputation grew as the two-year junior college expanded largely due to the Great Depression when less people became able to afford four-year college.
10. Reorientation Branch, Office of Occupied Areas and Office of the Secretary of the Army, *Semi-Annual Report of Stateside Activities Supporting the Reorientation Program in Japan and the Ryukyu Islands*, January 1951. Joseph C. Trainor Paper. Box 76. Hoover Institution Archives, Stanford University.
11. Walter Crosby Eells, *Communism in Education in Asia, Africa, and the Far Pacific* (Washington, DC: American Council on Education, 1954).
12. Teruo Takei, "Tatakia no naka kara Umareta Zengakuren Kessei to Sonogo no Tenkai [The development of Zengakuren that emerged in the midst of a struggle]," *Tatakau Seishun no Kaiko*, ed. Chūō Daigaku Gakusei Undō, Shashin to Kaiko Kankō Kai, in Takei, *Takei Teruo Gakusei Undō Ronshū: Sō to Shiteno Gakusei Undō, Zengakuren Sōseiki no Shisō to Kōdō* [A collection of Takei Teruo student movement papers: the student movement as a class struggle, the ideology and activities of Zengakuren in the early period] (hereafter cited as *Takei Student Movement Papers*) (Tokyo: Supesu Kaya, 2005), 19.
13. Ibid.
14. Akira Yamanaka, *Sengo Gakusei Undōshi* [A history of the postwar student movement] (Tokyo: Aoki Shoten, 1961), 49; Taro Murakami, "Arashi no Naka no Zengaukren [Zengakuren in the storm]," *Kaizo* 33, no. 6 (1952): 149.

15. "Kyōiku Fukkō Gakusei Kekki Taikai [The opening rally of students for the reconstruction of education]," *Gakusei Shimbun*, June 15, 1948. Document no. 132 in *Zengakuren Documents*, vol. 1, 1945–1949, 252.

16. Zai-Nihon Chōsen Minshu Seinen Dōmei Tokyo Honbu [The Korean Democratic Youth League in Japan, Tokyo headquarters], "Zainichi Chōsen Minshu Seinen Dōmei kara no Messēji [A message from the Korean Democratic Youth League in Japan]," July 7, 1948 in ibid., 270–271; This message was sent to the Federation of the National Public University and Technical College Self-Governing Associations (*Zenkoku Kankōritsu Daigaku Kōsen Gakusei Jichukai Rengōkai*).

17. Yamanaka, *Sengo Gakusei Undōshi*, 50–51.

18. Kokutetsu Rōdō Kumiai Jyōhō Sendenbu [The information and publicity office of the National Railway Union], "Zenkoku Jichiren 'Kyōiku Fukkō Tōsō' ['The struggle for the reconstruction of education' of All-Japan Prefectural and Municipal Workers Union]," September 1948. Document no. 140 in *Zengakuren Documents*, vol. 1, 1945–1949, 273.

19. "Kyōiku Fukko Gakusei Kekki Taikai," *Gakusei Shimbun*, June 15, 1948, 252.

20. Yamanaka, *Sengo Gakusei Undōshi*, 51.

21. Takei, "Zengakuren Kessei no Zengo: Sore wa Gyakuryū tono Tatakai no Makubiraki datta [Around the time of the founding of Zengakuren: it was the beginning of the fight against opposing currents]," *Waseda 1950-nen Shiryō to Shōgen*, ed. Waseda 1950-nen Kirokunokai in *Takei Student Movement Papers*, 59.

22. "Ware Ware wa Fashizumu to Sensō ni Hantai Suru: Zengakuren Kessei Taikai Sengen [We oppose fascism and war: a declaration made at Zengakuren's inaugural convention]," September 18, 1948. Document no. 146 in *Zengakuren Documents*, vol. 1, 1945–1949, 300.

23. "Zenkoku Gakusei Jichikai Sōrengō (Zengakuren) Kessei Taikai Gijiroku [Proceedings of Zengakuren's inaugural convention]," September 18–20, 1948. Document no. 145 in ibid., 287.

24. Nihon Gakusei Undō Kenkyūkai, *Gakusei Undō no Kenkyū* [A study on the student movement] (Tokyo: Nikkan Rōdō Tsushin Sha, 1966), 13–14.

25. Ibid.

26. The number of college and university students in Japan was 409,650 in 1945 and 405,310 in 1950, see Michiya Shimbori, "Zengakuren: A Japanese Case Study of a Student Political Movement," *Sociology of Education* 37, no. 3 (1964): 232.

27. "Zenkoku Gakusei Jichikai Sōrengō (Zengakuren) Kessei Taikai Gijiroku," September 18–20, 1948, 291.

28. "General Student Rally at Tokyo University," Education Division, Civil Information and Education Section, October 1, 1948. File: Communist Activities in Universities. RG 331. Box 5642. NARA II.

29. In the March 15 incident of 1928, the government arrested about 1,500 Communists and alleged Communist sympathizers under the 1925 Peace Preservation Laws. The Takigawa Incident of 1933 was the case involving the cabinet dismissal of Takigawa Yukitoki, a liberal law professor, for his alleged sympathies toward Communism. These are considered as one of the most notorious cases of governmental suppression of academic freedom.

30. Kansai-chihō Gakusei Jichikai Rengō [The Federation of Students' Self-Governing Associations of the Kansai region], "Daigakuhō Hantai Suto Sengen [A declaration of strikes against the University Law]," May 5, 1949 in *Zengakuren Documents*, vol. 1, 1945–1949, 406–7; "Ware Ware wa Fashizumu to Sensō ni Hantai Suru," September 18, 1948, 300.

31. "Ware Ware wa Fashizumu to Sensō ni Hantai Suru," September 18, 1948, 300.

32. Teruo Takei, "Tenkanki ni Tatsu Gakusei Undō [The student movement in the period of transition]," *Gakusei Hyōron* (November 1948) in *Takei Student Movement Papers*, 167.

33. Kokugakuren Shokikyoku [The Secretariat of the Federation of the National University Students' Self-Governing Associations], "Kyōiku Seido Kaikaku o Meguru Shomondai [The problems related to the reform of the education system]," June 28, 1948. Document no. 138 in *Zengakuren Documents*, vol. 1, 1945–1949, 263–69.

34. Takei, "Zengakuren Kessei no Zengo," 65.

35. Yamanaka, *Sengo Gakusei Undōshi*, 61.

36. Ibid., 64.

37. Ibid.

38. Ibid., 79; Takei, "Zengakuren Kessei no Zengo," 69.

39. Ibid.

40. Dower, *Embracing Defeat*, 72.

41. Tetsuo Hirata, *Reddo Pāji no Shi-teki Kyūmei* [Historical investigation of the red purge] (Tokyo: Shin Nihon Shuppansha, 2002), 22.

42. *The New York Times*, June 5, 1950.

43. The Acting United States Political Adviser for Japan (Sebald) to the Director of the Office of Northeast Asian Affairs (Allison), March 24, 1950 in *FRUS*, 1950, vol. VI, East Asia and the Pacific (Washington, DC: United States Government Printing Office, 1976), 1154–56.

44. Ibid.

45. Full text of General MacArthur's letter to Prime Minister released by the GHQ on June 6,1950, enclosed in the telegram from Sebald to the Department of State on June 6, 1950. RG 59. Box 4237. NARA II.

46. Telegram from Sebald to the Department of State on June 6, 1950. RG 59. Box 4237. NARA II.

47. SCAP's Letter to the Prime Minister Directing Indefinite Suspension of *Akahata* and Similar Communist Publications, July 18, 1950. RG 59. Box 4237. NARA II.

48. Anti-Communist Activities of Bin Akao, August 15, 1950, from USPOLAD [the United States Political Adviser] to the Department of State. RG 59. Box 4237. NARA II.

49. Ibid.

50. Special Investigation Bureau (*Tokubetsu Shinsakyoku*) was reorganized as the Public Security Intelligence Agency (*Kōan Chōsachō*) in 1951 when the Subversive Activities Prevention Act was put into force.

51. Baerwald, *The Purge of Japanese Leaders under the Occupation*, 1.

52. Takemae, *Sengo Rōdō Kaikaku*, 424.

53. Baerwald, *The Purge of Japanese Leaders under the Occupation*, 71–72.

54. Takemae, *Sengo Rōdō Kaikaku*, 425.

55. OISR, *The Labor Year Book of Japan*, 1952, vol. 24 (Tokyo: Jiji Tsūshinsha, 1951), 215–222.

56. Conference Reports, Education Division—Eells, "Excepts from address given by Walter C. Eells at Niigata University on July 19, 1949." File: Eells. RG331. Box 5359. NARAII; the full text of the speech is available in Japanese translation in *Kyōiku Gyōsei no Genjyō: Īruzu Seimei Kara Rinkyōsin* [The present state of the administration of education: from the Eells statement to the Provisional Council on education reform], ed. Ōkura Zaisei Chōsakai: Kyōiku Kenkyūbu (Tokyo: Okura Zaisei Chosakai, 1984), 215–22.

57. Conference Reports, Education Division—Eells, "Excepts from address given by Walter C. Eells at Niigata University on July 19, 1949." (emphasis in original).

58. Ibid.

59. Ibid.

60. Dower, *Embracing Defeat*, 72.

61. Hirata, *Reddo Pāji no Shi-teki Kyūmei*, 115.

62. Torigai Risaburo, "Communism and Education," [date unknown], Torigai Risaburo Documents, no. 21. Kyoto University Archive.

63. Ibid.

64. *Yomiuri Shimbun*, October 19, 1949.

65. "Asks Early Peace Past: Nanbara Seeks Neutral Status in Address to US Council on Education," International News Service, Washington. RG 331. Box 2642. NARA II.

66. Ibid.

67. Zengakuren Chūō Tōsō Iinkai [The central action committee of Zengakuren], "Dantai-tō Kiseirei Tekiō ni yoru Danastu o Hane Kaese! (Shiji 8-gō) [Oppose the repression of the application of the organization reformation order! (order number 8)]," August 18, 1949. Document no. 212 in *Zengakuren Documents*, vol. 1, 1945–1949, 492.

68. Hirata, *Reddo Pāji no Shi-teki Kyūmei*, 73.

69. Ibid.

70. Yamanaka, *Sengo Gakusei Undōshi*, 92.

71. "Zengakuren Jyōhō Dai16-gō [Zengakuren Information, number 6]," September 23, 1949, in *Zengakuren Documents*, vol. 1, 1945–1949, 503–4.

72. "Amerika ni Okeru Akairo Kyōjyu Tuihō no Shinsō, [A truth about the purge of red professors in America]," *Gakusei Hyōron*, no. 3 (1949): 71–78.

73. Ibid.; *The New York Times*, December 24, 1945; ———, March 7, 1946.

74. *The New York Times*, March 7, 1946.

75. Zengakuren Taikai Jimukyoku [The convention office of Zengakuren], "Zengakuren Dai3-kai Zenkoku Taikai Gijiroku [The proceedings of the third Zengakuren national convention]," November 2–3, 1949. Document no. 221 in *Zengakuren Documents*, vol. 1, 1945–1949, 509–16.

76. "Depurge" was the term used by Hans H. Baerwald in *The Purge of Japanese Leaders Under the Occupation*, to indicate the act of exonerating former fascists who had been purged before the reverse course.

77. Baerwald, *The Purge of Japanese Leaders under the Occupation*, 99.
78. Zengakuren Taikai Jimukyoku, "Zengakuren Dai3-kai Zenkoku Taikai Gijiroku," November 2–3, 1949, 515–516.
79. Comments on CIE Secret Report, "Communist Penetration of Japanese Schools and Universities," August 11, 1948. File: Student Movement. RG 331. Box 5642. NARA II.
80. Ibid.
81. Eells, *Communism in Education in Asia, Africa, and the Far Pacific*, 2–3.
82. Myojin, "Red Purge in Universities in Occupied Japan (3): A Study on 'Eells Whirlwind'," *Journal of Hokkaido University of Education* 47, no. 2 (1996): 33, 36.
83. Eells, *Communism in Education in Asia, Africa, and the Far Pacific*, 30.
84. "Tohoku Daigaku Jiken: Rupotājyu, [The Tohoku University incident: a reportage]," *Gakusei Hyōron*, no. 6 (1950): 117.
85. Hirata, *Reddo Pāji no Shi-teki Kyūmei*, 126.
86. Tohokudai Zengaku Kekki Taikai, Tohoku Heiwa o Mamorukai [An inaugural meeting of all-Tohoku University students, Tohoku group on defending peace], "Tohokudai Īruzu Jiken [The Tohoku University Eells incident]," May 4, 1950. Document no. 10 in *Zengakuren Documents*, vol. 2, 1950–1952 (Tokyo: San-Ichi Shobo, 1969), 93–100.
87. Ibid.
88. "Tohoku Daigaku Jiken," 118.
89. Tohokudai Zengaku Kekki Taikai, Tohoku Heiwa o Mamorukai, "Tohokudai Īruzu Jiken," May 4, 1950, 98.
90. Ibid., 93.
91. Ibid.
92. Ibid., 98.
93. "Tohoku Daigaku Jiken," 118.
94. Zengakuren Chuō Shikkō Iinkai, "Tohokudai Tōsō ni tsuite no Zengakuren Seimei [Zengakuren's statement in regard to the struggle at Tohoku University]," May 4, 1950. Document no. 11 in *Zengakuren Documents*, vol. 2, 1950–1952, 100.
95. Tokyo Daigaku Gakusei Undō Kenkyūkai, *Nihon no Gakusei Undō: Sono Riron to Rekishi* [The Japanese student movement: its theories and history] (Tokyo: Shinko Shuppansha, 1956), 201.
96. "Tohoku Daigaku Jiken: Rupotājyu," 114.
97. *Japan Times*, May 15, 1950. RG 331. Box 2642. NARA II.
98. *Hokkaido Daigaku Shimbun*, May 10, 1950 in Hokkaido Daigaku Shimbunkai, ed. *Hokkaido Daigaku Shimbun (Fukkoku-Ban)* [Hokkaido University Newspaper (reprint edition)], vol. 4 (Ōzorasha, 1989), 7.
99. Eells, *Communism in Education in Asia, Africa, and the Far Pacific*, 30.
100. Myojin, "Īruzu Tōsō: Kenkyūsha no Tachiba Kara (a View from the Scholar of the Eells Incident)," in *Sōkū ni Kozue Tsuranete: Īruzu Tōsō 60-shūnen Anpo Tōsō 50-shūnen no Toshi ni Hokudai no Jiyū Jichi no Rekishi o Kangaeru*, ed. Hokudai 5.16 Shūkai Hōkokusho Henshū Iinkai (Sapporo: Hakurosha, 2011), 39.

101. ———, "Red Purge in Universities in Occupied Japan (1): A Study on the Eells Incident in Hokkaido University," *Journal of Hokkaido University of Education* 45, no. 1 (1994): 21.

102. *Hokkaido Daigaku Shimbun*, May 30, 1950 in *Hokkaido Daigaku Shimbun—Fukkoku-Ban*, 10.

103. Masataka Yanada, *Hokudai no Īruzu Tōsō: Sono Shinjitu o Akiraka ni Suru Tameni* [The struggle against Eells at Hokkaido University: to clarify the truth] (Tokyo: Kōyō Shuppan Sha, 2006), 58; Myojin, "Īruzu Tōsō," 40.

104. Kudo Nobuhiko's letter to his father, May 18, 1950. File: Kudo Nobuhiko (Īruzu jiken) 0002. Hokkaido University Archives; In this letter to his father, Kudo, then a student at Hokkaido University, provided a detailed first-hand account of the event.

105. Ibid.

106. *Hokkaido Daigaku Shimbun*, May 17, 1950 (gōgai [a special edition]). File: Kudo Nobuhiko (Īruzu jiken) 0001. Hokkaido University Archives.

107. Ibid.

108. Ibid.

109. Masaru Matsui, "Īruzu Jiken: Sono Genzai ni okeru Igi [The Eells incident: its significance today]," October 4, 1964. File: Īruzu Jiken 0003. Hokkaido University Archives.

110. Yanada, *Hokudai no Īruzu Tōsō*, 48, 58.

111. Jyoji Ogura, Etsuji Sumiya, and Suehide Takakuwa, *Nihon Gakusei Shakai Undō Shi: Kyoto o Chūshin ni* [A history of the social movements of Japanese Students: a focus on Kyoto] (Kyoto: Doshisha Daigaku Shuppanbu, 1953), 264.

112. Takei, "Nihongakusei Undō ni Okeru Hantei-teki Dentō no Kenji to Hatten no Tameni [For the adherence to the tradition of anti-imperialism of the Japanese student movement and for its development]," *Gakusei Hyōron*, no. 7 (1950): 48.

113. Ibid., 34.

114. Ibid., 44.

115. Ogura, Sumiya, and Takakuwa, *Nihon Gakusei Shakai Undō Shi*, 262.

116. Student groups from non-Communist countries maintained their membership in the IUS at that time, despite their deteriorating relationship with their counterparts in Communist states. The outbreak of the Korean War would complete the Cold War split within the IUS in June and lead to the creation of a separate non-Communist international student federation, the International Student Conference in December 1950; the letter from the IUS was printed in *Hokkaido Daigaku Shimbun* (Hokkaido University Newspaper) on May 30, 1950.

117. Mosukuwa Hōsō [Radio Moscow], "Nihon Saisho no Hantei Demo [The first anti-imperialism demonstrations in Japan]," in *Zengakuren Documents*, vol. 2, 1950–1952, 115.

118. *Nippon Times*, May 18, 1950. RG 331. Box 2642. NARA II.

119. *Mainichi Shimbun*, May 19, 1950. RG 331. Box 2642. NARA II.

120. *The New York Times*, May 19, 1950.

121. [Unknown newspaper] [date unknown]. RG 331. Box 279. NARA II

122. Yoshiaki Kobayashi, *Sengo Kakumei Undō Ronsōshi* [A history of debates about postwar revolutionary movements] (Tokyo: San-Ichi Shobo, 1971), 53–4; Cominform was a forum established by the Soviet and eight other European Communist Parties in 1947 to keep the international Communist movement in line with the Soviet ideological direction.

123. J. Victor Koschmann, "Intellectuals and Politics," *Postwar Japan as History*, ed. Andrew Gordon (Berkeley: University of California Press, 1993), 397–98.

124. Kobayashi, *Sengo Kakumei Undō Ronsōshi*, 59.

125. Nihon Kyōsantō Zengakuren Chuō Gurūpu [JCP-affiliated Zengakuren central group], "Saikin no Gakusei Undō, Zengakuren Ikensho [The recent student movement: a Zengakuren opinion]," March 1950. Document no. 4 in *Zengakuren Documents*, vol. 2, 1950–1952, 9–78.

126. *Nippon Times*, May 11, 1950. RG 331. Box 2642. NARA II.

127. Zengakuren, "Zengakuren Dai4-kai Rinji Zenkoku Taikai Gian Taikai Sengen (Sōan) [The 4th Zengakuren special national convention, its agenda and statement (draft)]," Document no. 14 in *Zengakuren Documents*, vol. 2, 1950–1952, 106–10.

128. Ogura, Sumiya and Takakuwa, *Nihon Gakusei Shakai Undō Shi*, 262.

129. Zengakuren Dai4-kai Rinji Zenkoku Taikai Gian Taikai Sengen (Sōan), 111.

130. *The New York Times*, June 12, 1950.

131. Ibid.

132. Ibid.

133. "Wholesale Searching of the National Federation of Students Self-Government Association (Zengakuren)." RG 331. Box 279. NARA II; "Real State of Military Bases" is reprinted in Zengakuren Shokikyoku [Zengakuren Secretariat], "Gunjikichika no Jittai o Miyo! [Look at the real situation of military bases!]," Document no. 20 in *Zengakuren Documents, 1950–1952*, vol. 2, 147–49.

134. "Wholesale Searching of the National Federation of Students Self-Government Association (Zengakuren)."

135. Ibid.

136. Ibid.

137. *Asahi Shimbun-Nippon Times* [date unknown]. RG 331. Box 279. NARA II.

138. "State of Investigation After the Wholesale Investigation of the National Federation of Students Self-Government Association (Zengakuren)," July 18, 1950. RG 331. Box 279. NARA II.

139. "Special Investigation, Attorney General's Office," November 1, 1950. File: Tokyo Daigaku Saibō. RG 331. Box 2275DD. NARA II.

140. The Educational Policies Commission of the National Education Association of the United States and the American Association of School Administrators and the Executive Committee of the American Council on Education, *Education and National Security* (Washington, DC: American Council on Education, 1951).

141. Ibid., 3.

142. Ibid., 5.

143. Ibid., 12.

144. Ibid.

145. Memorandum by the Director of the Office of Northeast Asian Affairs (Allison) to the Consultant to the Secretary (Dulles), August 24, 1950 in *FRUS*, 1950, vol. VI, East Asia and the Pacific, 1289–90; Article 8 of the draft mentioned here is identical to Articles II of the draft attached to Memorandum by the Director of the Office of Northeast Asian Affairs (Allison) to the Consultant to the Secretary (Dulles), July 11, 1950 in ibid., 1242.

146. Memorandum by the Director of the Office of Northeast Asian Affairs (Allison) to the Secretary of State, August 29, 1950 in ibid., 1289.

147. The Secretary of State to the Secretary of Defense (Johnson), enclosure: Memorandum for the President, September 7, 1950 in ibid., 1293–94.

148. Ibid.

149. Memorandum of Conversation, Department State, January 17, 1951. Reel 1. President Harry S. Truman's Office Files, 1945–1953. Part 4: Korean War Files. Microfilm copy at Doshisha University Library.

150. Report by Ralph J. Watkins, attached to memorandum sent from Frank Pace, Secretary of the Army to President Truman, September 29, 1952. Reel 1. President Harry S. Truman's Office, Part 4: Korean War Files. Microfilm copy at Doshisha University Library.

151. Foreign Service Despatch from American Consulate General (Ralph J. Blake) to the Department of State, Washington, Subject: Communism in Japanese Universities, August 7, 1952. RG 59. Box 5676. NARAII.

152. Ibid.

153. Ibid.

154. Foreign Service Despatch from Glen Bruner, American Council, Kobe to the Department of State, Washington, Subject: An Example of the Failure of Material Success to Eliminate Student Leftism, July 31, 1953. RG 59. Box 4238. NARA II.

155. Ibid.

156. Ibid.

157. Ibid.

158. Ibid.

159. Foreign Service Despatch from John M. Allison, American Embassy, Tokyo to the Department of State, Washington. Subject: Transmittal of "An Appraisal of the Capabilities of the Japanese Communist Party as They Appear in June 1954," July 16. RG 59. Box 4238. NARA II.

160. Ibid.

161. Ibid.

162. Ibid.

163. Shin Sayoku Riron Zenshi Henshū Iinkai, *Shin Sayoku Riron Zenshi* [A complete history of the theories of the New Left] (Tokyo: Ryūdo Shuppan, 1979), 12.

164. Yamanaka, *Sengo Gakusei Undōshi*, 108–9.

165. *Bunto* is the Japanese pronunciation of the German word Bund.

166. Morita Minoru in an interview with the author in Tokyo on February 8, 2017.

Chapter Three

Clashing Concepts of National Security and the Beginning of the *Anpo* Struggle

The CIA reported in July 1949 that Japan was the "key to the development of a self-sufficient war-making complex in the Far East" because of its industrial potential and geographical location.[1] It predicted that Japan would serve as "the strongest anti-Communist center in Asia" with an "enthusiastically pro-US" regime in power.[2] On January 12, 1950, Dean Acheson made his famous "defensive perimeter" speech to the National Press Club in which he defined America's collective security system in the Pacific that "runs along the Aleutians to Japan and then goes to the Ryukyus."[3] America's involvement in the military defense of Japan, he argued, was required "in the interest of our security and in the interests of the security of the entire Pacific area and, in all honor, in the interest of Japanese security."[4] On April 14, the National Security Council (NSC) issued its historical NSC-68 that exhibited the growing emphasis on the necessity for a military build-up in order to defend the "free world" economic and political systems from the threat of Communism. With the outbreak of the Korean War, the geostrategic importance of the US military bases in Japan grew as its commitment to Pacific security increased. Securing the US position in the defense system envisioned by Acheson proved to be not only a military but also a political process of crystalizing hegemony. It had to demonstrate the solidarity of interests between the United States and Japan in the process of consolidating the US military sphere in the Pacific. The Japanese concepts of security had to be subsumed under the Cold War American discourse in order to fulfill American interest in the region.

The US Cold War security system that ran across the globe not only was connected to geopolitical, strategic, and security measures against the Soviet bloc but also intertwined with the internal relations of the host country. The direct confrontation with the US military empire, most notably in the small town of Sunagawa in Tokyo, contributed to the development of a powerful leftist student movement in Japan. Between 1951 and 1955, Zengakuren had suffered from years of confusion and bitter internal conflicts. The British Embassy in Tokyo observed in August 1953 that Zengakuren was growing less powerful due to factors such as "apathy on the part of the large majority of its members" that led to a decline in its total membership and affiliated chapters.[5] Zengakuren, however, would overcome its years of dormancy through the protests against the extension of the runway of Tachikawa Air Base. This chapter looks at this Sunagawa struggle as the beginning of the movement against the US-Japan Security Treaty, which climaxed in May and June 1960.

After World War II, the US military expanded its bases of operation, filling a vacuum left by European and Japanese empires. The signing of a separate peace treaty and the Security Treaty with the US confirmed Japan's official entry into the free world alliance system. On September 8, 1951, delegates from forty-eight countries signed the Peace Treaty with Japan in San Francisco, in the absence of the Communist states in the Eastern Bloc and China. It formally ended the occupation and restored Japan's sovereignty, except over the Ryukyu Islands and Bonin Islands, which remained under American control under the US-Japan Security Treaty that was signed a few hours later, also in San Francisco. This new bilateral security treaty granted the United States the right to maintain military bases in the Japanese mainland and established an innovative, if ill-defined, "residual sovereignty" over the Ryukyu Islands in order to permit the American occupation and administration of the islands. As Maria Höhn and Seungsook Moon argue, "It was in South Korea, Japan, and Okinawa, and West Germany that the bulk of the US overseas military empire would be anchored and where the battle lines would be drawn between the so-called Free World and the Communist bloc. Together, these three countries provided the basing locations that allowed the United States to span the globe during the Cold War."[6] Through the Cold War, US forces were deployed from Japan, in particular from Okinawa to engage in military conflicts in places like Korea, Lebanon, and Vietnam. In the 1950s, American policymakers thought that Japan would play a "leading and stabilizing role in Asia," and the United States had to assure Japan's present alignment with the United States structured by the Security Treaty signed in 1951.[7]

CONTAINING JAPANESE DESIRE FOR A "NEW DIPLOMACY"

In the mid-1950s, the Japanese government's growing tendency to conduct more independent diplomacy concerned American Cold War strategists. In December 1954, the new administration of Hatoyama Ichiro of the conservative Democratic Party replaced the administration of Yoshida Shigeru.

Hatoyama and Foreign Minister Shigemitsu Mamoru initiated what they called the "new diplomacy" which aimed to change the relationship between Japan and the US, demanding that the US treat Japan as an equal partner. In order to achieve this goal, Hatoyama and Shigemitsu sought to reduce Japan's dependency on the United States, first by recovering diplomatic and trade relations with the USSR and Communist China. In particular, the prospect of a huge market in China was irresistible to Japanese businesses.[8] American policymakers understood the growing Japanese tendency to conduct an independent diplomacy as the result of a decline in Japanese economic dependency on the United States. They thus thought that Japan's alignment with the United States could no longer be based solely on economic dependence. An NSC report in April 1955 concluded that "As Japan's strength grows, dependence will lessen and should be replaced by a new sense of common purpose, mutual interests and working partnership."[9]

Hatoyama and Shigemitsu were not willing to risk Japan's relationship with the United States for the "new diplomacy." They sought to trade with Communist countries while avoiding antagonizing the relationship with the United States and giving the US government the wrong idea that Japan was challenging the US or the bipolar world structure. Yet, Washington reacted against both Japan's efforts to develop close ties with the USSR and Japan's intention to recognize Communist China. John Foster Dulles warned that "[the] US does not want [to] be put [in a] position suffering from major public diplomatic defeat . . . and Japan's establishment [of the] relations [with] Communist China could have dangerous effect on [the] rest [of] Asia and its will [to] resist Communist expansion."[10] Japan was free to conduct its own diplomacy as a sovereign country, but it must not be, Dulles insisted, "inconsistent with [the] San Francisco treaty."[11] In response, Hatoyama and Shigemitsu tried to renegotiate the Security Treaty and replace it with a mutual defense agreement that would elevate Japan's status to from a junior partner to an equal partner of the United States.

On April 7, the NSC met to reassess US policy toward Japan. At the meeting, Secretary Dulles expressed his frustration with Japan's unwillingness to play a more active role on the behalf of the "free world" despite the economic recovery that Japan achieved through massive US procurement during the Korean War. Dulles disparaged the country by saying, "We have done everything that we could think of to stir up in Japan a desire to assume a position of international influence once again, and the results had been markedly unsuccessful. Indeed, the Japanese were utterly lethargic and lacking in any perceptible ambition to recover their pre-war international prestige."[12] The Acting Secretary of Defense, Robert Anderson, expressed his concern that the Japanese public might not be ready for a large-scale rearmament plan, and "the resultant psychological repercussions would be very unfortunate for us in view of the situation in the Far East."[13] Dulles expressed his frustration toward Japanese sensitivity to war and the armed forces, but he agreed with Anderson that the United States could not pressure Japan too much to rearm itself "because it was manifest that there was a strong pacifist sentiment abroad in Japan" and added, "In part, we ourselves were responsible for this, since we had imposed a pacifist constitution on the Japanese."[14] If the US should change the policy toward Japan, Dulles demanded, the change should not "mean that the United States would have to forgo its *right* to maintain forces and bases in Japan, and the privilege of doing so would be dependent on the agreement of the Japanese Government."[15]

The meeting resulted in the development of *The Statement of the US Policy Proposed by the National Security Council on Japan* (NSC 5516/1). This policy proposal recommended softening American demands for rearmament of Japan to safeguard the political and economic stability achieved during the Korean War. Sayuri Guthrie-Shimizu argued that such strategic reassessment resulted from "drastically reduced military tensions in Asia" after the armistices were concluded in Korea in 1953 and in Indochina in 1954.[16] Yet, as Dulles insisted, the US military bases in mainland Japan and Okinawa continued to possess strategic value to Washington for military conflicts in the future. The cease-fire in the Korean War did not mean the end of America's fight against Communism in Asia. The French defeat in Vietnam had made the United States the only power that could prevent the "fall" of Vietnam to Communism. Covert American "paramilitary operations in Communist areas" in Vietnam began "simultaneously with their final signing [of the Geneva Accords] on July 21, 1954."[17]

Washington was aware that the Japanese concept of security had to be in unison with that of Cold War America in order to promote a Pacific collective defense arrangement. At that time, the Korean War, the US test of the hydrogen bombs, and the formation of the Warsaw Pact increased the Japanese fear of eventually being exposed to the Cold War violence and even a nuclear war. The desire for peace and neutrality among the Japanese was certainly growing. In January, General John E. Hull, Commander in Chief of the Far East Command (CINCFE), had remarked that a major obstacle to the accomplishment of US objectives was "a growing tendency among the Japanese to participate in flights from reality which lead them to entertain hopes of neutralism and of prosperous coexistence with both the East and the West. These obstacles serve to increase the challenge placed on the US policy and, for the best interests of the US, should be overcome."[18] For the US, the Japanese tendency toward neutrality had to be overcome, for it was incompatible with the rules of the game in the bipolar system of the Cold War. In April,

Dulles argued that growing security did not simply mean the expansion of a Washington-centered military alliance bloc but also indicated "the growing acceptance of the collective security concept we describe."[19] NSC 5516/1 similarly pointed out the importance of crafting a homogeneous concept of "security" between the two nations. It concluded, "Japan currently considers alignment with the United States and cooperation with the democratic nations to be in its national interest . . . because it expects that the United States will if necessary defend Japan against attack."[20] It continued, "While the Japanese look upon US bases in Japan as protection for Japan, they also regard them as serving US strategic interests and as dangerously exposing Japan to nuclear attack in the event of war."[21] In other words, as long as the Japanese recognized the US bases as necessary for its security, the US would not face a serious challenge to the military bases that anchored America's military empire in the Pacific. NSC 5516/1 further insisted that the development of a "community of interests" among the Western pacific allies would be crucial in its fight against Communism.[22]

At the NSC meeting, President Eisenhower exhibited particular interest in the issue of nationalism. By 1953, the president and Dulles had begun to get the first clear sense of what Third World nationalism was all about. Westad has described the moment: "The '1948 Jakarta Axiom'—the idea that radical Third World nationalism of the nativist kind could be of long-term advantage to the United States—was ultimately defeated in Teheran in 1953."[23] During the NSC meeting, the president said, "It was very alarming to observe how the Communists had managed to identify themselves and their purposes with this emergent nationalism. The United States, on the other hand, had failed to utilize this new spirit of nationalism in its own interest."[24] Yet, this was not the case for Japan. He continued, "While this phenomenon was general, Japan was a notable illustration. Accordingly, if Japan grew more strongly nationalist, we should play up more to this development in order to bend it to our advantage."[25] Eisenhower suggested stressing the US record in the Philippines as "evidence of our sympathy for nationalist aspirations." Unlike neutralism, nationalism had potential usefulness for America. It was believed that Japanese nationalism, if it ever caught fire, would not be the wrong kind—the Third World version that the Communist might easily exploit—but something that the US could take advantage of. Yet, as the Sunagawa struggle would demonstrate, the close defense collaboration between the two countries and the struggle against the US military empire instead stimulated an anti-imperialist nationalism of precisely the sort that so concerned Eisenhower and Dulles.

In Tokyo, the Hatoyama administration had concluded that it had to make some efforts to strengthen Japan's defense force so as to convince Washington to revise the security treaty. In the progress report on the US policy towards Japan (NSC 125/2 and 125/6), the Operations Coordinating Board that was created in 1953 by Eisenhower had concluded that Japan's "Economic difficulties, ineffectual governmental leadership, pressure from Communist areas, and reluctance in moving positively toward self-defense have not been solved."[26] Furthermore, the Board pointed out the problem of "a serious increase in neutralist sentiment, periodic flare-ups of anti-Americanism and an intensification of communist overtures to Japan," despite the fact that "vigorous programs have been carried on to give the Japanese a better understanding of the United States and of world problems and combat leftist and neutralist influences."[27] Thus, the Board recommended that the Japan's conservatives overcome personal rivalries and focus on developing "legal measures against Communists, and to combat the neutralist, anti-American tendencies of many of the individuals in Japan's educated groups."[28] Basically, the Japanese government felt it had to give Americans more confidence in Japan's ability to resist and combat Communism and neutralism in order to gain more autonomy in the bilateral relationship.

Despite the public sensitivity to rearmament, the Japanese government agreed to make some efforts to strengthen Japan's defense forces. In July 1954, Japan upgraded the National Safety Agency to the Defense Agency which would command the newly promulgated Self Defense Forces. The ground, naval, and air forces were expanded under the plan, and the reserve system, which initially consisted of approximately 15,000 persons, was introduced.[29] These measures symbolized the Hatoyama administration's willingness to carry a greater burden in the collective security system and give the US government the terms it wanted in order to get them to agree to Japan's worthiness as an equal US partner. In the mid-1950s, the US-Japan bilateral defense cooperation grew accordingly. As a sweetener, the US Air Force signed a contract in 1955 to allow the production of about 500 jet fighter aircraft, in addition to seventy F-86 jet aircrafts, at the total cost of 40.6 million dollars.[30]

The Japanese government also agreed to America's demands for extensions of military bases. The plan included the extension of the runway at Tachikawa Air Base, located in the Tama region to the west of the Tokyo metropolitan area. The airbase was originally built in 1922 for the Imperial Japanese Army Air Force and hosted its elite units until the end of the war. During the occupation, the American military forces seized it, along with other military bases and facilities in Japan. With the signing of the Security Treaty in 1951, the US Air Force headquarter was moved to Tachikawa. It was one of the US military bases and facilities governed by the Administrative Agreement under the treaty. During the Korean War, the airbase became one of the most crucial supply depots for UN troops fighting in Korea. Yet, in order to accommodate modern US jet aircrafts, its runway had to be extended. To safely land on Tachikawa Air Base, American jet aircrafts, most notably C-124s that were used for heavy-lift transport, had to limit the size of cargo to two-third of its maximum capacity and reduce the weight by leaving unused gas at Johnson Air Base in Saitama prefecture before landing at Tachikawa.[31]

After the Korean War ended with a truce, the US military requested the Japanese government to help reorganize its military bases to make it better serve their common purpose, tto protect Japan as well as the entire region of Asia from the Communist expansion. On March 15, 1954, the US military sent a formal letter of request to the Yoshida cabinet, demanding the Japanese government to agree to the expansions of the US bases in Niigata, Komaki, Yokota, Itami, and Tachikawa. In the areas that hosted the US military bases, there had already been protests by local citizens against the continued presence of the US military after the truce in Korea. Labor unions and oppositional political parties had taken up the issue and raised their voices against the conservative-dominated government that tried to push the extension plan through the Diet. On July 28, 1955, the Assistant Secretary of State for Far Eastern Affairs, Walter S. Robertson, reported that "the Japanese Government has recently been much firmer in its support of the necessary extensions and firing ranges for the United States forces and in its public recognition of the necessity of such measures for the defense of Japan."[32] To his delight, the Japanese policymakers successfully adopted the plan to extend the runway of Tachikawa Air Base from 5,500 feet to 7,000 feet at the cabinet meeting held on September 20.[33] In addition, they also agreed to offer 120,000 m² (36,300 *tsubo* in a Japanese unit of area measurement) for the runway extension and designate another 55,210 m² (16,700 *tsubo*) as an obstacle-free zone for the US forces.[34] The plan required farmers to give up their lands and 130 houses to relocate.[35] According to the 316-page detailed record created by the students of the Self-Governing Association at Chuo University, this extension plan required the runway to extend into a small town called Sunagawa with a population of 12,655 (2,542 families), mostly small landowning farmers.[36]

It was the Procurement Agency that was in charge of obtaining land from the local residents. This agency itself was a product of the occupation. SCAP had created the Special Procurement Agency to allow the occupation to proceed with procurement dealings effectively.[37] The agency was, however, a nominal corporation staffed with government officials and supervised by the Prime Minister's office. In June 1949, the agency was formally transformed into an extra-ministerial board of the Prime Minister's Office, staffed with about seven thousand employees and operating eight regional offices in Sapporo, Sendai, Yokohama, Nagoya, Kyoto, Osaka, Kure, and Fukuoka.[38] In

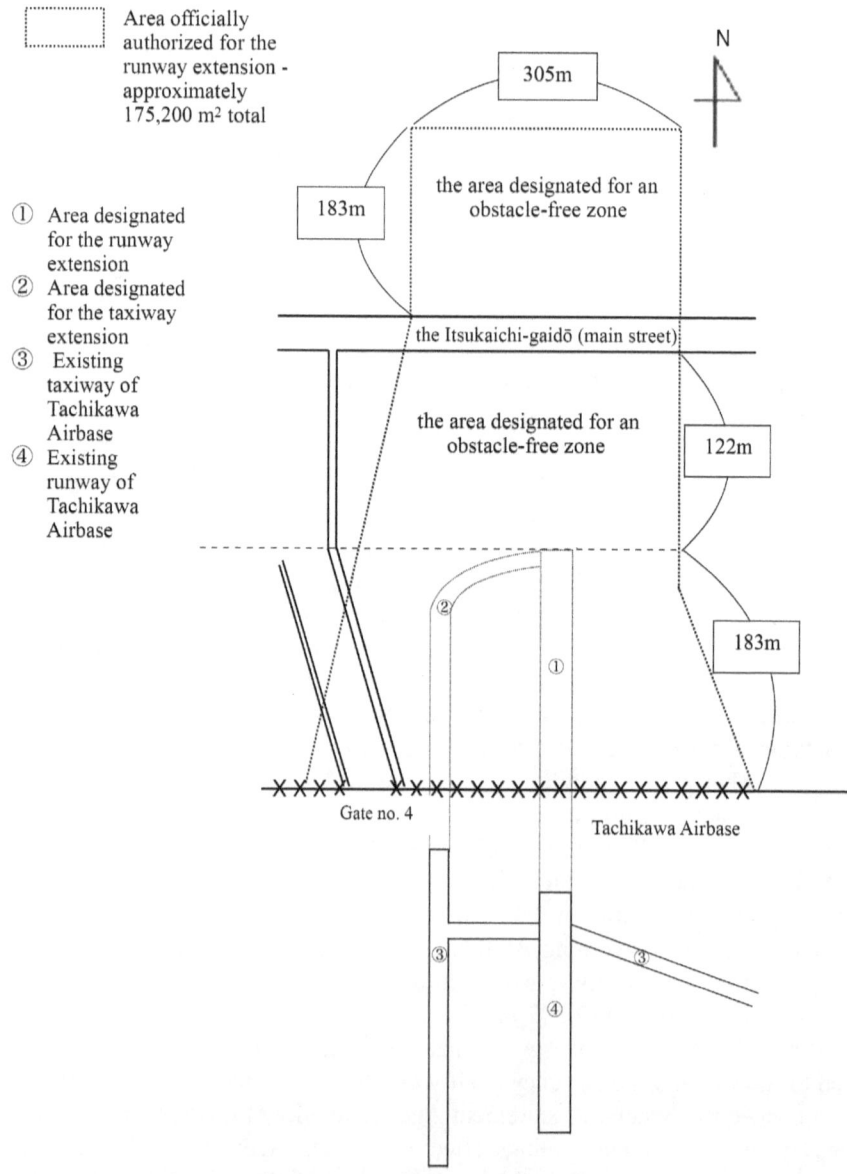

Tachikawa Airbase Extension Plan. *Created by author using information from Bōei Shisetsuchōshi Hensan Iinkai, ed. Bōei Shisetsuchōshi: Kichimondai to Tomoni Ayunda 45-Nen no Kiseki, 27; Chuo Daigaku Gakusei Jichikai Chōsabu,* Sunagawa-machi ni Okeru Kichi Kakuchō Hantai Tōsō o Megurite, *21.*

May 1951, SCAPIN-2154 had authorized the agency to directly "contract with procurement agents of the United States Government for furnishing such goods and services as they may desire to buy and to bill the United States Government for goods and services supplied in accordance with such contracts."[39] With the signing of the San Francisco treaties, the Special Procurement Agency was renamed as the Procurement Agency and continued to fulfill procurement demands of the US military forces in Japan, in accordance with the US-Japan Administrative Agreement, the Article 3 of the new bilateral Security Treaty.

On May 6, 1955, the Tokyo Procurement Agency announced that the runway of Tachikawa Air Base would be extended to the lands owned by Sunagawa residents. Immediately after the plan was made public, it provoked fierce opposition from the local residents of Sunagawa. A rumor that the US was planning to station aircrafts that carried nuclear bombs soon became widely circulated among the residents. The plan to accommodate modern US jets increased the Japanese fear of destructive, possibly nuclear, war between the superpowers on its soil. It was not only rumors, but local residents' actual war experience also deepened the local opposition against the plan. During World War II, Sunagawa and other nearby towns had experienced US bombings that targeted the Tachikawa airbase, which burnt 160 houses, killing twenty-five people in Sunagawa alone.[40] In addition, the recent crash of a B-29, which damaged a hundred houses near Tachikawa Air Base, helped evoke the strong local opposition against the extension plan.[41]

The fear of a nuclear war involving Japan had gained more ground between 1953 and 1954. A series of international and domestic events evoked a real sense of urgency. In August 1953, the Soviet Union detonated its first thermonuclear weapon, challenging the American lead in nuclear technology that had succeeded in producing the hydrogen bomb in the fall of 1952. On January 12, 1954, Dulles delivered the famous "massive retaliation" speech to the Council on Foreign Relations. Falsely assuming that the American nuclear power deterred the Chinese Communists from taking a more aggressive position in negotiating over the Korean conflict, Dulles insisted, "We need allies and collective security. Our purpose is to make these relations more effective, less costly. This can be done by placing more reliance on *deterrent power* and less dependence on local defensive power."[42] The Japanese, like the American people, became alarmed by the "massive retaliation" speech, which was widely interpreted as America's renewed faith in the power of nuclear weapons in its fight against Moscow or Peking in case of a local war. Furthermore, the hydrogen explosion at Bikini on March 1, 1954, heightened Japanese sensitivity to nuclear weapons and triggered large-scale public protests. The first hydrogen bomb test, codenamed Castle Bravo, accidentally exposed

Japanese fishermen on the fishing boat *Daigo Fukuryū Maru* (Lucky Dragon No. 5), to severe radiation, resulting in the death of a crew member. The media immediately placed the story on their front pages and also reported the high level of radioactive contamination of fish brought by the *Daigo Fukuryū Maru* to the Tukiji central wholesale market in Tokyo.[43] The incident sparked powerful anti-nuclear movements across Japan. Ordinary citizens joined the campaign against the nuclear bombs, which was first initiated by housewives in Tokyo who stood up against the contaminated fish that endangered their families' health. The growing public opposition against American nuclear weapons raised a serious concern for anti-Communists who feared that the Communists would take advantage of the incident. Suzuki Hiromasa, the president of the Japan National Student Association (*Nihon Gakusei Kyōkai*) that supported the fight against Communism, for instance, sent a letter to the US Embassy in Japan, warning that the Bikini affair had "aroused some anti-American feelings . . . giving a chance for the Soviet Russia's 'Peace Offensive' policy" and urged the US to "counteract such work as Zengakuren which Communists now dominating."[44] Dulles's speech and the Bikini incident reawakened general fears of nuclear weapons and invigorated the anti-nuclear movement in Japan. In Sunagawa, many residents feared that the runway extension plan was a part of the US preparation for potential retaliatory nuclear strikes against the Soviet Union and China. Mayor of Sunagawa Miyazaki Denzaemon, who firmly opposed the extension plan, said, "We don't want the same things to happen here as happened in Hiroshima and Nagasaki."[45]

Despite the local opposition, the Procurement Agency began acting upon the extension plan and surveying the land between June 30 and July 2, 1955.[46] By the end of the summer, the town was clearly divided between the opponents and the people who were willing to give up their lands for some compensation. The former created the Alliance against the Extension of the Air Base (*Kichi Kakuchō Hantai Dōmei*) while the latter organized the Federation for Measures for the Extension of the Air Base (*Kichi Kakuchō Taisaku Renmei*).[47] Of 131 owners of the land required for the runway extension, sixty-five people who owned about 66 percent (78,680 m^2) of the total land area of 120,000 m^2 opposed the plan and sixty-six people who owned the rest (41,320 m^2) agreed to take the payment of compensation and give up their land.[48] The local opposition groups demanded that the Tokyo district court issue a provisional disposition order to ban the survey team from entering their private lands, but the court rejected it on July 21.[49] Following the court decision, the Japanese government pushed ahead with the scheduled survey.

On August 26, Prime Minister Hatoyama announced that the extension of the airbase was "essential" to Japan's security.[50] A periodical report of the Procurement Agency criticized anti-military base demonstrations for not recognizing that times had changed since the end of World War II and the world had entered the age of collective security in which the security of a country could no longer depend on the national force and be guaranteed only through further treaties for mutual defense.[51] In fact, many Japanese people shared this view, especially when it came to Okinawa. The Assistant Secretary of State for Far Eastern Affairs, Walter S. Robertson, expressed the view that he "was impressed by Japanese recognition of the fact that our occupation of Okinawa is essential to the security of Japan and the rest of the Far East."[52]

The Sunagawa struggle took place during a critical time for the Hatoyama administration. Shigemitsu was going to Washington with the Secretary General of the Democratic Party, Kishi Nobusuke, to explain the Hatoyama administration's new diplomacy and to request the replacement of the Security Treaty signed in San Francisco at the end of the occupation with a treaty of mutual defense. During the three-day meeting that took place between August 29 and 31, Dulles informed Shigemitsu that the ratification of a new treaty would be possible, but the United States was not confident about Japan's capacity to operate under such a treaty.[53] Dulles pointed out the lack of unity and cohesion within the Japanese government and questioned its ability to pass necessary measures required for the build-up of its defense system.[54] Dulles said to Shigemitsu, "Pro-Communists and neutralist elements would attack a revised treaty" and Japan must counter "indirect aggression" of the Communists if it should sign the new mutual defense treaty with the United States.[55]

Hatoyama and Shigemitsu followed Dulles' logic of equal partnership and made a gesture to build up a sound defense system. At the meeting on August 30, Dulles responded to Shigemitsu's request to end Japan's "semi-independent position" and told him that "every treaty involves a partial surrender of sovereignty and that interdependence ad cooperation rather than independence are the requirements. For Japan to consider itself as unequal is wrong; this is not the way the United States treats Japan."[56] In other words, the subordinate position that Japan felt was not the problem with the Security Treaty itself and changing the treaty did not guarantee it greater autonomy.

Unfortunately for the Hatoyama government, the difficulty facing it in carrying out the runway extension seemed to support Dulles's claim about the strength of Communists in Japan. At the meeting at the Department of State on August 30, the Assistant Secretary of Defense for International Security Affairs, Gordon Gray, informed the Japanese delegation that the Defense Department recognized the Japanese government's efforts to carry out the runway extension plan, but that it also considered "the scope and organization of demonstrations in opposition to this program [to] have been discouraging."[57] Gray told Japanese representatives that "It is important that the Japanese people understand that this program is in their own interest, particularly since

Japanese aircraft will eventually need the extended space for their operations. Countermeasures against the current demonstrations are desirable and the United States is willing to assist."[58] American representatives told Shigemitsu that it was the Japanese government's responsibility to persuade its people on the issue of the runway extension.[59] Shigemitsu protested, saying that it was the initial phase of the occupation that deprived the Japanese government of the legal means to effectively combat Communism in Japan.[60] He went on to inform American officials, perhaps in reference to the situation in Sunagawa, of the existence of an intransigent leftist opposition to the extension plan despite the Japanese government's efforts.

THE BEGINNING OF THE SUNAGAWA STRUGGLE

Indeed, by September, the Sunagawa case was boiling up into a serious national controversy joined by the Socialist Party (JSP) and labor unions. Labor unions, especially in the Tama region, had organized their own groups to provide support for the struggle against the expansion of Tachikawa Air Base during the summer.[61] The Socialist Party also sent representatives to Sunagawa to support the local opponents on July 1.[62] The JCP supported the Sunagawa struggle, but it was the recently reunited Socialist Party that played a more active role. The Japanese Socialists, who had been divided between right and left wings, reunited in 1955 and promised to fight the conservatives in order to maintain peace and security, strengthen people's democracy, and improve ordinary people's lives.[63] In pursuit of this platform, the Socialists made a major effort in Sunagawa, demanding that the public understand that the issue went well beyond Sunagawa to the heart of the problems embedded in the Security Treaty and the ongoing occupation of Okinawa.[64] The JSP leaders led by Asanuma Inejiro and Shimagami Zengoro demanded that the Chief Cabinet Secretary Nemoto Ryutaro withdraw the police force, but Nemoto refused, saying that the police force was a countermeasure against the labor unions that were sending its foot soldiers to instigate the opposition protests.[65]

Zengakuren was still in no shape to mobilize for the Sunagawa protest. At the eighth annual national convention held in June, Zengakuren announced that it would fight the plan to extend US military bases in the name of "world peace and independence of Japan."[66] Yet, there were only a few student activists left to carry out such a task. Morita Minoru, who would become the peace leader of Zengakuren under the leadership of chairman Koyama in 1956, recalled, "It was difficult for Zengakuren to engage in any movement. It was too busy condemning the JCP leaders during the summer and fall of 1955."[67] Yet, the authorities remained wary of Zengakuren. In response to the situation in Sunagawa, the officers of the Political Division of the US Embassy and the Japanese Public Security Investigation Agency held a meeting on "Communist Subversion in Japan" to discuss the Communist strength among the Japanese. At the meeting, the chief officer of the agency, Seki Itaru warned Americans that "the greatest danger comes from the educated youth and intellectuals."[68] Yet, it was not until the fall of 1956 that Zengakuren could be so.

On September 10, the *Yomiuri Shimbun* reported the first "*Anpo* discharges," the firing of Japanese workers by the US military at Tachikawa Air Base for their protest activities. Eighty workers among them who lived on the planned extension site faced a dilemma: whether to risk their jobs or defend their privately-owned lands, and some of them joined the protest.[69] Some Japanese workers employed at US military bases hesitated to openly oppose the plan, fearing that they might lose their jobs, while others joined local protests to defend their lands. Two Japanese workers who supported the opposition group in Sunagawa were discharged. When labor unions protested the discharge, Japanese and American authorities denied the charge and claimed that their discharge was not the result of their protest activities when labor.[70]

On September 13, the first physical confrontations in Sunagawa occurred as the surveying squad, backed by the police force, attempted to enter the scheduled survey area, which had been barricaded with barbed wires and the protestors who held sit-in strikes.[71] The General Council of Japanese Trade Unions (*Nihon Rōdō Kumiai Sōhyōgikai*, abbreviated as *Sōhyō*) sent its members to the site to help form a "human wave" against the survey team.[72] The Metropolitan Police Department had assigned its force to provide protection to the survey squad. A phalanx of police pushed the "human wave" resisters, who in turn pushed back to prevent the survey team from entering the survey area. The Socialist Party issued a statement condemning the Hatoyama government for deploying the police force that had violently attacked peaceful demonstrators and trampled the villagers' vegetable gardens.[73] The periodical *Keisatsu Kōron* (Police Review) ran an article to justify its actions against the protestors, claiming that they were aimed to secure the traffic in the town, not to back up the extension plan.[74] Indeed, the violation of the traffic law, together with the law that prohibited interference with government officials in the execution of their duties, gave the police the power to arrest the protestors on *Itsukaichi-gaidō*, the main street outside Tachikawa Air Base.[75]

The American mainstream news media reported the issue and often criticized the leftist agitators for provoking villagers to engage in violent resistance. The *Los Angeles Times* called the protests at Sunagawa "anti-America disorders" that were "obviously encouraged if not actually promoted by the recently revived Communist Party."[76] The *Christian Science Monitor* reported that violence erupted between about 2,000 "tough but well-disciplined" Japanese police and 4,000 "angry Sunakawa [sic] villagers and union supporters from nearby Tokyo."⁷⁷ It read, "The extensions are violently opposed by anti-American, pro-Communist union leaders and politicians, as well as by more or less nonpolitical farmers embittered by loss of their ancestral lands."⁷⁸ The newspaper also ran a special section on the protest in Sunagawa and anti-Americanism in Japan. Its correspondent, Frank Robertson wrote, "The movement by the people of Sunakawa [sic] . . . was not organized as an anti-American campaign. . . . But then, Sōhyō, the largest national labor organization in Japan stepped in, and the whole character of the agitation was changed."⁷⁹ Similarly, *The New York Times* reported that small, but active leftist groups were making efforts to influence the rest of the public and commented, "today's development seemed to indicate that the Leftists have only begun to fight."⁸⁰ The Japanese conservatives voiced similar criticism against the opposition group for "violating the laws" and called for the labor unions to leave the town.⁸¹

The survey was resumed on November 1, but protestors firmly blocked the survey team from entering the land. The government officially authorized compulsory acquisition of lands for US airbases and ordered to forcibly proceed to survey the lands. The survey team, consisting of twenty-two men from the Special Procurement Agency and contracted private survey companies sent by the Tokyo Metropolitan Government, arrived at Sunagawa in the morning while the protestors gathered on the main street and prepared for sit-in to block the surveyors. ⁸² Men and women of the village, joined by the left-wing Socialist Party members, union workers and student protestors, formed lines to block the survey team. "Women sympathizers stood by with straw mops dripping with sewage waving them at police," reported the *Chicago Tribune*.⁸³ The confrontation between the "human wave" protestors and the police forces continued for about a week. Three demonstrators were arrested for obstructing police officials.⁸⁴ On November 9, the survey team reported completing the necessary survey of the area located on the edge of Tachikawa Air Base, and the government proceeded to open talks with Americans about the amount of compensation to be paid for the landowners.⁸⁵ The survey of residential area was left unfinished, but the Japanese procurement authority announced the end of the first survey.⁸⁶ At the end of the year, the Sunagawa case ranked third in *Yomiuri's* top ten news stories of the year.⁸⁷

During the winter, the government authority had made several attempts to negotiate, but failed to reconcile with the local opponents. On January 25, 1956, the Governor of Tokyo, Yasui Seiichiro, met the opposition group representatives, but failed to convince them to accept the plan. The Procurement Agency approached each landowner individually, yet still about half of the landowners adamantly refused to give up their lands.

Meanwhile, the opposition groups came to put their forces together. Before the second round of the survey which started in the fall of 1956, a total of twelve leftist-progressive organizations, including Zengakuren, together formed the National Liaison Council Against the Military Bases (*Zenkoku Gunji Kichi Hantai Renraku Kaigi*) to organize opposition against the presence of military bases throughout Japan.[88] Its periodical, *Kichij Jyōhō* (Military Base Information), served as a bulletin that circulated information coming from different military base sites throughout Japan. The group initiated a fundraising campaign to support the anti-military base protests. The formation of the national council was crucial in connecting anti-military base movements scattered throughout Japan.

ZENGAKUREN AND A NEW BEGINNING

By then, the pro-JCP faction's dominance of Zengakuren came to an end, and powerful anti-Stalinist factions were emerging within Zengakuren that were more critical of the JCP leadership. The news of Khrushchev's criticism of Stalin in February 1956 and the Soviet military invasion of Hungary in the fall had empowered anti-JCP factions of the student left and contributed to the downfall of the pro-JCP faction in Zengakuren. According to Historian Silvio Pons, Khrushchev's attack on Stalin "triggered a crisis of trust amongst communists around the world" and "many communists, at the time and then in their memories, experienced 1956 as an *annus terribilis*, although more in Europe than elsewhere."[89] The impact of the crisis reverberated rather slowly in the Japanese Communist movement. JCP leaders assumed that, having previously completed similar self-criticism at the Sixth National Party Congress in 1955, the JCP, unlike European counterparts, could regard this crisis as having little impact on the Japanese Communist movement.[90] In *Sengo Kakumei Undō Ronsōshi*, Kobayashi Yoshiaki concluded that the Japanese communists, including the students, interpreted the anti-Stalin speech as a criticism of Stalin's personality, rather than that of the Soviet system as a whole, and did not seriously question the Soviet version of socialism.[91]

Yet, the self-criticism of the JCP in 1955 and the Soviet Premier's criticism of Stalinism unleashed a new wave of enthusiasm and interests in reaching the "correct" understanding revolutionary Marxism among the student left. Tomioka Masuo, a founding member of the anti-Stalinist *Bunto* faction, recalled, "The criticism of Stalin might have made us think that the Soviet could be wrong," but many of the student left remained firmly Marxist in their ideological orientation.[92] Indeed, Marxism remained the ideological basis of the student left in Japan. Kuroda Hirokazu (known as Kuroda Kanichi), who became a Zengakuren leader in the 1960s, then claimed that communism had been "tainted by Stalinism, Maoism, and so on, thus students need to form a movement based on the true Marxist-Leninist doctrine."[93] A few months after the Soviet invasion of Hungary, Uchida Hideo, Kurihara Toichi (alias Ota Ryu), and Kuroda Kanichi formed a Trotskyist league.[94] These anti-Stalinist student leftists tried to promote a revolution based on "correct" understanding of Marxist principles.

Disillusioned with Stalinist Communism, some of the leftist students in Japan found a source of inspiration in the nationalist revolutions in the Third World. Zengakuren called for peace and national independence, which they saw as threatened by capitalist imperialism led by the United States. On June 19, they sent a petition to President Eisenhower and protested in front of the US Embassy building against the recommendations made by the Price Subcommittee of the House Armed Services Committee, which was widely interpreted in Japan as indicating the intention of the US to establish a permanent occupation of Okinawa.[95] In fact, the US occupation of Okinawa provided the leftists with a major reference point for calling for a national independence movement. US Ambassador to Japan John Moore Allison had remarked that the United States was vulnerable to the leftist "anti-colonial" criticism since "we are the sole Western nation which has taken over a large Asian population bloc (in the Ryukyus) since the end of the war."[96] The US presence in Japan had provided the student radicals with a sense of solidarity with the Third World nationalists.

The Third World revolutionaries seemed to offer an alternative form of revolutionary struggle against capitalist imperialism. The Sunagawa struggle coincided with the rise of Arab nationalism, which became a serious problem for the United States. In July 1956, Egypt's leader Gamal Abdel Nasser nationalized the Suez Canal, and the British, French, and Israeli forces invaded Egypt in late October. In response, the United States took punitive measures against its European allies and demanded the withdrawal of forces from Egypt. The Arab crisis led Eisenhower to request a significant increase in the US efforts to support pro-Western leaders against Communist influence in the Middle East. In his "Special Message to the Congress on the Situation in the Middle East" delivered on January 5, 1957, President Eisenhower proposed economically assisting nations in the Middle East and to "authorize the Executive to take in the same region programs of military assistance and cooperation with any nation or group of nations which desires such aid."[97] More importantly and problematically, the President requested "to employ the armed forces of the United States to assist to defend the territorial integrity and the political independence of any nation in the area against Communist armed aggression," in reference to the situation in the Middle East.[98] Zengakuren criticized the Eisenhower doctrine as a declaration of

America's intention to expand into the Arab world, even at the cost of peace. Zengakuren's central office accused "The US imperialists of advancing into the Middle East, replacing the British and French empires."[99] The President's statement seemed to convince the Zengakuren students that America was willing to use military force in the Cold War if necessary to fulfill its imperial ambition. Some Zengakuren students saw a mirror image of the Third World nationalist movement in the Sunagawa protest.

The Sunagawa struggle played a crucial role in uniting the splintered Zengakuren, providing it with a clear organizational objective. The pro-JCP faction's dominance in the early 1950s had alienated many student activists from Zengakuren, and the Sunagawa struggle helped Zengakuren win them back. In June, Zengakuren proclaimed the "new beginning" of the student movement and admitted its "past mistakes" at the ninth national convention.[100] It formally announced a shift in its organizational line and put an end to the participation in the JCP-directed Mountain-Village operation that was aimed to stimulate an armed uprising in Japan. At the convention, Zengakuren officially reunited with the Antiwar Student League as well as members of the central office who had been expelled under the Centralist leadership.

ZENGAKUREN AND THE PROTESTS AT SUNAGAWA

In 1956, Zengakuren formally joined the Sunagawa struggle. Shimizu Ikutaro, who was a prominent postwar progressive scholar active in the anti-base struggle, visited Morita, accompanied by labor union leader Takano Minoru and local opposition leader Aoki Ichigoro. They asked Morita to mobilize Zengakuren for Sunagawa. Morita said, "They were so insistent that I could not say no, but the problem was that there was not anyone left to lead Zengakuren for Sunagawa at University of Tokyo, except me."[101] Morita recalled:

> I was left alone to mobilize students for Sunagawa. So, I came up with the idea of renting a bus from a bus company and asked students to get on the bus to join the Sunagawa protest at the front gate of Komaba campus [of University of Tokyo]. At first, there were only three students who joined me on the bus to Sunagawa.... Then, there were ten students for the second trip and thirty on the third. Then, the bus became full, and we needed another bus for the fifth trip.... After that, we did the same at other universities in Tokyo, including Meiji, Hosei, Chuo and Waseda. We made these bus trips between May and August, and then I held a press conference and made the statement that Zengakuren would send 3,000 students to Sunagawa in the fall.... Yet to tell you the truth, I did not know whether we could gather 3,000 students at that time.... But they actually showed up in the fall.[102]

By September, Zengakuren gradually gained support from fellow students for its Sunagawa protest. Student groups outside Tokyo responded the Zengakuren leadership's call for fund raising campaigns for Sunagawa. Students in Tokyo continued the trips to Sunagawa to join the protest.[103] On September 22, the *Yomiuri Shimbun* gave special coverage entitled "Recovering Student Movement."[104] It reported that Zengakuren's membership was growing quickly from 170,000 in April to 230,000 in September and it "matured enough so that it could take a careful action in Sunagawa."[105] According to the *Yomiuri*, Zengakuren collected 250,000 signatures and raised 1.09 million yen in support for the Sunagawa struggle against the runway extension plan.[106] The newspaper stated, "The student movement indeed resurrected . . . but we do not yet know whether it will follow the right path."[107] Moreover, Zengakuren had proven itself within the opposition movement. On September 19, the representatives from the local opposition group visited Zengakuren, along with those from labor unions, to express their appreciation to Zengakuren's contribution and asked for continuing support in Sunagawa.[108]

The second round of the land survey began on October 1, 1956, and lasted for two weeks. On October 1, about 150 artists and intellectuals concerned with the US military bases in Japan arrived at noon, followed by roughly five hundred Zengakuren students.[109] Zengakuren by that time had set up a local branch in Sunagawa.[110] During the two-week resistance against the survey, Zengakuren sent over 1,500 members to Sunagawa, and each day had between 500 and 1,000 students staying in the town.[111] The sympathetic residents opened their homes to the Zengakuren students to sleep at night. One local woman recalled:

> We had students sleeping in our house every day, nine students at the most. . . . The members of the Japan Federation of Women's Organizations from Tokyo were in charge of cooking meals for the students, but their breakfast was not ready until about 9 o'clock. So, we offered the students rice balls or some food to eat in the morning, but they refused any food from us, saying that they were thankful that we put them up for the nights and they could not trouble us more . . . . The people in the village were by and large welcoming these students. . . . I believe that such solidarity between the local residents and the students brought the final victory for us.[112]

In the following days, each side anticipated a physical confrontation. On October 3, the local opponents and those from supporting labor unions, the Socialist Party, and Zengakuren held a meeting outside the local shrine. They proclaimed that the Sunagawa struggle against the extension plan for the US military base was "a part of the international struggles of the people who want peace and independence throughout the world from Ireland to Sunagawa and

Okinawa . . . to Suez."[113] On October 4, a soup kitchen was set up to provide foods for the protestors from outside Sunagawa.

A total of nineteen female students participated in the Sunagawa struggle between October 4 and 14. Upon their arrival in Sunagawa, they were assigned "not dangerous" routine and trivial tasks: preparing meals and taking care of injured protestors.[114] A female student recalled, "I came with three other female students to Sunagawa. We were told that we could only spend less than ten yen per meal. . . . When we went to buy fish, the person at the store sold fish at cost for us. After the morning grocery shopping, then we 'engaged in a 'fierce battle,' keeping in mind that we could not spend more than ten yen per meal."[115] These female students were at first seemed perplexed but grudgingly accepted their tasks. Another female student said, "We [female students] were told not to join protests on demonstrations because it would be dangerous; instead, they asked us to do the paperwork. I told myself that such work was no less important than protesting on the street, but I felt somehow disappointed."[116]

A physical confrontation started on October 4 as the survey team left the gate of the US military base to enter the village. The Tokyo Procurement survey team, which consisted of fifty men, appeared in Sunagawa in the

Photo of Socialist Party members welcoming Zengakuren students at a protest rally against the extension of the runway of Tachikawa Airbase on October 4, 1956. The flag on the left belongs to the students' self-governing association of the College of Arts and Science of the University of Tokyo. © *Kyodo News Agency*

morning.[117] The Socialist Party representatives and lawyers blocked their way into the scheduled survey areas and pushed the survey team back to inside the gate of the base. The survey team continuously made attempts but was forced by the demonstrators to the US military base by each time.[118] The following day, 1,500 Zengakuren students arrived at Sunagawa, including those from Hokkaido University, Fukushima University, Niigata University, Nagoya University, Kyoto University, Ritsumeikan University, Doshisha University, Osaka University, Hiroshima University, and Kyushu University.[119] About 2,000 Zengakuren students gathered at the local shrine and held a meeting, and about 4,000 protestors from other organizations and groups joined them, expressing their support for the Zengakuren students.[120]

In the following days, the survey team and demonstrators repeatedly clashed back and forth near the gate. On October 7, about 2,000 union activists, 1,000 Zengakuren students, 400 Socialist party members, and 500 people from other groups joined the local protestors.[121] On October 8, the leaders of the Socialist Party met Foreign Minister Shigemitsu, who was acting for the Prime Minister Hatoyama (who was in Moscow at the time, attempting to restore good relations with the Soviet Union). The JCP leaders asked Shigemitsu to stop the survey at least until Hatoyama came back from Moscow, but he rejected this.[122] Hatoyama and Shigemitsu worried that the domestic protests against the US military bases in Japan in the midst of their talk with the USSR would give the US the "wrong idea." Shigemitsu feared that the escalation of the Sunagawa struggle might invite an insurmountable American reaction against their diplomatic activities. Still, the situation in Sunagawa intensified. On October 9, the Tokyo Metropolitan Police Department discussed the possible deployment of the police force against the protestors in Sunagawa, although it understood the difficulty of justifying its intervention as long as the opponents were calling for "peaceful negotiation."[123] For two days, the survey team made attempts to enter the privately-owned lands but was blocked by the demonstrators who firmly guarded them.[124] Having failed to break the human blockade, the survey team retreated into the US military base each time.

Finally, the police were called to accompany the survey team that was entering the land scheduled to be surveyed from the fourth gate of Tachikawa Air Base on October 12.[125] It arrived in the afternoon in a total of fifty armored vehicles, transport trucks, and ambulances.[126] For some, police actions in Sunagawa evoked memories of wartime suppression. Hironaka Toshio, a law professor who specialized in the study of Japanese police, deplored that the police force deployed to Sunagawa was a special unit called the Police Reserve Force, which in fact was the successor to the wartime Japanese military unit that had been in charge of domestic policing.[127] He argued that this unit had inherited the spirit of anti-Communism and ultra-nationalism.[128] As the protestors blocked the survey team's access to the land scheduled for survey, a violent skirmish broke out between 2,000 police officers and about 4,500 demonstrators near the gate number 4.[129] Over 200 people, including seventy-five policemen, were injured.[130]

Violence between the police force and the demonstrators culminated on October 13. At around 2 pm, about 2,000 police officers wearing blue helmets "stormed and violently attacked everyone they saw on the streets."[131] The demonstrators cried, "Please do not make the town a military base for a nuclear war" and "Please go home."[132] Others shouted against the police officers, "thief," "America's dogs," and "don't sell out Japanese land."[133] The police continued clashing against the protestors. A student protestor recalled, "A policeman hit my stomach repeatedly with his club . . . and grabbed me around my neck and hit my head, face, and shoulder with the club in his other hand."[134] In the confusion of the struggle, one police officer whispered to a student, "You all are fooled. We are not going against you, but the Reds behind you that deceived you. You were provoked by temporary heroism and the wrong sense of justice."[135] The violent confrontation continued until five o'clock in the evening. At the end, about 700 demonstrators were sent to the hospital, including female students who went out to the streets to help the injured people.[136] The *Washington Post* described the scene: "Scores of injured lay groaning in a sea of mud littered with bamboo poles, stones, and broken glass."[137] The Tokyo Procurement Agency announced the cancellation of the survey scheduled for the next day. About 4,000 opponents gathered outside the local shrine and proclaimed their victory.

THE SUNAGAWA STRUGGLE AND THE DEVELOPMENT OF THE MOVEMENT AGAINST THE US-JAPAN SECURITY TREATY

The violent confrontation in Sunagawa resulted in growing public awareness of the costs associated with the Security Treaty. The *Washington Post* reported that the resistance was "capitalized by the Opposition factions seeking to embarrass the Government, which until today sought to avoid the use of force" and that it was primarily aimed against the Japanese government, not the United States.[138] Yet, the Sunagawa struggle drew public attention to the security treaty with the US. A local woman cried foul over the deployment of the police force, saying, "The police cannot deny that it is a watch dog for the government that represses the citizens, neglecting its duty to protect the people. Doesn't the government care to see the blood of the Japanese people as long as it could extend the runway for the US military?"[139] After the violent struggle, a police officer who had been assigned to Sunagawa committed suicide, leaving a note saying, "I can criticize neither side of the struggle. One thing clear is that the Sunagawa struggle changed my perspective of my life."[140] It was not clear how the event changed his perspective, but many Japanese people interpreted his death as the result of being caught in the crossfire of the American and Japanese governments and the ordinary Japanese citizens.

After these events, the focus of the public debate inevitably moved to the issue of the US-Japan Security Treaty after the events in October 1956. The novelist Hotta Yoshie, who later became a founding member of the anti-Vietnam War organization called *Beheiren*, wrote in 1956 that he had a great sympathy toward the police officer as well as the injured Zengakuren students who were violently attacked by the police officers. The Sunagawa struggle was, he argued, a part of the new resistance movements taking place across the globe from Hungary and Poland to Algeria and India, developing the "international belt" of resistance.[141] In Japan, he insisted that the resistance in places like Sunagawa was aimed against "the power called the San Francisco system" and the magnitude of the Sunagawa struggle proved that "the San Francisco system was dying in the hearts of the Japanese people."[142]

Uehara Senroku, a professor of European history, thought that the Sunagawa struggle signaled the emergence of new nationalism in Japan, which was already rampant in other Asian and African countries. He claimed that the "new nationalism" born in Asia and Africa, in contrast to one rooted in the Western world, was born out of the people's desire for independence and peace in response to the Western imperialism from which they suffered for a long time.[143] The Bandung Conference, argued Uehara, "manifested the strong desire of Asian and African countries for world peace." The Sunagawa struggle, for Uehara, seemed to signal the Japanese awakening to a new nationalism and the end of the isolation from the Asian and African new nationalist movement. In 1959, Uehara formed the *Anpo Mondai Kenkyū Kai* (the Study Group of the US-Japan Security Treaty Problems) with prominent liberal intellectuals including Shimizu Ikutaro.[144]

The Japanese conservatives, on the other hand, blamed the leftists for not acknowledging the legitimacy and benefits of the treaty. The special editorial of the journal *Shin Seikai* (New Political World) defended the actions taken by the Tokyo Procurement Agency and insisted that the Japanese public should admit that these US military bases were to provide defense for Japan rather than to serve US strategic interests. The journal tried to convince its readers that the extension plan, furthermore, would not mean that the US would steal the Japanese land. It claimed a landlord would not lose his or her rights even after a tenant occupied his or her property; rather, the landlord still had rights as a landlord while the tenant could claim rights as a tenant. In its logic, Japan, the landlord and the US, the tenant had different rights and duties legitimately agreed by the two.[145]

For many of the student activists, the Sunagawa struggle was a formative experience. In its newsletter issued on October 29, the Tokyo Metropolitan Federation of Students' Self-Governing Associations (*Tokyo-to Gakusei Jichikai Rengō*, abbreviated as *Togakuren*) published an article entitled "The Great Victory and Lessons: the Political Meaning of the Sunagawa Struggle" and proclaimed, "Our movement entered a new stage."[146] In the eyes of the student radicals, the victory in the Sunagawa struggle seemed to prove the student movement's ability to play a crucial role in leading a mass movement and bring a political change. The *Togakuren* students wrote in the article that the victory in Sunagawa demonstrated that student activists could win further victories against military bases in Japan. Zengakuren's leadership celebrated the remarkable solidarity among the local farmers, union workers, leftist political organizations, intellectuals and artists, and students that constituted a powerful mass movement that transcended political and ideological differences.[147] It claimed, "We no longer have the sense of defeat in the fight against the US-Japan reactionary forces that abuse the state power and use violence. The development of the mass movement showed us a new possibility."[148] At the tenth national convention held in June 1957, Zengakuren exhibited its renewed confidence, assuming a central role in the people's movement in Japan. It claimed that the Sunagawa struggle demonstrated Zengakuren's strength and heightened national and international expectations about its role.[149]

The Sunagawa struggle nurtured leftist students' imagination of international "anti-imperial" nationalist solidarity. At the tenth national convention, Zengakuren passed a resolution supporting the Algerian people's national liberation movement.[150] Celebrating it as a heroic struggle against the imperialists, an epitome of anti-Stalinist revolutionary struggle, the Antiwar Student League and Zengakuren leaders sent a letter to the Algerian National Liberation Front (NLF) expressing their strong protest against "the common enemy of imperialism and the violent oppression against the people."[151] They wrote, "We know that your fight against imperialism occupies the important place for the people in the world and your victory would offer great opportunities for the liberation of the oppressed people."[152] A group of socialist students also issued a statement that "the French counterrevolutionary war in Algeria" revealed the true motives of the capitalist imperialists to dominate the world with the bourgeoisie rule by suppressing the people and destroying peace.[153] In a similar vein, the leftist students in Japan celebrated the peoples' struggle in Lebanon, Indochina, Bolivia, and Venezuela against the international capitalist imperialism.[154] Defining their protest at Sunagawa as the people's struggle against US and Japanese imperialism, they expressed a strong sense of solidarity with the Third World liberation movements.

The Sunagawa struggle resumed in 1957. In the early morning on July 8, a confrontation took place between the survey team and about 2,000 protestors who had formed an approximately 500-meter-long line along the fence that guarded Tachikawa Air Base.[155] Zengakuren regularly had between 500 and 1,000 members staying in Sunagawa until July 11.[156] The students expressed a stronger sense of urgency in this third round of the Sunagawa struggle. The Eisenhower administration's emphasis on nuclear weapons had renewed the fear of a global nuclear war, which made the Sunagawa struggle evermore important for the Zengakuren activists. *Yomiuri* reported that the total of about 2,500 Zengakuren students and other demonstrators clashed with the 1,900-strong police contingent that stood guarding the fence.[157] When a part of the fence was toppled during the skirmish, some 200 protestors including Zengakuren students pushed themselves into the military base and held a sit-down strike there.[158] The protestors' entry to the US military base resulted in the arrest of nine Zengakuren and fourteen labor union protestors under Article 2 of the Special Criminal Law enacted under the Administrative Agreement under Article III of the US-Japan Security Treaty, which prohibited unauthorized entry into American military facilities in Japan.[159]

Zengakuren, along with the *Sōhyō* federation of labor and the Socialist Party, fiercely protested the arrests as unjust political repression of Japan's peace movement. On September 23, Zengakuren decided to respond to the arrest with a nationwide strike.[160] Two days later, students across Japan went out into the streets protesting the arrest of the Sunagawa protestors, and in Tokyo, over 2,000 students showed up for the rally.[161] It was reported that a total of 20,000 students showed up for the meetings held on university campuses around Tokyo in protest against the arrest of their fellow students at Sunagawa.[162] The Sunagawa struggle against the runway extension plan developed into a movement against Sunagawa "political repression" by the end of September. Despite Zengakuren's protests against the arrest of protestors, seven activists—an employee at the National Railway, three factory workers, and three students—were going to face prosecution.

By the end of 1950s, the student left, which had grown more powerful over time through the participation in the Sunagawa struggle, confronted the JCP with new vigor. Anti-JCP students of Zengakuren now openly criticized the JCP's lack of militancy in the struggle against imperialism and condemned the Old Left as the "non-revolutionary" Left. The students argued that this "non-revolutionary" Left had failed to understand the class struggle, and this resulted in their failure to harness the revolutionary energy of the working class. Zengakuren students also criticized JCP theorists' misunderstanding of Japan's place in the global capitalist structure. While the JCP advocated, based on their understanding of the Russian revolutionary model, that the Japanese first had to complete a democratic revolution before taking further steps toward socialism, the student left argued that Japan's anti-imperial struggle should aim not only against American imperialism but also Japanese capitalism, which was about to reach the highest stage once again after the Korean War economic boom.[163] In January 1958, student activist Yamaguchi Hajime's article, published in the organ of the University of Tokyo Communist cell, *Marukusu Rēnin Shugi* (Marx-Leninism), provided the most influential criticism of the JCP. Yamaguchi argued that the JCP's sole focus on the fight against American imperialism misled the working class and caused a serious setback for Japan's revolutionary movement.[164] In April, the students of the Communist cell at University of Tokyo issued an Opinion Paper that openly criticized the JCP's policy.

The eleventh national convention held between May 28 and 31 marked the official formation of an anti-JCP Zengakuren. As a result of the dispute with Zengakuren, the JCP purged Zengakuren-affiliated students from the party on July 7, 1958.[165] In the editorial of the JCP party newspaper *Akahata* published on July 14, the JCP firmly stated, "We must correct this incorrect theory and the action of a group of student party members within the party" for the survival of the student movement that could effectively promote peace and democracy against the international reactionary forces.[166] Two months later, at the special national convention gathered on September 4, Zengakuren officially adopted the policy of combatting US-Japan imperialism and declared a second front against the JCP.[167] At the convention, the Zengakuren Secretariat (*Shoki Kyoku*) proclaimed, "We will support the struggles against colonial imperialism of the people of Arab, Africa, and Asia" to internationally "isolate imperialists."[168] It further argued that the rebirth of Japanese imperialism, backed by the United States and protected by the "military alliance" with it, urgently demanded the student movement to shift its focus to blocking Japanese rearmament and imperial expansion into Asia.[169]

During 1958, the Zengakuren student movement underwent historic organizational transformations. In May, the Antiwar Student League changed its name to the Socialist Student League (*Shakai Shugi Gakusei Dōmei*, abbreviated as *Shagakudō*) in order to reflect their aim to make their movement more revolutionarily based on the socialist principles.[170] At its inaugural meeting, the *Shagakudō* leaders declared that the rebirth of Japanese imperialism was imminent, and this invited JCP's criticism.[171] The most crucial development of 1958 was the creation of the Communist League (*Kyōsan Shugi Gakusei Dōmei*, abbreviated as *Kyōsandō*). A group of students led by former JCP members Shima Shigeo, Hiromatsu Wataru, and Tomioka Masuo founded this new anti-JCP faction, commonly known as the *Bunto*, in December 1958. The *Bunto* was characterized by its fierce anti-Stalinism and the principle of "real struggle." It called for rethinking of orthodox Marxism, which had been distorted and misrepresented, most notably by Stalin and the JCP. Hiromatsu attacked Stalin for distorting Marx's theory of state, calling his "Dialectical and Historical Materialism (1938)" and "Marxism and Problems of Linguistics (1950)" nonsense.[172] As for tactics, these student activists called for more confrontational direct actions, or "real" political struggles, against the reactionary forces. In 1960, the *Bunto* would put this in practice in the protest against the revision of the US-Japan Security Treaty.

Meanwhile, Ambassador Douglas MacArthur II, preparing for the revision of the Security Treaty, believed that the fulfillment of America's long-term security objectives depended on the long-term alignment of Japan. He understood that "that only possible approach [for Japan] was through alignment with the United States" because of Japan's historical isolation from both Asia and the West.[173] He observed, however, "While Japan is now in practice aligned with the United States, it is not yet a dependable alignment *because of the feeling of many Japanese that the alignment was forced on them by us in a one-sided manner for our own purposes rather than for mutual benefit.*"[174] He went on: "There are unquestionably elements in Japan which suggest a disengagement from close ties with the United States and toward neutrality or non-involvement as to security commitments. The motivations of such elements are to some extent based on neutralism and pacifism."[175] Yet, MacArthur failed to see that he would be confronting a powerful student movement in 1960.

In March 1959, the Sunagawa struggle moved to court as the trial for the convicted protestors who crossed the fence into the US military base in July 1957 began. The trial was held at the Tokyo District Court, headed by Justice Date Akio. The prosecutors' argument was that the demonstrators violated Article 2 of the Special Criminal Law of the Security Treaty, agreed upon by the US and Japanese governments, and it was the country's responsibility as generally expected by the international community to provide security for foreign troops. The defense pointed out that the presence of the US military force contradicted Article 9 of the Japanese Constitution which stated:

> Aspiring sincerely to an international peace based on justice and order, the Japanese people forever renounce war as a sovereign right of the nation and the threat or use of force as means of settling international disputes.
> In order to accomplish the aim of the preceding paragraph, land, sea, and air forces, as well as other war potential, will never be maintained. The right of belligerency of the state will not be recognized.[176]

The prosecutors argued that the peace clause of the Constitution prohibited maintaining war potential, not the defense force. Furthermore, Japan did not have any control over the use of American forces stationed in Japan.[177] On March 30, 1959, the Tokyo District Court ruled the defendants not guilty and called the maintaining of an armed force, either Japanese or American, as unconstitutional under Article 9.[178] The decision encouraged the groups that opposed the Security Treaty, whose revision was now being negotiated between the US and Japanese governments.

The Tokyo District Court's ruling posed a serious problem for Japanese conservatives and American officials. Prime Minister Kishi Nobusuke, who replaced Ishibashi Tanzan after he fell ill, responded to the court's decision by stating: "It is not necessary to change the government's interpretation of the constitution by the first ruling. Of course, the government will respect a Supreme Court decision, but it is not bound by any decision by lower courts on the way to a Supreme Court ruling."[179] MacArthur called for a meeting with Foreign Minister Fujiyama Aiichiro to discuss the Sunagawa case. In the meeting, the ambassador said, "While I was not familiar with many aspects of Japanese jurisprudence, I understood two possibilities were available to GOJ [Government of Japan]. 1. To appeal decision of Tokyo District Court to Appellate Court or 2. To appeal decision direct to [the] Japanese Supreme Court."[180] MacArthur hoped not only to overturn the unacceptable decision made by the district court but also to put an end to the debate over the constitutionality of the Security Treaty by silencing the anti-treaty elements. He wrote in the report, "I felt personally it was most important for GOJ to appeal directly to [the] Supreme Court, since socialists and leftists would not . . . accept decision of [the] Appellate Court as final and appeal to Appellate Court would only extend period of debate till Supreme Court says final word."[181] In April, Fujiyama privately assured MacArthur that it would directly appeal the case to the Supreme Court and "it has no doubt whatsoever that [the] Tokyo Court decision will be reversed."[182] Within two days, the Japanese government announced its decision to appeal to the Supreme Court, bypassing the Appellate Court. Once decided, the Sunagawa case was given priority over pending cases, and the Supreme Court delivered the final verdict by the end of the year.

On December 16, the Supreme Court annulled the verdict issued by the Tokyo District Court and proclaimed, "the pacifism advocated in our Constitution was never intended to mean defenseness [sic] or non-resistance."[183] The Court delivered its unanimous decision declaring that Japan could constitutionally maintain or host the armed forces that were not "war potential of its own."[184] In addition, it ruled that the Japanese courts did not possess the power to overrule international treaties signed with a foreign country. For the first time, the legal system recognized the priority of the Security Treaty over Article 9. By doing so, the Court interpreted the US-Japan Security and the presence of American military bases in Japan as providing peace and security and declared that Article 9 prohibited war potential, not armed forces as a whole. The Supreme Court embraced the government position that Japan's peace and security rested on the alliance with the United States.

The leftists argued that the presence of the US military force endangered Japan's national independence and security, but the Court's argument was that exercising the right to self-defense, to which all sovereign nations were entitled, proved Japan's independence. In his supplementary opinion, Chief Justice Tanaka Kotaro stated, "Self-defense is one of the most fundamental missions and functions of the state" and argued that the Security Treaty was not incompatible with the "spirit of pacifism" since it was aimed to maintain peace and security of Japan.[185] Justice Kawamura Daisuke similarly argued, "The Treaty of Peace recognizes that Japan as a sovereign nation has the right to enter into collective security arrangements, and further, the Charter of the United Nations recognized that all nations possess the inherent right of individual and collective self-defense."[186] The Supreme Court's adjudication removed the legal obstacles to a new security treaty. At the end of 1959, the treaty negotiations between the US and Japanese governments made significant progress, and the signing of the revised treaty of security and mutual cooperation was only a matter of time.

The Sunagawa case raised serious questions for the first time about the "security" granted by the treaty and made the Japanese aware of the real cost of the Security Treaty. The Court's decision did not end the *Anpo* struggle; rather it had invigorated the opposition against the treaty, in particular among the student left. By that time, Zengakuren had not only recovered but grown more powerful and confident. It now perceived its role as the vanguard of the mass "proletariat" movement. Despite the ruling of the Supreme Court, the Sunagawa struggle demonstrated that the student left could mobilize and lead a mass opposition against militarism in Japan. This sense of power gained through the Sunagawa struggle became a crucial factor that encouraged the students to lead a major *Anpo* struggle of 1960.

NOTES

1. Central Intelligence Agency (CIA), Intelligence Memorandum No. 197, July 25, 1949, *Documentary History of the Truman Presidency*, vol. 5, 348.
2. Ibid., 357.
3. Remarks by Dean Acheson before the National Press Club, January 1950. Elsey Papers. The Harry S. Truman Library, http://www.trumanlibrary.org/whistle

stop/study_collections/koreanwar/index.php?action=docs (accessed on December 7, 2012).

4. Ibid.

5. Dispatches from the British Embassy, "Tokyo, in regard to Communism in Japan, and Japanese Universities, particularly Communism therein," September 1, 1953. RG 59. Box 5676. NARAII.

6. Maria Höhn and Seungsook Moon, "Introduction: The Politics of Gender, Sexuality, Race, and Class in the US Military Empire," in *Over There: Living with the U.S. Military Empire from World War Two to the Present*, ed. Maria Höhn and Seungsook Moon (Durham, NC: Duke University Press, 2010), 8.

7. National Security Council Report, April 9, 1955 in *FRUS*, 1955–1957, vol. XXIII, Part 1, Japan (Washington, DC: United States Government Printing Office, 1991), 53.

8. Liu Xing, "Rethinking Shigemitsu's Visit to US in Japan-US Security Relations," *Journal of Law and Politics (Nagoya Daigaku Hōsei Ronshū)* 207 (2005): 9.

9. National Security Council Report, April 9, 1955 in FRUS, 1955–1957, vol. XXIII, Part 1, Japan, 55.

10. Telegram from the Department of State to the Embassy in Japan, January 10, 1955 in ibid., 5–6.

11. Ibid., 11–12.

12. Memorandum of Discussion at the 244th meeting of the National Security Council, Washington, April 7, 1955 in ibid., 40–41.

13. Ibid., 43.

14. Ibid., 44.

15. Ibid, 42 (emphasis in original).

16. Sayuri Guthrie-Shimizu, "Japan, the United States, and the Cold War, 1945–1960," in *The Cambridge History of the Cold War, Volume 1: Origin*, ed. Melvyn P. Leffler and Odd Arne Westad (New York: Cambridge University Press, 2010), 256.

17. Young, *The Vietnam Wars, 1945–1990*, 45.

18. Editorial Note in *FRUS*, 1955–1957, vol. XXIII, Part 1, Japan, 4; The quotation is taken from the summary of "the telegram CINCFE [Commander in Chief, Far East Command] from Tokyo, January 7, 1955, General Hull transmitted his Commands' view to the Department of the Army," which was attached to the memorandum on February 10 to the Operations Coordinating Board.

19. John Foster Dulles, "Policy for Security and Peace," *Foreign Affairs* 32, no. 3 (1954): 335–56.

20. National Security Council Report, April 9, 1955 in *FRUS*, 1955–1957, vol. XXIII, Part1, Japan, 55.

21. Ibid.

22. Ibid., 58.

23. In 1953, the United States and the United Kingdom launched operations against the democratically elected government of Mohammad Mosaddegh who attempted to nationalize and take control of the concessions of the Anglo-Iranian Oil Company. The Iranian crisis significantly increased the Eisenhower administration's concern over nationalism in the Third World; Westad, *The Global Cold* War, 119.

24. Memorandum of Discussion at the 244th meeting of the National Security Council, Washington, April 7, 1955 in *FRUS*, 1955–1957, vol. XXIII, Part 1, Japan, 41.

25. Ibid.

26. Memorandum by the Executive Officer of the Operations Coordinating Board (Staats) to the Executive Secretary of the National Security Council (Lay), Progress Report on National Security Council (NSC) 125/2 and 125/6: United States Objectives and Courses of Action with Respect to Japan, October 28, 1954 in *FRUS*, 1952–1954, vol. XIV, Part 2, China and Japan (Washington, DC: United States Government Printing Office, 1985), 1762; The Operations Coordinating Board, chaired by the Under Secretary of State, was created by President Eisenhower's Executive Order 10483 in September 1953. The board was in charge of overseeing the implementation of national security policies and provide review to the NSC.

27. Ibid.

28. Ibid.

29. The Ambassador in Japan (Allison) to the Japanese Foreign Minister (Okazaki), April 6, 1954 in *FRUS*, 1955–1957, vol. XXIII, Part1, Japan, 1628–9.

30. Memorandum from the Director of the Office of Northeast Asian Affairs (McClurkin) to the Assistant Secretary of State for Far Eastern Affairs (Robertson), February 1, 1955 in ibid., 15.

31. Chōtatsuchō Sōmubu Sōmuka [the General Affairs Section of the General Affairs Department of the Procurement Agency], "Hikōjyō Kakuchō ni Kansuru Shomondai ni Tsuite [On the problems of the airbase extension]." *Chōtatsuchō Chōsa Jihō*, no. 15 (1957): 5.

32. Memorandum from the Assistance Secretary of State for Far Eastern Affairs (Robertson) to the Secretary of State, July 28, 1955 in *FRUS*, 1955–1957, vol. XXIII, Part 1, Japan, 78–79.

33. Chōtatsuchō Sōmubu Sōmuka, "Hikōjyō Kakuchō ni Kansuru Shomondai ni Tsuite," 5–6.

34. Ibid.

35. *Yomiuri Shimbun*, July 2, 1955.

36. Chuo Daigaku Gakusei Jichikai Chōsabu [A research group of Chuo University Self-Governing Association], *Sunagawa-machi ni Okeru Kichi Kakuchō Hantai Tōsō o Megurite* [About the struggle against the military base extension in Sunagawa] (Tokyo: Chuo Daigaku Gakusei Jichikai, 1956), 27, 41.

37. Bōei Shisetsuchōshi Hensan Iinkai [The Editorial Committee of Defense Facilities Administration Agency], ed. *Bōei Shisetsuchōshi: Kichimondai to Tomoni Ayunda 45-Nen no Kiseki* [A history of the Defense Facilities Administration Agency: the historical trajectory of the 45 Years with military base problems] (Tokyo: Bōei Shisetsu-cho, 2007), 7.

38. Ibid.

39. The Supreme Commander for the Allied Powers Instruction (SCAPIN) 2154: Authorization of Special Procurement Agency to Furnish Goods and Services on Contract to Occupation Forces, May 26, 1951 in Takemae, ed. *GHQ Shirei (SCAPIN) Sōshūsei* [A collection of GHQ SCAPINs], Vol. 15: SCAPIN 2051–2204 (Tokyo: Emutei Shuppan, 1993), 7206–07.

40. Chōtatsuchō Sōmubu Sōmuka, "Hikōjyō Kakuchō ni Kansuru Shomondai ni Tsuite," 18.

41. *Yomiuri Shimbun,* November 19, 1951.

42. John Foster Dulles, "The New Look: The Evolution of Foreign Policy," January 12, 1954 in Sam C. Sarkesian and Robert A. Vitas, eds., *US National Security Policy and Strategy: Documents and Policy Proposals* (New York: Greenwood Press, 1988), 53 (emphasis added); Neal Rosendorf, "John Foster Dulles' Nuclear Schizophrenia," in *Cold War Statesmen Confront the Bomb: Nuclear Diplomacy since 1945,* ed. Philip H. Gordon, et al. (New York: Oxford University Press, 1999), 73.

43. Lisa Yoneyama, *Hiroshima Traces: Time, Space, and the Dialectics of Memory* (Berkeley: University of California Press, 1999), 14.

44. Letter from Hiromasa H. Suzuki to Robert D. Murphy, September 20, 1954. RG 59. Box 5677. NARAII.

45. *Washington Post,* October 13, 1956.

46. Bōei Shisetsuchōshi Hensan Iinkai, *Bōei Shisetsuchōshi,* 25.

47. Chuo Daigaku Gakusei Jichikai Chōsabu, *Sunagawa-machi ni Okeru Kichi Kakuchō Hantai Tōsō o Megurite,* 30–32.

48. Chōtatsuchō Sōmubu Sōmuka, "Hikōjyō Kakuchō ni Kansuru Shomondai ni Tsuite," 6; Shinseikai Henshūkyoku, "Kichi to Sunagawa Mondai Tokushū [A special issue on military bases and the Sunagawa problem]," *Shinseikai* 2, no. 13 (1956): 21.

49. *Yomiuri Shimbun,* evening edition, July 21, 1955; Shinseikai Henshūkyoku, Shinseikai Henshūkyoku, "Kichi to Sunagawa Mondai Tokushū," 21.

50. *The New York Times,* August 26, 1955.

51. Chōtatsuchō Sōmubu Sōmuka, "Hikōjyō Kakuchō ni Kansuru Shomondai ni Tsuite," 2.

52. Ibid.

53. Memorandum of a Conversation, Department of State, Washington, August 30, 1955 in *FRUS,* 1955–1957, vol. XXIII, Part1, Japan, 98.

54. Ibid.

55. Ibid.

56. Ibid., 102.

57. Ibid., 101.

58. Ibid.

59. Ibid.

60. Ibid.

61. Ibid., 31.

62. Shinseikai Henshūkyoku, "Kichi to Sunagawa Mondai Tokushū," 21.

63. Yoshiaki Kobayashi, *Sengo Kakumei Undō Ronsōshi* [A history of debates about postwar revolutionary movements] (Tokyo: San-Ichi Shobo, 1971), 134.

64. Chuo Daigaku Gakusei Jichikai Chōsabu, *Sunagawa-machi ni Okeru Kichi Kakuchō Hantai Tōsō o Megurite,* 81.

65. Ibid., 34.

66. Zengakuren Shoki Kyoku, "Zengakuren Dai8-kai Zenkoku Taikai Ketsugi, Taikai Sengen [The declaration and resolution of the 8th Zengakuren national

convention]," June 10–14, 1955. Document no. 96 in *Zengakuren Documents*, vol. 3,1952–1955 (Tokyo: San-Ichi Shobō, 1969), 432.

67. Morita Minoru in an interview with the author in Tokyo on February 8, 2017.

68. Memorandum of Conversation, Subject: Communist Subversion in Japan, July 19, 1955. RG 59. Box 3964. NARAII.

69. *Yomiuri Shimbun*, September 10, 1955.

70. Ibid.

71. *Yomiuri Shimbun*, September 14, 1955.

72. The General Council of Japanese Trade Unions (*Sōhyō*) was one of the largest labor federations in Japan. It provided a solid base of support for the JSP.

73. Nihon Shakaitō [The Japan Socialist Party], "Shakitō no Seifu e no Moushiire [The Japan Socialist Party's request to the government]," September 12, 1955, reprinted in Chuo Daigaku Gakusei Jichikai Chōsabu, *Sunagawa-machi ni Okeru Kichi Kakuchō Hantai Tōsō o Megurite*, 54–55.

74. Keisatsu Kōron Henshūbu, "Sunagawa Jiken ni Tsuite: Kichimondai no Ichi Danmen [About the Sunagawa incident: one aspect of military base problems]," *Keisatsu Kōron* 10, no. 11 (1955): 30.

75. Ibid.

76. *Los Angeles Times*, September 14, 1955.

77. *Christian Science Monitor*, September 13, 1955.

78. Ibid.

79. Ibid., May 23, 1956.

80. *The New York Times*, September 17, 1955.

81. *Yomiuri Shimbun*, September 14, 1955.

82. ———, November 1, 1955.

83. *Chicago Tribune*, November 6, 1955.

84. Ibid.

85. Chuo Daigaku Gakusei Jichikai Chōsabu, *Sunagawa-machi ni Okeru Kichi Kakuchō Hantai Tōsō o Megurite*, 37–38.

86. *Yomiuri Shimbun*, November 10, 1955.

87. ———, December 20, 1955.

88. Chuo Daigaku Gakusei Jichikai Chōsabu, *Sunagawa-machi ni Okeru Kichi Kakuchō Hantai Tōsō o Megurite*, 82.

89. Silvio Pons, *The Global Revolution: A History of International Communism 1917–1991* (Oxford: Oxford University Press, 2014), 210.

90. Kobayashi, *Sengo Kakumei Undō Ronsōshi*, 127.

91. Ibid.

92. Ibid., 128.

93. Ibid., 132–33.

94. In December 1967, the group changed its name to the Revolutionary Communist League (*Kakumeiteki Kyōsan Shugisha Dōmei*, abbreviated as *Kakukyōdō*).

95. Memorandum from the Assistant Secretary of State for Far Eastern Affairs (Robertson) to the Secretary of State, June 25, 1956, *FRUS*, 1955–1957, vol. XXIII, Part 1, Japan, 192.

96. Chiefs of Mission Conferences, American Embassy Tokyo, March 19–21, 1956, 26. Papers of John Foster Dulles: State Department Declassified Documents. Box 1. Folder 9. Princeton University Library.

97. "Special Message to the Congress on the Situation in the Middle East," January 5, 1957 in Dwight D. Eisenhower, *Public Papers of the Presidents of the United States: Dwight D. Eisenhower, 1957* ed. National Archives and Records Service Office of the Federal Register, General Services Administration (Washington DC: US Government Printing Office, 1958), 13.

98. Ibid., 15.

99. Zengakuren Shoki Kyoku, "Zengakuren Dai10-kai Zenkoku Taikai Ippan Hōkoku, Hōsin [The 10th Zengakuren national convention, a general report, policy]," June 3–6, 1957. Document no. 30 in *Zengakuren Documents*, vol. 4, 1956–1958 (Tokyo: San-Ichi Shobō, 1969), 168.

100. Ibid., 162–3.

101. Morita Minoru in interview with the author in Tokyo on February 8, 2017; According to Morita, Koyama was in Prague, attending the meeting of the International Union of Students in Prague and Shima was suffering from asthma.

102. Ibid.

103. Zengakuren Shoki Kyoku, "Sunagawa ni tuite [About Sunagawa]," *Zengakuren Tūshin*, October 8, 1956. Document no. 17 in *Zengakuren Documents*, vol. 4, 1956–1958, 118–120.

104. *Yomiuri Shimbun*, September 22, 1956.

105. Ibid.

106. Ibid.

107. Ibid.

108. Zenkoku Gunji Kichi Hantai Renraku Kaigi [The National Liaison Council Against the Military Bases], "Kyōsei Sokuryō o Meguru Sunagawa Tōsō no Keika [The progress of the struggle against the forcible land survey in Sunagawa]," *Kichijyōhō*, no. 30 (November 5, 1956), 3. Sengo Shakai Undō 50-3, Kichi Mondai no. 641. OISR Archive.

109. Chuo Daigaku Gakusei Jichikai Chōsabu, *Sunagawa-machi ni Okeru Kichi Kakuchō Hantai Tōsō o Megurite*, 84–85.

110. Zengakuren Shoki Kyoku, "Sunagawa-machi Daini Tochi Shūyō Nintei Happyō ni Saishite no Seimei [The statement on the second round of the land survey in Sunagawa]," September 13, 1956. Document no. 16 in *Zengakuren Documents Zengakuren Documents*, vol. 4, 1956–1958, 116–118.

111. Zengakuren Shoki Kyoku, "Sunagawa ni tsuite," *Zengakuren Tūshin*. Document no. 17 in ibid., 118–120.

112. Chuo Daigaku Gakusei Jichikai Chōsabu, *Sunagawa-machi ni Okeru Kichi Kakuchō Hantai Tōsō o Megurite*, 273.

113. Ibid., 146.

114. Ibid., 216.

115. Ibid., 215–6.

116. Ibid., 212.

117. Zenkoku Gunji Kichi Hantai Renraku Kaigi, "Kyōsei Sokuryō o Meguru Sunagawa Tōsō no Keika," *Kichij Jyōhō*, 30. Sengo Shakai Undō 50–3, Kichi Mondai no. 641. OISR Archive.

118. "Sunagawa no Shufu Nikki [Diary of a housewife in Sunagawa]," *Fujin Kōron* 41, no. 12 (December 1956): 79.

119. Zengakuren Chūō Shikkō Iinkai, "Zengakuren dai10-kai Chūō Iinkai ni taisuru Chūō Shikkō Iinkai Houkoku [The report of the Central Executive Committee of Zengakuren on the 10th Zengakuren national convention]," January 19–21, 1957. Document no. 22 in *Zengakuren* Documents, vol. 4, 1956–1958, 140.

120. Zenkoku Gunji Kichi Hantai Renraku Kaigi, "Kyōsei Sokuryō o Meguru Sunagawa Tōsō no Keika," *Kichij Jyōhō*, 30. Sengo Shakai Undō 50-3, Kichi Mondai no. 641. OISR Archive.

121. Ibid.

122. Chuo Daigaku Gakusei Jichikai Chōsabu, *Sunagawa-machi ni Okeru Kichi Kakuchō Hantai Tōsō o Megurite*, 95.

123. Ibid., 97.

124. Ibid., 98–99.

125. Ibid., 105.

126. Ibid.

127. Toshio Hironaka, "Keisatsukan no Higeki [A tragedy of the police]," *Chūō Kōron* 71, no. 13 (December 1956): 40.

128. Ibid.

129. "Sunagawa no Shufu Nikki," 106.

130. Hironaka, "Keisatsukan no Higeki," 40.

131. Ibid.

132. Kazuya Amano, "Sunagawa no 3-Jikan: Gakusei Kara Mita 2-Ji Kara 5-Ji Made [3 hours in Sunagawa: what a student saw from 2pm to 5pm]," *Bungeishunju* 34, no. 12 (December, 1956): 118.

133. Zenkoku Gunji Kichi Hantai Renraku Kaigi, "Kyōsei Sokuryō o Meguru Sunagawa Tōsō no Keika," *Kichij Jyōhō*, 33. Kichi Mondai no. 640, 50–3. OISR Archive.

134. Hironaka, "Keisatsukan no Higeki," 41.

135. Amano, "Sunagawa no 3-Jikan," 121.

136. Hironaka, "Keisatsukan no Higeki," 41.

137. *Washington Post*, October 13, 1956.

138. ———, October 14, 1956.

139. Hironaka, "Keisatsukan no Higeki," 80–81.

140. Yoshie Hotta, "Sunagawa Kara Budapesuto Made: Rekishi ni Tsuite [From Budapest to Sunagawa: about history]," *Chūō Kōron* 71, no. 13 (December 1956): 21.

141. Ibid., 23–24.

142. Ibid., 25–27.

143. Chuo Daigaku Gakusei Jichikai Chōsabu, *Sunagawa-machi ni Okeru Kichi Kakuchō Hantai Tōsō o Megurite*, 312–14.

144. Rokuro Hidaka, *1960-nen 5-Gatu 19-Nichi* [May 19, 1960] (Tokyo: Iwanami Shoten, 1960), 90.

145. Ibid.
146. Togakuren Shoki Kyoku [Secretariat of the Tokyo Metropolitan Federation of Students' Self-Governing Associations], "Idai na Shōri to Kyōkun: Sunagawa Tōsō to Sējiteki Igi [The great victory and lessons: the Sunagawa struggle and its political significance]," *Togakuren Nyūsu,* October 29, 1956. Document no. 18 in *Zengakuren Documents,* vol. 4, 1956–1958, 120.
147. Zengakuren Chūō Shikkō Iinkai, "Zengakuren dai10-kai Chūō Iinkai ni taisuru Chūō Shikkō Iinkai Houkoku," 137–138.
148. Ibid., 138.
149. Zengakuren Shoki Kyoku, "Zengakuren dai10-kai Zenkoku Taikai Ippan Hōkoku, Hōsin," 176.
150. Zengakuren, "Zengakuren Dai10-kai Zenkoku Taikai Shoketsugi, Taikai Sengen [The declaration and resolution pledged at the 10th Zengakuren national convention]," June 7, 1957. Document no. 31 in *Zengakuren Documents,* vol. 4, 1956–1958, 227.
151. Nihon Hansen Gakusei Dōmei [The Japan Antiwar Student Association], Dai 11-kai Zenkoku Iinkai [The 11th national committee of the Japan Antiwar Student League], "Arugeria Minzoku Kaihō Sensen to Arugeria Zengakuren no Sien Ketsugi [The Algerian people's liberation front and Zengakuren's resolution to support Algeria]," March 30, 1958 in *Zengakuren Documents,* vol. 4, 1956–1958, 288–90.
152. Ibid.
153. Shakai Shugi Gakusei Dōmei Zenkoku Shikkō Iinkai [The National Executive Committee of the Socialist Student League], "Shakai Shugi Gakusei Dōmei Dai1-kai Zenkoku Taikai [The 11th national convention of the Socialist Student League]," Document no. 42 in *Zengakuren Documents,* vol. 4, 1956–1958, 274–275.
154. Ibid., 267.
155. *Yomiuri Shimbun,* July 8, 1957.
156. ———, June 30, 1957.
157. ———, July 8, 1957.
158. Ibid.
159. *Yomiuri Shimbun,* September 22, 1957.
160. Zengakuren Shokikyoku, "Sunagawa Futō Danatsu Hantai Tōsō no Sōkatsu [A summary of the struggle against unjust oppression]," *Zengakuren Tsūshin,* no. 26 and 27, September 30, 1957. Document no. 35 in *Zengakuren Documents,* vol. 4, 1956–1958, 241.
161. Ibid.
162. *Yomiuri Shimbun,* September 25, 1957.
163. Kobayashi, *Sengo Kakumei Undō Ronsōshi,* 146.
164. Ibid., 143–44.
165. Ibid., 154.
166. *Akahata,* July 14, 1958. CIA-RDP78-00915R000900200006-4; Database of Declassified CIA documents (cited as CREST hereafter), NARAII.
167. Ibid.
168. Zengakuren Shoki Kyoku, "Zengakuren Dai12-kai Rinji Zenkoku Taikai Keika Hōkoku, Tōmensuru Kinkyū Ninmu [The 12th Zengakuren special national

convention, a progress report, urgent tasks]," September 4–5, 1958. Document no. 49 in *Zengakuren Documents,* vol. 4, 1956–1958, 371.

169. Ibid., 373.

170. Kobayashi, *Sengo Kakumei Undō Ronsōshi*, 149.

171. Ibid., 150.

172. Tokyo Daigaku Gakusei Undō Kenkyūkai, *Nihon no Gakusei Undō: Sono Riron to Rekishi*, 11–12.

173. Memorandum of Conversation, September 8, 1958, *FRUS*, 1958–1960, vol. XVIII, Japan and Korea (Washington, DC: United States Government Printing Office, 1994), 63.

174. Letter from the Ambassador to Japan (MacArthur) to the Assistant Secretary of State for Far Eastern Affairs (Robertson), ibid., 24. (emphasis in original).

175. Ibid., 25.

176. Chapter II: Renunciation of War, Article 9 of the Japanese Constitution.

177. *Yomiuri Shimbun*, December 16, 1959.

178. Ibid.

179. *Los Angeles Times*, March 31, 1959.

180. Incoming Telegram from Tokyo to Secretary of State, March 31, 1959. RG 59. Box 2918. NARAII. Reprinted in Reiko Fukawa and Shoji Niihara, "The Declassified Documents of US Government Concerning the Decision of Tokyo District Court on the Sunagawa Case Judged by Akio Date," *Yamashina Gakuin Law Review* 64 (2010): 200.

181. Fukawa and Niihara, "The Declassified Documents of US Government Concerning the Decision of Tokyo District Court on the Sunagawa Case Judged by Akio Date,"197–8.

182. Ibid., 192.

183. Judgment Upon Case of the So-called "Sunakawa [*sic.*] Case, Series of Prominent Judgments of the Supreme Court upon Questions of Constitutionality No. 4, General Secretariat, Supreme Court of Japan, 1960. RG 84. Box 201. NARAII.

184. Ibid.

185. Ibid.

186. Ibid.

Chapter Four

The *Anpo*

During the Eisenhower administration, special emphasis was placed on the further development of collective security and regional alliance systems. Eisenhower and Dulles initiated the period characterized by "pactomania," seeking to strengthen a network of alliance system radiating from Washington.[1] Expansion and consolidation of the alliance system was believed to enhance the security of the free world through collective defense efforts and pave the way for the universal allure of American values to prevail throughout the world. In January 1959, Eisenhower declared that mutual cooperation in defense of the capitalist world "strengthens the stability of free nations and lessens opportunities for Communist subversion and penetration."[2] The establishment of Southeast Asia Treaty Organization (SEATO) in 1954 and the Baghdad Pact in 1955 reflected the President's perspective.[3] At the same time, it was equally important for the United States to maintain and strengthen existing anti-Communist alliances. The North Atlantic Treaty Organization (NATO) added the Federal Republic of Germany in 1955 and the Australia, New Zealand and United States Security Treaty (ANZUS), which was signed at the San Francisco Conference in 1951, was linked to SEATO by inviting these two countries to participate in SEATO activities. For a similar purposes, American and Japanese policymakers began working on the revision of the US-Japan Security Treaty and established the Japanese-American Committee on Security (*Nichibei Anpo Iinkai*) in 1957.[4] The official decision to revise the US-Japan Security Treaty sparked vigorous public opposition in 1960 and brought new intensity to the Zengakuren student movement.

The *Anpo* crisis of 1960 is one of the most cited Japan's Cold War stories. By the fall of 1960, sixteen million Japanese people were reported to have participated in the anti-*Anpo* demonstrations.[5] Historian Wesley Sasaki-Uemura argued that the participation of various citizen groups was "spontaneous" and the anti-*Anpo* struggles were made possible and sustained by independent activities that aroused from their concerns for various issues linked to the *Anpo* treaty. The existence of a multitude of diverse groups in the anti-*Anpo* movement attests that their heterogeneous experiences cannot be confined within a monolithic narrative of a national history. This chapter presents Zengakuren's *Anpo* struggle within broader Cold War international contexts. The anti-*Anpo* demonstrations were events that brought significant changes within the Zengakuren student movement and to Washington's approach to Japanese student radicalism.

By the late 1950s, after the Soviet success of launching the world's first artificial satellite, Sputnik, American officials had expressed optimism in the construction of an East Asian political and economic stability. Japan's Cold War economy seemed to be finally taking off, a real reward of American postwar investment. During the period between 1945 and 1964, Japan received $3.8 billion in US aid and trade began to grow, as the US helped open foreign markets for Japanese exports and guaranteed Japanese access to raw materials.[6] The year 1959 was reported as a year of "vast growth" in Japan that exceeded the economic boom of 1957.[7] Japan's GNP reached $28 billion for the 1958 fiscal year and was estimated to grow by 11.2 percent to $32 billion by the end of 1959.[8] The *Washington Post* reported, "In 1959, Japan again enjoyed the respect of the world as a country which, following a recovery that represents one of the most spectacular events of the postwar era, has resumed its role as the workshop of Asia and one of the leading industrial powers of the world."[9] It celebrated Japan's economic and political progress achieved based on Western principles even though it remained "less than perfect when measured by Western standards." Japan's "progress" toward a Western capitalist model increased its importance as a showcase for the non-Western world. The Assistant Secretary of State for Far Eastern Affairs, Walter Robertson, who worked closely with Dulles for the containment of Communism in Asia, wrote to the Secretary of State that America's "entire strategic position in the Western Pacific is anchored on Japan" and moreover that the country would also play an important role in dealing with "uncommitted Asia and Africa."[10]

It was not only Japan that Washington viewed as making proper progress. On January 14, 1959, Dulles stated before the Senate Foreign Relations Committee, "In general, I believe the leaders and peoples of Asia now understand better the sincerity of American policy favoring their independence and our willingness to support unconditionally their efforts to stay free and do so in their own way, which may indeed be a non-Western way."[11] The Under Secretary of State, Clarence Douglas Dillon, went further to state that America's vision was shared by not only powerful elites in Asia, but he was "confident that our hope is shared by the peoples of free Asia, who are crying out today for economic and social progress."[12] Dillon continued, "They are at the beginning stage of the continuing Asian revolution, a profound social and political upheaval which has drawn much of its inspiration from our own liberal revolution."[13] He believed that mutual understanding and consensus between the United States and Asian allies were successfully being built. In the view of these American policymakers, Asia was economically, politically, and socially on the right track in catching up to the West, and its "progress" was stressed as proof of American superiority to the Soviet system.

Japan's record of economic and political successes not only improved American self-confidence but also imposed pressure on the United States to make certain adjustment in US-Japan relations. Dissatisfaction with the current security treaty with the United States was growing within the Japanese conservatives who dominated the government. Japan had agreed to build up its defense forces and make greater contribution to the collective security system for the capitalist world. It overcame the conservative split in 1955, which had been a concern for American Cold War strategists, through the merger of two major conservative parties. The Japanese conservative leaders now saw the treaty signed at the end of the US occupation as no longer relevant and demanded "equality" with the United States.

The proposed revision of the security treaty reflected America's intention to ameliorate Japan's subordinate position, or more accurately, the Japanese feeling of subordination. The most significant changes proposed to the revision of the *Anpo* treaty were the elimination of the clause that allowed the US to deploy its forces against internal riots in Japan and creation of a "prior consultation" clause that would require the US to obtain the Japanese government's approval before deployment of its forces from Japan.[14] These changes were thought to give the Japanese a greater sense of the sovereignty and equality they demanded. In addition, the United States agreed to reduce the number of ground forces stationed in Japan. The unpopularity of US bases in mainland Japan, as seen in Sunagawa, made the reduction of the US troops a plausible decision. Moreover, the end of the Korean War and the adoption of the Radford Plan that proposed a shift in emphasis to air and atomic power by making drastic reduction of the ground forces, mostly from the Army and Navy, affected the decision to revise the US-Japan Security Treaty.[15] Dulles also believed that bringing ground troops home would "provide a most eloquent rebuttal to the Communist charge of 'imperialism'."[16]

The purpose of the treaty revision for Washington was to keep its basic structure unchanged. In the process of revising the treaty, the United States made clear that the revision would not militate against basic American security interests. The revised treaty, for instance would not change the status of the Ryukyu Islands and the Bonin southern islands that were placed under the American military occupation with Japan's "residual sovereignty." It was aimed to give the Japanese the impression that the US-Japan Cold War alliance rested on "a solid foundation of sovereign equality, mutual interest and cooperation beneficial to both nations," as declared in the Joint Communiqués issued by Prime Minister Kishi Nobusuke and President Dwight Eisenhower in 1957.[17]

At the end of the 1950s, public criticism of the treaty was also becoming louder, but for different reasons. The debates over the extension of Tachikawa Air Base had inevitably generated public debate on the *Anpo* treaty. The anti-*Anpo* opposition had become a nationwide political movement joined by various groups of people as debate over the treaty revision began proving the focal public interest. Pointing out the growing Japanese discontent with its status in the relationship with the United States, Robertson recommended that the United States recognize "the ground swell which is taking place in Japan" and to make necessary adjustment to satisfy the Japanese.[18] He predicted that the US would face challenges of the anti-colonial nationalist kind if it failed to react to the current Japanese domestic discontent. He wrote in a report submitted to the Secretary of State in January 1957:

> We risk seeing all the unrelated contentious issues coming together in a focal point of hostility in the Japanese mind resulting in domestic Japanese convulsions impairing permanently our future relations with Japan. In other words, if we do not act in a timely fashion to meet the evolutionary changes occurring in Japan which we now see clearly, we risk finding ourselves in the same position in which the British, and particularly the French, have found themselves in their relations with various Asian and African countries.[19]

Robertson urged Washington to take Japanese public opinion seriously for the purpose of maintaining the basic structure of US-Japan relations. He warned, "These signs of discontent are still subtle and under control, but if they break out into the open it will be too late to influence Japan's policies in the direction which best serves the interests of the United States."[20] Robertson suggested that only way the US could avoid jeopardizing the current US position in the Pacific was to revise the Security Treaty to "foster greater mutuality in Japanese-American relations."[21]

In the spring of 1958, the United States encountered the first direct popular agitations against promotion of American policy among its Cold War allies, which resulted in deepening Washington's concern about Communist diplomacy. A wave of demonstrations swept across Latin America against Vice President Richard Nixon during his seventeen-day goodwill visit to Uruguay, Argentina, Paraguay, Bolivia, Peru, Ecuador, Colombia, and Venezuela. A series of US interventions in Latin America carried under the name of alliance, including its involvement in the Guatemalan coup d'état and granting the military dictator Marcos Pérez Jiménez asylum, were the primary grievance that spurred the protests.[22] On April 28, forty students from Uruguay's National University protested against "North American imperialism," chanting "Out with Nixon!" as Nixon's car moved from the airport.[23] In Paraguay and Bolivia, Nixon faced similar challenges as the crowds of protestors called for him to go home.[24] In Lima, the San Marcos University students protested against the "plutocratic imperialist." Nixon observed, "There were some very old students in the crowd. I'd say a majority of the noisemakers were real pros at this thing."[25] The most serious protests against Nixon on the tour occurred in Caracas on May 13 as his car moved toward the tomb of Venezuelan liberator Simon Bolivar for a ceremony.[26] It was later reported in Washington, "the spearhead of the agitation was the excitable, Communist-controlled and penetrated student organizations."[27] On that day, Eisenhower ordered US troops to fly to Cuba and Puerto Rico in case he had to help Nixon get out of the country. Nixon blamed the "infamy of Communists" for instigating anti-American riots.[28]

These "anti-American" riots in Latin America were largely perceived as a clear sign of the success of manipulative Communist diplomacy to cultivate anti-American resentment. The conspicuous presence of students in the demonstrations led the *Los Angeles Times* to write, "Both in Europe and other parts of the world university students are more vocal and more active than our own when it comes to political agitation. Such being the case, one must acknowledge that it was Moscow that first capitalized on this student psychology and background, especially since the passing of Stalin."[29] Serafino Romualdi, who was an anti-Communist representative of AFL-CIO in Latin America, observed, "The intellectuals field, in all its many ramifications, still represents, in my opinion, the main immediate goal of the Communists south of the Rio Grande" and they were effectively building resentment against the United States in the intellectual and student circles in Latin America.[30] In the same light, the Japanese anti-*Anpo* demonstrations were to be viewed as irrational anti-Americanism, if not the work of the Communist diplomacy.

ZENGAKUREN'S PROTESTS AGAINST THE US-JAPAN "IMPERIALIST" TREATY

After the Sunagawa struggle, Zengakuren had grown more enthusiastic and was prepared to take its protest against the *Anpo* treaty to the next level. The feeling of power was widespread among the student left. The Sunagawa struggle had given Zengakuren a positive "revolutionary" self-image. Zengakuren membership grew accordingly. The eleventh National Convention of Zengakuren held in May 1958 was attended by 300 student self-government associations from 120 universities, representing 300,000 students, the largest number in the history of Zengakuren.[31] In June 1959, the students of the Communist League (*Bunto*) faction that was critical of the JCP leadership took over Zengakuren leadership. The *Bunto*-led Zengakuren declared that they would lead the Japanese proletariat movement in the right direction and called for all the proletariats in Japan to join their revolutionary movement against imperialism and exploitative capitalism.[32]

Growing self-confidence accelerated their criticism of the JCP. The anti-JCP student radicals now viewed the party as a tenacious obstacle to Japan's new Marxist movement which was moving history forward. Shima Shigeo, a founding member of the *Bunto* recalled, "We no longer expected to receive any guidance from the Party. No, we could not carry out our movement without fighting against the Party that tried to interfere and control us under their leadership."[33] The student radicals had begun to project themselves as a new vanguard of a revolution, contrasting themselves to the JCP and other old "non-revolutionary" leftist organizations. After the Eleventh National Party Congress, the JCP carried out a large-scale purge of the Zengakuren leaders who were critical of the party leadership, including Koyama, Morita and Shima. Morita recalled, "When I was purged from the Party, I personally did not suffer any sense of alienation."[34]

Zengakuren expressed strong confidence in building a mass movement bounded by "remarkable solidarity among the workers, students, and farmers who together created a new page in history of Japanese liberation struggle."[35] Zengakuren students sought to repeat the "monumental achievement" of the Sunagawa struggle. The presence of the active working class furthermore had given student radicals hope that they could make significant political changes with the consolidation of the revolutionary forces. In 1959–1960, the workers led by the *hyō* labor federation launched militant strikes against large-scale discharges being carried out under economic rationalization programs.[36] The strikes at the Mistui Miike Coal Mine in Fukuoka in particular were receiving public attention and were considered the last bastion of the militant labor struggle against the rationalization, for it was the largest coal mine in Japan. Zengakuren students pledged to take the Japanese mass movement down the correct revolutionary road by harnessing the revolutionary energy of these militant workers. The real test came in the opposition against the Security Treaty. Shima said, "Through fighting against the Security Treaty, we began to ask ourselves whether and how it was within our means to make a revolution in Japan."[37] Arguing that the purpose of the revision was strengthening US-Japan economic and military "imperial" cooperation, Zengakuren concentrated its forces on opposition against the US-Japan Security Treaty, defining it as "the most important political mission" to bring down the "Japanese imperialists" led by Kishi, a former Class A war criminal.[38]

Japan's renewed regionalism also had given the student left a new sense of urgency. The idea of Japanese economic development through accessing markets of Japan's wartime Greater East Asia was not new, but it was during Kishi's administration that the idea began to have a concrete form with the Japanese government's proposal for the creation of the Southeast Asian Development Fund (*Tōnan Ajia Kaihatsu Kikin*), which was aimed to use American financial power and Japanese technological skills to aid economic development of the region to prevent it from falling into Communism.[39] On May 20, 1957, Kishi embarked on a Southeast Asian tour to visit six countries: Burma, India, Pakistan, Dominion of Ceylon, Thailand, and Nationalist China, in sixteen days in order to access the popularity of the Southeast Asian Development Fund among Asian leaders.[40] Kishi believed that his new regionalism and the demonstration of his willingness to contribute to the development of Asia would convince the United States that Japan was the nucleus of America's anti-Communist sphere and persuade it to revise the unequal Security Treaty.[41]

Zengakuren saw Japan's new regionalism as deeply connected to the US-Japan Security Treaty. It charged that the purpose of the US-Japan "intra-bourgeoisie" alliance was to make Japan economically expand into Southeast Asia and ultimately reconstruct the Greater East Asia Co-Prosperity Sphere.[42] History had proven, the student radicals argued, the Japanese capitalists would pursue their economic interests in Asia, even at the cost of peace and the national independence of others.[43] This time, however, the security treaty would ensure that Japan's economic expansion would mutually benefit the imperial ambitions of both Japan and the United States. Zengakuren students claimed that this "intra-imperial" alliance between the United States and Japan would allow, if not encourage, the US to use military means to deal with issues in Asia. In its newspaper, *Zengakuren Tūshin* (Zengakuren Correspondence), Zengakuren declared that the Japanese and American governments were now united by the common objective to suppress the people's movements and "stabilize" East Asia.[44]

Despite the language employed by Zengakuren leaders, it was genuine anxiety about the Cold War tensions that motivated many students to join the anti-*Anpo* demonstrations. A large segment of students, including those who did not share Zengakuren's view of the treaty, joined the anti-*Anpo* struggle out of fear of being dragged into a Sino-US military conflict. A survey conducted by Kazuko Tsurumi showed that 44 out of 100 students surveyed responded that the meaning of the anti-Security Treaty demonstrations was the expression of antiwar sentiments.[45] The desire for Cold War neutralism remained high among the Japanese in general. When the revision of the treaty began to dominate public debate, many people interpreted that the revision of the *Anpo* treaty meant a closer alliance with the United States and thus an increase in Japan's chances of being exposed to the Cold War's hot war.

Communist opposition further fueled the anxiety felt over the revision of the security treaty with the US. In late 1958, the Soviet Union and Communist China sent direct messages to the Japanese, expressing their opposition to the revision of the Security Treaty with the United States. On December 2, 1958, the Soviet Foreign Minister, Andrei Andreevich Gromyko, met Japanese Ambassador to the Soviet Union, Kadowaki Suemitsu, and handed over the Soviet government's statement on the revision of the US-Japan "military" treaty that denounced the United States as the "instigators of the new military treaty" that sought "to embroil Japan in military preparations designed to turn the Japanese people into cannon fodder for new ventures."[46] The Soviet government expressed, "It is easy to see that the conclusion of the new American-Japanese military treaty can only complicate the situation in the Far East even more and further aggravate the danger of a military conflict in this area."[47] On November 19, 1959, the Chinese Foreign Minister, Chén Yì, publicly supported Japanese national independence and neutrality in the Cold War, implying his opposition to close US-Japan alliance.[48] On December 2, Gromyko warned again that the Soviet Union would regard the revised treaty as a military alliance aimed against the Soviet Union and Communist China in his memorandum to the Soviet Embassy in Tokyo.[49] The Communist states' opposition to the US-Japan "military alliance" added a strong sense of urgency among the Japanese to stop the revision to avert another Cold War confrontation in East Asia.

ZENGAKUREN: MAKING ITS OWN ANTI-*ANPO*

The anti-*Anpo* movement was rapidly growing, following the Supreme Court's ruling on the Sunagawa case. On March 24, 1959, the People's Council to Stop the Revised Security Treaty (*Anpo Kaitei Soshi Kokumin Kaigi*) consisting of thirty-four political and social organizations was established as a national organization to coordinate anti-*Anpo* demonstrations.[50] On April 2, Zengakuren led the creation of the Joint Struggle Council of the Youth and Students against the revision of the US-Japan Security Treaty as a branch of the People's Council.[51] On April 15, the People's Council to Stop the Revised Security Treaty held the first joint rally against the revision of the Security

Treaty on the grounds of supporting the Tokyo District Court's Sunagawa decision that declared the Security Treaty unconstitutional, and Zengakuren organized its rally a month later at the Hibiya Park. The Newspaper of the People's Council to Stop the Revised Security Treaty (*Anpo Jyōyaku Kaitei Soshi Kokumin Kaigi Nyūsu*) celebrated their success.[52] By the summer of 1959, the anti-*Anpo* movement had had a solid basis of support from various progressive-leftist groups, and a series of anti-*Anpo* protests began to take place across the country.

As the signing of the treaty revision became imminent, Zengakuren began expressing a greater sense of urgency and grew more militant in their opposition to the revision of the treaty. Frustration spread among the student radicals over the People's Council to Stop the Revised Security Treaty, which hesitated to move demonstrations beyond Hibiya Park. Zengakuren radicals disparaged the council's demonstrations as self-effacing "*shōkō demo* (burning incense demonstrations)," equating it with a line of people quietly moving to make incense offering during a Buddhist funeral rite. On November 27, the Zengakuren students, disregarding the People's Council's warning, entered the Diet building ground and clashed with a cordon of police officers. A total of about 30,000 students and workers occupied the area surrounding the Diet premises. [53] The leaders of the JCP, JSP, and *Sōhyō* unions told the young protestors to leave the Diet grounds using loudspeakers.[54]

The student radicals' growing militancy deepened the schism with other affiliated groups of the People's Council. The student-run *Tokyo Daigaku Shimbun* (The University of Tokyo Newspaper) declared the November protests to be the beginning of the final struggle against the *Anpo*.[55] On December 10, 1959, about 18,000 Zengakuren students from over eighty universities participated in a demonstration sponsored by the People's Council.[56] Zengakuren students expressed their desire to storm the Diet building again, but the People's Council tried to convince the student radicals that such actions would disintegrate the anti-treaty revision movement.[57] Some militant union workers similarly advocated surrounding the Diet building, but the leaders of the *Sōhyō* labor federation ordered them to engage in strikes at production centers instead of the political site.[58] The *Bunto* students lamented that these old activists failed to "keep up with the growing belligerence of fellow proletariats."[59]

The November demonstrations sharpened American officials' interest in Zengakuren activities. Counselor of US Embassy Coburn B. Kidd studied a detailed report of Zengakuren by the Japanese Public Safety Investigation Agency (PSIA) several months ago. [60] He then reported his findings and observation of the recent events to the State Department.[61] In a report entitled "Status of Zengakuren and its Actions since the November 27 Diet

Demonstrations," Kidd concluded that Zengakuren was an "extremely small Communist or radical minority" that "appear to speak for Japanese students in general," dismissing the PSIA's estimate of Zengakuren membership as around 290,000 as somewhat overestimated.[62] Kidd's report reflected the long-standing assumption that a popular demonstration against the US government or the alliance with the United States was incited by Communist agitators, but it also pointed out that Zengakuren's "excess" invited criticism from not only the general public but also leftist organizations, predicting Zengakuren's eventual isolation. Ambassador MacArthur shared this view and believed that "like other communist parties in Free World, JCP seems much more disturbed by rivals within the family and possible challenge of its 'leadership of proletariat' than by conservative enemies on the outside."[63] Despite the criticism it invited from older generations of the left, Zengakuren, with 300,000 affiliated members in over 140 campuses, was, as described by historian Setsu Shigematsu, "gearing up for the 1960 Anpo Protest" in 1959.[64]

American military officers in Okinawa, however, did not share such optimism expressed by Kidd and MacArthur. Most troubling was Zengakuren's "peace movement." Okinawa was by then one of the most heavily armed places on the globe. Americans on the island feared that Zengakuren's "peace movement" could stir anti-base, anti-armament sentiments in Okinawa. On December 3, the intelligence section of United States Army Ryukyu Islands (USARYIS) sent the United States Civil Administration of the Ryukyu Islands (USCAR) an intelligent report that informed that Zengakuren had repeatedly attempted to extend its influence to align the Ryukyu University Students' Association (RUSA).[65] It warned that Zengakuren had sought to place RUSA under its control since 1955 and would "continue to dictate guidance policies to RUSA in hope of an eventual weakening on the part of university authorities" that tried to prevent the extension of Zengakuren influence over students in Okinawa.[66] USCAR had been informed that the RUSA had already "carried out activities in conjunction with Zengakuren radical movements."[67] Their analyses of Zengakuren activities reflected the underlying assumption that Zengakuren Communists would attempt to spread their anti-American "peace" campaigns to the ideologically defenseless Ryukyu Islands.

As 1960 began, Zengakuren took more direct actions to block the signing of the revised security treaty. The *Bunto* faction that dominated the Zengakuren leadership circle prepared to stage a protest at the Haneda Airport to block Prime Minister Kishi from leaving Japan for the United States. The student activists tried to engage in physical resistance of the same kind seen in the Sunagawa struggle.[68] During the night of January 15, over 1,000 students stormed into the Haneda Airport, and about 700 of those occupied the lobby and barricaded themselves with chairs and tables.[69] Karoji Kentaro, then the Zengakuren chairman, shouted to the crowd, "The People's Council cancelled a direct confrontation plan at the Haneda. They betrayed us. Zengakuren will fight against the police repression alone."[70] The Haneda struggle further deteriorated the relationships between the student left and the older generation of the left whom the young radicals denounced as "reformist" or "non-revolutionary" left.[71]

The protest at the Haneda Airport was put to an end when the police forcibly moved the sit-in strikers who occupied the airport. *The New York Times* reported that 78 protestors were arrested.[72] Kishi departed from the airport in the morning to sign the treaty revision in Washington. The failure to block Kishi from leaving Japan invited criticism of the *Bunto* leadership from fellow student activists. The Revolutionary Communist League (RCL) (*Kakumeiteki Kyōsan Shugi Dōmei*, abbreviated as *Kakukyōdō*), an anti-Stalinist faction of Zengakuren, condemned the Haneda protest as the "tragedy of the extremists of the left," referring to the *Bunto* activists.[73]

American officials thought that the Haneda protest would be the final major act of Zengakuren. In a report entitled "Zengakuren on Defensive," Kidd wrote to MacArthur, "Zengakuren, the Trotskyite-led university student organization, has suffered a number of reverses since its abortive attempt to prevent Prime Minister Kisi's departure for the Security Treaty signing ceremonies."[74] He pointed out the lack of financial resources, alienation from the general public, internal factional conflicts, and government agencies' increased effort to crack down student radicals, especially on the grounds of violating the Subversive Activities Prevention Law, had put Zengakuren in "a severe crisis."[75] Kidd concluded, "Zengakuren's ability to stimulate mass demonstrations or carry out plans for extensive anti-Treaty activities appears to have been greatly curtailed."[76] MacArthur agreed with Kidd and wrote a similar report addressed to the Secretary of State, in which he expressed his conviction that Zengakuren would implode sooner or later, suffering from intense internal disputes between the mainstream group that led the Haneda protest and other factions that criticized it as a tactical error. He added, "Leaders of both groups have denied that there was any split in Zengakuren or that they have even harbored any such intention. Both sides expressed conviction they would be able [to] win other side over. None of this can disguise [the] fact that [the] split in leadership already exists."[77] MacArthur assured that the intensifying internal disputes and radicalization of Zengakuren would eventually lead to the disintegration of the leftist insurgency.

In Washington, Kishi tried not to discourage Americans from signing the revision. He believed that the revision was necessary for Japan in order to "sweep away residues of the Occupation" and open a "new era of US-Japan relations" grounded on mutuality between the two countries.[78] In Washington, Kishi met Eisenhower on January 19 to discuss the US-Japan relations.[79] During the meeting, when Eisenhower asked about Japanese public opinion on treaty revision, Kishi responded by saying that the recent protests against revision were a matter of "leftists and Communist subversive elements in Japan and the Sino-Soviet bloc [who] are attempting to neutralize Japan and separate it from the United States."[80] He then assured the President that his Liberal Democratic Party, which then held over two-thirds of the Diet seats, would be able to secure the ratification of the revised treaty and the majority of the Japanese people approved of the revision.[81]

Washington agreed with Kishi and shared his confidence. On February 9, the CIA, the intelligence organization of the Department of State, the Army, the Navy, the Air Force, and the Joint Chiefs of Staff produced a joint report entitled "National Intelligence Estimate: Probable Developments in Japan." As long as Japan depended heavily on the US for defense and trade, they estimated, Japan's foreign policy would not undergo any major shift. The report also pointed out that "under the revised security treaty, the US will probably be able to maintain a substantial military position in Japan."[82] It read, "Despite continued left-wing opposition to US forces and bases in Japan, and the dependence of these bases upon Japanese labor for effective operations, we believe that the US will be able to use them for logistical support of security actions in the Far East."[83] In sum, Washington officials concluded that Kishi would be able to secure the treaty revision in the Diet and that ongoing leftist opposition to the revision might not harm basic American interests.

The mainstream American press accepted the official analysis of the situation involving the treaty revision with Japan. Mainstream newspapers shared the view that the protests were more or less controlled by a small group of Communists and carried out by the isolated leftist extremists. The *Chicago Daily Tribune* reported that Zengakuren followed "the Russian and Red Chinese communist line and have been objecting loudly to the new treaty on the grounds it will entangle Japan in 'American imperialistic military adventures'."[84] It also criticized the Japanese dissidents for not understanding that the treaty would actually give Japan "virtual veto power over the use of American military forces in Japan," probably referring to the new prior consultation clause.[85] *The New York Times* also called the Haneda protestors isolated extremists who represented the "hard core" of Zengakuren and mentioned that they were considered "too radical" even by the Communist Party.[86]

In the United States, Zengakuren received a different kind of attention as well. The *Young Socialist*, a Trotskyist monthly published in New York City, printed a first-hand account of Zengakuren's Haneda protest that was written by Kurihara Toichi (alias Ota Ryu), a member of the Trotskyist faction of Zengakuren. In the article, Kurihara condemned the undemocratic use of suppressive state violence employed against the protestors at the Haneda Airport.[87] Writing for American readers, he probably modified his criticism of the United States; instead, he criticized police violence at Haneda and emphasized Zengakuren's stand for pacifism. In another article, a Japanese student named Nakada Kei explained that a series of recent demonstrations in Japan were not rooted in anti-American sentiment but popular desire for peace. To achieve this goal, he wrote, the Japanese students were engaging in the "proletarian antiwar struggle" against the belligerent capitalist class.[88]

To the distress of the US Embassy, the response of the Japanese government to student radicalism was more lenient than Kurihara's description would be. By the end of the spring, the student insurgencies and Japanese government's lackadaisical efforts to crack down on them were increasingly getting on MacArthur's nerves. The US Embassy in Tokyo began directly contacting Japanese professors and students to discuss the issues of Zengakuren. On April 14, Professor Takeishi Haruki and two students, Omori Tomonari and Tazawa Tomoharu, all from Nihon University, were invited to the US Embassy to discuss the role of the National Federation of Private University Students Self-Government Associations (*Zenkoku Shiritu Daigaku Gakusei Jichikai Rengō*, abbreviated as *Shigakuren*). Professor Takeishi had informed MacArthur earlier that students at Nihon University played a leading role in *Shigakuren*, in which the Ambassador expressed particular interest.[89] Tazawa, who later became an LDP member of the Diet and the Minister of Justice, was a former student leader of *Shigakuren* who was then active in organizing a new National Students Liaison Council (*Zenkoku Gakusei Renraku Kaigi*), another alternative organization to Zengakuren. Tazawa informed the US Embassy officials that *Shigakuren* was an "anti-Zengakuren organization" that aimed to address issues that directly related to student life, rather than engaging in political affairs.[90] He told Americans that the organization had "no intention of entering into open debate with Zengakuren," but the development of these alternative organizations would eventually erode Zengakuren's dominant position in the student movement by attracting students.

MacArthur lamented that none of the measures put forth by the Japanese so far proved effective against Zengakuren. In the report to the State Department, he wrote:

> Embassy believes that the awakening of university and Education Ministry interest in doing something about Zengakuren is worth nothing. Whether the method proposed (faculty guidance through staff of trained specialists) will overcome student predilections for "do it yourself" association and romanticized student-revolutionary leaders remains to be seen. It is now the case of a very small tail wagging a very large dog. If this muddy tail can be thoroughly

discredited, or the student body be convinced that their proper interests lie elsewhere, the authorities will have restored the situation. Until now, however, many of the authorities themselves (particularly at Tokyo University) have invited trouble by their own lenience.[91]

MacArthur expressed his frustration with the Japanese authorities' handling of the situation as well as the general public that still seemed to tolerate of radical Zengakuren even after the Haneda "violence."

After being called to account, so to speak, by the Ambassador, the Education Ministry began to act to control Zengakuren activities on campus. On April 30, the Ministry sent out letters to universities, asking what measures were required to control student radicals' activities.[92] The vice Minister, Ogata Shinichi, told the press that the Ministry intended to control Zengakuren activities by prohibiting self-government associations from affiliating with Zengakuren and imposing stricter punitive measures for students who engaged in illegal political activities.[93] Following the publication of Ogata's statement, Nishida Kikuo, an Education Ministry official who was in charge of student affairs of the higher education, met an US Embassy officer to discuss the issue of Zengakuren. Nishida admitted Japanese universities' lackadaisical responses to recent student riots and tried to have Americans understand that any governmental intervention in university affairs could instigate public accusations of the government of resorting to suppressive measures similar to those used by the wartime thought police. Nishida said, "The universities, faculty and students alike, are jealous of their rights and regard guidance from the central government as an attempt to revive prewar 'thought control'."[94] He warned that the Education Ministry's direct interference in the university affairs could be counterproductive and further radicalize the student left. Both American and Japanese officials were aware of the seriousness of the Zengakuren issue but were unable to agree on how to deal with it.

MacArthur had another concern related to the security revision: the disunity within the ruling conservative party, which, he feared, might empower the leftwing opposition against the treaty revision. He wanted the Japanese conservatives to improve the fragile LDP unity. The Ambassador informed Assistant Secretary J. Graham Parsons that Kishi was losing support within the LDP and he might not survive if anti-Kishi factions grew within the party.[95] The fall of Kishi, MacArthur warned, would jeopardize the ratification of the treaty revision.[96] In order to secure the passage of the revision, MacArthur approached key figures of the LDP including the party tycoon Yoshida who was in the United States at that time. He urged Parsons to "get in touch with Yoshida at once . . . to tell him on private personal basis that reports from Tokyo indicate that Ikeda [Hayato], Ohno [Banboku], and Ishii [Mitsujiro] have stopped actively supporting Kishi following favorable vote on treaty and are adopting neutral position that appears generally to be playing into hands of pro-Communist and neutralist elements in Japan."[97] MacArthur told Parsons that Ikeda was [the] "key to situation" and asked him to press Yoshida to communicate with Ikeda to support Kishi in the process of ratification of the revised treaty. MacArthur advised Parsons, "You should say [at a meeting with Yoshida] that if anything happens to the treaty it will be the greatest victory Communists could gain in Asia and a terrible blow not only to US-Japan relations but particularly for Japan itself."[98] McArthur then informed Parsons that he would approach Ikeda to "urge him to support Kishi."[99]

Circumstances demanded that Kishi act quickly if he hoped to secure passage of the treaty revision. On May 1, the Soviet downing of the American U-2 aircraft flying over the Soviet territory increased the Japanese anxiety toward renewing the Cold War alliance with the United States. Even within the LDP, some members began agitating against Kishi, demanding further deliberation before a vote was taken in the House.[100] Kishi requested an American statement to subdue the public uproar over the incident, and the State Department, in response, reassured the Japanese government that "U-2 aircraft flying from airbases in Japan have been utilized only for legitimate normal purposes and not intelligence overflight missions."[101] Yet, this statement did little, if anything, to diminish the public anxiety over a close alliance with the United States. Before the anti-Kishi factions gained too much power within the LDP and before the leftist anti-*Anpo* movement gained further momentum, Prime Minister Kishi had to employ blitzkrieg tactics to pass the treaty revision.

On May 19, the anti-*Anpo* struggle entered a new phrase as Kishi's LDP steamrolled the Security Treaty revision through the House of Representatives. Since the signing of the treaty revision, which was done in Washington on January 19, it had been debated in the Diet, especially in a special committee established to examine the proposal at the request of the Socialists and the Social Democrats in February. Despite the opposition members' deliberate efforts to prolong the special committee session, the proposal was put to the vote in the House of Representatives on May 19. The ruling LDP called their secretaries into the Diet and prepared to forcibly push the treaty revision, and the Socialist and Communist opposition members responded by barricading the chamber. They confined the Speaker of the House, Kiyose Ichirō, in his office to prevent him from reaching the floor of the House, until the police were called in at 11 pm, six hours after the barricade started.[102] Outside the Diet building, a large crowd of demonstrators surrounded the Diet premise guarded by 3,000 policemen.[103] The initial police report estimated the number of the demonstrators to be 7,000 while the opposition groups claimed it to be over 20,000.

Kishi managed to declare the opening of the plenary session before midnight and the LDP then voted for the revision of the Security Treaty in the total absence of Socialist and Communist opposition groups who had been removed from the floor.[104] 248 LDP members out of a total of 286 who were present voted for the passage past midnight.[105] The treaty revision passed the House of Representatives on May 19. It now became only a matter of time before the revision became law since a treaty passed by the House of Representatives would automatically become effective without a vote by the House of Councilors after thirty days. MacArthur reported, "Party leaders [were] especially relieved that final Diet action virtually assured before President arrives in Japan."[106] Although the revision of the treaty became law as he wished, Prime Minister Kishi bewailed that the procedure was "legally effective but politically, the worst disaster." [107]

Indeed, public criticism mounted against Kishi's "undemocratic" handling at the Diet, adding intensity to the anti-*Anpo* movement. Kishi's naked use of police forces to secure the passage of the treaty revision triggered serious public outrage, not only over the treaty revision but also his "undemocratic" handling of the situation. Maruyama Masao, one of the most prominent postwar political philosophers, observed that the event on May 19 and 20 "simplified" political struggles and taught a critical lesson to the Japanese people that "those in power could do anything."[108] He argued, "If we were to approve what happened on May 19 and 20, it means we accept that those in power could do anything, the omnipotence of power, but then we can no longer say that democracy exists [in Japan]."[109] Maruyama asserted, the *Anpo* struggle now posed the logic of "you must be either anti-*Anpo* or anti-democracy."

Like Maruyama, many Japanese now saw that the *Anpo* threatened the very existence of postwar democracy. Takeuchi Yoshimi, a prominent Sinologist at Tokyo Metropolitan University, resigned in protest against Kishi's "undemocratic" handling of the situation, and Tsurumi Shunsuke, Professor of Political Philosophy at Tokyo Institute of Technology, followed suit.[110] On May 24, about 800 professors and university employees engaged in sit-in demonstrations, and they were joined by 1,500 people from various cultural circles in Kanda, Tokyo.[111] The demonstrators demanded Kishi resign and dissolve the Diet. The National Association of Scholars and Researchers to Defend Democracy (*Minshu Shugi o Mamoru Zenkoku Gakusha Kenkyūsha no Kai*) was immediately organized, and it held its first major rally on June 2.[112] The anti-*Anpo* struggle was developing into Japan's most significant postwar democratic struggle.

Kishi appeared at a press conference on May 28 and tried to convince the public that he protected parliamentary democracy imperiled by the violence of the extremists by standing firm against the protest. He declared that he would not succumb to the angry protestors and only listen to "*koe naki koe*," the voices of the voiceless.[113] Kishi believed that ordinary people had no reason to oppose that the treaty revision because it would not militate against the Japanese interest. He rather viewed it as benefiting the Japanese because it "is said to be equal and reciprocal, but it in fact put the security burden only on the United States to protect Japan."[114] The reverse was not the case; the peace clause of the Japanese Constitution still held.[115] Thus, Kishi viewed that the demonstrations against the treaty were irrational, if not the work of Communist traitors who served foreign interests.

The leftist opposition raised another serious problem for Kishi. Preparation had been made for President Eisenhower's visit to Japan, which was scheduled to take place from June 19 to 23. It was going to be a part of Eisenhower's tour in Asia, an international publicity campaign to gain and maintain support for America's international role. The President's visit to Japan was aimed to publicize the new era of the US-Japan partnership under the revised treaty. Kishi personally believed that Eisenhower's visit was particularly important since it would allow him to elevate Japan's international standing and increase Japanese public confidence in his leadership. The problem was that the issue of the mass anti-*Anpo* demonstrations was far from resolved. Nationwide anti-*Anpo* protests continued relentlessly even after the vote in the House of Representatives.

On May 26, Ambassador MacArthur secretly met Foreign Minister Fujiyama Aiichiro to discuss the Eisenhower's visit to Tokyo. He intentionally avoided meeting with Kishi because he thought such a personal meeting would be "unhelpful" for Kishi's political life in this crucial moment.[116] At the meeting, Fujiyama told the Ambassador that the Japanese government could "fully assure safety of President [Eisenhower] and that there is no personal risk involved for him."[117] There would be "some demonstrators along road from airport waving red banners and like and while there might be certain 'other undesirable scenes'," but, Fujiyama promised, the president would be safe in Japan.[118] He expressed the Japanese government's strong desire to invite Eisenhower and told the Ambassador that the President's visit would surely create a favorable political atmosphere for the US-Japanese partnership and the revised treaty.[119]

Despite the Japanese government's assurance, MacArthur felt some reservation about proceeding with the plan as scheduled. He understood that not only the physical security of the president but also the image of the United States was at stake. The large-scale popular protests against the US president in the allied country would create a negative image both at home and abroad. In his report to Secretary of State, MacArthur wrote, "In their [demonstrators'] efforts to drive wedge between Japan and US, creation of such an image was, I felt, one of basic objectives of communists."[120] At the same time, as MacArthur told Fujiyama, the cancellation of the presidents' visit was not a good idea because it would be seen as a "great victory of communist elements in Japan."[121] He suggested to Fujiyama that the best solution would be to postpone his visit in order to save the dignity of the US president and the international image of the United States as well as to avoid appearing weak to Communist pressure.

The demonstrations against the revision of the Security Treaty continued and culminated in June. The People's Council to Stop the Revised Security Treaty held rallies in twenty-six places in Tokyo, attended by over 100,000 people in total on May 20.[122] On the same day, Zengakuren students held a large rally in front of the Diet and the Prime Minister's residence.[123] Zengakuren leaders described the rally as follows: "In particular, at the Prime Minister's residence, workers and students' rage culminated. They confronted a phalanx of police forces that violently grabbed and hit their heads, eyes, faces, stomachs, and so on with their clubs."[124] A nationwide general strike took place on June 4, which was participated in by 830,000 people throughout Japan.[125] The Public Safety police reported that Zengakuren's demonstrations gathered 11,000 students in Tokyo and 7,000 in Kyoto. A total of 55,000 students of over one hundred schools participated in demonstrations throughout Japan.[126]

On Saturday, June 4, the anti-*Anpo* protest drew an unprecedented number of participants across the country. The police reported that 254 anti-*Anpo* meetings attended by a total of 222,604 people were held, and there were demonstrations in seventy-eight places, which were participated by a total of 171,018 people.[127] A total of 605,979 workers were reported as having engaged in anti-*Anpo* strikes, which took place in 9,758 workplaces in total.[128] The public transportation workers were among those who engaged in the largest strikes, which paralyzed the transportation system in Tokyo. Zengakuren organized a massive nationwide strike to support the labor unions' anti-*Anpo* demonstrations. In Tokyo, they snake danced around the Diet building and moved to the Prime Minister's residence where they clashed with the police.[129] About 1,500 students, on their return from the Zengakuren-sponsored protest at the Prime Minister's residence, joined the transportation workers' work stoppage in the Shinagawa station and engaged in a sit-in protest at eighth platform to stop a long-distance express train, *Kodama*.[130] Throughout Japan, 759 trains were either affected or canceled because of these strikes.[131] At Shinagawa Station, protestors proclaimed, "Today's demonstration is intended to prevent war. Workers are demonstrating not for ourselves but on behalf of all the Japanese people."[132]

Public interviews conducted by the *Yomiuri Shimbun* at train stations in Tokyo showed that many ordinary citizens were sympathetic to the protester's anti-*Anpo* and anti-Kishi messages. In this public interview of "the voiceless voices," *Yomiuri* asked passengers about their views of the strikes. In the interview, a 26-year-old woman responded by saying, "It is a citizens' natural response to the government's handling, so I would not mind being late for work."[133] At Shibuya station, a 46-year-old man said that the reason why these public transportation workers' strikes did not create utter chaos was that the most of people agreed with their anti-*Anpo* messages.[134] A 57-year-old man said, "This [strike] is the voice of the Japanese citizen. Although I believe that we need the *Anpo*, but the irregular Diet sessions started on [May] 19th have been very disturbing."[135] There were people who criticized the strikers but, the *Yomiuri* reported, the majority of the passengers interviewed did not.[136]

By then, the prospect of Eisenhower's visit to Tokyo had become more improbable. American mainstream newspapers reported about the demonstrations, highlighting the most anti-American part of the event. *Chicago Daily Tribune* and *Los Angeles Times* both reported JCP-affiliated students' protest at the US Embassy, which the Zengakuren newspaper criticized for being overly anti-American.[137] These newspapers wrote that more than 15,000 people picketed in front of the US Embassy building in Tokyo against Eisenhower's visit, carrying English-written signs such as "Stop Coming Mr. Ike" and "You Too (U-2) Fly Back to Your Own Home" and chanted "Yankee, go home," "Ike, don't come to Japan," and "Americans get out of Asia."[138] Such media coverage probably alarmed the US officials. White House Press Secretary James C. Hagerty, who was in Honolulu at that time, declined to comment on the June 4 demonstrations and announced further information regarding the President's visit would be given in Tokyo.[139]

On June 10, Hagerty and Eisenhower's Appointments Secretary Thomas E. Stephens arrived at the Haneda Airport to discuss the president's planned visit. Upon their arrival, JCP-affiliated Zengakuren students stormed their car.[140] MacArthur was also in the car, and they were heading towards the US Embassy. The police reported that 2,000 Zengakuren students and 6,000 from labor unions and other leftist groups violently shook and threw stones against their car.[141] A US military helicopter was summoned to rescue them from the sea of angry demonstrators who completely surrounded the car. Immediately after the incident, Foreign Minister Fujiyama wrote to MacArthur, "it is highly deplorable that these acts of violence should have occurred, involving you and distinguished visitors from the United States, but I am sure that such acts do not reflect the sentiment of the Japanese people."[142]

The public demonstrations against the *Anpo* reached their zenith over the weekend of June 11 and 12. The police reported that a total of 330,000 people were out on the street throughout Japan, protesting against the *Anpo*.[143] According to the police report, demonstrations erupted in 353 places across the country.[144] In Tokyo, 230,000 protestors marched from the Hibiya Park to the Diet building, denouncing the treaty and calling for Kishi's resignation.[145] Many of them were ordinary citizens, including housewives, senior citizens, and small shop owners. There were various citizen groups who joined anti-*Anpo* activities. In Hamamatsu city in Shizuoka, an anti-*Anpo* demonstration gathered people from citizens' choir groups, *Tanka* poem groups, women's associations, religious groups and so on.[146] Kishi continued to stress that the anti-*Anpo* protests was the work of international Communism "organized left-wing, powerfully supported and subsidized by Soviet Union and Communist China" that were carrying out "its campaign of forces, agitation and intimidation."[147] However, it was clear by then that the anti-*Anpo* movement, which was initially dominated by the leftwing organizations, had been transformed into a citizen-based political alliance to defend democracy in Japan, especially after May 19.

June 15 became the most memorable day for Zegakuren's anti-*Anpo* protesters. In the morning, a group of student activists in the University of Tokyo gathered on the campus and discussed whether they should break into the Diet building premises, even at the risk of isolating themselves from the general public. Suzuki Hajime, who was then a student in the group, recalled, "Our final decision was that we would try to fight along with others, but we would also fight alone if necessary."[148] Around 2 pm, student protestors began arriving outside the Diet building. About 7,000 students from universities in the Tokyo metropolitan area gathered by 3 pm, followed by 2,000 students from Waseda University, and Zengakuren's car also arrived, equipped with speakerphones.[149] They held a rally and began marching toward the south gate of the Diet building. Another 10,000 students arrived a few hours later and joined the march.[150] The police began attacking the student protestors with water from fire hoses when students pulled a truck parked inside the gate.[151] Student protestors continued their effort to enter the Diet building, and when they did, they confronted 800 police guards.[152] 1,500 students stepped inside the gate, and the police responded by mobilizing 3,000 forces and attacked them with their cudgels, driving them out of the Diet premises.[153] Around the Diet premises, Zengakuren and labor union snake-dancers filled the streets, carrying various signs against the revision of *Anpo* and the Kishi government.

In the evening, the physical confrontation with the police injured 270 students and killed Kanba Michiko, a female Zengakuren student of the University of Tokyo.[154] The death of Kanba shocked and infuriated Zengakuren students, as well as many ordinary citizens, who viewed it as the result of state violence employed against an innocent citizen. *Yomiuri* newspaper reported that Kanba died from compression and intracerebral hemorrhage, reportedly after having been severely attacked and trampled.[155] According to *Tokyo Daigaku Shimbun*, the police forces acted differently on that day. It reported that they came running toward protestors, brandishing clubs, instead of trying to move demonstrators out of the Diet premises.[156] Through the night, students continued to clash the police phalanxes aggressively, expressing their anger toward the government, which they saw as responsible for the death of Kanba. The subsequent student protests received wide media attention both in Japan and the US. *Yomiuri* reported that fifteen police trucks had been burned, and 386 police officers and 495 student protestors had been injured by 1 am.[157] A total of 182 student protestors and 53 right-wing counter-demonstrators were arrested that day.[158] Kishi tried to convince the public that it was the anti-*Anpo* mob that initiated violence and defined the struggle as the conflict between democracy and Communism, condemning the latter for violently threatening Japanese parliamentary democracy. Yet, protest against police violence soon spread. *The New York Times* reported that in Sapporo, about 2,600 students from Hokkaido University went on to the streets and clashed with 300 police officers in protest against the police violence that caused Kanba's death.[159]

Kanba's death became a rallying cry for the student protestors. *Bunto* students issued a statement on June 23 and announced that Kanba was "the most capable, most brave activist," a "great revolutionary," and sacrificed herself for the "liberation of the international proletariat."[160] They declared they would complete the "proletariat international revolution," to which Kanba had devoted herself.[161] Zengakuren leadership dominated by non-JCP affiliated students also criticized the JCP affiliated groups for still focusing on attacking their rival factions within Zengakuren. They urged students to keep the anti-imperial tradition of the Japanese student movement, rather than blindly following anti-Americanism and acting like the puppets of the JCP and thus the Soviet Union on a string.[162] During the anti-*Anpo* demonstration, the schism between the JCP-affiliated and anti-JCP mainstream students became widened, with the former revolting against American imperialism and the latter against domestic monopoly capital and the conservative forces led by the LDP.[163]

President Eisenhower received the news of the June 15 demonstrations in Tokyo while in Manila. He mentioned neither the Tokyo demonstrations nor Communism in the speech he delivered to the students of the University of the Philippines, but criticized "those who are allied against us," claiming their hearts and minds were "chained in the dictates of a tyrannic [*sic*] master plan," which ultimately ignited riots.[164] During his parade in Manila, the president learned that Japan was going to request a postponement of his visit to Tokyo.[165] The fear of possible repercussions around the world, especially in the areas that hosted American military bases, emerged between the president and his staff who were on the tour.[166] The anti-*Anpo* demonstrations coincided with the powerful demonstrations against the US-backed President Syngman Rhee, driven by high school and university students in South Korea, and the coup d'état led by young military officers in Turkey that toppled the government led by Prime Minister Adnan Menderes in May.[167] According to *The New York Times*, the US government "feared that the wave of student uprisings that has triggered political explosions in South Korea, Turkey, and Japan might now receive additional momentum, affecting other areas of unstable political structure."[168] These "political explosions," in addition to the anti-Nixon protest in Latin America, were interpreted as signs of a growing anti-Americanism and perhaps a confirmation of the validity of the domino theory enunciated by Eisenhower.

The anti-*Anpo* movement continued without losing its intensity after June 15. The police reported that over 310,000 people in 265 different places throughout Japan participated in demonstrations against the ratification of the *Anpo* treaty on June 18.[169] And it had even reached the United States. Some members of the Young Socialist Alliance (YSA) protested against the signing of the US-Japan Security Treaty in solidarity with Zengakuren students. The YSA activists from Boston picketed at the Japanese Embassy and those from NYC, Philadelphia, and Baltimore gathered in front of the White House protesting against the *Anpo* treaty with Japan.[170] The summer issue of *The Young Socialist* celebrated antiwar protests abroad and sent supporting messages to student protesters in Tokyo, as well as dissidents in South Africa, South Korea, Turkey, San Francisco, Chicago, Madison, Seattle, and the American South.[171]

The American mainstream media provided coverage of the "anti-American" riots in Tokyo, mostly blaming Communists for instigating anti-American riots. *Time* magazine reported, "Zengakuren, the tightly disciplined Communist-led student federation mobilized its forces for a supreme assault on the government of Japan's wispy Premier Nobusuke Kishi."[172] It criticized the Soviet Union and Communist China's conspiratorial influence in bringing about the revolt against the United States and warned, "As the Security Treaty fight began, Communist activity in Japan was vastly stepped up. . . . Moscow and Peking have made it abundantly clear that the neutralization and eventual takeover of Japan is their No.1 objective in Asia."[173] The *Los Angeles Times'* title of the coverage of demonstrations implied militant characteristics of the protesters, which read, "Japan Mobs Set for New Outbreaks: Plans Made After Forcing President to Call Off Visit 'Battlefield' Where the Japanese Reds

Anti-*Anpo* protestors surrounding the car in which White House Press Secretary James C. Hagerty, Presidential Appointments Secretary Thomas E. Stephens, and Ambassador Douglas MacArthur II rode on June 10, 1960. They were rescued by a US military helicopter. © *Kyodo News Agency*

Zengakuren students doing a snake-dance down the street toward the Diet building in Tokyo, June 18, 1960. This was part of the demonstration against the US-Japan Security Treaty. © *AP Photo*

Scored Triumph Over Kishi."[174] *The New York Times* expressed its concern with the international publicity of the events that took in Tokyo and wrote, "the postponement of the Presidential visit because of the current political disorders was taken both here and abroad as a stunning victory for the Communists in the Far East, where Japan is considered the strongest ally of the United States."[175]

President Eisenhower's visit to Tokyo had been officially cancelled following the June 15 demonstrations. The president grudgingly accepted the decision. His Asian tour was resumed without a visit to Japan. Believing in the effectiveness of public diplomacy, President Eisenhower had visited eleven countries in Europe, the Middle East, Asia, and North Africa, but had never been forced to stay out of America's allied country.[176] *The New York Times* reported that the forced cancellation cast "an atmosphere of heavy gloom over the Presidential party."[177] The President and his party now sailed from Manila to Taiwan, protected by 100 planes, two aircraft carriers, and four destroyers navigated by the Seventh Fleet, "the world's most powerful peacetime naval force," without stopping at Japan.[178]

At midnight on June 19, the revised US-Japan Security Treaty was automatically ratified. Kishi announced his resignation. The revised security treaty was put into effect on June 23. On June 27, President Eisenhower appeared on national television and radio and declared to the American public, "The ratification of the mutual security between the United States and Japan represents an important victory for the free world—a defeat for international communism."[179] Yet, it failed to boost a feeling of victory since the shock of the cancelation of the presidential visit overshadowed it.

The forced cancellation of the president's visit to one of its principal allies resulting from the local "anti-American" riots raised concerns about the dignity of the capitalist democracy among the US Cold War allies. After observing the protests that occurred upon the arrival of Hagerty and White House officials in Tokyo, the French government had insisted that the Eisenhower's visit to Tokyo had to proceed as planned to preserve the "dignity of the free world."[180] The *Times* of London published an editorial that called the cancellation "the biggest blow to the prestige of an American President, and of the United States Government, since the war. . . . It is that the disturbances in Tokyo are likely to provide new anxieties everywhere in the west."[181] The *News Chronicle*, a British daily, criticized the US State Department for having "become too accustomed to blame anything that goes wrong on the Communists and to believe that any objection to American policy must be automatically Communist-led and inspired."[182] It further added, "This was untrue in South Korea and Turkey. It is untrue of Japan. The damage cannot be repaired until this illusion is dispelled."[183]

After skirting mainland Japan, the President's team stopped at Okinawa on June 19. By the time of his arrival at Naha Air Base, local demonstrators had gathered near the government compound to protest against his visit. In the capital city, Naha, 2,000 protestors snake-danced, demanding the return of the Ryukyu Islands to Japan.[184] American major newspapers, including the *Boston Globe*, the *Chicago Daily Tribune*, and *The New York Times*, reported that the student demonstrators chanted "Yankee, go home," waving red flags in the demonstrations. The demonstrations forced President Eisenhower to take a back road and escape by a helicopter on his return to Naha Air Base.[185]

On that day, the US military government in Okinawa for the first-time deployed forces against the student protestors. After warning the demonstrators to clear the site, "a column of Marines in full battle gear with drawn bayonets marched down" the streets to disperse the crowd."[186] A student who had participated in the demonstration wrote in anger, "I think, to threaten a person by military force is in contempt of human beings. . . . I think perhaps such an attitude is the manifestation of [Americans'] distrust and contempt for the Okinawans. When I saw the display of arms, I felt anger from the bottom of my heart."[187] The student furiously questioned: How could a person advocate peace while pointing bayonets at unarmed people and advocate "pure" democracy while refusing to listen to the voices of the people?[188] On June 29, a student leader of the RUSA told an interviewer from the *Pacific Stars and Stripes*, "I am a reversionist but not a communist or an anti-American. In fact, I personally like Americans," yet what happened on June 19 was intolerable.[189] The use of forces resulted in the irrevocable disillusionment with the United States among many Okinawan students.

The use of military force against the student protestors also alienated more moderate students in Okinawa. The *Ryudai Taimusu* (Ryukyu University Times), a student-run newspaper, issued the editorial titled, "Appeal to Americans: Friendship Cannot be Bought with a Sword." It read, "Following the end of the war, we had this spirit [of democracy] passed to us from you," yet on June 19, America's action against the demonstrations lacked "respect for humanity," a prerequisite for democracy.[190] The editorial concluded, "We, as the proud Japanese, shall never forget the scene on June 19, 1960. The quiet anger of that day will eventually, as a natural process, explode thunderously. By telling you that friendship cannot be brought with a sword, we earnestly hope that you will deeply reconsider about it."[191]

In 1960, the anti-*Anpo* struggle brought mainland and Okinawan student activists closer. Some students of RUSA had been in contact with Zengakuren since 1955, but it was not until 1959 that they began to work closer. In 1959, the intelligence division of US Army, Ryukyu Islands (G2 USARYIS) informed the Special Assistant to the High Commissioner in

Okinawa about increasing Zengakuren attempts to "dictate their guidance policies" to RUSA.[192] The Japanese Ministry of Education also warned about Zengakuren's spreading influence in Okinawa in its "secret" letters to the university authorities in Okinawa.[193]

Quite contrary to their misconceptions, however, student activists in Okinawa had taken initiative, especially to organize protests against the US occupation. In July 1956, for instance, the USCAR administrator General Vonna Burger became so upset when a group of Ryukyu University students marched on the street calling "Yankee, go home," that he demanded the university punish the students more severely and expel them from the university.[194] Following his order, six students were expelled in August, and this triggered vigorous student protests against the USCAR. One of the largest student protests took place when the US military government issued HICOM (High Commissioner) Ordinance Number 23: Penal Code and Procedures for the Ryukyus Islands in order to deal with Okinawan "mob" actions.[195] This Ordinance prohibited Okinawans from engaging in activities against the US occupation, including the distribution of unregistered printed material, unauthorized protests, sabotage, and espionage, and political activities by unregistered organized groups.[196] The passage of this code further radicalized the students' demand to abolish the "colonial law making" in Okinawa.[197]

Yet, the common stereotypes attributed to Okinawans in general made USCAR assume Zengakuren in mainland Japan was attempting to spread their revolution into the ideologically pristine land of Okinawa. With the outbreak of the massive anti-*Anpo* demonstrations in the Japanese mainland, the fear of Zengakuren influence on Okinawa, which hosted America's most strategically crucial base in the Pacific, grew, and it made the US officials more closely monitor Zengakuren. An American anthropologist who was doing a field study in Okinawa reported to the US authority in Japan that a student from the University of Tokyo, allegedly affiliated with Zengakuren, had arrived in Okinawa on July 1.[198] On July 19, USCAR reported that it had discovered that four Okinawan students, including the president of RUSA, were attempting to travel to the mainland to establish a firm relationship with the mainland student organizations in order to gain their support.[199] The USARYIS intelligence section informed the Education Department of USCAR that USARYIS was anticipating "action by Zengakuren to further influence radical student movements on Okinawa in the near future either by attempting to send delegates to Okinawa or to invite Okinawan students to Japan."[200]

Yet, the June 19 demonstrations had given a lesson to USCAR that suppressing "anti-American" demonstrations by force could lead to the intensification of anti-American sentiments. USCAR thus made more cautious efforts to deal with the student movement in Okinawa. In July, when four Okinawan students applied for visas to travel to mainland Japan, USCAR thought that it could not simply deny issuing the visas for them since it might provoke another "anti-American" protests against "thought control."[201] The director of the liaison office of HICOM reported to USCAR that placing restrictions on the students' travel between Okinawa and the mainland would "increase awareness of Okinawa issues in Japan . . . and can be expected to rekindle and intensify the interests of the Japanese left in Okinawa," and "this is what is wanted by Zengakuren."[202]

The *Anpo* demonstrations of 1960 in Japan and Okinawa drew international attention. Observers interpreted these events very differently, within their own frameworks. Moscow celebrated the anti-*Anpo* struggle in the context of "national liberation." What happened in Japan seemed to provide moral support for Khrushchev's vision for the revival of revolutionary diplomacy. On May 28, Khrushchev said at a labor conference in Moscow, "It is no accident that the voice of the people is resounding with growing volume in Japan— people who have risen to the struggle for the independence of their homeland, for the creation of a government which would really meet the interests of the Japanese people and would be guided by them in its activities."[203]

Progressives and radicals in the capitalist world, however, interpreted the protest in Japan was not just challenging the United States but revolting against the Cold War. American sociologist C. Wright Mills referred to it as one of the examples of the emerging New Left movement, in his historically prominent article entitled "Letter to the New Left," which provided one of the first intellectual analyses of the New Left. In defining the contours of a New Left movement, Mills questioned, "Who is it that is getting fed up with what Marx called all the old crap? Who is it that is thinking and acting in radical ways?" His answer was:

> In the spring and early summer of 1960—more of the returns from the American decision and default are coming in. . . . On Okinawa—a US military base—the people get their first chance since World War II ended to demonstrate against US seizure of their island and some students take that chance, snake-dancing and chanting angrily to the visiting President: "Go home, go home—take away your missiles" (Don't worry, 12,000 US troops easily handled the generally grateful crowds; also the President was "spirited out the rear end of the United States compound" -and so by helicopter to the airport). . . . In Japan, weeks of student rioting succeeded in rejecting the President's visit, jeopardise a new treaty with the U.S.A., displace the big-business, pro-American Prime Minister, Kishi. And even in our own pleasant Southland, Negro and white students are— but let us keep that quiet: it really *is* disgraceful.[204]

Mills saw that this emerging new leftist movement, led by young intelligentsia like those in the Japanese anti-*Anpo* protests, would play a significant role in challenging the flaws of American liberalism as well as Soviet-style socialism.

The members of the conservative political establishment in the United States, on the other hand, believed that Communism was the major source of the "mob violence" in Tokyo, maintaining a traditional Cold War framework. On August 26, the Subcommittee to Investigate the Administration of the Internal Security Act and Other Internal Security Laws of the Senate Committee on the Judiciary, published a sixty-page report titled *Communist Anti-American Riots: Mob violence as an Instrument of Red Diplomacy, Bogotá—Caracas—La Paz—Tokyo* to the Committee on the Judiciary and devoted nearly half of the pages to "The Red Riots in Tokyo." The subcommittee's chair was Senator James Eastland of Mississippi, a powerful southern Democrat who was unabashedly a supporter of racial segregation and a notorious anti-Communist. The report's purpose was stated to determine "the techniques employed and the purposes sought" by "anti-American riots" that took place in Latin America against Nixon in 1958 and in Tokyo against the US-Japan Security Treaty in 1960.[205] The authors of the report blamed Communists for staging "a series of anti-American riots in Latin America and Asia" and said that "these actions have done serious injury to the United States and to its relations with Latin American and Asian nations."[206]

Preoccupied with its task of investigating the work of Communist agents operating under the Soviet guidance, the subcommittee concluded that the anti-security treaty demonstrations in Japan were provoked by outside "agitators" mainly from Communist China and North Korea.[207] The authors of the report warned, "This would set a pattern for the nations of the Far East, Africa and Latin America" and demanded that the United States take more seriously the possible loss of its key strategic point in the Pacific."[208] Quoting Ambassador MacArthur's statement, the report continued, "Without the great arc of free Asia of which Japan is the key stone, [the US system] could never survive."[209] The "mob violence" of 1960 in Japan became a reference point for the traditional anti-Communists in America who demanded that the US take tougher actions against international Communism.

In addition to Communism, there was "anti-Americanism" to be blamed, though they were conceptually linked closely. By 1954, the concept of "anti-Americanism" had gained broader meaning than resistance against American military activities and economic interests.[210] Historian Greg Grandin has argued that the idea of "anti-Americanism" began to indicate emotional and psychological resistance against capitalist modernity and liberal democracy, of which the US identified its society as the "apex."[211] "Irrational" protests in rapidly transforming societies indeed were considered another source of communist-like demonstrations against the United States. This view was also reflected in the subcommittee's report on Zengakuren. It explained that a reason why the majority of Zengakuren students, who were not professional Communists, ended up having "wittingly or unwittingly served Communist purposes" was that they had suffered from "emotional unrest" after the war.[212]

The liberal Democrats in Washington exploited the demonstrations in Tokyo as the failure of the Republican leadership. On July 15 at the Democratic National Convention, the young presidential candidate, John F. Kennedy, criticized the old style of Republican leadership for having failed to block the spread of Communist influence in the world. Kennedy said, "Friends have slipped into neutrality—and neutrals into hostility. As our keynoter reminded us, the President who began his career by going to Korea ends it by staying away from Japan."[213] The Tokyo riot brought another shock to American self-confidence in the Republic leadership that had remained low since the Soviet success of launching Sputnik on October 4, 1957. During his campaign in Virginia, Kennedy further criticized the Republican leadership for "successive blows to our security and prestige—Indo-China, Hungary, Suez, Sputnik, the riots in Venezuela, the collapse of the Summit, the riots in Japan, the collapse of the Baghdad Pact, the failure of disarmament, the U-2 fiasco, and now Cuba and Congo."[214]

At the Republican National Convention, the Presidential nominee, Vice President Richard Nixon, responded by insisting that his party must not be blamed for Communist conspiratorial activities. Referring to Kennedy's speech at the Democratic National Convention, Nixon said, "We heard the United States [being] blamed for the actions of communist-led mobs in Caracas and Tokyo. We heard that American education and American scientists are inferior. We heard that America militarily and economically is a second-rate country. We heard that America's prestige is at an all-time low. This is my answer: I say that at a time the Communists are running us down abroad it's time to speak up."[215] Nixon's repetition of such familiar accusations against Communists failed to attract the majority of voters.

In November, Americans voted not for the old anti-Communist, but youthful Kennedy who promised a "New Frontier." The new President expressed his ambition to provide new, youthful leadership for the nation that had suffered from consequent setbacks in their fight against Communism. In respect to US-Japan relations, the coming era of the new Kennedy administration meant the end of the old MacArthur era and the beginning of a new liberal approach under the leadership of John F. Kennedy and his appointed Ambassador to Japan, Edwin O. Reischauer, which the Japanese left termed the "Kennedy-Reischauer offensive."

NOTES

1. Message of the President on the State of the Union, January 9, 1958, in Paul E. Zinner, ed. *Documents on American Foreign Relations, 1958* (New York: Harper and Row, 1959), 2.

2. Security in the Free World: Radio-TV Address to the Nation by the President, March 16, 1959 in Zinner, ed. *Documents on American Foreign Relations, 1959* (New York: Harper and Row, 1960), 33.

3. The Baghdad Pact was renamed the Central Treaty Organization (CENTO) in 1959.

4. Memorandum from the Assistant Secretary of State for Far Eastern Affairs (Robertson) to the Secretary of State, August 16, 1957 in *FRUS*, 1955–1957, vol. XXIII, Part 1, Japan, 444.

5. Wesley Sasaki-Uemura, *Organizing the Spontaneous: Citizen Protest in Postwar Japan* (Honolulu: University of Hawai'i Press, 2001), 16.

6. Joyce Kolko, *American and the Crisis of World Capitalism* (Boston: Beacon Press, 1974), 84–85.

7. *The New York Times*, January 12, 1960.

8. Ibid.

9. *Washington Post*, January 10, 1960.

10. Memorandum from the Assistant Secretary of State for Far Eastern Affairs (Robertson) to the Secretary of State, January 7, 1957 in *FRUS*, 1955–1957, vol. XXIII, Part 1, Japan, 240.

11. "Freedom—the Predominant Force," Statement by the Secretary of State (Dulles) before the Senate Foreign Relations Committee, January 14, 1959 in Zinner, ed., *Documents on American Foreign Relations, 1959*, 21.

12. Address by the Under Secretary of State (Dillon) before the Far East-America Council of Commerce and Industry, New York, October 7, 1959 in ibid., 445.

13. Ibid.

14. John Swenson-Wright, *Unequal Allies?: United States Security and Alliance Policy toward Japan* (Stanford: Stanford University Press, 2005), 224, 39.

15. *The New York Times*, July 15, 1956; Frank Langdon, *Japan's Foreign Policy* (Vancouver: The University of British Columbia Press, 1973), 38.

16. John Foster Dulles, "The Evolution of Foreign Policy," *The Department of State Bulletin*, vol. XXX, no. 761, January 25, 1954, in Marc Trachtenberg, ed. *The Development of American Strategic Thought: Basic Documents from the Eisenhower and Kennedy Periods, Including the Basic National Security Policy Papers from 1953 to 1959* (New York: Garland Publishing, Inc., 1988), 283.

17. Joint Communiqués of Japanese Prime Minister Kishi and US President Eisenhower, June 21, 1957. The World and Japan Database Project, Database of Japanese Politics and International Relations, Institute of Oriental Culture, University of Tokyo. http://worldjpn.grips.ac.jp/documents/texts/JPUS/19570621.D1E.html. (Accessed on March 22, 2018.)

18. Memorandum from the Assistant Secretary of State for Far Eastern Affairs (Robertson) to the Secretary of State, January 7, 1957 in *FRUS, 1955–1957*, vol. XXIII, Part 1, Japan, 241.

19. Ibid., 242.

20. Ibid., 241.

21. Ibid.

22. Max Paul Friedman, *Rethinking Anti-Americanism: The History of an Exceptional Concept in American Foreign Relations* (New York: Cambridge University Press, 2012), 147–8.

23. *Chicago Daily Tribune*, April 19, 1958; The protest was organized by the Federation of University Students of Uruguay.

24. *Newsday*, May 10, 1958.

25. *The Wall Street Journal*, May 9, 1958.

26. *Daily Boston Globe*, May 14, 1958.

27. Senate Committee on the Judiciary, *Communist Anti-American Riots: Mob Violence as an Instrument of Red Diplomacy. Bogotá—Caracas—La Paz—Tokyo, August 26, 1960*, Cong. (Washington DC: United States Government Printing Office, 1960), 17.

28. *The Hartford Courant*, May 9, 1958.

29. *Los Angeles Times*, May 9, 1958.

30. Senate Committee on the Judiciary, *Communist Anti-American Riots*, 17.

31. Kazuko Tsurumi, "The Japanese Student Movement (1) Its Milieu," *Japan Quartely* 15, no. 4 (1968): 445.

32. "Kyōsan Shugisha Dōmei Kōryō Sōan [The policy draft of the Communist League]," September 8, 1959. File 1. Shima Shigeo Kyōsan Shugisha Dōmei (Bunto) Kankei Shiryō (hereafter cited as Shima Collection). The National Diet Library, Tokyo.

33. Shima Shigeo and Takazawa Koji, *Bunto (Kyōsan Shugisha Dōmei) no Shisō* [The ideology of *Bunto* (Communist League)], vol. 1 (Tokyo: Hihyō Sha, 1992), 19.

34. Quoted in Tsurumi, "The Japanese Student Movement (1) Its Milieu," 445.

35. "Nihon Kyōsantō no Kiki to Gakusei Undō—Zengakuren Ikensho [The crisis of the JCP and the student movement—a Zengakuren statement." Document no. 1 in San-Ichi Shobō Henshūbu, ed. *Shiryō Sengo Gakusei Undō: Zengakuren Documents*, vol. 5, 1959–1960 (Tokyo: San-Ichi Shobō, 1969), 26.

36. The workers were reacting to a new wave of economic rationalization sweeping throughout Japan in 1959 and their situation being deteriorated due to the shift in energy policy that was intended to reduce dependency on coal by supplementing it with alternative energy, oil.

37. Quoted in Tsurumi, "The Japanese Student Movement (1) Its Milieu," 446.

38. Zengakuren Shoki Kyoku, "Zengakuren Kinkyū Tsūtatsu [Zengakuren emergency notification]," August 4, 1959. File 38-1. OISR Archive.

39. Shintaro Hamanaka, *Asian Regionalism and Japan: The Politics of Membership in Regional Diplomatic, Financial and Trade Groups* (New York: Routledge, 2010), 83; According to historian Hara Yoshihisa, there were certain levels of suspicion among Asian states, especially Burma and India, about political strings attached

to the package of the economic assistance, see Yoshihisa Hara, *Sengo Nihon to Kokusai Seiji: Anpo Kaitei no Seiji* [Postwar Japan and international politics: the political dynamics of the security treaty revision] (Tokyo: Chūō Kōron Sha, 1988), 111–12.

40. Hara, *Sengo Nihon to Kokusai Seiji*, 111–12.

41. Ibid.

42. Zengakuren Shoki Kyoku, "Zengakuren Kinkyū Tūtatsu," August 4, 1959. File 38-1. OISR Archive.

43. Ibid.

44. *Zengakuren Tūshin*, no. 39 (January 23, 1959). File 38-1. OISR Archive.

45. Among the 100 students surveyed, 47 identified as "Activist," 30 as "Interested," 23 as "Apathetic." In the survey, the respondents were free to choose more than one item. 26 students selected "Opposition to Kishi," 3 selected "Stop Eisenhower Visit to Japan," 5 selected "Expression of Anti-American Sentiment," 49 selected "Opposition to Security Treaty," 44 selected "Expression of Antiwar," 16 selected "Defense of the Constitution," and no one selected "Against Japanese Imperialism," 21 selected "Other Reasons," and 7 selected "Do not Know." For more details, see Tsurumi, "The Japanese Student Movement (1) Its Milieu."

46. "Soviet Government Statement," *Current Digest of the Soviet Press* 10, no. 48 (January 1959): 21–22.

47. Ibid.

48. Shinichi Uemura, "Guromuiko Oboegaki no Nerai: Nichibei Kōshō Kara Kongo no Nisso Kankei Made [The intention of the Gromyko memorandum: from the US-Japan agreement to the USSR-Japan relations in the Future]," *Sekai Shūhō* 47, no. 7 (February 1960): 38.

49. Ibid.

50. Kōan Chōsachō, *Anpo Tōsō no Gaiyō: Tōsō no Keika to Bunseki* [A summary of the anti-*Anpo* struggle: a progress report and analysis of the struggle] (Tokyo: Kōan Chōsachō, 1960), 39–43.

51. Ibid.

52. *Anpo Jyōyaku Kaitei Soshi Kokumin Kaigi Nyūsu*, no. 2 (May 23, 1959). File 42-1. OISR Archive.

53. Kobayashi, *Sengo Kakumei Undō Ronsōshi*, 206.

54. Ibid.

55. *Tokyo Daigaku Shimbun*, January 11, 1960.

56. Kōan Chōsachō, *Anpo Tōsō no Gaiyō*, 164.

57. Ibid.

58. Zengakuren Anpo Hikokudan [Zengakuren *Anpo* defense team], "6. 15 Ware Ware no Genzai [June 15, our current situation]." File 37. Shima Collection. The National Diet Library, Tokyo.

59. Kakumei-teki Kyōsan Shugisha Dōmei (Dai4 Intānashonaru) [The Revolutionary Communist League (the Fourth International)], *Sekai Kakumei*, no. 60 (January 30, 1960). Shima Collection, file 10. The National Diet Library, Tokyo.

60. Coburn B. Kidd, "Status of Zengakuren and its Actions since the November 27 Diet Demonstrations," Foreign Service Despatch from US Embassy, Tokyo to the Department of State, December 7, 1959. RG 84. Box 74. NARA II.

61. Ibid.
62. Ibid.
63. Airgram from US Embassy, Tokyo to Secretary of State, December 24, 1959. RG 84. Box 74. NARA II.
64. Setsu Shigematsu, *Scream from the Shadows: The Women's Liberation Movement in Japan* (Minneapolis: University of Minnesota Press, 2012), 211.
65. Disposition Form to Special Assistant to the High Commissioner from Assistant Chief of Staff, G2 R. B. Self, "National Federation of Students' Self-Government Association (Zengakuren)," December 3, 1959. The United States Civil Administration of the Ryukyu Islands Records (hereafter cited as USCAR Records). Sheet no. 08630. The National Diet Library, Tokyo.
66. Ibid.
67. Ibid.
68. Zengakuren Shoki Kyoku, "Nokosareta Hi o Haneda Dōin no tame Shiryoku o Tukuse [Devote the remaining days for mobilization for the Haneda protest]," January 8, 1960. Document no. 19 in *Zengakuren Documents*, vol. 5, 1959–1960, 245.
69. *Tokyo Daigaku Shimbun* reported that 1,500 protestors were at Haneda on January 20, 1960; Japanese Public Security Intelligence Agency (Kōan Chōsachō) reported that 1,000 Zengakuren students stormed into the Haneda Airport in Kōan Chōsachō, *Anpo Tōsō no Gaiyō: Tōsō no Keika to Bunseki*, 165.
70. *Tokyo Daigaku Shimbun*, January 20, 1960 in *Zengakuren Documents*, vol. 5, 1959–1960, 257.
71. Kakumei-teki Kyōsan Shugi sha Dōmei (Dai4 Intānashonaru), *Sekai Kakumei*, no. 60 (January 30, 1960). File 10. Shima Collection. The National Diet Library, Tokyo.
72. *The New York Times*, January 17, 1960.
73. Kakumei-teki Kyōsan Shugi sha Dōmei (Dai4 Intānashonaru), *Sekai Kakumei Sekai Kakumei*, Special Edition, January 17, 1960. Shima Collection, file 10. The National Diet Library, Tokyo.
74. Coburn B. Kidd, "Zengakuren on Defensive," Foreign Service Despatch from US Embassy, Tokyo to the Department of State, February 15, 1960. RG 84. Box 74. NARA II.
75. Ibid.
76. Ibid.
77. Airgram from US Embassy, Tokyo (MacArthur) to Secretary of State, March 22, 1960. RG 84. Box 74. NARA II.
78. Nobusuke Kishi, *Anpo Jyōyaku Kaitei no Ikisatsu to Sono Haikei* [The background and development of the *Anpo* treaty revision] (Tokyo: Jiyū Minshutō Kōhō Iinkai, 1969), 21.
79. Foreign Minister Fujiyama Aiichiro, Ambassador Asakai Koichiro, Ambassador MacArthur, and Assistant Secretary of State for East Asian and Pacific Affairs J. Graham Parsons were also present at the meeting.
80. Memorandum of Conversation, "Japanese Domestic Political Situation," January 19, 1960 in *FRUS*, 1958–1960, vol. XVIII, Japan and Korea, 261.
81. Ibid.

82. National Intelligence Estimate, "Probable Developments in Japan," February 9, 1960 in *FRUS*, 1958–1960, vol. XVIII, Japan and Korea, 287.

83. Ibid.

84. *Chicago Daily Tribune*, January 16, 1960.

85. Ibid.

86. *New York Times*, January 17, 1960.

87. Toichi Kurihara, "Japanese Students Push Anti-War Action," *The Young Socialist* 3, no. 5 (March 1960), 3. Microfilm Film R-7271. Tamiment Library and Robert F. Wagner Archives, New York University.

88. Ibid.

89. Memorandum of Conversation, Subject: Shigakuren and the National Student Liaison Council, April 14, 1960. RG84. Box 74. NARAII; Takei Teruo has criticized *Shigakuren* as the organization that blindly took a pro-government stance on every political and social issue, see Takei, "Zengakuren Kessei no Zengo," 66.

90. Memorandum of Conversation, Subject: Shigakuren and the National Student Liaison Council, April 14, 1960. RG84. Box 74. NARAII.

91. Incoming Airgram from US Embassy, Tokyo to Secretary of State, April 15, 1960. RG 59. Box 2900. NARA II; By "Tokyo University," MacArthur probably meant "University of Tokyo" here.

92. Foreign Service Despatch from US Embassy, Tokyo to the Department of States, Subject: Education Ministry Efforts to Obtain Greater Discipline of Zengakuren by University Administrators, May 10, 1960. RG 84. Box 74. NARA II.

93. Ibid.

94. Ibid.

95. Telegram from the Embassy in Japan to the Department of State, May 23, 1960 in *FRUS*, 1958–1960, vol. XVIII, Japan and Korea, 299–300.

96. Ibid.

97. Ibid.

98. Ibid.

99. Ibid.

100. Telegram from the Embassy in Japan to the Department of State, May 11, 1960 in ibid., 293.

101. Telegram from the Department of State to the Embassy in Japan, May 9, 1960 in ibid., 292.

102. Telegram from the Embassy in Japan to the Department of State, May 20, 1960 in ibid., 295.

103. *Tokyo Daigaku Shimbun*, July 11, 1960.

104. Ibid.

105. Telegram from the Embassy in Japan to the Department of State, May 20, 1960 in *FRUS*, 1958–1960, vol. XVIII, Japan and Korea, 296.

106. Ibid.

107. Quoted in Hara, *Sengo Nihon to Kokusai Seiji*, 398.

108. Maruyama Masao, "Sentaku no Toki [Time to choose]," *Tokyo Daigaku Shimbun*, July 11, 1960.

109. Ibid.

110. *Tokyo Daigaku Shimbun*, July 11, 1960.
111. Ibid.
112. Ibid.
113. *Asahi Shimbun*, May 28, 1960.
114. Kishi, *Anpo Jyōyaku Kaitei no Ikisatsu to Sono Haikei*, 24.
115. Ibid.
116. Telegram from MacArthur to Secretary of State, May 26, 1960. RG 84. Box 73. NARA II.
117. Ibid.
118. Ibid.
119. Ibid.
120. Ibid.
121. Ibid.
122. *Yomiuri Shimbun*, May 21, 1960.
123. *Tokyo Daigaku Shimbun*, May 25, 1960 in *Zengakuren Documents*, vol. 5, 1959–1960, 348.
124. Zengakuren Shoki Kyoku, "5. 26 'Kishi Datō, Sokuji Kokkai Kaisan,' Anpo Funsai Zenkoku Suto, Kokkai Demo de Kekki Seyo! (tūtatsu)," [May 26, 'overthrow Kishi, dissolve the Diet immediately,' national Strike against the *Anpo*, rise up in the demonstration at the Diet]," May 21, 1960. Document no. 32 in ibid., 348.
125. *Yomiuri Shimbun*, June 5, 1960.
126. Kōan Chōsachō, *Anpo Tōsō no Gaiyō*, 168.
127. *Yomiuri Shimbun*, June 4, 1960.
128. Ibid.
129. "Rupo, 6.4 Zene Suto Shien Tōsō [A report, the struggle supporting for the general strike on June 4]," June 8, 1960, *Waseda Daigaku Shimbun* in *Zengakuren Documents*, vol. 5, 1959–1960, 358–9; snake dance was a demonstration technique widely used by student activists in Japan. It was also called *zigzag demo* by Japanese activists.
130. Ibid.
131. Ibid.
132. *Chicago Daily Tribune*, June 4, 1960.
133. *Yomiuri Shimbun*, June 4, 1960.
134. Ibid.
135. Ibid.
136. Ibid.
137. Zengakuren Shoki Kyoku, "6.3–4 genesuto ha kishi datō heno kyodaina ichigeki to natta! Sarani 6.15 ni mukete bakushin [June 3–4 general strike caused a huge damage to Kishi. Again, dash for 6.15]," Document no. 33 in *Zengakuren Documents*, vol. 5, 1959–1960, 351–357.
138. *Chicago Daily Tribune*, June 5, 1960; *Los Angeles Times*, June 5, 1960.
139. *Chicago Daily Tribune*, June 5, 1960.
140. The JCP announced that these students acted without the permission of the party and later expelled the student leaders who led the anti-Hagerty protest at Haneda for their "theoretical revisionism, see Hisato Harada, "The Anti-Ampo Struggle,"

Zengakuren: Japan's Revolutionary Students, ed. Stuart J. Dowsey (Berkeley: Ishi Press, 1970), 95.

141. Kōan Chōsachō, *Anpo Tōsō no Gaiyō*, 169.

142. Telegram from US Embassy, Tokyo to the Secretary of State, June 11, 1960. RG 84. Box 73. NARA II.

143. *Tokyo Daigaku Shimbun*, January 11, 1960.

144. "Hanbei, Han Fassho (Kishi) no Ikari Bakuhatsu [Anti-America, anti-fascism (Kishi) anger exploded]," *Shūkan Rōdō Jyohō*, no. 260 (June 15, 1960), 3.

145. Ibid.

146. *Tokyo Daigaku Shimbun*, June 11, 1960.

147. Telegram from US Embassy, Tokyo to the Secretary of State, June 8, 1960. RG 84. Box 73. NARA II.

148. Hajime Suzuki, "Tatakai no Kiroku, 6.15 [The record of the struggle, June 15]," Gendai Shichōsha, ed. *Sōkōsha to Seishun: Zengakuren Gakusei no Shuki* (Tokyo: Gendai Shichōsha, 1960), 155.

149. Ibid.

150. *Yomiuri Shimbun*, June 16, 1960.

151. Ibid.

152. Ibid.

153. Ibid.

154. Kanba belonged to the *Bunto* faction.

155. *Yomiuri Shimbun*, June 16, 1960.

156. *Tokyo Daigaku Shimbun*, June 18 in *Zengakuren Documents*, vol. 5, 1959–1960, 382–383.

157. *Yomiuri Shimbun*, June 16, 1960.

158. Ibid.

159. *The New York Times*, June 17, 1960.

160. Kyōsan Shugisha Dōmei [The Communist League], "Dōshi Kanba no Shi o Itamu [Mourn for comrade Kanba's death]," in Gendai Shichōsha, *Sōkōsha to Seishun*, 176–80.

161. Ibid.

162. Zengakuren Chūō Shikkō Iinkai, Kanba San no Shi wa Ikani Tsugunawareru Bekika—Ware Ware wa Fukai Ikidōri o Motte Nihon Kyōsantō ni Kougi Suru [How Kanba's death should be compensated—we protest against the JCP with deep indignation]," June 24, 1960. Document no. 42 in *Zengakuren Documents*, vol. 5, 1959–1960, 375–377.

163. Nick Kapur, *Japan at the Crossroads: Conflict and Compromise after Anpo* (Cambridge, MA: Harvard University Press, 2018).

164. *Washington Post*, June 16, 1960.

165. Ibid.

166. *The New York Times*, June 17, 1960.

167. For further discussion on the South Korean student protests in 1960, see Charles R. Kim, "Moral Imperatives: South Korean Studenthood and April 19th," *The Journal of Asian Studies* 71 (May 2012), pp. 399–422.

168. *The New York Times*, June 17, 1960.

169. *Yomiuri Shimbun*, June 19, 1960.
170. "YSA Demonstrates Against Treaty," *The Young Socialist* 3, no. 9 (Summer 1960). Tamiment Library and Robert F. Wagner Archives, New York University.
171. Ibid.
172. *Time*, June 27, 1960.
173. Ibid.
174. *Los Angeles Times*, June 17, 1960.
175. *The New York Times*, June 17, 1960.
176. *The Christian Science Monitor*, January 6, 1960; *The New York Times*, January 7, 1960.
177. *The New York Times*, June 17, 1960.
178. Ibid.
179. Dwight D. Eisenhower, "Radio and Television Report to the American People on the Trip to the Far East," Address by the President (Eisenhower) to the Nation, June 27, 1960. Document no. 209 in *Public Papers of the Presidents of the United States: Dwight D. Eisenhower, 1960–1961*, ed. Office of the Federal Register, National Archives and Records Service, General Services Administration (Washington DC: US Government Printing Office, 1961), 529.
180. *Asahi Shimbun*, June 11, 1960.
181. *Times* (London), June 17, 1960.
182. Quoted in *New York Times*, June 17, 1960.
183. Ibid.
184. *Daily Tribune*, June 19, 1960.
185. Agent Report, Subject: Subversive Activities of Ryukyus University Students," June 29, 1960. RG260. Box111. NARAII.
186. Ibid.
187. "Participating in the Petitionary Demonstration Armed Soldiers Conducted Themselves with Contemptuous Disregard for Human Beings—by Shimabukuro Tetsuo," Subversive Activities of Ryukyus University Students, Agent Report, August 29, 1960. RG 260. Box 111. NARA II.
188. Ibid.
189. Agent Report, Subject: Subversive Activities of Ryukyus University Students, June 29, 1960. NARAII. RG 260. Box 111; reversionists supported the reversion of Okinawa to Japan.
190. "Editorial: Appeal to Americans. Friendship Cannot Be Brought with a Sword," Subversive Activities of Ryukyus University Students, Agent Report, August 29, 1960. RG 260. Box 111. NARA II.
191. Ibid.
192. Disposition Form, Subject: National Federation of Students' Self-Government Association (Zengakuren), From G2 USARYIS to Special Assistant to the High Commissioner, Dec. 3, 1959. RG260. Box 138. NARA II.
193. Ibid.
194. Summary of Subversive Activities of Ryukyus University Students: Covering Reports Dated 4 June 1953 Through 23 April 1957." RG 260. Box 111. NARA II.
195. This ordinance became effective on June 5, 1959.

196. United States Civil Administration of the Ryukyu Islands, Office of the High Commissioner, Ordinance no. 23. Code of Penal Law and Procedure for the Ryukyu Islands, 1959. Arthur W. Diamond Law Library, Columbia University.

197. Agent Report, Subversive Activities of Ryukyus University Students, July 20, 1959. RG260. Box 111. NARAII.

198. Memorandum for Record, Subject: Zengakuren on Okinawa. July 20, 1960. RG260. Box 138. NARA II.

199. Memorandum for the Deputy Civil Administrator, Subject: Travel of Four University Students to Japan, July 19, 1960. RG260. Box 111. NARA II.

200. To USCAR Education Department from Assistant Chief of Staff, G2 R. B. Self. USCAR Records. Sheet no. 08630. The National Diet Library, Tokyo.

201. Memorandum for the Deputy Civil Administrator, Subject: Travel of Four University Students to Japan, July 19, 1960. RG260. Box 111. NARA II.

202. Ibid.

203. *Current Intelligence Weekly Summary*, July 16, 1960, Central Intelligence Agency. CIA-RDP79-00927A002800050001-7, CREST, NARAII.

204. C. Wright Mills, "Letter to the New Left," *New Left Review*, no. 5 (September–October) (1960).

205. Senate Committee on the Judiciary, *Communist Anti-American* Riots, 1.

206. Ibid.

207. Ibid., 31.

208. Ibid., 33.

209. Ibid.

210. Greg Grandin, "Your Americanism and Mine: Americanism and Anti-Americanism in the Americas," *The American Historical Review* 111, no. 4 (2006): 1059.

211. Ibid., 1046.

212. Senate Committee on the Judiciary, *Communist Anti-American Riots, 1960*, 44.

213. John F. Kennedy, "The New Frontier," Acceptance Speech of Senator John F. Kennedy, Democratic National Convention, July 15, 1960. The Papers of President Kennedy: Pre-Presidential Papers, Box 1027. John F. Kennedy Presidential Library (hereafter cited as JFK Library).

214. John F. Kennedy, "The Basic Issue: Experience," an address delivered by Senator John F. Kennedy in Alexandria, Virginia on August 24, 1960, 1960. The Papers of President Kennedy: Pre-Presidential Papers. Box 1027. JFK Library.

215. Richard Nixon, "Address Accepting the Presidential Nomination at the Republican National Convention in Chicago," July 28, 1960. Online by Gerhard Peters and John T. Woolley, *The American Presidency Project*. http://www.presidency.ucsb.edu/ws/?pid=25974. (Accessed on March 28, 2018).

Chapter Five

The Reischauer Offensive
Promoting a Different Kind of Past

Recalling his appointment as Ambassador to Japan, Edwin O. Reischauer said, "I had been chosen [by President Kennedy] specifically to make better intellectual contact with all the people of Japan, especially with those not in government circles or in the opposition camp from the government in power."[1] Large-scale uprisings that demonstrated students' power in places such as Latin America, Korea, Turkey, and Tokyo had made American policymakers place greater emphasis on the importance of developing communications with the citizens of the allied countries. Reischauer described the anti-*Anpo* demonstrations as "the Broken Dialogue with Japan" and was highly motivated to repair it while serving at the US Embassy in Tokyo.

After arriving in Tokyo, Reischauer made a conscious effort not just to foster a mutual dialogue with the Japanese intellectuals, but to have them, especially Marxists, embrace the American dialogue, which then meant the modernizationist understanding of social progress and political development. During the Kennedy administration, modernization theory played a pivotal role in shaping American Cold War policy. Historian Michael E. Latham has argued that modernization theory was not merely an academic discourse but the driving ideology of the Kennedy administration.[2] The proximity of modernization theory and political power revealed their mutual reinforcement and limitation of academic independence placed by Cold War anti-Communism. The prominent position that modernization theory achieved in academia and Kennedy's enthusiasm for the new "scientific" and "objective" knowledge gave modernizationist scholars significant political leverage in shaping the administrations' policy objectives and strategies.

In Japan, this ideology of modernization came to play an important role in shaping its political and social fabric under Reischauer. Once liberated from the old shackles of Marxist briefs, Reischauer believed, the Japanese would come to embrace rationality and understand the real benefits of American liberalism. He aimed to diminish the prominence of Marxism in the intellectual quarter of Japan by articulating this capitalist alternative theory on social progress and modernization, and such effort proved to be a psychological, rather than intellectual, campaign against Japanese Marxists. Modernization theorists' renarrativization of the Japanese national history as a successful modernization story in particular was effective in countering Marxist influence. It proved fitting to the desire of Japan to reemerge as the nation at the forefront of modernization in non-Western world. Japanese Marxists, including the student left, criticized modernization theory for granting amnesty to Japan's history of imperial militarism and aggression. Yet, in the 1960s, it was Reischauer's history of modern Japan that gained popularity among the Japanese who were willing to leave the past behind.

WHAT WENT WRONG?

After the massive *Anpo* demonstrations in June, Zengakuren students struggled to reach a correct analysis of their *Anpo* struggle. The student activists still shared a belief in the power of their movement; the *Anpo* protest of 1960 had heightened it, but there was little, if any, agreement among Zengakuren factions over how to effectively employ it. Anti-*Bunto* factions of student radicals emphasized *Bunto* leaders' "failure" in their analyses of the June 1960. *Zenshin* (Moving Forward), the organ of the *Kakukyōdō* faction, commented acerbically that the *Bunto*-led *Anpo* demonstrations failed to damage the basic economic and political structures of Japan, even though it had gained an unprecedented number of supporters.[3] They argued, like many other student activists did, that the students' anti-*Anpo* protest failed to block the passage of the treaty revision and prevent another LDP man, Ikeda Hayato, from replacing Kishi.[4] To reinforce such a conclusion, some employed Lenin's theory of revolution that stated: "For the revolution it is necessary that the exploiters should not be able to live and rule as of old. Only when the masses *do not want* the old regime, and when the rulers *are unable* to govern as of old, then only can the revolution succeed."[5] Many student radicals felt that the anti-*Anpo* mass movement of 1960 was a failed revolution that could not transform the old structure of power and class domination.[6] The Cell of the Communist League at the University of Tokyo faction issued an opinion paper on August 14, 1960 that demanded the "revolutionary subjects" admit their fault.[7]

Probably the most significant outcome of the June *Anpo* struggle for Zengakuren was the intensifying factional rivalries unleashed by the disintegration of the *Bunto* faction. Placing the blame on *Bunto* leaders, many rank-

and-file members left to join other groups. As the *Bunto* disappeared from the scene, rivaling factions put more energy to competing with others to fill the leadership vacuum. In the 1960s, a number of small factions emerged. The Japan Marxist Student League (*Nippon Marukusu Shugi Gakusei Dōmei*, abbreviated as *Marugakudo*), an anti-JCP faction, was one of those that gained members from the implosion of the *Bunto*.[8] At the same time, some student activists began forming new groups, either by refusing to join or splitting the existing ones. In 1962, *Marugakudo* was divided into two factions, and its rivaling factions, the Socialist Student League, the League of Socialist Youth of Japan (*Nihon Shakai Shugi Seinen Dōmei*, as *Shaseidō*), and the Structural Reform Faction (*Kōzō Kaikaku-ha*) formed the Triple Alliance (*Sanpa Zengakuren*) to counter *Marugakudo*.[9] In the same year, the JCP-affiliated groups left Zengakuren, dominated by anti-JCP factions, and established another Zengakuren, calling it *Heimin Gakuren*.[10] These factional antagonisms among the student activists intensified after the *Anpo* struggle of June 1960, consuming time and energy of the student activists.

Besides the *Bunto* leadership, some intellectuals and student activists thought that the anti-*Anpo* movement manifested the problem of the political backwardness and indifference of the rural mass. A few days after the June 19 anti-*Anpo* demonstrations, a group of student activists formed the Association to Defend Democracy with Everyone (*Minnade Minshu Shugi o Mamoru-kai*).[11] It then cooperated with other leftist groups such as The National Association of Scholars and Researchers to Defend Democracy and organized the so-called Homecoming Movement (*Kikyō Undō*) during the summer of 1960.[12] Their aim was to spread democracy, "enlighten" the rural population, and expand the anti-*Anpo* movement beyond the urban centers. The Homecoming Movement tried to foster the political consciousness of the rural mass through lectures, workshops, and round-table discussions on the issue of democracy and the *Anpo* treaty.[13] Yet, their effort to "teach" democracy to spur protest against the *Anpo* in rural areas revealed their naïve ignorance of rural lives. The land reform during the US occupation had established a solid LDP electoral base in rural Japan after the war. The idea that support for the LDP and Japan's close cooperation with the United States would assure economic prosperity and stability had been more strongly cemented in rural places. During the Homecoming Movement, intellectuals and student activists learned that most people in these rural areas expected them to give lectures on agriculture and trade, rather than democracy.[14] Ambassador MacArthur probably derided such experiments and reported, "Discouraging results of Kikyo Undo revival were eye-opener to leftists, who have counted heavily on expansion of mass organizational techniques in hinterlands where leftwing is weak."[15]

The people's movement was not over yet, but few knew how to proceed in practice in the immediate aftermath of the June 1960.

Cold War strategists and policymakers in Washington meanwhile were also asking themselves what had been wrong with their policy. The unprecedented scale of the mass opposition in Japan invited the call for reassessment of current US policy and attitude toward Japan. At the meeting of the Pacific Coast Branch of the American Historical Association on September 8, 1960, George Kennan called for more "realistic" American policy in East Asia. He thought that the US had pushed Japan too hard and insisted, "Our stake in Japan's independence does not mean that Japanese policy must be at all times identical with our own in all areas, or that we should expect of the Japanese enthusiastic support for all our global cold war objectives."[16] He continued, "To expect from her a complete identity of outlook and policy with our own is to provoke precisely those reactions of protests which took so unfortunate a form, and were so unscrupulously exploited, earlier this summer."[17] Kennan believed that the US should allow the Japanese a space to independently maneuver within the free world in order to prevent another anti-US crisis and said, "let them discover the limits for themselves. They are not children. They have memories and experience."[18] The anti-*Anpo* demonstrations in Tokyo evoked bitter memories of the "loss of China." Kennan emphasized, "Let us be careful not to apply to them that self-indulgent patronizing favor that misled us so grievously in the case of China."[19] The US could not risk repeating such a major Cold War setback in East Asia.

Cold War liberals spoke out against American arrogance and indifference to ordinary people in foreign countries. In the anti-Communist socialist weekly *New Leader*, Reinhold Niebuhr, a renowned theologian, insisted, in more sympathetic tone to the Japanese, that the crisis in Tokyo and the cancellation of Eisenhower's trip to Japan "accentuated the catastrophic character of the American defeat in the world situation," as the result of "the failure of American leadership" in the free world.[20] He argued that American arrogance toward Japan blinded the US policymakers to resentment being accumulated in Japan over the years "against our domination of Japanese policy, against wresting Okinawa from Japanese sovereignty, against dropping the first atomic bombs on Japanese city, against prohibition of trade with mainland China, and against the neutralism and pacifism enforced through the MacArthur Constitution."[21] Niebuhr criticized that the "vanity" of Eisenhower's personal diplomacy that only focused on political elites resulted in American indifference to the Japanese local plight. Reischauer's appointment as US Ambassador to Japan was, in a way, an answer to such criticism.

A SCHOLAR-AMBASSADOR: REISCHAUER AND THE PROBLEM OF MARXIST TENDENCY IN JAPAN

The appointment of Reischauer reflected President Kennedy's criticism of American diplomats in general. This was the time when American representatives' lack of cultural sensitivity and knowledge of local cultures and languages abroad were increasingly seen as posing serious problems for America's Cold War. *The Ugly American*, written by Eugene Burdick and William Lederer, which portrayed American diplomats' blatantly arrogant behavior and lack of knowledge of local realities as a major obstacle to America's fight against Communism, was a best-selling novel in 1958. Reischauer's personal background promised the Kennedy administration that he would not be the case. Born in 1910 in Tokyo as the son of the Presbyterian educational missionaries, Reischauer was fluent in Japanese.[22] In 1938, he took the position of a teaching fellow in the Department of Far Eastern Languages at Harvard.[23] During the war, Reischauer served in the Division of Far Eastern Affairs of the State Department.[24] After the war, he came back to Harvard and pursued his academic career as Professor of Japanese Studies. While at Harvard, he published numerous articles and books on Japan and the US policy in Asia, including *Wanted: An Asian Policy* published in 1955 in which he advocated the employment of an "arsenal of ideas" to combat Communist influence in Asia.[25]

In October 1960, Reischauer published an article titled "The Broken Dialogue with Japan" in *Foreign Affairs*, which became one of the most influential analyses of the anti-*Anpo* protest published in America. He explained that the *Anpo* crisis was in part rooted in lack of unifying ideals, which he called "gulfs," existing within the Japanese society. Comparing to America and England, Reischauer argued that Japan's "dangerous ideological gulfs," or the loss of "a central core of ideals on which all groups can agree" was "inescapable result of the tremendous rate of social, political and ideological change over the last century."[26] In addition, Reischauer insisted that Japan suffered from the wide gap between generations and said, "The fact that the 'main stream' group of Zengakuren is engaged in bitter fighting with the Communist Party can be cited as a typical example of youth revolting against the older generation—even when the two are on the same side."[27] Reischauer thought it was time for Japan to develop a liberal consensus, as in Anglo-American societies, believing that such consensus was vital for the country to successfully resist Communism and play a larger role in the world.

In the article, Reischauer warned that Washington must come up with more innovative policies to prevent its allies from falling into Communism or even neutralism. Referring to the Tokyo riots, Reischauer stated, "Ever since the end of the war has the gap in understanding between Americans and Japanese been wider than over this incident." [28] He warned that neutral, if not Communist, Japan "might well mean the inevitable withdrawal of the American defense line to the mid-Pacific," a serious strategic setback for the United States.[29] The fundamental problem was, he suggested, that the majority of the Japanese had not been convinced that siding with one power in the Cold War would provide them security and still believed, "Naked defenselessness would be safer."[30] "The Broken Dialogue with Japan" was Reischauer's warning to Americans.

Reischauer's background distinguished him as the best-suited ambassador to the post-*Anpo* Japan. He proved to have both a "sympathetic understanding" of the Japanese and an American anti-Communism stance. At the hearings before the Committee on Foreign Relations on Ambassadorial nomination held on March 23 and 24, 1961, Reischauer stated, "I think there has been a great misunderstanding of the American position, American ideals, and what we stand for in the Far East, on the part of certain elements in Japanese society, and I think it is important to correct some of these misunderstandings."[31] He then continued, "Quite obviously, the Communists had done their best to stir things up as they had on many occasions before. The dangerous aspect of the happenings of May and June was that there was such a large response on the part of many people who felt themselves to be not pro-Communists, even anti-Communists, but felt themselves to be acting in behalf of democracy and peace. This was a rather frightening phenomenon."[32] His appointment met some opposition in Washington. Secretary of State Dean Rusk was particularly mistrustful of Reischauer's "dovish views on China."[33] Yet, on March 29, the Senate unanimously approved Reischauer's appointment as Ambassador to Japan.[34]

Reischauer and his Japanese wife, Haru, arrived in Tokyo on April 19, 1961. Haru was the granddaughter of the former Prime Minister of Japan Matsukata Masayoshi. She had her own "dual background." Her mother, Miyo, was born and raised in New York and was "much more American than Japanese."[35] Haru received American schooling in Japan and pursued her education in the United States.[36] In 1955, she met Reischauer for the first time. Haru described her first impression of Reischauer as the person who was "as devoted as I to Japanese-American understanding and friendship" and "he combined my two cultures, though in his own way."[37] When Reischauer was appointed to Ambassador to Japan, she thought it would be their great opportunity to devote for promoting greater friendship between the two countries. Upon their arrival at the Haneda Airport, the Reischauers addressed to the Japanese, "To us it is like coming home."[38] Haru soon received public admiration as a "world-standard," stylish, well-educated, "modern" wife and mother who combined American female modernity and affection for Japan.

Photo of Edwin O. Reischauer and his wife Haru at the US Embassy in Tokyo. © *Kyodo News Agency*

ENDING THE MACARTHUR ERA: REISCHAUER AND A NEW "PARTNERSHIP" WITH JAPAN

Reischauer believed that the occupation mentality of the US Embassy in Japan had been partly responsible for the Japanese hostility toward the US. During his term in Tokyo, he brought a new term "partnership" to describe the US-Japan relations to "prod the Japanese into regarding themselves as equals and into playing a more important role" in the capitalist world.[39] The use of the term "partnership" was not so much aimed at changing the US traditional Cold War demands, as at boosting Japan's willingness to share not only benefits but also the Cold War burdens. Reischauer had expressed his frustration with Japan acting like a "big boy who prefers to sit in the back row of the classroom in the hope that no one will notice him."[40] He perceived that the shift from the Japanese self-perception from the defeated evil to the model "partner" could make the Japanese more willing to act as an active member of the international community while showing the goodwill of the United States.

The emphasis on "partnership" was in part Reischauer's response to the leftist criticism of the Japanese "military alliance" with the United States as well. He believed that the Eisenhower placed too much emphasis on Japan's value as a military ally, and his administration's close tie with the former Class A war criminal Kishi had alienated a large segment of the Japanese public.[41] Reischauer thus sought to replace the aggressive and militaristic image of the United States with that of a partner who supported world peace.[42] Moreover, Reischauer tried to convince the Japanese public that the US forces' presence in Japan was in fact functioning as a deterrent against the militaristic right-wing Japanese pushing for a for a large-scale rearmament.[43]

Another major change that took place in the US Embassy in Tokyo under Reischauer was its policy toward the non-Communist left and progressive forces in the Japanese society. He made significant efforts in making alliance with a wide range of the non-Communist Japanese. To reach out to the formerly alienated forces, Reischauer opened the US Embassy, which was largely restricted to the conservative business leaders and politicians under Ambassador MacArthur, to the ordinary Japanese, most remarkably the non-Communist left. Recommended by Assistant Secretary for Far Eastern Affairs Averell Harriman, Reischauer appointed John Emmerson as his chief deputy and put him in charge of bridging the US Embassy and the non-Communist Japanese left and progressives.[44]

Inviting Emmerson to the US Embassy was a bold decision of Reischauer. First of all, he was one of the Far Eastern specialists in the State Department who were accused of "losing China."[45] During the height of McCarthyism, furthermore, Emmerson had become the subject of the State Department's Loyalty Security Board for his alleged friendly relationship with the imprisoned Japanese Communist leaders during the early occupation period when he worked as the Political Adviser to General Douglas MacArthur. Even though his loyalty to the US government was confirmed by December 1951, the issue of his suspected affinity with the Japanese Communists resurfaced when the White House announced his appointment on June 18, 1961. Emmerson recalled that his appointment met vigorous protests by the Japanese rightists and conservatives who feared that it would militate against their interests.[46] Before his arrival in Japan, the Japanese right wingers and conservatives protested his appointment by sending a letter to Reischauer, accusing Emmerson of being "ultra-leftist."[47] Emmerson recalled that the copies of the letter were also sent to "numerous Japanese businessmen, politicians, journalists, and other prominent citizens, as well as some two hundred Americans, including members of Congress."[48] The conservative Japanese media ran stories that sensationalized his association with the Japanese Communist leaders.[49] Despite such opposition, Emmerson's appointment was confirmed. He returned to Japan in 1962, over twenty-one years since he had left with the end of the US occupation, but this time, his task was to "rid the relationship of the occupation psychology."[50]

To reach out to students in Japan, Reischauer appointed a graduate student of Asian Studies at Harvard, Ernest Young, to work with him in Tokyo. This was a recommendation made by Under Secretary of State Chester Bowles who told Reischauer to take an aide, someone who was outside the Foreign Service bureaucracy and "could be a kind of protection against hostile maneuvering," with him to Tokyo.[51] Young was expected to improve communication with the Japanese youth and probably to serve as a model student for them. Reischauer recalled, "I had specially selected and brought with me a graduate student in Asian studies to be my personal aide in making contacts with the students of Japan, and from the start I devoted my major effort toward making contacts of all sorts."[52] Young recalled, "His [Reischauer's] idea, as expressed to me, was to have someone close to him who would focus on the world of Japanese university students. He knew that I was somewhat of a dissenter from US foreign policy and thought that would be an advantage in contacts with Japanese students, radicalized by the recent 'Anpo *hantai* [opposition]' movement."[53]

In January, *Time* honored Reischauer for his popularity and quality as the "cultural ambassador." It reported, "To the Japanese, gentle Reischauer has 'low posture,' the degree of humanity that permits frankness. He eagerly talks to labor-union leaders, journalists, university professors, industrialists, and sees more of opposition leaders and intellectuals than his predecessor."[54] *Time* selected Reischauer, along with George Kennan and John Kenneth Galbraith, for its front cover featuring its article on the new US Ambassadors.[55]

"I SHALL DEAL WITH IT AS A HISTORIAN": REISCHAUER AND THE PROBLEM OF MARXISM IN JAPAN

As a scholar, Reischauer thought that one of the most urgent tasks was to deal with the persistent tendency of the Japanese intellectuals and students to "think in Marxian terms."[56] Their continuing adherence to Marxism, he argued, naturally produced "a very different picture of the world situation than that prevalent in the United States."[57] In a long run, Reischauer thought such tendency of the intellectuals and student would be an obstacle for the two countries to develop a common vision for the future world, because these intellectuals and students were the "ideological pathfinders and the generation to which the future Japan belongs."[58]

Such concerns over the popularity of Marxism in Japan was widely shared among American scholars, who, like Reischauer, believed in the superiority of American modernization theory in explaining capitalist development. One of the most noteworthy events was the Hakone Conference held in the summer of 1960 in Japan. To deal with the problem, a group of American social scientists working in the field related to Japan organized a conference called "The Conference of Modern Japan," or more commonly known as the Hakone Conference. It was attended by both American and Japanese scholars and funded by the Ford Foundation.[59] The conference had a clear Cold War objective. Historian John Whitney Hall, an organizer of the conference, described the conference as aiming to "devise a unified and objective conception of modernization" and deal with "the acceptability of previously unchallenged Marxist concepts" of modernization and social progress.[60]

The conference confirmed to American scholars that the discussions of democracy in Japan did not necessarily produce support for the free world as they were supposed. Hall described the problem of overly theoretical nature of the Japanese discourse as follows:

> We [Western scholars] were confronted at Hakone with a number of stereotyped answers derive[d] in the main from theories about social behavior which rested on the magnification of certain aspects of social change in preference to others. The Marxist emphasis on class tension as the moving force in social change, Marx Weber's stress upon the role of changing values. . . . We have no quarrel with these theories as such. . . . But we must be skeptical of them as dogmas or as unitary explanations of modernization.[61]

American participants agreed that the Japanese should pay less attention to the vague ideas of democracy and peace and more to the supposedly value-free "rational" and "scientific" analysis of society and history. On the other hand, there was a certain frustration on the Japanese side that attempted to engage in the discussion of democracy, capitalism, and modernization. Maruyama Masao, a leading political philosopher of University of Tokyo, observed:

> The American participants, in their papers, hesitated to introduce any ideologically charged concepts into the definition of "modernization," the Japanese side in the main insisted that it would be meaningless to discuss modernization, especially that of Japan, without paying due consideration to these concepts. It would be an over-simplification to understand this difference in approach merely in terms of the "ideologists" opposing the "non-ideologists."[62]

American scholars' unwillingness to engage in the discussion of any "value-oriented" subjects, including those of individualism, democracy, communism, or fascism seemed incomprehensible for the Japanese participants. The Hakone Conference seemed to deepen American scholars' belief in the effectiveness of modernization theory. Reischauer, who was also present at the conference, wrote, "The Japanese participants perceived the basically positive view of the Americans regarding the changes that had been sweeping Japan for the past century as a direct challenge to their own deeply entrenched Marxist concepts."[63]

Reischauer also criticized the Japanese understanding of democracy as being misguided. In "On Japanese Democracy: Concerning Communication between the US and Japan," aimed at Japanese readers, he contrasted Japanese society with "the Anglo-Saxon society where such things as the anti-*Anpo* demonstrations were condemned as undemocratic" and concluded that the Japanese were still unaware of the incompatibility between violent demonstrations and representative democracy.[64] He further argued that the Japanese were, compared to people of the Anglo-Saxon culture, more emotional, and the same thing could be said of Latin Americans, whose democracy was not working well either. For this reason, he insisted, the Japanese had to rigidly follow democratic institutional forms and laws in order to secure democracy.[65] History had proven, Reischauer thought, Japanese were susceptible to the extremism of both right and left.[66]

As the liberal critique of the old anti-Communism gained increased prominence, more attention was given to values and psychology of the student radicals. The Communist conspiracy theories were increasingly becoming anachronistic, being replaced by "scientific" theories. As in the previous decade, Marxism remained popular among the Japanese students. In June 1960, Saul Padover, an American historian who then lectured at University of Tokyo, wrote to the US Embassy that "it would be conservative to say that fifty percent of all Japan's professors and even more of her students were devoted Marxists."[67] It was reported that many Japanese university students "unwittingly absorbed the concepts of class struggle, imperialism, and an alarming number of the inverted social and political definitions of Marxism-Leninism."[68]

Modernization scholars viewed the student unrest as a passing phrase or struggle in the process of modernization. In "The Source of Protest in Japan," Herbert Passin, a distinguished sociologist, lamented, "the fabric of consensus is seriously torn" and "politics is sharply polarized" in Japan.[69] Quoting the renowned modernization theorist Walt Rostow's idea of reactive nationalism, Passin categorized Japan as an "old 'new' state" and explained that the Japanese share Western rationality and affluence on the one hand, "assertive nationalism" and "great hyper-sensitivity" of traditional society on the other.[70] This dual characteristic of Japanese society was, to Passin, the source of the student protest for it prompted a historical circle of Westernization and anti-Western reactionary protests.[71] For him, the anti-*Anpo* was another phrase of Japan's historical circle that was rooted in its "constant tension of tradition and modernity."[72] He concluded that the protest against the security treaty resulted from Japan's traditional emotional reactions to changes and progress.

Official documents reflected these assumptions about the popularity of Marxism among the Japanese university students. On June 24, 1960, the US embassy in Tokyo produced a report entitled "Japanese Student Mentality" based on the information it gathered from both Japanese and American sources. It pointed out that common problems of the Japanese students were "the nihilism among the students, the discrediting of older standards of value and the lack of anything in their place, the compulsion toward group conformity, the fascination or fashionableness of Marxist theories, the opposition to any manifestation of militarism, and *the obsession with a concept of 'democracy' that is free of any restraints or responsibilities.*"[73] Their susceptibility to Marxism was identified as a symptom of their psychological resistance to modern values and rationality as well as the failure to adjust to the rapidly changing world.

The problems of Marxism and the student unrest in Japan were also perceived through cultural relativism. After the June demonstrations, *Time* magazine wrote that the Japanese still had unique cultural patterns that were a "mystery to the Western mind," which resulted in misuse of political freedom and going "back to Marx."[74] It stated, "To Occidental observers, the reasoning behind the uproar seemed inscrutably Oriental . . . much is irrational in Japan's politics these days."[75] In Cold War America, such cultural explanation remained a powerful analytical tool to understand events and situations that did not fit to the established paradigm of Cold War culture.

To deal with such problems, Reischauer acted both as a scholar and an American official on campuses, although two were indistinguishable. Being motivated by his desire to encourage the Japanese to share the Anglo-American dialogue, Reischauer aimed to improve the embassy's ties with students, in particular those in the moderate oppositional campuses, and visited universities on many occasions. The Japanese university authorities had been hesitant to invite any American officials, fearing the possible eruption of violence on campuses, but Reischauer successfully gained access as a renowned scholar.[76] *Time* magazine reported, "Ed Reischauer has an entrée to Japanese universities that is jealously denied other foreign officials. In every campus appearance he has scrupulously avoided propaganda but manages nonetheless to get in some pertinent points."[77]

During such occasions, Reischauer skillfully oscillated between being a scholar and an official US representative. At Chuo University on November 16, he gave a lecture on campus based on questions from students that had been collected prior to his visit, which contained a wide range of topics. In response to the question on the difference between American and Japanese students' interests in world affairs, for instance, Reischauer argued that American and Japanese youth did not vary so much in terms of interests in world affairs, but in their attitude. He said, while American students tend to ask what they could do for peace and democracy and the nation and the world, Japanese students tend to look at things negatively and to "criticize rather than to think of a problem as starting with oneself."[78] He also openly criticized Communism as the theory that had "developed into a system in which the emphasis is one the state and its power, in other words on society as a whole, and not on the individual."[79] Yet, in response to the question about Japan's position in Asia, he said to the audience, "I shall deal with it as a historian" and went on to explain the process of modernization.[80] He said, "Society always changes," and that the ideas that people had 300 years ago about our society are entirely different from the ideas we have today, because society itself is entirely different."[81] Similarly, in his message to students at St. Paul's (*Rikkyo*) University, Reischauer wrote, "We must develop our critical capacities for clear thinking, for seeing past words, slogans, and simple theories to the complex realities behind them, and for developing constructive, realistic concepts in place of vague wishful thinking."[82] This time, without making a direct reference to Marxism, Reischauer attacked the inability of "old theories" to comprehend today's society and called for rational and more critical thinking.

THE HISTORY OF MODERN JAPAN AND THE FUTURE OF THE US-JAPAN ALLIANCE

The modernization theorists posited their ideas on the hierarchical dualism of West-East dialectic. Since the mid-19th century, many American intellectuals tried to explain the process of modernization and modernity through cultural pecurialism and "Asia" came to signify an unchanging cultural space that was isolated from the modern world in that intellectual tradition.[83] In *Modernization from the Other Shore,* David C. Engerman has shown that American concepts of modernity had been connected with the ideas of national characteristics and cultural peculiarism. These cultural and national peculiarities were considered a hindrance to achieving the level of modernity of Western Europe and North America. Characterization of Japan as occupying a place somewhere between Eastern Europe and Asia on the barometer of modernity was not new. In 1904, Russian expert George Kennan, a great-uncle of George F. Kennan, for instance, characterized Japan as a "civilized and modern" Asiatic power, as compared to "semi-barbarous and mediaeval" Russia.[84] Between the late 1950s and 1960s, Japanese "in-betweeness" regained its usefulness as a major reference to explain the Japanese economic success and modernization within the Cold War context.

Assuming such ambiguity of Japan's place in the hierarchy of modernity, modernization theorists in the 1960s emphasized Japan's successful modernization as proof that a country with non-Western cultural peculiarities could successfully follow a Western model of modernization. During the late 1950s and early 1960s, modernizationist scholars in the field of Japan studies produced various analyses on Japanese modernization, largely agreeing on the idea that the Meiji Restoration had successfully triggered Japan's transition from feudal Asiatic society to the nation that embraced Western values and its capitalist development model. Reischauer viewed Japan as a "mixed case" that occupied the place between northern Europe and "primitive" Africa, sharing "cultural peculiarities" of countries such as China and Korea.[85] To serve the US Cold War purpose, Japan was expected to be the showcase that would prove "affluence and personal freedom are not necessarily limited to the Occidental sector of mankind but can be achieved by others too," to quote Reischauer's words.[86]

A new look at Japanese modern history was also necessary to help the Japanese play a larger role in the Cold War. Too much emphasis on Japan's colonial past appeared to be inflicting undesirable limitations on Japan's ability to share America's burden. The State Department reported the attempt to send the Japanese Peace Corps to Southeast Asia failed because of its susceptibility to "leftist charges in Japan and abroad of the revival of 'Co-Prosperity Sphere' ambitions."[87] As the result, the Japanese program was revised to be "a kind of 'stay-at-home' Peace Corps program that invited young people in less developed countries to Japan.[88]

Promoting modernization as the universal process of development and Japan as a model for the non-Western societies inevitably led to trivializing the legacy of Japanese colonialism. In general, modernization theorists presented Japan's ultra-nationalism and wartime aggression as a brief period of "aberrations."[89] Historian Sheldon Garon wrote, "The generation [of the modernization theorists] of the 1960s . . . had concentrated on the apparent achievements of the Meiji era. . . . However, when it came to the period of 1931 to 1945, the years of authoritarianism and war, there was a curious void."[90] Modernization theory posited that every country could embark on the process of modernization, a linear path toward liberal capitalism, dismissing their historical diversities. Professor Itagaki Yoichi, who specialized in the study of colonialism and political economy of Asia, insisted on the importance of "drawing a clear distinction between the two fundamentally different patterns of societies; namely, autonomous vs. colonial society" at the International Conference on Problems of Modernization in Asia held in Seoul in 1965.[91] Though Itagaki did not challenge the modernization theory per se, he questioned, out of his intellectual inquisitiveness, the applicability of the theory of the progress in colonized societies, where "Westernization" had long meant conquests and colonization. Critical scholars in the United States voiced similar criticism of the modernization theory that failed to take colonialism into account in the analysis of the development of society.[92]

Despite such criticism, modernizationist views of Japanese modern history was popularized in Japan by Reischauer, under the name of a new non-ideologically tainted "scientific" approach. On May 10, 1962, Reischauer appeared at the Tenth Annual Convention of National Association of Commercial Broadcasters, where he gave a speech titled, "A New Look at Modern History." His speech, which was given in Japanese, was broadcast on national television and published in the *Asahi Journal* on June 10 at full-length. Presenting his methodology as scientific and objective, Reischauer pointed out shortcomings of Marxist theories. Reischauer argued that his theory was grounded on his discoveries and was an explanation of what was taking place, not the prediction of the future, unlike Marxism. He said to the audience, "One can learn from the sad case of Karl Marx how dangerous it is to attempt to do the latter."[93] Besides its scientific, objective nature, Reischauer emphasized the advantage of modernization theory being newer than the theory of Marx, who only knew capitalism of the nineteenth century.

Like other modernizationist views of history, Reischauer's "A New Look at Modern History" focused on Japan's successful modernization. In the speech, Reischauer explained that societies were categorized into four groups. By using his "two-dimensional" charts, he quadrisected societies by placing each of them on a political axis that ranged from "absolute democracy" and "absolute dictatorship" intersecting with an economic axis that run from "completely controlled economy" to "completely free economy."[94] He then went on to explain that Japan modernized itself after the Meiji Restoration, but unlike the "old democracies" of North Western Europe, North America, Australia, and New Zealand, it failed to establish stable democracy. Reischauer stated, "Modernized states, it would seem, inevitably slip off the middle political ground toward one extreme or the other."[95] Comparing Fascist Italy and Germany and the Soviet Union on the chart, Reischauer concluded that militarist Japan was "the least dictatorial of the four."[96]

PROTESTING "THE REISCHAUER LINE"

By the mid 1960s, the debates over modernization theory came to dominate the intellectual milieu in Japan. Marxist scholars argued that modernizationist theorists' interpretations of Japanese modern history was not "value-free" as it claimed. On August 31, 1963, Chinese, Korean, and Japanese scholars issued a joint statement against "American imperialism" in academic and cultural fields. Vice Chairman of the Chinese People's Association for Cultural Relations with Foreign Countries Chu Kuang was probably the central figure in organizing this group in Peking. Ando Hikotaro and Furuya Sadao who specialized in Chinese and Korean affairs respectively were the Japanese signatures of the statement. They attacked modernization theory for promoting "American cultural imperialism." The statement proclaimed, "US imperialism is spreading in various parts of Asia its reactionary, decadent culture and the so-called American way of life to poison the minds of the people and vitiate their militant will so as to insure its domination over Asia in the cultural sphere."[97] It continued, "The Chinese and Korean peoples were resolutely opposing US imperialist aggression, thoroughly exposing its policy of fake peace and its imperialist nature . . . This struggle is closely linked and is in common with that currently waged by the farsighted scholars, researchers, and other intellectuals of Japan against the Reischauer line."[98] They insisted that modernization theory's fundamental objective was to create more favorable conditions for American imperialism in Asia.

At Kyoto University, the protest against the "Reischauer Offensive" was organized by leftist scholars, students, and university employees when the university announced its decision to create a new research institute, the Center for Southeast Asian Studies (CSEAS), in 1962. The plan was first drafted in 1958 and made a rapid progress during Reischauer's time in Japan. By 1962, it had received enough funding from supporters both in the US and Japan; the largest funding came from the Ford Foundation. In addition to its potential contribution to the field of Southeast Asia area studies, the establishment of the CSEAS was also considered to play an important role in promoting a greater "intellectual unity" between American and Japanese academia. The leftists on the campus formed a central committee to organize protest activities against the plan. They accused that CSEAS' fundamental mission was to fulfill the objective of "Reischauer Offensive" to transform Japanese academia into the intellectual ally of Cold War America, arguing that the creation of the CSEAS would be a step toward the formation of "academic NEATO [North East Asia Treaty Organization]."[99]

The opponents of the plan argued that the structure of the knowledge production of the "areas" defined based on Washington's Cold War map would further make Japan a burden-sharing junior collaborator of US "imperialist" policy in Asia.[100] As proof, they cited an official document published by the university's committee to establish the CSEAS that had reported that the researchers at the CSEAS were expected to engage in the studies of Southeast Asia, except Thailand which had been fairly covered by scholars in the United States, especially those at Cornell University.[101] The opponents on the campus claimed that the creation of the CSEAS would erode academic integrity of the university and problematized the center's "political characteristic" that was associated with Kennedy's Southeast Asia policy and the containment of Communist China.[102]

Protesting the establishment of the CSEAS, the dissidents on the campus asserted historical continuity between the official purpose of the CSEAS and Japan's wartime imperial rhetoric of development and modernization that was used to legitimize colonial rule in Asia. The official purpose of the CSEAS that was announced to the faculty members was allegedly as follows: "Given the international status of our country, it is needless to say that it is important for us to conduct academic research on not only the advanced countries but also underdeveloped countries. . . . The importance of studying this region had increasingly grown. Rather, it is considered as the duty of the Japanese to conduct academic research of the Southeast Asia."[103] The opponents criticized that the production of knowledge at the CSEAS was not aimed to support self-determinism and democratization of the region, but its main objective was to find out "How to promote Japan-style 'modernization' in Asia."[104] A group of students at the Faculty of Letters wrote that "By positing Japan as the only successful 'modernization' model, there is an effort to replicate Japanese experience in less developed countries in Southeast Asia in order to prevent Communism, and this is called the Kennedy-Reischauer Offensive. . . . Isn't it similar to the ideology of the Great East Asian Co-Prosperity Sphere?"[105] Despite the over a year-long protest against the plan, the CSEAS was founded in 1963 as Kyoto University's research institute that would cover the studies of Southeast Asian countries, with special emphasis on Burma and Malaya.

The students of Western history at the University of Tokyo made similar criticisms against modernization theory's failure to take the history of Japanese imperialism seriously. At the school festival, *Gogatsu Sai* (May Festival) of 1966, a group of history students held the "Refutation of Reischauer and Rostow" exhibition.[106] It consisted of three parts: "What is Imperialism," "the Modernization Theory," and "Critique on the Modernization Theory."[107] The introduction of the analytical paper they prepared for the exhibition stated, "Is 'imperialism' no longer applicable today? . . . It seems that imperialism exists today with little change in its essence but covered by a different mask, and the 'modernization theory' is such a veil that covers up the essence."[108] The chapter on "Critique on the Modernization Theory" was aimed to intellectually, not politically, challenge modernization theory although, the authors admitted, these two kinds of critique might be indistinguishable.[109] It was indeed a critique of US Cold War policy in Asia. They argued that given the current situations in the Third World, in particular Vietnam, it made little sense to insist that the age of imperialism had ended.[110] They insisted that "It is clear to us that South Vietnam is a *'seimeisen* (lifeline)' of the United States today," in the way Manchukuo was for the Japanese imperialism.[111]

The analytical paper presented a strong argument on the history of Japan and modernity. The authors argued that "modernization" was not a value-free promotion of development. They problematized the definition of "modernity" as the path to the capitalist "bourgeoisie" democracy modeled on former imperial societies. The students argued in the paper, "Today, when we look back on Japanese history of modernization, we think we must not repeat the same mistake of the past."[112] Modernity should not only satisfy the greed of imperialists, they insisted, instead "modernization should be for the people and by the people."[113] The most powerful argument made in the paper was that modernization after the Meiji Restoration must not be admired for having created the Great Japanese Empire, but its "nature" that had "inevitably created the Great Japanese Empire" should be carefully analyzed as a lesson from the past.[114] They went on to argue that the Meiji modernization was the process of Japanese industrialization, but it simultaneously had a deep connection with "plunder and violent extraction committed against the peoples in neighboring countries, like Korea and China, and the modernization theory must be able to analyze this side as well."[115] The students drew an ideological similarity between the Japanese developmentalist imperialism in the past and capitalist modernization promoted under the Cold War and concluded that imperialism was neither a brief period of aberration nor anachronism, but the present reality.

The protest against the CSEAS at Kyoto University and the panel presented at the school festival of the University of Tokyo substantiate the existence of strong criticism of modernization theory among leftist students. Yet, the dearth of Zengakuren-issued documents that directly engage in the discussion of Reischauer or modernization theories suggests that Zengakuren did not mobilize itself fully against American liberal campaigns. The reasons can be only speculated on here. First, such movement against American liberal offensive lacked urgency, compared to issues such as the runway extension plan in Sunagawa and the revision of the *Anpo* treaty. Furthermore, American liberal efforts to combat Japanese Marxism was more subtle than previous American anti-Communist campaigns in Japan, making it difficult to generate public sympathy. Finally, Japanese liberal and Marxist intellectuals could not provide effective theoretical tools for student radicals. After the *Anpo* protest of 1960, according to historian Nick Kapur, many of these intellectuals who had provided theoretical underpinnings to the progressive and leftist movement withdrew from political activism.[116]

Outside the leftist student circle, in contrast, the celebration of Meiji as successful modernization led the Japanese to halt the postwar effort to complete the democratic revolution. Meiji held a special place in the history of modern Japan. Maruyama Masao had argued that the condemnation of Meiji was "future-focused" in his study of "the internal obstacles to the growth and establishment of a democratic polity" after the war.[117] In the 1960s, modernization theorists celebrated the Meiji era as Japan's "take-off" point. It also helped spread the illusion of completeness of the postwar democratization and epistemologically shifted the role of individual subjectivity by identifying modernization as a process that would naturally enlighten the mass to embrace equality and liberty as well as rationality. In other words, democratization was presented as a process that required little, if any, popular efforts. By the end of 1960s, historian Victor Koschmann has argued, "the peculiarly American combination of 'objective' social science and anti-Communist fervor encouraged the trend in Japan away from self-critical concern about peace and democracy toward a preoccupation with becoming a 'great power' through economic prosperity."[118] This preoccupation became a sort of national purpose for the Japanese in the mid-1960s. Economic prosperity became something that could be openly pursued as a national goal once again without raising the issue of imperialism or colonialism, and so was expressing national pride.

American modernizationists' interpretation of Japanese modern history proved effective in fostering positive national self-image among the Japanese. Seki Yoshihiko, Professor of Social Philosophy and also an active member of the Democratic Socialist Party, applauded Reischauer's study of Japanese modern history in the *Yomiuri* newspaper published on November 11, 1965. He wrote that Reischauer's study not only had the "scholarly value of providing objective analysis of Japanese history" but also reflected the "Ambassador's compassion for Japan," his wish to help Japanese intellectuals regain lost national confidence.[119] Seki wrote, "I would like to recommend his book to those who love the past and the present of Japan, in particular those who teach history in high school" and praised it as "the best book that would allow us to overcome Marxist historical interpretations."[120] Modernization theory gave a strong moral endorsement to Japan's efforts to reemerge as a normal state in the international arena. With the past increasingly being redefined, it became difficult for student radicals to establish legitimacy for their anti-imperial movement by referring to Japan's past.

"It became clear in 1966 that Japan had indeed come a long way since 1960," Reischauer stated in his article "Our Dialogue with Japan" published in January 1967.[121] He thought that the debate of modernization had successfully led the Japanese to realize how important Japan was as a nation for "what it might have to offer in this regard to the less modernized countries of the world."[122] In Washington, Republican Senator George Aiken of the Committee on Foreign Relations called Reischauer "one of the highest grade Ambassadors we have in any country" and honored his "open-minded approach to both diplomacy and history."[123] He continued, "Once in Japan, Reischauer launched into his self-appointed task of the broken dialogue in a long effort of intellectual contacts, which soon became known, partly in administration and party with apprehension, as the 'Reischauer offensive'."[124] Indeed, Reischauer had remarkable success in repairing the broken dialogue, not through reciprocal exchanges but by encouraging the Japanese to reach the existing Anglo-American dialogue. By the 1960s, the Japanese largely perceived modernization in terms of technological development and growth in productivity, rather than a social transformation and its modern history was now widely interpreted as a successful model of modernization.

As Reischauer pointed out in the article, the shift away from democracy and peace to obsession with economic growth was not a sole victory of American modernization theorists. Prime Minister Ikeda "drew attention away from the controversial areas of defense and international alignment toward the safer field of economic growth."[125] Indeed, coming into office after the *Anpo* crisis, Ikeda concentrated on less politically controversial issues, namely the economy. His Income Doubling Plan, which committed the government to promoting economic growth, deemphasized political conflicts by mobilizing the nation for economic growth. During his cabinet, the Japanese economy surpassed that of Great Britain, France, and West Germany. In terms of GNP, Japan ranked the world's third largest economy by the late 1960s, only after the US and Soviet Union. These factors were as effective as modernization theory in creating national obsession with economic growth and the depoliticalization of modernity. Supported by the high economic growth of the 1960s, modernization theory successfully motivated Japan's desire to reposition in the world as the model for capitalist modernization. This posed a serious challenge to Marx-Leninist anti-imperialists. The student radicals attacked modernization theory's failure to accurately account the legacy of colonialism and more importantly history of Japanese imperialism, but it was Reischauer's version of history that made the Japanese feel better. Both sides would agree that interpreting history was about a way of understanding the future.

NOTES

1. Edwin O. Reischauer, Letter to Thomas M. Bowman, March 21, 1981. Thomas M. Bowman Papers. Box 1. JFK Library.
2. Michael E. Latham, *Modernization as Ideology: American Social Science and "Nation Building" in the Kennedy Era* (Chapel Hill, NC: The University of North Carolina Press, 2000), 169.
3. Kakumeiteki Kyōsan Shugisha Dōmei, *Zenshin*, August 30, 1960. File 10, Shima Collection. The National Diet Library, Tokyo; *Zenshin* was later published by the Central Core Faction (*Chūkaku-ha*).
4. Ibid.
5. Vladimir I. Lenin, *"Left Wing" Communism: An Infantile Disorder* (Detroit: Marxian Educational Society, 1921), 83. (emphasis in original).
6. Keisei Kurata, *Anpo Zengakuren* (Tokyo: San-Ichi Shobo, 1969), 203
7. Kyōsan Shugisha Dōmei, Tokyo Daigaku Saibō, "*Anpo Tōsō no Zasetsu to Ikeda Naikaku no Seiritsu* [The failure of the anti-*Anpo* struggle and the birth of the Ikeda cabinet]," August 14, 1960. File 7. Shima Collection. The National Diet Library, Tokyo.
8. Harada, "The Anti-Ampo Struggle," 95.
9. Nihon Gakusei Undō Kenkyūkai, *Gakusei Undō no Kenkyū*, 130–1.
10. *Heimin Gakuren* is the abbreviation of *Anpo Hantai, Heiwa to Minshu Shugi o Mamoru Zenkoku Gakusei Jichikai Rengō* (The National Student Federation of Student Self- Governing Associations Against *Anpo*, Defend Peace and Democracy).
11. Takemasa Ando, *Japan's New Left Movements: Legacies for Civil Society* (New York: Routledge, 2013), 38.
12. Ibid.
13. Douglas MacArthur II, Airgram from US Embassy, Tokyo to the Secretary of States, August 19, 1960. RG 84. Box 74. NARA II.
14. Ibid.
15. Ibid.
16. George Kennan, "Russian and American Interests in East Asia," Speech at Pacific Branch, American Historical Association, September 8, 1960. George F. Kennan Papers. Box 302. Folder 16. Princeton University Library.
17. Ibid.
18. Ibid.
19. Ibid.
20. Reinhold Niebuhr, "The Failure of US Diplomacy," *New Leader* 43, no. 31 (August 1960): 6.
21. Ibid.
22. US Congress, Senate, Committee on Foreign Relations, *Ambassadorial Nominations, Nomination of Edwin O. Reischauer to Be Ambassador to Japan: Hearings before the Committee on Foreign Relations United States*, March 23 and 24, 1961. Cong. 87, sess. 1 (Washington, DC: US Government Printing Office, 1961), 2.
23. Ibid.
24. Ibid.

25. E. O. Reischauer, *Wanted: An Asian Policy* (New York: Knopf, 1955).

26. ———, "Nihon no Minshu Shugi ni Tsuite: Nichi Beikan no Kōryū o Zentei ni [On Japanese democracy: premised on the US-Japan exchanges]," *Sekai* 178 (October 1960): 18.

27. Ibid., 19.

28. Ibid., 11.

29. Ibid.

30. Ibid., 17.

31. US Congress, Senate, Committee on Foreign Relations, *Ambassadorial Nominations, Nomination of Edwin O. Reischauer to Be Ambassador to Japan: Hearings before the Committee on Foreign Relations United States*, March 23 and 24, 1961.

32. Ibid.

33. Schaller, *Altered States: The United States and Japan since the Occupation* (New York: Oxford University Press, 1997), 167.

34. George R. Packard, *Edwin O. Reischauer and the American Discovery of Japan* (New York: Columbia University Press, 2010), 151.

35. Haru Matsukata Reischauer, *Samurai and Silk: A Japanese and American Heritage* (Cambridge, MA: Belknap Press of Harvard University Press, 1986), 1.

36. Ibid., 3.

37. Ibid., 15.

38. "Like Coming Home, says Reischauer at Haneda," *Yomiuri Newspaper* (English edition), April 20, 1961, 1. HUG (FP) 73.50. Box 1. Harvard University Archive.

39. John K. Emmerson, *The Japanese Thread: A Life in the US Foreign Service* (New York: Holt, Rinehart and Winston, 1978), 373.

40. Ibid., 374.

41. Schaller, *Altered States*, 163.

42. Ibid., 167.

43. Ibid.

44. Emmerson, *The Japanese Thread*, 365.

45. Ibid., 378.

46. Ibid., 365–6.

47. Ibid.

48. Ibid.

49. Ibid., 366–7.

50. Ibid., 371, 73.

51. Author's interview with Ernest Young, February 16, 2015.

52. Letter from Edwin O. Reischauer to Thomas M. Bowman, March 21, 1981. Thomas M. Bowman Papers. Box 1. JFK Library.

53. Author's interview with Ernest Young, February 16, 2015.

54. "The Natural Americans," *Time*, January 12, 1962, 17.

55. Ibid.

56. E. O. Reischauer, "Nihon no Minshu Shugi ni Tsuite," 20.

57. Ibid.

58. Ibid., 13.

59. American participants of the Hakone Conference included Norton S. Ginsburg from University of Chicago, Marion Levy, Jr. from Princeton University, Robert Lifton from Yale University, and Edwin O. Reischauer from Harvard University. Japanese participants included Furushima Toshio, Maruyama Masao, Nakano Takashi, Numata Jiro and Ouchi Tsutomu, all from the University of Tokyo, Kosaka Masaaki, Horie Yasuzo and Sakata Yohsio from Kyoto University, and Okita Saburo from the Economic Planning Board of the Japanese government, see Koschmann, "Modernization and Democratic Values: The 'Japanese Model' in the 1960s," in *Staging Growth: Modernization, Development, and the Global Cold War*, ed. David Engermann, et al. (Amherst, MA: University of Massachusetts Press, 2003), 227.

60. John Whitney Hall, "Changing Conceptions of the Modernization of Japan," in *Changing Japanese Attitudes toward Modernization*, ed. Marius B. Jansen (Princeton: Princeton University Press, 1965), 14; This is the first volume of the five-volume series published for the Conference on Modern Japan of the Association for Asian Studies.

61. Ibid., 32.

62. Maruyama, "Patterns of Individuation and the Case of Japan: A Conceptual Scheme," in *Changing Japanese Attitudes toward Modernization*, ed. Marius B. Jansen (Princeton: Princeton University Press, 1965), 490.

63. E. O. Reischauer, *My Life between Japan and America* (New York: Harper & Row Publishers, 1986), 155.

64. E. O. Reischauer, "Nihon no Minshu Shugi ni Tsuite," 219.

65. Ibid., 221.

66. Ibid.

67. Memorandum of Conversation, "Padover's Impression of Japanese Intelligentsia," June 22, 1960. RG 84. Box 74. NARAII.

68. Ibid.

69. Herbert Passin, "The Sources of Protest in Japan," *The American Political Science Review* 56, no. 2 (1962): 395.

70. Ibid.

71. Ibid., 395–7.

72. Ibid., 395.

73. Foreign Service Despatch, "Japanese Student Mentality," US Embassy, Tokyo, June 24, 1960. RG 84. Box 74. NARAII. (emphasis in original).

74. "Foreign Relations: The No.1 Objective," *Time*, June 27, 1960, 11–13.

75. "Japan: The Anti-Kishi Riots," *Time*, June 6, 1960, 22.

76. Emmerson, *The Japanese Thread*, 375.

77. "The Natural Americans," *Time*, January 12, 1962, 17.

78. "Lecture made by Ambassador Reischauer at Chūō University," November 16, 1961. HUG (FP) 73.50. Box 1. Harvard University Archive.

79. Ibid.

80. Ibid.

81. Ibid.

82. "Message to Students by the Honorable Edwin O. Reischauer, United States Ambassador to Japan," November 3, 1961," HUG (FP) 73.50. Box 1. Harvard University Archive.

83. David C. Engerman, *Modernization from the Other Shore: American Intellectuals and the Romance of Russian Development* (Cambridge, MA: Harvard University Press, 2003), 3–4.

84. George Kennan, "Which Is the Civilized Power," *Outlook*, no. 78 (1904): 515.

85. Hall, "Changing Conceptions of the Modernization of Japan," 35–6.

86. E. O. Reischauer, *Beyond Vietnam: The United States and Asia* (New York: Alfred A. Knopf, Inc., 1967), 117.

87. Department of State, "Policy on The Future of Japan," June 26, 1964, National Security File (hereafter cited as NSF), Country File: Japan, Box 250 (1 of 2). Lyndon Baines Johnson Presidential Library (hereafter cited as LBJ Library).

88. Ibid.

89. Hall, "Changing Conceptions of the Modernization of Japan," 9–10.

90. Sheldon Garon, "Rethinking Modernization and Modernity in Japanese History: A Focus on State-Society Relations," *The Journal of Asian Studies* 53, no. 2 (1994): 348.

91. Yoichi Itagaki, "The Developmental Patterns of Political and Economic Modernization in Asia in Transitional Stage from a Point of View of Culture Contact with Special Reference to the Vestige of Colonialism," in *Report: International Conference on the Problems of Modernization in Asia, June 28–July 7, 1965* (Seoul: Korea University, 1966).

92. Ron Robin, *The Making of the Cold War Enemy: Culture and Politics in the Military-Intellectual Complex* (Princeton: Princeton University Press, 2001), 222.

93. E. O. Reischauer, "A New Look at Modern History," HUG (FP) 73.12. Box 1. Harvard University Archive.

94. Ibid.

95. Ibid.

96. Ibid.

97. "Joint Statement on the Promotion of Academic and Cultural Exchange," August 31, 1963. HUG (FP) 73.12. Box 1. Harvard University Archive.

98. Ibid.

99. "Tōgi Shiryō, 'Tōnan Ajia Kenkyū Sentā' Mondai [Materials for the debate, the problem with 'the Center for Southeast Asian Studies']," Sengo Gakusei Undo Kankei Shiryō III, 4–92. Kyoto University Archive.

100. Ibid.

101. Ibid.

102. Kyoto Daigaku Tōnan-A Ken Mondai Zengaku Taisaku Kyōgikai [The council for the problem of the Center for Southeast Asian Studies in Kyoto University], "Apīru [An appeal]," Sengo Gakusei Undo Kankei Shiryō, III, 3–351. Kyoto University Archive.

103. Quoted in "Tōgi Shiryō, 'Tōnan Ajia Kenkyū Sentā' Mondai."

104. Ibid.

105. Bungakubu Gakuyūkai, Tōitsuha Jichikai Gurūpu [The friends of the Faculty of Letters, the unification faction of self-governing associations], "Bungakubu Jichikai Saiken no Tameni [For the reconstruction of the self-governing association of the Faculty of Letters]," Sengo Gakusei Undo Kankei Shiryō, III, 4–118. Kyoto University Archive.

106. Letter from David M. Chalmers to Edwin O. Reischauer, May 25, 1966, HUG (FP) 73.12. Box 1. Harvard University Archive.

107. "Teikoku Shugi no Shomondai, Gendai Teikoku Shugi to Kindaika [The problems of imperialism: modern imperialism and modernization], HUG (FP) 73.12. Box 1. Harvard University Archive.

108. Ibid.
109. Ibid.
110. Ibid.
111. Ibid.
112. Ibid.
113. Ibid.
114. Ibid.
115. Ibid.
116. Kapur, *Japan at the Crossroads*, 167.
117. Rikki Kersten, *Democracy in Postwar Japan: Maruyama Masao and the Search for Autonomy* (New York: Routledge, 1996), 119.
118. Koschmann, "Modernization and Democratic Values," 226–7.
119. *Yomiuri Shimbun*, November 11, 1965.
120. Ibid.
121. E. O. Reischauer, "Our Dialogue with Japan," *Foreign Affairs* 45, no. 2 (January 1967): 220.
122. Ibid., 223.
123. Senator George Aiken, speaking on "Our Ambassador to Japan, Edwin O. Reischauer," US Congress, Senate, *Congressional Record*, June 15, 1966. Cong. 89, sess. 2, 13169.
124. Ibid.
125. E. O. Reischauer, "Our Dialogue with Japan," 216.

Chapter Six

Robert Kennedy and Zengakuren

Seeking a Newer World

Between the end of the *Anpo* crisis of 1960 and the beginning of the US bombing in North Vietnam in 1964, the Japanese student movement faced an American liberal offensive and, in the face of it, appeared defensive. Attorney General Robert F. Kennedy's visit to Tokyo and Osaka in February 1962 was a key moment. During his trip, Kennedy made a conscious effort to improve the image of the United States in Japanese society. He tried to meet ordinary Japanese, in particular workers and students, rather than just politicians, government high officials, and business leaders, whom he did not think it was necessary to woo as they were the unquestionable allies of the United States in Japan. What seemed promising for the United States was its JFK-style youthful image that symbolized American liberalism, which would challenge Marxist disdain for America's version of bourgeois liberal capitalism.

Kennedy wanted to appeal to the Japanese public by advocating the New Frontier, promised by his brother President Kennedy in his speech accepting the Democratic presidential nomination in July 1960. A briefing paper prepared for RFK before the trip stated, "One of our greatest psychological assets in Japan is the wide popular appeal of the New Frontier—an image of a dynamic, questing America seeking a brighter future of itself and all mankind. We believe that your appearance before student and worker groups will materially reinforce this image and will dispel many of the stereotypes now held in Japan."[1] As recommended, Kennedy presented American democracy and its historical experience as exceptional, not conforming to classical Marxist historical analysis during his tour in Japan. In addition to Kennedy's effective campaign to counter the "stereotypes" of American liberalism, Zengakuren's post-1960 factionalism and the declining public support and tolerance for its activities made it difficult for Zengakuren to advance its movement against the US Cold War policy.

"WE STAND FOR A WORLD OF DIVERSITY"

Prior to his visit to Japan, the State Department had informed RFK that the popularity of Marxism among Japanese intellectuals was one of the major problems in Japan. The briefing paper, informing Kennedy about Japan before his departure, stated, "One of the outstanding, long-term problems which we face in Japan arises from the Marxist orientation of the bulk of the intellectual-academic community."[2] The telegram sent from the US Embassy in Tokyo to the State Department on January 6, 1962 had also warned the Attorney General that many students, labor union leaders, and some people in the media in Japan would "exhibit standard Marxist stereotypes about American 'imperialism', monopoly capitalism, etc."[3] Because of this Marxist tradition in Japan, it stated, socialism was often associated with "national independence, peace and the full flowering of the human spirits" and capitalism was often referred to the system associated with colonialism, war, and oppression.[4] Kennedy's trip to Japan was thus in part motivated by a sense of mission to correct misconceptions about the United States and capitalist democracy.

Arthur Schlesinger, Jr. provided RFK with a five-page paper titled, "Themes for Meetings with Students," to help him prepare for his trip. Schlesinger, the author of the 1949 book, *The Vital Center: The Politics of Freedom*, was an advocate for "pragmatic" liberalism in contrast to "ideological" "utopian" idealism or radicalism.[5] Invited by Robert Kennedy to join the administration in 1961, after declining JFK's offer of an ambassadorship, Schlesinger worked closely with the Kennedys as a Special Assistant to the President in the White House and played an important role in shaping the political thought behind the New Frontier policies.[6] Schlesinger, a history professor at Harvard and the author of Pulitzer-winning books, was "an intellectual gadfly, skittling here and there to seek out new ideas and sting the slothful bureaucratic beast into action," as the press secretary to Robert Kennedy, Patrick Anderson, described.[7] Schlesinger, who had visited Japan to attend a meeting of the US-Japan Committee on Education and Cultural Cooperation in Tokyo a few days before the Kennedys arrived, wrote to RFK, "The Japanese are a practical people too, and we should therefore be in intellectual harmony."[8]

Schlesinger urged RFK to encourage Japanese students to move beyond classical ideology and correct their stereotypes of the American political system. He also emphasized the pragmatism of mainstream liberalism in contrast to the utopian and prophetic radicalism of the New Left he witnessed in the United States and elsewhere. Schlesinger's "Themes for Meetings with Students" consisted of the following seven points:

1. The role of young people in American politics (including the Freedom Riders).
2. The Things we have done to secure better opportunities for Negroes.
3. The nature of trade unionism and collective bargaining in the United States.
4. The Nature of American capitalism—it is *not* the system of uncontrolled laissez-faire imagined by Karl Marx. . . .
5. The essential American approach to social problems is practical rather than ideological. . . .
6. We stand for a world of diversity in which each nation seeks fulfillment according to its own national traditions and genius. . . .
7. Communism's greatest appeal today is the theory that it must inevitably triumph. . . .[9]

Unlike his predecessors in Washington, Schlesinger saw little value in unconditional denial of Communism and stressed that America's ability to live within a diversity of ideas. He stressed the importance of presenting the United States as the society that appreciated a diversity of ideas and views, contrasting it to the "monolithic" world of Communism.[10] According to Stephen P. Depoe, the author of *Arthur M. Schlesinger, Jr., and the Ideological History of American Liberalism*, Schlesinger believed that the liberal consensus would be "strong enough to absorb the growing diversity of viewpoints in America."[11] In his paper, Schlesinger advised RFK to advance this argument by linking it to the issue of self-determination in dealing with Japanese student radicals. He wrote that respecting diversity of opinion at home and diversity in the system of capitalist democracy was tantamount to guaranteeing freedom for each nation to seek "fulfillment according its own national traditions and genius."[12]

Quoting Rostow's modernization view of progress, Schlesinger identified Communism as a "disease" of the modernization process, rather than its destination. He thought that the future belonged to those who achieve what the United States stood for: national independence, freedom, and peace.[13] He believed that the modernization process would naturally lead a nation "not toward Marx, but away from Marx."[14] Schlesinger thought that RFK had to convince the Japanese that history was not progress toward Marxism. He wrote to RFK, "Communism's greatest appeal today is the theory that it must inevitably triumph; and that therefore, whether you like it or not, you had better come to terms with it or face the certainty of obliteration. But the historical evidence suggests that, on the contrary, Communism is *not* the wave of the future."[15]

KENNEDY AND THE "DEMOCRATIC" EXCHANGE OF VIEWS WITH JAPANESE STUDENTS

With Schlesinger's memorandum in hand, Robert Kennedy and his wife Ethel arrived in Tokyo in the evening of February 4, capturing significant media attention. Reischauer wrote in his report to the State Department, "Attorney Generals' arrival headlined front pages of all major papers. Comment exceptionally friendly and sustained all media. . . . Editorial comment has sympathetic enthusiasm as news coverage and lacks slightest critical note."[16] The Ambassador believed that Kennedy's visit would transmit "a feeling of youthful vigor of New Frontier" to Japan.[17] Reischauer had been concerned that "some mass media people may exhibit standard Marxist stereotypes about American 'imperialism,' monopoly capitalism," but it was Kennedys' youthful and energetic image that spread triumphantly throughout the country.[18] The Robert Kennedy Reception Committee had been created by individuals from social organizations and business and political circles who worked closely with the government to welcome RFK and his wife.[19] Its members included the future Prime Minister Nakasone Yasuhiro, then a young LDP politician, who was put in charge of scheduling and coordinating Kennedy's activities in Japan.[20] Prior to Kennedy's arrival in Japan, the committee had arranged meetings with prominent individuals for him, yet, to their surprise, Kennedy showed more interest in meeting with ordinary Japanese, particularly those in the opposition camp, including the Socialists, labor union members, and student activists, rather than high-ranking government and business leaders.

On February 6, Kennedy visited Nihon University, a private university in Tokyo, to attend an honorary degree award ceremony, where he delivered a speech, "Our Generation, Our World, Our Future." In the speech, he told the students in the audience that American society was not a passing process of evolution, but the living evidence of the errors Marx had made in the nineteenth century. He said, "Roosevelt and the Americans of his generation created a new society, far different from the unregulated and brutal economic order of the 19th century, the order on which Marx based his theories of capitalism."[21] Kennedy's speech contained not only an attack on Communism and Marxism but also by implication that the United States shared the same ideals and aspirations expressed by the young generation of the "free world" and Third World countries. In his speech, RFK emphasized America's historical dedication to freedom, liberty and national independence. He told the audience that the young generation in the world was crucial for the construction of American's world, America's future.

After the ceremony at Nihon University, the Robert Kennedy Reception Committee had scheduled the Kennedys to attend a tea ceremony with the Emperor and Empress at the Imperial Court. However, Kennedy requested cancelling the tea ceremony and asked the committee to arrange a meeting with Zengakuren instead.[22] The committee members grudgingly accepted the request and tried to set up a meeting at Waseda University. Professor Nakatani Hiroshi, who was in charge of handling the university's guest lectures at Waseda, recalled that the university initially declined Kennedy's visit to its campus, on the pretext that students would be too busy studying for exams to attend his lecture.[23] The committee replied to Waseda, "In fact, it does not matter whether students would be Waseda students or not, he [Kennedy] wants to 'talk with Japanese students' so you can satisfy his request by gathering students from other nearby universities as well."[24] Nakatani reluctantly agreed, hoping that the event would be quickly carried out in a small lecture room, yet he soon discovered that this would not be the case. Kennedy had requested that the committee arrange a debate with students, rather than a simple lecture for his visit to Waseda University, and it was going to take place in the Okuma Auditorium, the largest lecture hall on campus with a seating capacity of 2,500 people.[25] For the members of the Welcoming Committee and Waseda, the most troubling request from Kennedy was to invite Zengakuren students to attend the debate session. Nakatani recalled, "It was not in my power to mobilize Zengakuren, so I thought if they come, that would be fine."[26] Yet, during preparation, Nakatani decided to design flyers for the event that would be attractive to the radicals.[27]

In the afternoon, Kennedy and his company, including Reischauer, arrived at Waseda University, and they were escorted to the Okuma Auditorium, which had been filled with students and professors. Probably taking Schlesinger's advice, Kennedy expressed his eagerness to engage in the exchange of views and to listen to dissenting voices in a "democratic way." After being introduced, Kennedy said to the audience:

> The great advantage of the system under which we live—you and I—is that we can exchange views and exchange ideas in a frank manner with both of us benefiting. It is very possible that there are those here today who will disagree with what I say. But under a democracy we have a right to say what we think, and we have the right to disagree.[28]

Students also prepared to debate with Kennedy at Waseda. Having learned about the debate session, student activists at Waseda and from other nearby universities had quickly drafted a paper entitled "Open Questionnaire to Kennedy."

The "Open Questionnaire to Kennedy" consisted of questions regarding the US Cold War policy. The first question was about the provisions of the US-Japan Security Treaty.[29] The students wanted to ask Kennedy whether the US was willing to return Okinawa and whether it had any intention of removing its forces from its military bases in Japan. They also planned to ask Kennedy's view of American democracy, especially the repression of Communists in the United States, referring to red baiting symbolized by McCarthyism, which seemed to contradict the idea of freedom of speech and expression. The next question was about Kennedy's view on the US commitment to world peace, particularly in regard to Asia and the issue of nuclear weapons. The final question was about the issue of self-determination for countries in the Third World, referring to the US intervention in Cuba and support for undemocratic governments in South Korea, South Vietnam, and Taiwan. Commenting on the students' questionnaire, Professor Matsumoto Kaoru, who was in charge of organizing the event at Waseda, later recalled, "In fact these questions were not so violently provocative, rather they were what most Japanese wanted to ask."[30]

The problem was that this "Open Questionnaire to Kennedy" included a long statement reflecting leftist student views along with the questions, which provoked some opposition from other students. When Kennedy made his way up to the podium and started talking, the "right wing looking" students began pushing the two students who had the prepared paper in their hands to prevent them from speaking to Kennedy.[31] Kennedy saw this from the podium and said, "Now there is a gentleman down in front who evidently disagrees with me and the position of my country."[32] Having been invited by Kennedy to the podium, one of the students walked up and began reading the prepared paper to Kennedy. The student began by saying, "The United States, which has this glorious tradition of freedom and independence, who should be a prime force leading these colonial peoples who are trying to gain their freedom and independence, I find, is acting to the contrary."[33] Kennedy told his interpreter to tell the student to get to a question, but the student continued reading the long statement, presenting their views on the issue of Okinawa and finally asked Kennedy how the United States, which was admired for its promise for independence and freedom, could continue "colonialism" of Okinawa against the Charter of the United Nation and more importantly against the will of the people in Okinawa.[34]

When RFK was about to respond, his microphone was accidentally disconnected. The students in the audience started filling the silence with their voices. The student on the podium told the audience to be quiet and "behave as Waseda students should."[35] In the midst of the disturbance, Kennedy started speaking, "We [Americans] were born and raised in revolution. We had many years in which to develop."[36] He then told the audience that the United States did not try to control any country in the world but assist their efforts while respecting the principle of self-determination. He then shifted his discussion to the topic of the diversity of views and stressed that even those students who oppose US policy should have "the right to speak out" as citizens of the democratic world.[37] The audience responded with applause. When Kennedy said that it was impossible for people to freely express different views in a Communist state, some student in the audience called out, "How about in America?"[38] Responding to the student's question, Kennedy stressed that the US was committed to spread freedom and make a better life for everyone. He told the audience that the United States respected self-determination of others and the Japanese people, especially young people, had the freedom to determine the future of the country. He continued, "This world is in the hands of people like ourselves."[39] This was Kennedy's message to the Japanese students.

Photo of students protesting against the visit of Attorney General Robert Kennedy in the campus of Waseda University, Tokyo on January 18, 1964. The placard reads: "We are opposed to Kennedy's visit to our university." "Get out of Panama." "Hands-off South Vietnam." "Get out of Japan, return Okinawa." "End the talk on the normalization treaty between Japan and South Korea." "Against the stationing of F105D, a Yokota rally [to be held] on January 26." © *AP Photo*

Robert Kennedy visited Waseda University on February 6, 1962. Above: Kennedy trying to speak to students at Waseda University in the mayhem that followed the student's "long questionnaire to Kennedy." Below: Kennedy sitting on the podium and waiting for the crowd to calm down. © *Kyodo News Agency*

The questions and long statement, the microphone accident, and probably euphoric excitement generated by Kennedy's visit to Waseda soon led to confusion in the auditorium. The students in the audience began shouting, "I can't hear well," "Stop," "How about the United States?" "Kennedy, go home," and "Kennedy, fight!"[40] His aide told Kennedy to make a final farewell comment so that he could leave for a television show scheduled after the event at Waseda. When Kennedy prepared to leave, a student from a university marching band said in English, "We are so glad that you came here that we are going to sing the University song."[41] In this confusion, Kennedy managed to make a final comment, and then the school band started singing the university song for him. Meanwhile, some students tried to ask more questions and some others continued shouting, "Kennedy go home," "Imperialistic," and "Return Okinawa."[42] After an hour visit, Kennedy left Waseda expressing his appreciation to the university. After he left, a feeling of guilt about what had happened to Kennedy emerged among the audience. A group of students at Waseda organized an informal meeting for "self-reflection on [their behavior] at Mr. Kennedy's lecture meeting" and decided to make an apology to Kennedy.[43] A group of 150 students visited the US Embassy on that day as the representatives of Waseda University students and made a formal apology for their behavior toward Kennedy.

The Japanese public criticized Waseda students for their rudeness to the important foreign visitor. The US Embassy even received a letter to Kennedy from someone identified as "a sixth-grade elementary school student," which read, "I read an article saying that you were jostled in the crowd of students at Waseda University. I felt mortified as if my dear uncle had been spited. I wonder why those people who cannot talk quietly were even admitted to the university. . . . I regret the acts of those students at Waseda University."[44] A female high school student wrote in her letter to Kennedy that she would like to apologize as a young Japanese citizen "for rudeness of college students" at Waseda.[45] Being more sympathetic about the students at Waseda, this female student wrote, "We must not put the blame on only them and we must understand the young people, but it is shame for us to insult visitors from a far country. . . . I apologize to you heartily."[46] Some Japanese people criticized Zengakuren for being undemocratic while praising Kennedy for engaging in a democratic exchange of views. An American official in Kobe commented that Kennedy's "handling of Waseda heckling [was] uniformly praised and undemocratic ill manners [of] leftist students [were] heavily castigated" in the Japanese media and the public.[47]

Some people expressed their concern with the impact of the event at Waseda on the international image of Japan. It was the time when Japan was working to build its positive image as a "normal" country that had made a fresh start with positive aspirations. Historian Sandra Wilson has argued that Japan was trying to present itself as a country resuming its path towards modernity "not only equal to others, but actually at the forefront of the international scene" in the 1960s.[48] Critics who shared such national aspirations criticized the student unrest for harming the country's effort to present itself as a peace-loving modern nation. In the *Asahi* newspaper on February 7, Professor Ikeda Kiyoshi of Keio University, the famed author of *Discipline and Freedom: British School Life*, condemned the student protestors who, he thought, rejected a democratic way of exchanging views.[49] Viewing the student unrest as a sign of Japanese backwardness, Ikeda lamented, "This kind of thing would be unthinkable in universities in Britain, Germany, and the United States."[50]

Other critics shared Ikeda's view and argued that the Waseda students embarrassed Japan by showing how underdeveloped Japanese democracy really was. Some of them warned that their "undemocratic" behavior would be seen as a Japanese betrayal of American postwar tutelage. Moderate students at Waseda similarly criticized the student protestors for failing to respect "the freedom of thought and the principle of democracy."[51] A group of Waseda students jointly sent a letter to Kennedy, expressing their disdain for Zengakuren activists at Waseda whom they blamed for showing "their energies explosively" and disrupting the exchange of opinions.[52] They pleaded for Kennedy's forgiveness and wrote, "Remember that we are now making great efforts to bring up step by step, democratic and liberal spirit in our young minds."[53] In the letter, the students promised Kennedy that they would cultivate "real democracy throughout our country to compensate the faults we made."[54]

The JCP-affiliated members of Zengakuren in Tokyo responded to the public criticism and issued a statement, arguing that the confusion that occurred at Waseda University was caused by violence initiated by the right-wing students in the audience.[55] In the statement, the students advocated that the real purpose of Kennedy's "friendly" visit to Waseda was in fact to encourage the revival of Japanese militarism and to deepen Japanese submission to the United States. They also criticized Kennedy for not answering the questions on Japanese independence and America's threat to its peace and security straightforwardly and avoiding them with his gesture of "youth" and "democracy."[56] Beside this small group of JCP-affiliated students, the rest of Zengakuren remained silent. It failed to effectively counter growing public criticism in the midst of the Kennedy boom.

Reischauer reported to the State Department on February 15 that the incident at Waseda had a positive impact on US policy and the future of Japan. He observed, "unanimous verdict of non-Communist Japanese press, that Attorney General scored major victory in this affair, reflected primarily feeling that contrast between Attorney General's behavior and that of hecklers had further discredited and isolated Communist minority among students."[57] Reischauer believed that the Communist-led student movement discredited itself in the well-publicized event, and this "may have healthy consequences for the future of the student movement in Japan."[58] Reischauer concluded that RFK succeeded in engaging public support in his efforts to counter the challenges of the Communist student movement.

After Waseda, Kennedy continued to generate public excitement and positive comments. Kennedy resumed his goodwill tour of Japan and met with workers and students in the Kansai region. In Osaka, he visited the students at Maruzen Oil Technical High School in the morning and the factory workers at the Matsushita Electric Plant in the afternoon, where he ordered the same lunch as them in the workers' dining room and ate whale meat, which was served as a cheap meat substitute for proletariats.[59]

In Kyoto, a meeting between Kennedy and students from the Kyoto Federation of Zengakuren had been arranged. Prior to the meeting, the US Embassy in Japan had warned Kennedy that "the outspoken advocates of the most extreme leftist views" might be attending.[60] Yet, probably to Kennedy's disappointment, Zengakuren announced that the chairman and vice chairman of the Kyoto Federation would boycott the meeting with Kennedy.[61] Its motivation or argument behind the decision remains unknown, but it was arguably a sign of their weakness facing Kennedy. The meeting between students in Kyoto and Kennedy was held without the two Zengakuren leaders. At the meeting, students emphasized that they were not controlled by any Communist organizations and their criticism of US policy were their own views. Referring to the anti-*Anpo* demonstrations of 1960, the students told Kennedy that their call for neutrality was neither a flight from reality nor an expression of anti-Americanism but rooted in their sincere desire for peace. A student told Kennedy that the opposition against the *Anpo* treaty was in fact not aimed against the United States, and people joined the protest, believing that Japanese neutrality in the Cold War would help stabilize and maintain peace in Asia.[62] Kennedy responded by saying, "A matter such as whether you are going to be neutral or allied is something that is going be decided by the Japanese and Japan, not by us."[63]

Kennedy's response led the students to point out the contradiction between the Cold War reality and the rhetoric of US foreign policy. One of the students told Kennedy that the US support for undemocratic governments in the world and counter-revolutionary actions as seen in Guatemala and Cuba contradicted what Kennedy had said about neutrality being a matter to be decided by countries, not by the US. Another student argued, "If South Korea [under the military rule led by Park Chung-Hee] is called a free nation, then certainly the Soviet Union and Communist China should be called free nations as well."[64] Kennedy responded by emphasizing that the US respected self-determination of each nation and did not force foreign countries to follow US policy.[65] He also admitted that there had been cases that required US interventions such as in Cuba, where Castro had established a "complete police state."[66] Responding to the students' criticism of US support for undemocratic governments, Kennedy pointed out the South Korean case and explained that the US government supported Park Chung-Hee because he had "promised to return to democratic control" and the United States was "tolerant enough" to give Park time to accomplish things he promised.[67]

Kennedy then told the students that their arguments were similar to those made by American isolationists. He said, "We have groups in the United States who feel that our country has become too involved with others, that we should retreat within our own border."[68] Although he disagreed with American isolationists, Kennedy said, he recognized that these people who criticize US foreign policy also had freedom of expression, in contrast to dissidents in the Communist bloc. Whether individuals agree or disagree with each other, Kennedy told the students, the important thing was to engage in a "free discussion," not to "retreat within yourself and just exchange views with those who already agree with you, yell slogans, and march with signs."[69] He believed that a new world demanded cultivating a new attitude, and a willingness to engage in international efforts for the betterment of the "free world." This was his final comment in the meeting.

The appealing images of the Kennedys dominated the Japanese mass media. The *Asahi Shimbun* compared Kennedy to Anastas Mikoyan, the First Deputy Chairman of the Council of Ministers of the Soviet Union who had visited Japan before Kennedy. Referring to Mikoyan as the "Red salesman," it reported that Kennedy was the successful "Star-and-Stripes salesman" with greater mass appeal.[70] During his visit, Kennedy met students, workers and union leaders in the Kanto and Kansai areas.[71] Ethel, who accompanied RFK during the trip, had received wide media attention as the model of a "modern" lady. An American official in Kobe reported that Kennedy's visit to Kansai had created a "*Bobi-Esēru būmu* (Bobby-Ethel boom)."[72] Even the Socialist Party was reported having admitted that Kennedy was a young "understanding man."[73] His popularity in Japan arguably contributed to Kennedy's confidence in the New Frontier's power to weaken Communist influence in the free world. The New Frontier was, Kennedy defined, "the expression of perennial progressive impulse in American life—the impulse to redress the balance of social power in favor of those whom Andrew Jackson called, 'the humble members of society'."[74] Kennedy's experience in Japan showed that American liberalism could be appealing even to those were critical of the US policy.

In the midst of the Bobby-Ethel boom, Zengakuren had difficulty in mobilizing against the US foreign policy and the US-Japan Cold War alliance. In 1962, the issues brought up by the student activists, such as the US occupation of Okinawa and American support for undemocratic governments in the world, failed to mobilize public opposition. Some student activists called for a second "Eells-Hagerty" strike. The choice of the name reflected their desperate attempt to gain public support. Furthermore, the internal divisions of Zengakuren added to its difficulty in mobilizing student activists in various factions. Zengakuren in 1962 existed only nominally. In July 1960, the US Embassy reported that increasing tensions between different factions and conflicting views of strategy and program had "reduced capacity of Zengakuren to lead students in mass action campaigns."[75] The sense of euphoria generated by Kennedy's success dominated the US Embassy in Japan.

After visiting Japan, Kennedy arrived in Indonesia and achieved similar results. On February 15, 1962, the Attorney General delivered a speech at Gadjah Mada University in Yogyakarta. A group of students challenged Kennedy and called the United States a "capitalistic and monopolistic society" in their protest against America's ambivalent attitude toward Dutch efforts to retain its colonial claim of New Guinea.[76] Kennedy replied, "If you disagree with any aspect of American policy, step forward. Now come up and tell me."[77] *The New York Times* reported that Kennedy appeared "tough" and "bristled when students spoke of 'monopoly capitalism' and gave them a lecture on social reform in the United States."[78] Kennedy then repeated what he said to the students in Japan. "It's not that we haven't got faults in the United States or that we don't make mistakes," he said, but Marx's old idea of capitalism could not be applied to the current system of the United Stated that had made tremendous progress, which Marx failed to predict."[79] Kennedy thought that these students used words like capitalism and imperialism to criticize the United States without understanding what they really meant. At Bandung Technical Institute, in response to student protestors, Kennedy told the students they should be "more mature" and understand that they could not have everything they requested and the best thing the US could do was to encourage negotiations with the Dutch government.[80] As in Japan, the general public in Indonesia welcomed Kennedy. *The New York Times* commented, "He hardly converted Indonesia, but the favorable reaction of officials and the almost universal friendliness of crowds indicated that he did some good."[81]

RFK CALLS FOR A "MORE AGGRESSIVE" REPRESENTATION OF THE UNITED STATES ABROAD

After he returned to Washington from these trips, Robert Kennedy became an advocate of cultivating positive views of the United States among foreign youth. At a debriefing with President Kennedy, Vice President Johnson, and Secretary of State Dean Rusk, RFK told them that he had found a "tremendous reservoir of goodwill toward the United States and the democratic way of life" in the countries that he had visited during the trip.[82] Although, he thought, the United States had not taken advantage of it yet. A memorandum released by the State Department on the debriefing reported, "He [RFK] particularly was struck by this situation in Japan and Indonesia."[83] At the meeting, Kennedy expressed optimism and enthusiasm about America's ability to counter the Communist diplomacy which targeted young people in the world. RFK said, "I was particularly encouraged with the many student groups I met. They're not saying everything we do is right. But they're asking questions, asking [for] the truth. And that gives us a great advantage, because truth is on our side."[84] His confidence in America's natural ability to attract foreign youth and its system seemed to have grown through the trips. Kennedy said, "We don't have to say everything is right about the United States—we can admit our mistakes, as the Communists never can."[85] Yet, he regretted, the US had failed to take advantage of this and did not make "any significant contact with tomorrow's leaders, leaving the field open to our enemies."[86] Kennedy urged Washington policymakers to provide more attention to "the rising elements" abroad.[87] RFK strongly recommended to President Kennedy and Secretary Rusk that the United States should engage in "more aggressive representation abroad."[88]

The White House and State Department endorsed Kennedy's ideas. A special committee on international youth and student affairs was convened in Washington, which was soon officially named the Interagency Youth Committee (IAYC) in April 1962. This marked the historical emergence of a "definitive national policy" toward foreign youth in the United States.[89] It initially involved the Department of State, Department of Defense, Department of Justice, United States Information Agency, Peace Corps, Agency for International Development, and the CIA. On April 24, Secretary of State Dean Rusk delivered the news to American foreign posts and informed them about the administration's new emphasis on policy targeting the youth abroad. Rusk reported to the foreign posts that Kennedy's trip to Asia had confirmed the "belief that the phenomenon of youth unrest is worldwide and a serious obstacle to achievement of US objectives."[90] Benjamin H. Reed, Executive Secretary of the State Department recalled that the IAYC "came into being as a direct result of Attorney General Kennedy's trip to Asia in February, 1962."[91] In his biography of Robert Kennedy, Evan Thomas also noted that the creation of the IAYC owed much to RFK's meeting with "critical students" in Japan and Indonesia.[92]

The agency's mission was to make alliances with the idealism and aspirations of the young people abroad. This was now believed to be a crucial Cold War strategy to counter Communist influence abroad. The prominent roles played by the youth and students in demonstrations in Japan, Korea and Turkey had alarmed Washington. Whether or not Communists had been involved significantly, Washington viewed that these demonstrations had encouraged the Soviet Union to expand its efforts directed toward the youth. A memorandum circulated in the State Department regarding the development of an effective youth policy reported that the Communist-run press, *World Marxist Review*, had celebrated "new opportunities now for drawing the younger generation into the struggle for peace and democracy, and for the great ideals of communism."[93] In 1964, the Executive Secretary of the IAYC, Martin McLaughlin, stated in a seminar held at the Foreign Service Institute on the Emphasis on Youth policy, "Our goal in this competition with the Communist Bloc is not to coexist peacefully, any more than theirs is. Our goal in this respect is to frustrate and to destroy, totally and permanently, but without military conflict, the Communist thrust and offensive in the developing areas."[94] By 1964, Washington was seriously engaging in developing effective youth policy to win the Cold War.

In the effort, the US Embassies abroad became "the front line of the youth effort."[95] Until then, the US government had designated youth problems as simply a cultural matter. By 1964, the new emphasis on youth made them a political concern. The State Department ordered the political section of the US Embassies abroad to first identify potential leaders in their assigned countries and then build communication lines with them and learn their political concerns and attitudes so that they could provide Washington perspectives for problems and issues involving youth policy.[96] In Japan, most of these tasks had already been carried out independently under Ambassador Reischauer. At the debriefing meeting held after his returned to Washington, RFK informed the attendees that he was particularly impressed by the work of Ambassador Reischauer and his wife, who had made a "tremendous difference" by engaging in direct contacts with the ordinary Japanese.[97] Reischauer's campaigns in Japan probably convinced RFK that the United States should provide foreign youth opportunities to correct their misunderstanding of American values and systems by engaging in direct communication with them.

In the summer of 1963, President Kennedy gave the IAYC further endorsement. On August 21, the committee sent a memorandum requesting that

President Kennedy issue a formal mandate to give the IAYC, which currently functioned on an ad hoc basis, a permanent status. He stated in his reply to the memorandum:

> I want to emphasize again how important I consider our efforts directed toward young people throughout the world, and therefore the particular significance I attached to the work of the Interagency Youth Committee. It is essential to the successful conduct of our foreign affairs that we reach young people abroad to obtain their understanding and support.[98]

By "youth," Kennedy emphasized, he did not simply indicate an age group, but young leaders and potential leaders who "have a capacity, in the classroom or in the streets, to frustrate the achievement of our objectives."[99] Recognizing the importance of winning hearts and minds of the future leaders, Kennedy promised to provide any additional governmental support necessary for the operation of the IAYC. This memorandum, signed on November 20, 1963, became one of the last documents signed by President Kennedy.

By the end of the Kennedy administration, the dialogue between the US and Japan was not only restored but seemed stronger than ever. The State Department's report on "The Future of Japan," released on June 26, 1964, concluded that Japan would make economic gains and healthy political development in the next ten years. It optimistically predicted that Japan would assume a greater role in the Cold War in Asia, sharing America's burden. It continued that Japan would overcome the most troubling trait of backwardness: political extremism. The report argued that the possibility of "the sudden and unforeseen" revolts remained, but now Washington could be more certain that the "seizures of irrationality in the Japanese character are now happily matters of the past."[100]

The popularity of the Kennedy administration among the Japanese was apparent. When President Kennedy was assassinated, John Emmerson observed in Tokyo that the President's death "shocked the Japanese as if the president had been one of their own."[101] A number of Japanese people visited the US Embassy and formed long lines in front of the Embassy building, mourning his death and offering their sympathy and gifts. Emmerson wrote in his autobiography, "The outpouring of genuine grief and respect, in the form of mass media eulogies, personal calls, communications, gifts, and the unending file of mourners at the special memorial service, together with similar manifestations throughout the country, proved Japanese goodwill for the United States."[102] What the Japanese left termed, "the Kennedy-Reischauer offensive" succeeded in generating positive publicity, making the *Anpo* crisis a thing of the past.

Though the Marxist-Leninist critique of imperialism remained powerful among Zengakuren students, there was more ambivalence toward American democracy among the student radicals. Their resistance to American "bourgeois" democracy seemed to be weaker in the early 1960s compared to those in the 1950s. What made Kennedy successful in Japan was arguably not his challenge to Marxism, rather it was the demonstration of his commitment to American democracy, his emphasis on personal freedom of thought and speech. Zengakuren seemed unable to launch any effective counterattack in the face of Kennedy's liberal approach.

President Lyndon B. Johnson promised to continue Kennedy's programs, including the IAYC. After Johnson moved to the office, RFK left the cabinet to run for the Senate from New York. The IAYC continued to operate under the shadow of the Kennedys until 1973.[103] During that period, Kennedy's memorandum on November 20, 1963 was frequently quoted in the agency's documents as if to remind IAYC officials the spirits of the Kennedys. The new President worried "if youth would go away with the Kennedys."[104] To his dismay, the youth world did move away, yet it was not because of his age but because of US policy in Vietnam.

NOTES

1. Attorney General's Visit, Japan, February 4–10, 1962: Scope Paper. Papers of Robert F. Kennedy: Attorney General Papers. Series 13. Box 260. JFK Library.

2. Ibid.

3. Ibid.

4. Ibid.

5. Stephen P. Dope, *Arthur M. Schlesinger, Jr., and the Ideological History of American Liberalism* (Tuscaloosa, AL: The University of Alabama Press, 1994), 14.

6. Ibid., ix, 62; Richard Aldous, *Schlesinger: The Imperial Historian* (New York: W.W. Norton, 2017), 217–8.

7. Quoted in Aldous, *Schlesinger*, 225.

8. Memorandum for Attorney General Robert Kennedy from Arthur Schlesinger, Jr., Special Assistance to the President, January 20, 1962. Papers of Robert F. Kennedy: Attorney General Papers, Series 13. Box 260. JFK Library.

9. Ibid. (emphasis in original).

10. Ibid.

11. Dope, *Arthur M. Schlesinger, Jr., and the Ideological History of American Liberalism*, 68.

12. Memorandum for Attorney General Robert Kennedy from Arthur Schlesinger, Jr., Special Assistance to the President, January 20, 1962.

13. Ibid.

14. Dope, *Arthur M. Schlesinger, Jr., and the Ideological History of American Liberalism*, 67.

15. Memorandum for Attorney General Robert Kennedy from Arthur Schlesinger, Jr., Special Assistance to the President, January 20, 1962. (emphasis in original).

16. Incoming Telegram from Tokyo to Secretary State, February 5, 1962, Papers of Robert F. Kennedy: Attorney General Papers. Series 13. Box 261. JFK Library.

17. Ibid.

18. Incoming telegram from Tokyo to Secretary of State, January 6, 1962. Papers of Robert F. Kennedy: Attorney General Papers. Series 13. Box 260. JFK Library.

19. A Letter form Yasuhiro Nakasone to Robert F. Kennedy, November 14, 1961, Papers of Robert F. Kennedy: Attorney General Papers. Series 138.2. Box 263. JFK Library.

20. Ibid.

21. "Our Generation, Our World, Our Future," Address by United States Attorney General Robert F. Kennedy at Ceremonies of Conferment of Honorary Degree at Nihon University Auditorium, Tokyo, February 6, 1962, Attorney General Visit," Papers of Robert F. Kennedy: Attorney General Papers. Series 138.2. Box 267. JFK Library.

22. Gakusei Mondai Kenkyū Jyo [Research center for student problems], "Sōdai Kōdo no Tōronkai Mondai o Megutte [About the problem with the debate that took place on Waseda University campus]." Sengo Shakai Undō Kankei Shiryō. File 41-11. OISR Archive.

23. Ibid.
24. Ibid.
25. Ibid.
26. Ibid.
27. Ibid.

28. Robert F. Kennedy, Transcript, "Waseda University, Kyotsu Lecture Hall, Meet with 1200 students at 16:30 on February 6, 1962," Papers of Robert F. Kennedy. Series 13. Box 272. JFK Kennedy.

29. Nihon Kyōsantō Sōdai Gakusei Saibo, Tokyo Tonai Kaku Daigaku Gakusei Saibō [A JCP cell at Waseda University and student cells in universities in Tokyo], "Gakuyū Shokun ni Uttaeru: R. Kennedī no Tōronkai no Jijitu ni Tsuite [We appeal to fellow students: the truth about the debate with R. Kennedy]." Sengo Shakai Undō Kankei Shiryō. File 41-11. OISR Archive.

30. Ibid.
31. Ibid.

32. Events at Waseda: Transcribed from tape-recording. Papers of Robert F. Kennedy. Series 13. Box 272. JFK Kennedy.

33. Ibid.
34. Ibid.
35. Ibid.
36. Ibid.
37. Ibid.
38. Ibid.

39. Ibid.
40. *Asahi Shimbun*, February 7, 1962.
41. Events at Waseda: Transcribed from tape-recording.
42. Ibid.
43. Daily Summary of Japanese Press, February 8, 1960. *Mainichi* (Full), "Written Apology for Confusion at Waseda to be Requested by Students." Papers of Robert F. Kennedy. Series 13. Box 267. JFK Library.
44. A letter from a sixth-grade Japanese student, February 8, 1962. Papers of Robert F. Kennedy: Attorney General Papers. Series 138.2. Box 263. JFK Library; The letter was written in Japanese. The text was quoted from the English translation attached to the letter.
45. A letter from a Japanese high school student to Robert F. Kennedy, February 8, 1962. Papers of Robert F. Kennedy: Attorney General Papers. Series 138.2. Box 263. JFK Library.
46. Ibid.
47. Incoming telegram from Kobe (Chalker) to Secretary of State, February 8, 1960. Papers of Robert F. Kennedy. Series 13. Box 260. JFK Library.
48. Sandra Wilson, "Exhibiting a New Japan: The Tokyo Olympics of 1964 and Expo '70 in Osaka," 85, no. 227 (2012): 162.
49. *Asahi Shimbun*, February 7, 1962; The Japanese title of the book is *Jiyū to Kiristu: Igirisu no Gakkō Seikatsu*.
50. Ibid.
51. A letter from students of Waseda University, the members of Miss. Ohlsen's Conversation Class, February 9, 1962. Papers of Robert F. Kennedy: Attorney General Papers. Series 138.2. Box 263. JFK Library.
52. Ibid.
53. Ibid.
54. Ibid.
55. Nihon Kyōsantō Sōdai Gakusei Saibo, Tokyo Tonai Kaku Daigaku Gakusei Saibō, "Gakuyū Shokun ni Uttaeru: R. Kennedī no Tōronkai no Jijitu ni Tsuite."
56. Ibid.
57. Incoming telegram from Tokyo (Reischauer) to Secretary of State, February 15, 1962. Papers of Robert F. Kennedy: Attorney General Papers. Series 138.2. Box 261. JFK Library.
58. ———, February 7, 1960. Papers of Robert F. Kennedy: Attorney General Papers. Series 138.2. Box 261. JFK Library.
59. "Principal Events of Kennedy Visit," February 4–10, 1962. Papers of Robert F. Kennedy: Attorney General Papers. Series 138.2. Box 264. JFK Library.
60. Ibid.
61. Discussion Meeting with Students, February 8, 1962, Miyako Hotel, Trip Summary, Foreign Service Dispatch from Tokyo. Papers of Robert F. Kennedy: Attorney General Papers. Series 138.2. Box 264. JFK Library.
62. Ibid.
63. Ibid.
64. Ibid.

65. Ibid.
66. Ibid.
67. Ibid.
68. Ibid.
69. Ibid.
70. Incoming Telegram from Tokyo to Secretary of State, February 10, "Attorney General Visit." Papers of Robert F. Kennedy: Attorney General Papers. Series 13. Box 261. JFK Library.
71. Ibid.
72. Incoming telegram from Kobe (Chalker) to Secretary of State, February 8, 1960.
73. Daily Summary of Japanese Press, February 7, 1962. Asahi (Full), "JSP Finds Kennedy 'Understanding'." Papers of Robert F. Kennedy. Series 13. Box267. JFK Library.
74. Address by the Honorable Robert F. Kennedy, Attorney General of the United States of America, at the Earnest Reuter Society, Free University, Berlin, February 22, 1962. Papers of Robert F. Kennedy. Series 10. Box 253. JFK Library.
75. Airgram from American Embassy in Tokyo (David L. Osborn) to Department of State, July 20, 1962. RG 59. Box 216. NARAII.
76. *Chicago Tribune*, February 15, 1962.
77. Ibid.
78. *The New York Times*, February 19, 1962.
79. ———, April 24, 1962.
80. Ibid.
81. *The New York Times*, February 19, 1962.
82. ———, March 1, 1962.
83. Memorandum to [Philip] Coombs from William H. Brubeck, Deputy Executive Secretary, "Follow-up" to Attorney General's Debriefing, April 5, 1962. RG 353. Box 14. NARAII.
84. *The New York Times*, March 1, 1962.
85. Ibid.
86. Memorandum to [Philip] Coombs from William H. Brubeck, Deputy Executive Secretary, "Follow-up" to Attorney General's Debriefing, April 5, 1962.
87. *Emphasis on Youth: Potential Leaders*, Guidance Material Provided for the Use of Military Personnel Overseas. RG 353. Box 1. NARAII.
88. *The New York Times*, March 1, 1962.
89. *Emphasis on Youth: Potential Leaders*, Guidance Material Provided for the Use of Military Personnel Overseas.
90. Department of State Instruction, Subject: Educational Exchange: New Emphasis on Youth. To All US Chiefs of Mission from Secretary Rusk, April 24, 1962. RG 353. Box 14. NARA II.
91. Memorandum for Mr. McGeorge Bundy from Benjamin H. Reed, Subject: Interagency Youth Committee, August 21, 1963. RG 353. Box 14. NARA II.
92. Evan Thomas, *Robert Kennedy: His Life* (New York: Simon & Schuster Paperbacks, 2000), 418.

93. Memorandum from William R. Tyler, Subject: Proposals to improve the Department's effectiveness in dealing with International Youth and Student Affairs, March 21, 1960. RG 353. Box 14. NARAII.

94. Martin McLaughlin, Executive Secretary, Interagency Youth Committee in "Excerpts from Seminar 'Emphasis on Youth' Foreign Service Institute, October 19–20, 1964. RG353. Box 1. NARAII.

95. Memorandum to Mr. Richard F. Pedersen from Robert D. Cross, Subject: Inter-Agency Youth Committee, June 19, 1969. RG 353. Box 1. NARA II.

96. From Department of State, Inspector General, Foreign Service Inspection Corps to Foreign Service Inspectors, subject: The Youth Program, April 16, 1964. RG 353. Box 4. NARAII; Memorandum to Richard F. Pedersen from Robert D. Cross, Subject: Inter-Agency Youth Committee. RG 353. Box 1. NARA II.

97. *The New York Times*, March 1, 1962.

98. Memorandum for the Secretary of State from John F. Kennedy, November 20, 1963. RG353. Box 14. NARA II.

99. Ibid.

100. Department of State Policy on the Future of Japan, June 26, 1964. National Security File. Box 250 (1). LBJ Library.

101. Emmerson, *The Japanese Thread*, 378–9.

102. Ibid.

103. According to Klimke, IAYC's efforts were continued in different institutional and policy forms. See Klimke, *The Other Alliance*, 234.

104. "Inspection Corps Efficiency Reports," August 12, 1965. RG353. Box 4. NARA II.

Chapter Seven

Protesting across Borders
The Vietnam War and the Global 1968

The youth world, which the Kennedys sought to make an alliance with, was revolting against the US "imperialist" policy epitomized by the Vietnam War by the mid-1960s. The IAYC was aware of growing international networks and communication among the youth. On January 18, 1967, it reported that "there exists, of course, a tremendous flow of information and contacts" and "the young Berkeley radicals are said to have been discussing the Provos of Amsterdam as far back as a year and a half ago, before the general public had heard of them; they had their own informal contacts. University students in Japan were found by a visiting Berkeley professor to be at least as well informed as he about the unrest at Berkeley while it was going on" (underline in original).[1] The question was, "Which Americans have a wavelength with whom?" (underlines in original).[2]

The beginning of direct large-scale American military intervention in Vietnam in 1964 galvanized young radicals around the globe to rapidly mobilize against the war. In *1968: The World Transformed,* Carole Fink, Philipp Gassert, and Detlef Junker observed, "Activists throughout the world operated as part of formal and informal networks of communication and collaboration."[3] The escalation of the Vietnam War in the mid-1960s was the single most important event in the Cold War that stimulated the globalization of the protest movements. The young radicals rose up against the existing power structures and systems across the globe, regardless of whether they lived in the First, Second, or Third World. This "globality" of 1968 operated, Timothy Scott Brown argued, "not merely as a temporal designation but as a spatial one; through the combined weight of similar events taking place across the world around the same time, the date 1968, or the decade of the 1960s, are transformed into the world historical event '1968'."[4] The Vietnam War in particular had a significant influence on the rise of a global 1968. In opposition to the war, local and national protest movements converged and transformed student radicals into global players of 1968.

ZENGAKUREN'S QUEST FOR INTERNATIONAL SOLIDARITY

The *Anpo* crisis of 1960 had left Zengakuren divided without a single faction that could alone achieve the position of majority. In 1963, anti-JCP Zengakuren factions Socialist Student League, the League of Socialist Youth of Japan, and the Central Core Faction (*Chūkaku-ha*) of the Revolutionary Communist League formed the Triple Alliance (*Sanpa Rengō*), acting as a separate Zengakuren. The Triple Alliance, the Revolutionary Marxist Faction (*Kakumeiteki Marukusu Shugisha*, abbreviated as *Kakumaru-ha*) of the *Kakukyōdō*, and the pro-JCP factions were the dominant factions that competed against each other for the leadership of the student movement. According to an US intelligence estimate, pro-JCP Zengakuren claimed fifty-four percent of the total Zengakuren membership, representing roughly 372,000 members, and anti-JCP factions, including the Triple Alliance, the Revolutionary Marxist Zengakuren and the Structural Reform Faction, claimed forty-six percent, representing roughly 324,000 members.[5]

By the mid-1960s, Zengakuren's factionalism had proven almost impossible to overcome. The intensifying factionalism was mainly caused by conflicting interpretations of Marxist theories and the split over the best strategies and tactics to adopt as well as personal and institutional rivalries among student activists. Unable to solve factional divides, student radicals had begun engaging in what they called, *uchigeba*, or internal *Gewalt* (violence in German), against members of rival factions. On September 13, 1961, eighty students were reported to have violently raided a meeting held by other factions with wooden staves in Tokyo in order to disrupt the meeting.[6] This wooden stave, widely known as *gebabō* (*Gewalt* staves), came to symbolize the Japanese student movement as violence became more pervasive in the late 1960s. On December 9, 1963, thirteen members of a minority faction were locked in a room and attacked by roughly fifty members of the rival pro-JCP faction at Doshisha University, which resulted in serious injuries.[7]

Despite its irreparable factional schism, Zengakuren still maintained a united front in dealing with the United States and Japanese foreign policy. In the fall of 1963, Zengakuren announced the Japan-South Korea bilateral treaty talks as a pressing issue and called for the total mobilization of all student activists.[8] Zengakuren protested against the treaty, charging that its purpose was to facilitate Japan's capitalist expansion and economic and political domination in Asia. Their protest reached its greatest momentum within two years. Also, in South Korea, there was strong opposition among student groups to the bilateral talk. They demanded an apology and compensation for Japan's colonial rule, instead of the economic cooperation from Japan that the new treaty promised. On March 26, 1964, some 60,000 students marched in Seoul and twelve other cities, calling for President Park Chung-hee to halt the "humiliating diplomacy" with the former colonizers.[9] The protests in South Korea forced the South Korean government to postpone a bilateral negotiation for the treaty with Japan.

With the signing of the bilateral treaty, Japan would provide economic and technological assistance to South Korea in exchange for access to South Korea's cheap labor and markets. By 1963, Japanese exports had reached their highest level, nearly five billion dollars.[10] Japanese demands for overseas markets had grown and generated some trade friction with other countries, including the United States. In November 1962, Japanese business representatives visited Moscow to sign a new trade agreement, seeking to achieve a total of 1.3 billion dollar in exports to the Soviet Union.[11] Historian Kil J. Yi pointed out, "In the middle of Japan's desperate search for more overseas markets, South Korea remained a minor trading partner due to the state of no recognition between the two countries."[12] For Japan, South Korea represented great market potential for trade gains. In addition, the shift in Korean economic policy invited greater attention from Japanese government and business. In the early 1960s, South Korea, as well as Taiwan, began to reject the policy of protectionist import-substitution and embrace trade liberalization through promotion of exports by devaluing its currencies, lowering tariff barriers, and inviting foreign investment and loans.[13] Historian Bruce Cumings pointed out that South Korea and Taiwan became the potential source of "abundant and unorganized" low-paid labor forces for Japan.[14]

For Washington, the normalization of diplomatic relations between Japan and South Korea was an ideal blueprint that could benefit all the parties involved. From Washington's perspective, granting the Japanese access to South Korea's cheap labor and natural resources and opening South Korean markets for Japanese exports would ensure that the Japanese capitalist ambitions could be confined within the free world. For such reasons, the normalization of diplomatic relations between Japan and South Korea was considered mutually beneficial to not only the three parties involved but also to the health of the Japan-centered capitalist bloc of Asia as a whole.

The Cold War strategic concerns also prompted the United States to push for a normalization settlement between its two principle allies in East Asia. Victor D. Cha insisted that the two principle factors that explained the significant increase in US pressure for normalization in the mid-1960s were "rising threats from China, coupled with a deteriorating situation in Vietnam."[15] In

Washington's China, James Peck also pointed out that "the fear that China would be provoked into intervening in Vietnam was a real one" for Washington.[16] With Vietnam increasingly demanding Washington's attention and resources and the growing risk of war with China, the United States wanted economic cooperation between Japan and South Korea, which would allow the United States to allocate its resources to Vietnam.

The Japanese governments' ardent attempt to normalize diplomatic relations with South Korea, backed by the United States, and South Korea's popular resistance further convinced Zengakuren activists of the aggressive nature of the US-Japan "imperialism." The protest against the new treaty between South Korea and Japan marked the highest level of student mobilization after the anti-US-Japan Security Treaty movement of 1960.[17] The Japanese student radicals accused the treaty between Japan and South Korea and US policy toward Vietnam of being the two sides of the same coin, arguing that they were both aimed at subduing local resistance to a future of American and Japanese new capitalist domination in Asia.

Japan's growing willingness to share America's Cold War burden also compelled Zengakuren students to call for an Asian people's alliance against it. In spite of intense factionalism within the student movement, student activists agreed that this "imperial" cooperation between the United States and Japan posed a serious threat to peace in Asia.

The Socialist Student League faction called for Japanese students to play a leading role in "Asian international anti-imperial struggles."[18] In January 1965, the Triple Alliance proclaimed, "Our struggle in Japan would have decisive influence and encourage the students of South Korea and ignite the flames of the solidarity."[19] It proclaimed, "Now is the time when the workers and students in Japan must unite with the people of Asia, especially those in Vietnam and Korea, in the struggle against war and colonialism."[20] In May, the anti-JCP members in Kyoto and Tokyo jointly organized a rally to protest what they called the American imperial invasion of Vietnam and Japanese imperial efforts to make South Korea its stepping stone for capitalist expansion.[21]

Despite Zengakuren students' ample calls for anti-imperial solidarity with the "oppressed" peoples of Asia, it remained largely amorphous, although joint rallies were carried out along with *Zainichi* Korean students residing in Japan and the pro-JCP faction which maintained ties with Communist China. The struggle against the basic treaty between Japan and South Korea demonstrated how difficult it was for Japanese students to realize solidarity with the "oppressed" people of Asia. It exposed Japanese student radicals' lack of knowledge of local circumstances and their narcissistic preoccupation with their revolutionary self-images. For one thing, cooperating with the Japanese, no matter who they were, bore a political risk for South Korean protestors of the treaty. In their opposition against the treaty with Japan, South Korean protestors had condemned a key negotiator of the treaty, Kim Jong-pil, for being "too close to the Japanese" and associated him with Yi Wanyong, who signed the 1910 Annexation Past with Japan.[22] Historian Yoon Tae-Ryong pointed out that such accusations against the "pro-Japanist" were a common way of criticizing South Korean officials signing the normalization treaty in 1965.[23]

Such situations also cast doubt for Japanese students on the possibility of forging class solidarity with Asian revolutionaries. The Central Core Faction leaders pointed out that some of their fellow students raised the question about the applicability of Leninist "international proletariat" solidarity with the Korean anti-treaty movement, which, in their view, was motivated by pure nationalism, rather than anti-imperialism.[24] They admitted that there was a serious "gap" between Korean and Japanese anti-treaty movements and criticized the apathy of Japanese proletariats and leftist groups who failed to recognize this gap.[25] At the same time, the abundance of consumer goods, skyrocketing income, and the jubilant population with regained national pride added to the difficulty for the Japanese left to legitimize its "class" solidarity with the "oppressed peoples" of Asia. In sum, such solidarity posed both theoretical and practical problems for Zengakuren students.

In the early 1960s, Zengakuren also faced difficulty in pursuing Leninist proletariat internationalism, along with students in the Communist bloc through the International Union of Students. While most of the student groups of the capitalist world left, Zengakuren maintained its membership in the IUS and had regularly been sending delegations since 1949. Although the IUS was run by student organizations of the Communist states, Zengakuren openly maintained its anti-Stalinist position since the Soviet invasion of Hungary in 1956 and remained critical of Communist bureaucratism. As the internal schism within the Communist bloc deteriorated in the early 1960s, this "neutralist outlook" of Zengakuren became a serious concern for other members of the IUS. In particular, the Japanese delegates' criticism of Soviet nuclear bombs invited reproach from Communists who ordered them to concentrate their criticism on American nuclear possession and testing. In March 1962, Zengakuren Chairman Nemoto Hitoshi and some other students were reported to have been arrested for staging a demonstration in Red Square in Kremlin against the US and Soviet nuclear testing. At the seventh IUS Congress held in Leningrad from August 18 to 28, a Canadian student observed, "Undeterred by the experience of being arrested in Moscow for demonstrating, the Zengakuren delegation made an energetic effort to secure the condemnation of Soviet as well as American testing [of nuclear bombs]."[26]

Probably responding to the international pressure, the JCP-affiliated Japan Council Against Atomic and Hydrogen Weapons (*Gensuibaku Kinshi Nihon*

Kyoōgikai, abbreviated as *Gensuikyō*) expelled Zengakuren for picketing against Soviet nuclear testing in a demonstration that it sponsored in May 1962. Such experiences with Communist organizations deepened Japanese students' disillusionment with the Communist world and encouraged them to seek an alternative alliance. After declaring their decision to split with *Gensuikyō* Communists, for example, a group of student activists at Ryukyu University called for a peace campaign by joining "the international anti-war struggle by the British Hundred Committee, American Peace Students Association, West Germany's Socialist Students League and Zengakuren."[27]

The deterioration of Sino-Soviet relations and the JCP's pro-China policy further paralyzed the effort of Zengakuren to pursue an internationalist course as a member of the IUS. In January 1963, the JCP-affiliated *Heimin Gakuren* submitted a proposal backed by Beijing to replace the anti-JCP Zengakuren with *Heimin Gakuren*, which had been formed in August 1962.[28] The pro-Soviet Communists in the IUS rejected the proposal, fearing that the replacement of the current "neutralist" Zengakuren with pro-JCP Zengakuren as the Japanese delegate would militate against their position within the IUS because of the JCP-affiliated group's pro-China stance. Such multisided conflicts within the Communist bloc engulfed the IUS and made it increasingly difficult for "neutralist" Zengakuren to effectively pursue internationalism and fight alongside the student groups in the Communist world.

The rise of radical movements in Western Europe and the United States meanwhile had begun drawing Zengakuren students' attention. The common desire for peace was gradually fostering international consciousness among the progressive and leftist students in Western Europe, the United States, and Japan. On April 27, 1962, Zengakuren organized its first major international rally, the International Antiwar Assembly, against the slow progress of the nuclear test ban. A total of 30,000 students rallied in major cities throughout Japan protesting against nuclear testing on that day.[29] They called for united actions by peace activists around the world to pressure the American and Soviet governments to reach a nuclear test ban and control the arms race. Zengakuren Chairman Nemoto recalled that the Japanese student activists engaged in discussion on international solidarity.[30] On that day, Zengakuren for the first time directly appealed to their counterparts in the United States and Western Europe, expressing the desire to forge international solidarity with them.

Responding to Zengakuren's appeal for solidarity, peace activists in Western countries sent supporting messages to the Japanese students. Philip Altbach, representing the Student Peace Union (SPU) in the United States, wrote, "We thank you very much for your demonstration of solidarity with us here" and introduced their activities in the United States.[31] The Committee of 100, a British anti-war organization formed in 1960, declared the "international solidarity" with Zengakuren, and its representative Maurice Henry wrote to Zengakuren students, "As you say, it is vitally important that our movement should be thoroughly international in character . . ."[32] He suggested, "One thing we can do immediately is to hold simultaneous demonstrations in both countries, which thereby become really one demonstration, and correspondingly more effective."[33] The Socialist German Student Union (SDS) also appealed for united action and declared "full solidarity with the efforts of Zengakuren against the Imperialist and Stalinist policies to increase their military force, oppressing all the people in the world."[34] Michael Vester of the German SDS also informed Zengakuren about German student activism and their current task "to prepare a New Left in Germany."[35]

By 1963, Zengakuren students were publishing leaflets and newspapers in English to make them readable for their comrades abroad. The international edition of the Central Core Faction's official newspaper *Zenshin* (Moving Forward) was one of such publications. In the second issue published in November 1963, the Central Core Faction students argued that the Japanese Marxist-Leninist students "need to match new perceptions" of the international New Left that possessed the critical views of both Capitalist and Socialist systems, rejecting "an addiction to slogans, dogma, rhetoric."[36] These publications reflected their excitement about the possibilities of forging international solidarity between the Japanese student left and the New Left in the United States. They proclaimed, "We are told solidarity bet. [between] US & Japanese workers & People is unrealistic. Our way may be long. But we must. [We were] glad to hear [Howard] Zinn say there is new independent radicalism in America."[37] By the end of 1964, the Central Core Faction was regularly publishing international editions of its bulletins and reporting on Zengakuren activities in English.

WE ARE THE PEOPLES OF THE EMPIRES: THE VIETNAM WAR AND ANTI-IMPERIAL SOLIDARITY

The passage of the Tonkin Gulf Resolution of August 7, 1964, and the subsequent US bombings of North Vietnam that officially began on March 2, 1965, made Vietnam the focal point of radical movements everywhere. The first major anti-Vietnam War protest by Japanese students took place on April 22 against the arrival of the chairman of the State Department's Policy Planning Council, Walt W. Rostow who advocated US military intervention to combat Communist insurgencies in Vietnam. The *Christian Science Monitor* reported that the purpose of his visit to Japan was to encourage the Japanese to "stand

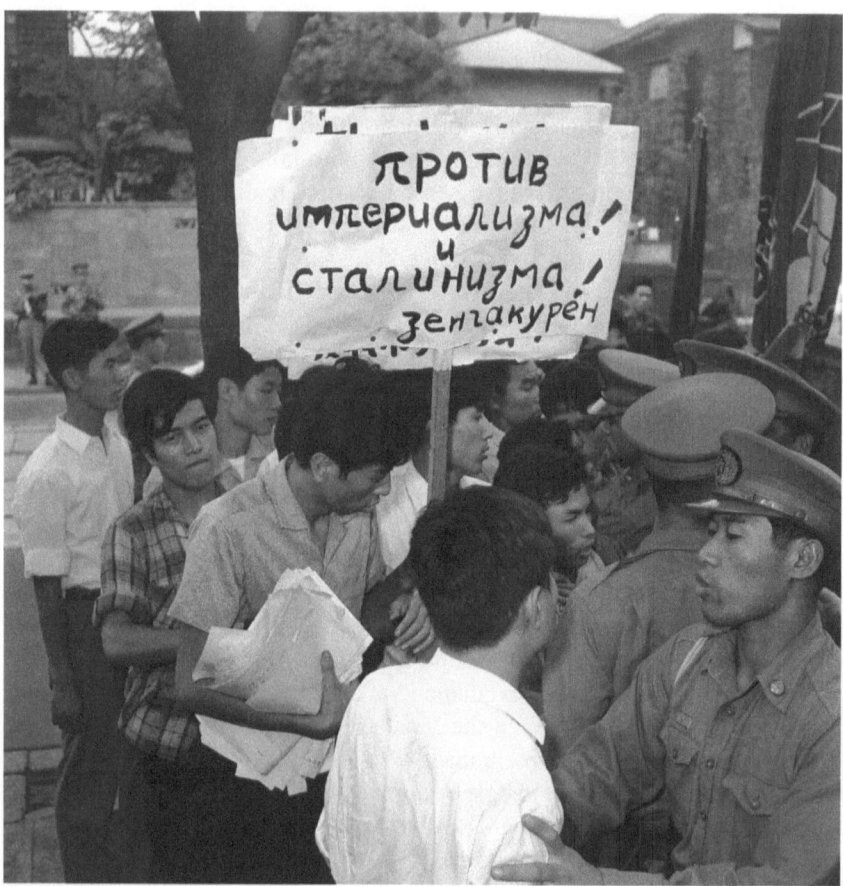

Photo of Zengakuren students protesting against the Soviet resumption of nuclear testing in front of the Soviet Embassy in Tokyo on September 8, 1961. The placard in Russian reads, "Against Imperialism and Stalinism! Zengakuren." The "neutralist outlook" of Zengakuren became a concern for the other member of the International Union of Students. © *AP Photo*

as a shining example of liberal democracy in Asia."[38] At the Haneda Airport, the JCP-affiliated Zengakuren students gathered to protest his arrival, raising a banner that read, "Rostow Go Home."[39] The *Los Angeles Times* reported that 700 students snake-danced inside the airport and another 900 protested outside.[40] The police arrived to disperse the crowd of protestors and forcibly removed the students from the observation tower.[41] Because of the protest, Rostow was forced to cancel a press conference scheduled at the airport.[42]

Rostow had planned to visit university campuses in Japan, but Japanese university authorities preemptively withdrew their initial acceptance of Rostow's offer to deliver a speech on their campuses, fearing possible disruptions.

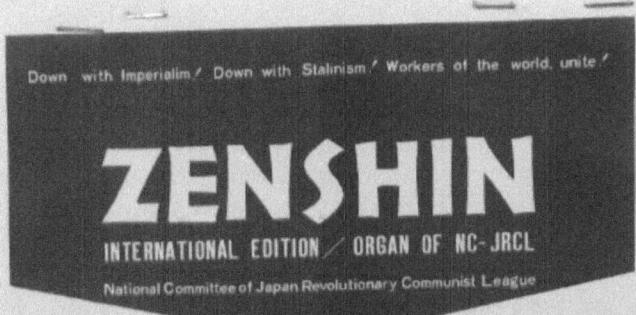

CONTENTS

THIRD NATIONAL CONGRESS
OF NC-JRCL

On the Fundamental Features of Situation
at home and International -- 2nd Report
On the Task of the Revolutionary Left Wing
in the crisis of the class struggle
-- 3rd Report

* * * * * * * * * * * *

Red Guards and Bankruptcy of Chinese
Stalinism ----- TAKEYO TAKEI
Socialism and Stalinism - Introduction
of 'profits' and Russian Stalinism
at standstil ----- KATSU YAMAMURA
CONTRIBUTION FROM USA
State Capitalism and Marx's Humanism or
Philosophy and Revolution
-- RAYA DUNAYEVSKAYA

MARCH, 1967   No.4
ZENSHINSHA, 1-50 Ikebukuro-higashi, Toshima-ku, Tokyo

A front cover of the international edition of *Zenshin* published by the Central Core Faction of Zengakuren. March 1967. Box 112. Library of Social History. Hoover Institution Archives, Stanford CA.

The chair of the Department of Economics at Kyoto University, Kishimoto Eitaro, said, "We feared student protests would break out on campus since he [Rostow] is known as the hard-liner on the Vietnam War and it had been confirmed that he will be meeting political and economic elites in Japan. We cannot allow him to bring political activities to the campus."[43] Probably feeling sorry for Rostow, fourteen scholars in Kyoto held a meeting with Rostow at Miyako Hotel to compensate him for the cancellation of on-campus talks. On that day, 300 student protesters rallied against Rostow outside the hotel.[44]

Many ordinary citizens in Japan also disapproved of the US military intervention in Vietnam. According to the survey conducted by the *Asahi* newspaper in August 1965, ninety-four percent of 3,000 respondents were aware of the conflict in Vietnam, and seventy-five percent of them disapproved of the US bombings of North Vietnam while only four percent approved.[45] In July 1966, Prime Minister Sato demanded of the Japanese public that an "increasing recognition should be made of the fact that the US is making a major contribution to security in the Far East, including my country."[46] Despite the unpopularity of America's war in Vietnam among the general public, Sato remained firmly supportive of the war, along with members of the ruling conservatives of the LDP. In particular, the LDP party's Asian Problems Study Group, which consisted of party members including those who had been closely associated with anti-Communists of the 1930s, gave firm support for the US policy in Vietnam, and Sato went along with this group.[47] Besides the concern with Communist expansionism, Sato feared that any Japanese hesitation to support the war would lead the US to bar Japanese products from American domestic market and make Americans more reluctant to give up Okinawa.

In addition, Japanese businesses also understood the risk of losing American support and followed the government's decision. After the US bombing of North Vietnam, Japanese shipping companies voluntarily suspended service to Hanoi. Between January and December 1965, Japanese exports to North Vietnam had totaled $11,456,000 and imports amounted $3,853,000.[48] The Japanese decision to halt trade with Hanoi and the devastated economy of North Vietnam due to the war eventually reduced trade between Japan and North Vietnam to a miniscule amount. Meanwhile, overall Japanese exports to other parts of Southeast Asia grew. Exports to South Vietnam skyrocketed from $37 to $138 million dollars between 1965 and 1966.[49] At the end of 1966, the Director of the Japanese Economic Planning Agency, Miyazawa Kiichi, estimated the overall Japanese economic benefits of the US military expenditures in Vietnam would reach $800 million in 1966.

It was widely known among the Japanese that the brutal violence in Vietnam had a profound link with the US-Japan Security Treaty and the US occupation of Okinawa. In *Fire Across the Sea,* Thomas R. H. Havens described Japan as America's "silent partner" in the Vietnam War for its significant but inconspicuous direct and indirect involvement. The US military bases and facilities in Japan were indispensable for the US fight in Vietnam, especially those in Okinawa, which was considered "the key stone of the Pacific" for the United States.[50] In March 1965, the first 15,000 American Marine and Army combat troops landed in Vietnam from Okinawa.[51] According to Havens, about 50,000 troops were regularly stationed in the Ryukyu islands, a logistical command center in Okinawa handled 400,000 tons of goods for the American troops, and the runways of the Kadena Airbase were used for taking off or landing every three minutes during the Vietnam War.[52] The jungles of Okinawa, moreover, served as training areas for not only American troops but also those from South Vietnam, the Philippines, Thailand, Taiwan, and South Korea that fought against Hanoi along with American troops.[53] In mainland Japan, US military bases and facilities, including the ports in Sasebo, military hospitals in Tokyo, the Tachikawa Airbase that hosted the 315th Air Transport Group, and communication centers in Kanagawa, all contributed to America's war effort in Vietnam.[54] Together with those in Okinawa, these US military facilities in mainland Japan, as Havens pointed out, "formed a network coordinated from Hawaii that was quickly activated to support Gen. William C. Westmoreland's military assistance command in Vietnam in early 1965."[55] The United States considered such cooperation "normal and expected" under the US-Japan Security Treaty.[56]

The close alliance between Japan and the United States compelled many Japanese to join the antiwar movement. One of the largest antiwar organizations developed in Japan was the Peace for Vietnam! Committee (*Betonamu ni Heiwa wo! Shimin Rengo*) formed in April 1965, which is more widely known as Beheiren.[57] The principle figures of Beheiren included Oda Makoto, Anai Fumihiko, Furuyama Yozo, Iida Momo, Muto Ichiyo, Takabatake Toshimichi, Tsurumi Shumsuke, and Yoshikawa Yuichi; many of them were in their thirties and forties. Beheiren was a non-partisan organization which grew out of the Voiceless Voices (*Koenaki Koe no Kai*) organized by intellectuals and novelists during the demonstrations against the US-Japan Security Treaty of 1960. The members of Beheiren came from various backgrounds. Iida and Yoshikawa had been members of the JCP and Muto had worked at the *Gensuikyō*. As Oda described it, Beheiren was miscellaneous, consisting of independent voluntary action-oriented groups. Rejecting factionalism, Beheiren welcomed anyone, regardless of their political or organizational affiliations, to join its movement to stop the war in Vietnam. A week after the formation of Beheiren in Tokyo, another Beheiren was established in Kyoto, followed by many other regional ones. Probably comparing Beheiren to other leftist organizations including Zengakuren, Oda said, "These groups do not take orders from anyone. Beheiren Tokyo is by no means a headquarter as in the way regional Beheiren groups are not branches. Sometimes, there are two Beheiren groups in one university campus, but there is no conflict over which is legitimate, and which is not."[58] Student activists also participated in Beheiren's demonstrations and activities. Beheiren and anti-JCP Zengakuren came to form a loose organizational association in their opposition against the Vietnam War.[59] Oda considered Beheiren to be a movement, rather than an organization.

Beheiren soon emerged as the forefront of trans-Pacific antiwar activism through its considerable effort to build a transnational network between American and Japanese antiwar activists. On April 24, when Beheiren organized its first major anti-Vietnam rally, it invited Philip Altbach of SPU. Altbach spoke in front of the crowd of somewhere between 1,000 and 1,500 on that day.[60] For many Beheiren activists, the American New Left epitomized a mass movement that they hoped to establish. Iida later recalled that she was struck by the American New Left described by Altbach, in particular its source of inspiration, which was "not Marx, Trotsky, Stalin, nor Max Shachtman, but [Albert] Camus, Paul Goodman, Bob Dylan, and the Student Nonviolent Coordinating Committee (SNCC)."[61] About a month later, Beheiren announced another antiwar demonstration on May 22 and named it "The First Japan-US Joint Demonstration," corresponding to the first Vietnam Teach-in organized by the Vietnam Day Committee (VDC) in Berkeley, California. 2,000 people were reported to have participated in the demonstration, which marked the largest march to date organized by Beheiren.[62] The picture image of the demonstration in Japan was later used by the VDC in its leaflet for the International Days of Protest on October 15 and 16 of that year at Berkeley.[63]

Beheiren members also traveled to the United States, facilitating the trans-Pacific flow of ideas and protests. Having observed a campus-based teach-in in Ann Arbor, Michigan, when he attended an international conference entitled "Alternative Perspectives on Vietnam," Oda organized their first teach-in at Akasaka Prince Hotel in Tokyo between August 14 and 15, inviting six hundred delegates. American representatives included individuals like Carl Oglesby, a former Students for a Democratic Society (SDS) leader.[64] It was nationally televised and attained "an audience of unprecedented magnitude."[65] In the US, the New York-based progressive weekly *National Guardian* provided coverage of the teach-in.[66] A month after the teach-in, Oda and Tsurumi Yoshiyuki traveled to the United States to attend an international conference on "Alternative Perspectives on Vietnam" held between September 14 and 18, organized by faculty and students at the University of Michigan. Beheiren sought to build an international antiwar mass movement that was organized around individuals' autonomous actions and the universal principle of humanity, rather than Marxist-Leninist anti-imperial "solidarity," which was the "shop-worn" word that Oda disliked.[67]

Zengakuren meanwhile sought international anti-imperial solidarity with the radicals in the West. Unlike Beheiren, Zengakuren framed their international solidarity in the contexts of war and imperialism. High economic

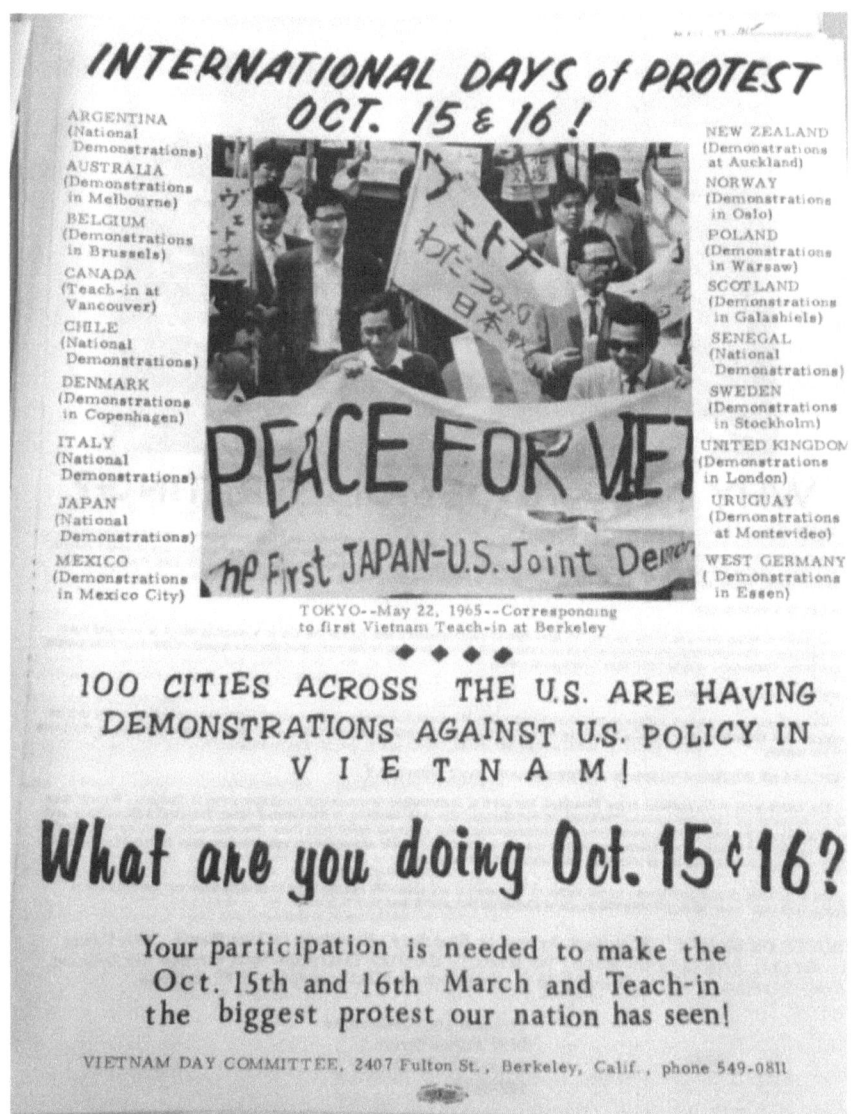

A leaflet by the Vietnam Day Committee in Berkeley, CA with the picture image of the anti-Vietnam War protest in Japan. *Box no. 60. Hardin Blair Jones papers. Hoover Institution Archives, Stanford CA.*

growth and deepening economic cooperation with the Western capitalist countries as epitomized by Japan's participation in the Organization for Economic Cooperation and Development (OECD) deepened the student left's conviction that Japanese imperialism had become *Jiritsu shita teikoku shugi* (full-grown, self-reliant imperialism). Zengakuren activists insisted on the importance of forming solidarity between the anti-imperial struggles within the empires and the liberation movements in the Third World in order to end the bourgeoisies' domination of the world. In its English-written bulletin published in October 1965, Zengakuren proclaimed:

> Since imperialists of US, Great Britain, Japan, West Germany and France are in international concert with local bourgeoisies of South Vietnam, South Korea, Philippines and Formosa in order to control politically and economically Asian people, American friends, as of Students for Democratic Society, British Committee of a Hundred, Japanese Zengakuren and other friends must fight in international solidarity with South Vietnamese National Liberation Front and Students Union of South Korea etc.[68]

Zengakuren's internationalism reflected its determination to engage in the global class struggle and challenge the structure of oppression by striking the empires from within.

ZENGAKUREN AND "PRACTICAL COOPERATION" WITH AMERICANS

During 1966, transnational activism blossomed through common opposition against the Vietnam War. Beheiren played a crucial role in providing Japanese antiwar activists with firsthand experience interacting with the "other America" by inviting American dissidents who opposed the war. On April 24, 1966, the members of the Committee for Non-Violent Action (CNVA) from the United States, including the eighty-two-year-old pacifist A. J. Muste visited Japan to join Beheiren's antiwar rally in Tokyo.[69] In June, Howard Zinn and Ralph Featherstone of SNCC traveled throughout Japan with Beheiren members to speak against the war. Zinn recalled, "Ralph and I traveled north to south through Japan, from Hokkaido to Hiroshima and Fukuoka, and across the East China Sea to Okinawa. We spoke at fourteen universities in nine different cities, at big meetings and small ones, at tea gatherings and beer sessions, with trade unionists and housewives."[70] Throughout the trip, Zinn and Featherstone engaged in conversations with Japanese student activists and answered their questions such as those about Beatniks and the peace movements in the US.[71] In Sendai, their talk gathered over 1,000 people in the audience, and somewhere between fifty and sixty students remained after the event to continue their conversation with Zinn and Featherstone, which lasted past midnight.[72] They spoke in front of a total of 15,000 Japanese during their Japan tour between June 1 and 15.[73] Muto Ichiyo, a Beheiren member, recollected that Zinn and Featherstone brought "thought shock" to Japan's antiwar movement. Without citing Marxist theories, Muto wrote, Zinn eloquently made the radical argument that the Vietnam War, or any other aggressive foreign policy was not paradoxical to American liberalism; rather, it was rooted in American liberalism, on which Japanese "postwar democracy" was based.[74] This experience led Muto to conclude that Japanese popular movements should no longer concentrate on the defense of this "postwar" democracy; rather, it must aim to expand or replace it with a new democracy, something more direct, as Zinn and the American New Left had been trying to achieve in the US.[75]

Unlike Beheiren members, Zengakuren students tried to figure out whether this political alliance between American and Japanese radicals could be an ideological affinity as well. Having attended a meeting with Zinn and Featherstone, the leader of the Revolutionary Marxist faction, Kinoshita Hiroshi, the International Secretary of Zengakuren, Kawahara Hiroshi, and the Chief Editor of Waseda University Newspaper, Terada (first name unknown), jointly wrote a letter to Zinn, making inquiries about American radicalism. Misunderstanding SNCC as a basically anti-Vietnam War organization because of the word "non-violence" in its name, they asked Zinn how SNCC was trying to develop the black liberation struggle within the anti-Vietnam War movement and its relation with the Berkeley Vietnam Day Committee and SDS.[76] They attempted to gain insight into the ideological orientation of American radicals by asking where SNCC stood in relation to "Marx's proletarian philosophy and John Dewey's pragmatism."[77] Although much remained unknown by the Japanese students about American radicalism, the letter reflected Zengakuren students' desire to form what they called "practical cooperation" with American radicals through their common opposition to aggressive capitalist imperialism.[78]

Between August 11 and 13, Beheiren held the Two-Nation Conference for Peace in Vietnam and invited American antiwar activists from a broad range of political views. Nine American antiwar activists traveled to Japan to attend the conference: the editor of the journal *Liberation*, David Dellinger; staff member of the War Resisters League (WRL), David McReynolds; Executive Director of the Committee for a SANE Nuclear Policy (SANE), Donald Keys; Boston University professors Howard Zinn and Murray Levin, Zinn's wife Roslyn, and Rabbi Israel Dresner; Robert Ockene of the Veterans and Reservists to End the War in Vietnam; and Quentin Bassett of America's

SDS.[79] Sixty-one Japanese representatives from a wide range of groups attended the conference, including an actress, Buddhist monks, university professors, artists, doctors, high schools students, and literary critics. In addition, there were fifteen observers from Argentina, Britain, Canada, France, India, Mongol, Pakistan, and the Soviet Union. 1,600 people packed the Sankei International Conference Hall in Tokyo for the two nation antiwar event.[80] At the final phrase of the two-nation conference, Dellinger and Oda, as the representatives of American and Japanese participants, signed the US-Japan Antiwar Peace Citizens' Treaty, as opposed to the US-Japan Security Treaty, declaring their opposition against the Vietnam War based on "moral conscience and human justice."[81] The conference gathered a wide range of antiwar protestors from many countries and was widely reported by the media. The success of the Two-Nation Conference manifested to the Japanese activists the possibility of building a global radical movement.

The flow of contacts and growing knowledge of radical movements across the Pacific mutually shaped the ways the student activists imagined their movement beyond Vietnam. In the United States, Allan Greene, a Baltimore SDSer, wrote a position paper on "SDS and the Japanese New Left," which was published in SDS's *New Left Notes* on August 19. Requesting for SDS to act more with other political and cultural organizations, Greene wrote, "Other student movements in other areas of the world are also moving toward these conclusions. Perhaps the most promising of the movements is the militant Zengakuren. . . ."[82] Greene described Zengakuren's radical Marxist critique of society and capitalism as an exemplar of radical critique developed outside the authoritarian framework of the Cold War that leads to radical action. He wrote, "SDS, SNCC, are radical *precisely* because they have moved in the direction of consciously tying up issues."[83] Greene advocated for closer relationships between SDS and SNCC and Zengakuren, which would allow them to compare experiences, common problems and issues, differences and theories of change.[84]

In a world engulfed in a wave of new radicalism, the engagement in local struggles with the US power deepened the global consciousness of the student radicals in Japan. Ishii Eiki, a former Zengakuren activist, recalled that words such as "the world (*sekai*)" and "international (*kokusai*)" became more frequently used among the student radicals in 1968.[85] The international "revolutionary" events such as the Prague Spring, Paris May, and the Chicago Democratic Convention, for instance, provided a global context for their ongoing local struggles. Believing that worldwide protests and mobilizations against imperialism would eventually bring about the crisis of liberal capitalism, Zengakuren students tried to reach out to their counterparts abroad. In 1968, a Zengakuren faction chaired by Matsumoto Reiji held the International Antiwar Conference between August 1 and 3, 1968, at Chuo University in Tokyo. To invite international participants, Kudo Kohei, then a member of Matsumoto's faction, traveled abroad. Kudo first flew to Rome where he unfortunately found an empty campus due to summer vacation. He then moved to Frankfurt looking for the German SDS office but was told that its main organizers were in London to attend a European student conference.[86] In Paris, Kudo met with the leaders of a French student group called the Revolutionary Communist Youth (JCR) and witnessed the French May revolt. He then traveled to London, Spain, Havana, Mexico, and Canada before he came back to Tokyo.[87] On the day of the conference, a total of about 2,000 representatives, including those from American SDS, SNCC, German SDS, and the JCR of France, attended, pledging their solidarity against the imperialist war.[88] Matsumoto stated in his opening speech that one of the purposes of the conference was to transform the anti-imperial movements that were simultaneously happening throughout the world into a single global movement.[89] Foreign participants seemed to share the idea. Ken Cloke, who represented American SDS at the conference, wrote that despite many differences between SDS and Zengakuren, "The inexorable fact of world history is that we are being moved closer together as imperialists around the world group together in joint defense," in his article on Japanese Zengakuren published in the September 16 issue of *New Left Notes*.[90] Cloke stated, "We have to recognize that America cannot merely be transformed at home, since it does not exist only within the boundaries of the US," calling for a global revolution to change the United States and the world as a whole.[91]

While Japanese student radicals increasingly put emphasis on framing their activism within global contexts, they possessed no consensus on how to transform their local protests into a global one. Reporting on the International Antiwar Conference for the *Kyoto Daigaku Shimbun* (Kyoto University Newspaper), Murauchi Mareto wrote that there was an important question raised in the conference: How could the local or regional struggles be fought within a global movement?[92] In response, American SDSers suggested for Japanese students to be a part of the antiwar movement of the American GIs in Japan and address the problem of race and exploitation, but Murauchi wrote that he felt it would only mean to fight an American struggle, not an international one. He went on, "Of course, it is an important issue, . . . but the question is 'how we [the Japanese radicals] can fight our own struggles for ourselves' within a global revolutionary movement?"[93] No one seemed capable of answering such questions.

By the mid-1960s, Washington faced increasing criticism of the US policy in Vietnam. People at home were organizing large-scale antiwar demonstrations and engaging in various forms of protests against the war. The demonstration hosted by the Spring Mobilization Committee to End the War in Vietnam in

New York on April 15, 1967, for instance, gathered over 100,000 participants. American officials often faced severe criticism against the war when they visited foreign countries. In Malaysia, antiwar protestors greeted President Johnson with banners that criticized "US imperialists in Asia" during his Southeast Asian tour in the fall of 1966.[94] At Oxford University in England, a student protest against American bombing raids in Vietnam forced Robert Kennedy, who was visiting the campus, to defend the US position by saying that people had to "recognize that the Government of North Vietnam also has a responsibility" over the situation in Vietnam.[95]

Despite intensifying criticism of the US policy in Vietnam, the war showed no sign of de-escalation. The number of American servicemen in South Vietnam increased from 184,000 at the end of 1965 to 400,000 by 1967. In January 1967, 6,978 Americans were killed in action and 39,977 had been wounded since January 1961.[96] In the first week of February 1966, the Vietcong death toll was 1,541, more than five times larger than the allied side.[97] In April 1967, the Joint Chiefs of Staff endorsed General William Westmoreland's request for an additional 100,000 American troops. The US government estimated that defense would account for 55 percent of the national budget, around $75.5 billion, and Vietnam was costing an average of $20 billion per year by the middle of 1967.[98] The national expenditure was estimated to increase from $153.6 billion in fiscal year 1967 to $169.2 billion in fiscal year 1968 and $5.8 billion out of the $15.6 billion hike was to cover the growing costs of Vietnam and other national defense spending.

The US military bases and facilities in Japan directly exposed the Japanese in the area to the horrific images of warfare in Vietnam. The escalation of the Vietnam War led to a rise in the number of American casualties transferred from Vietnam to American military bases in Japan. Seventy percent of the wounded American soldiers in Vietnam were transferred to US military hospitals in the Kanto region in Japan.[99] Okinawa provided temporary mortuaries for dead soldiers.[100] Okinawan base workers, mostly female workers, worked at these transshipment points. They cleaned the corpses of American soldiers before they were transported to their families in the United States. For many Japanese, especially those living in the areas that hosted American military facilities, it was not a distant war.

AMERICAN MILITARY BASES IN JAPAN AND TRANSNATIONAL SPACES OF DISSENT

Between 1967 and 1968, as the anti-Vietnam War movement in Japan grew more militant, protestors began directly targeting American military operations. The areas that hosted US military bases and facilities in Japan exhibited special vulnerability to antiwar activism. Zengakuren launched a series of strikes targeting the US military bases and facilities. Even Beheiren, which was known for employing more moderate tactics, began engaging in direct action against the war. On October 23, 1967, Beheiren assisted four young US sailors who had deserted from the aircraft carrier USS *Intrepid* that was harboring at the US base in Yokosuka before returning to the Gulf of Tonkin. Beheiren filmed the plight of the "Intrepid Four" and invited Ernest Young, who was then teaching East Asian history at Dartmouth College, the position he had taken after working at the US Embassy in Japan under Ambassador Reischauer, to interview the deserting soldiers in order to broadcast the case internationally. *The New York Times* reported alarmingly that Beheiren successfully "circulated [the film] around the world."[101] Because of their use of the Soviet Union as a temporary harbor for the Intrepid Four, US military intelligence fallaciously concluded that Beheiren was "influenced by the USSR rather than the Chinese Communists."[102] Beheiren's direct action was, in fact, something inspired by American antiwar dissenters. David McReynolds, one of the participants in the Two-Nation Conference of 1966, had written that the concepts of "direct action" or "civil disobedience," as opposed to formal demonstrations and publication of antiwar materials, had not been familiar to the Japanese before the conference.[103] The American-introduced idea of direct action was appealing to Beheiren for it offered a conceptual context in which they could expand their activities while maintaining its protest philosophy distinct from Zengakuren's. After the Intrepid Four case, Beheiren established the Japan Technical Committee to aid US Anti-War Deserters (JATEC) to make their activities to assist American deserters its permanent program.

These antiwar activities that were directed at American soldiers raised serious security concerns for American military authorities. The US Navy warned American sailors about "antiwar peace groups" trying to induce them to desert the service.[104] In an interview with *The New York Times*, Admiral Thomas H. Moorer, the Chief of Naval Operations lamented, "[I]t is difficult for the average member of the armed services to be able to distinguish between legitimate political minority group actions and subversive propaganda aimed at weakening the military effort. I am concerned that naval personnel be duped by subversive groups taking advantage of this situation and be led to erroneous conclusions."[105] The Navy warned of these peace groups that tried to approach and convert US soldiers, especially those on their rest-and-recreation leaves in such countries as Australia and Japan, "where antiwar activity is strong."[106] The US Navy authorities published such warnings in its newspapers and bulletin boards and broadcasted them on ships.

Between January 15 and 23, the Triple Alliance Zengakuren protested against the harboring of the nuclear-powered USS *Enterprise* at Sasebo Port in Nagasaki. Zengakuren students, as well as those in other leftist and pacifist groups, considered the Japanese government's approval of the entry of the USS *Enterprise*, along with the USS *Truxturn* and the USS *Halsey*, to Sasebo as indicating that their country was no longer interested in even pretending to be a pacifist state and was now willing to be nuclearized. Along with over 10,000 Zengakuren students, some 50,000 people from leftist political parties and labor unions joined demonstrations against the harboring of the *Enterprise*.[107]

In response, Washington tried to desensitize the Japanese public to American military activities to weaken antiwar protests. The US government was "virtually certain that it [the harboring of US military ships in Japan] would lead to violent demonstrations" and would give the Japanese leftist opposition an opportunity to "use the port call as a means of fighting an extension of the Security Treaty after 1970."[108] However, it was considered to serve the long-term interests of the United States. Rostow wrote to President Johnson that the "immediate reason" was to serve logistic and Rest & Recreation purposes of the Navy and, more importantly, the harboring of the ships was to provide the Japanese "visible demonstrations of close US-Japanese political relations."[109] He explained to the President that nuclear-powered submarines had been entering Japanese ports since 1964 and the leftist opposition had been mobilizing against them ever since, yet "they have tapered off to the point where visits are now considered routine by both the Navy and the Japanese people," alleviating the nuclear allergy of the Japanese.[110] Rostow added that the entry of these American ships to Sasebo was not an American imposition since Prime Minister Sato had been given an opportunity to deny it.

In March 1968, student protestors led a major campaign against the construction of a new US Army hospital in Camp Oji in Tokyo, which had been vacant since a US military team that had occupied the camp moved to Hawaii in 1966. Since the beginning of the Vietnam War, there had been a steady increase in beds in US military hospitals in Japan, but by 1968 there was a serious shortage as more wounded soldiers arrived from Vietnam.[111] The construction of a new hospital at Camp Oji was to meet this demand. The reactivation of Camp Oji met strong opposition. Between February and April, Zengakuren students engaged in a series of violent battles with the police in order to stop the plan. On February 20, according to the US intelligence report, 850 Zengakuren students protested in front of Camp Oji, and the number reached 2,000 on March 8.[112] On March 28, 3,800 Japanese riot police were mobilized against a crowd of 2,000 protestors, resulting in a violent confrontation between the police and protestors.[113] About thirty students made their way into the military compound and some even entered the hospital building on that day. Because the camp was located in a crowded Tokyo residential area, many local residents also joined the demonstrations. The new hospital began operating in April, but the protests had caused serious security concerns for the US Army.[114] This was probably one of the reasons why the Army hospital was shut down in November 1969.

Student protestors also targeted the transportation of American military supplies. On July 22, antiwar protestors, including about 120 Zengakuren students, disrupted the transportation of ammunition by demonstrating on railway tracks in Kyushu. A week later, 200 students tried to obstruct fuel-carrying trains to Tachikawa Air Base in Tokyo, protesting against the Vietnam War.[115] *The New York Times* reported, "The protests have not been without effect. Visits by nuclear-powered vessels have been halted for the time being. Fuel-carrying trains have been held up. And plans have been discussed to relocate the Tokyo hospital" due to militant student demonstrations.[116]

The Sunagawa struggle was revitalized as the antiwar protestors began pointing out America's desperate need for the extended runways to fight the war in Vietnam. Indeed, between 1967 and 1968, the Sunagawa struggle reached a new level of intensity, being connected to the Vietnam War. The extension of the runways remained unfinished because some twenty-three residents still refused to give up their land. As the anti-Vietnam War movement gained momentum, Sunagawa once again became a hotbed of student activism. Zengakuren organized a series of protests in Sunagawa against the extension plan and the Vietnam War. Zengakuren launched the February 26 Sunagawa Struggle, along with young labor union activists in the Tama region. The Triple Alliance Zengakuren organized another major demonstration, calling it the May 27 Sunagawa Struggle with other antiwar youth organizations. On that day, students from seventy universities throughout Japan were reported to having arrived at Sunagawa.[117] On July 9, 10,000 Zengakuren students arrived at Sunagawa and protested against the extension plan, together with 5,000 protestors.[118] Zengakuren students stressed the importance of obstructing the US-Japan "counterrevolutionary" policy against Asian liberation movements in their protests in Sunagawa. In December 1968, the United States finally announced the cancellation of the extension plan, and the Japanese government officially accepted the decision in April 1969.

There was little the US could do to counter the student protests in Japan. Ambassador Alexis Johnson wrote in his report to the Department of State that "US policymakers in Tokyo have frequent, often daily, reminders of the importance of student unrest to their planning and decision, but the limitations on action" was clear.[119] In 1969, the US Embassy in Japan further acknowledged that the US military, along with the Japanese government, would continue to be the chief target of the student movement and "violent riots" in Japan. A report to State Department sent from the US Embassy in Tokyo stated:

> If these internal trends and events go against us, nothing the US might reasonably do will keep 1970 from being a year of vast disorder. Even in this worst case, however, it would be important for the USG [US Government] to cooperate with the GOJ [Government of Japan] in keeping as small as possible the area of the target we jointly present to the mob; that is, in avoiding concrete manifestations of controversial aspects of our military relationship.[120]

Mounting criticism of the Vietnam War and the powerful Japanese student protests against the US-Japan alliance put the United States in Japan increasingly on the defensive.

The US government's concern with foreign youth and student upheavals in general reached its zenith in 1968. Klimke has shown that the foreign youth revolts of 1968 elevated the importance of the IAYC and expanded the US government's study programs on the subject of the youth revolts aimed to assess their impact on US foreign policy. On August 16, 1968, Thomas L. Hughes of the Bureau of Intelligence and Research of the State Department wrote in his report to the Secretary of State, Dean Rusk, "In the last few months, virtually every US country-team (except for those in Communist countries) has submitted at least one report on the development of political attitudes among the host-country youth and on the theme of student unrest."[121] Compiling information about the youth and student revolts in the world, the Department of State drafted two reports on the youth revolts in 1968, which were entitled "Generalizations on Student Unrest" and "General Action Recommendations on Student Unrest." The reports were sent out by Rusk on September 3 and shared among all American diplomatic posts.

The "Generalizations of Student Unrest" was a comprehensive report on the student unrest and assessment of possible impact on US foreign policy interests. The major concern with the student movement seemed no longer about Communism, since the idea of Communist manipulation of the student radicalism outside the Third World had been widely gainsaid. Moreover, Washington had been informed of Moscow's critical view of the New Left movement in the West. In 1968, student radicalism was viewed as a challenge to the collective identity and ideology of the capitalist world. The report stated, "The ultimate danger posed by student unrest is a possible weakening of the whole fabric, so painfully constructed over the years, which holds together the Community of Free World Nations."[122] Washington seemed deeply concerned with the grassroots challenge to the official ideology and perspectives of the nature and objectives of the "free world" alliance, which was crucial in sustaining "the worldwide functioning of our [US] business interests and our free enterprise economic system."[123]

In November, Alexis Johnson, who was then Ambassador to Japan, submitted his view regarding the applicability of the department's analysis and action recommendations provided in the report to the Japanese situations. While agreeing with the overall views of the State Department on student unrest, Johnson pointed out that its view that student protests abroad were primarily motived by national rather than international issues did not apply to the Japanese case. He thought that what united Zengakuren student radicals, despite their factional rivalry, was "the US and its Japanese 'lackeys' that are pictured as trying to re-militarize Japan."[124] He added, "For years the main 'issues' here have been 'international', rather than national, almost always connected with matters of war and peace (in Japanese thinking) and US-Japan relations."[125] Regarding action recommendations, Johnson advocated for the establishment of more efficient information gathering and sharing among the posts and institutions dealing with student unrest at home and abroad. He wrote that experiences of American university administrations in dealing with the student protestors, for instance, could be coordinated and made available for Japanese university authorities. Americans also could profit from experiences of other nations in dealing with the student revolts. Johnson pointed out that in particular, the Japanese riot police's tactics for handling student demonstrations, which was developed over two decades, could be a model to emulate for the police abroad. Johnson reported, the Japanese police were armed with an "impressive collection of special equipment," and most important of all, they act with "the clear understanding that they are engaged in a public relations battle."[126] On December 1, Robert W. Barnett, Deputy Assistant Secretary of East Asian and Pacific Affairs of State Department wrote to Johnson, congratulating him for his reports on the student unrest, which was "the best of those" he had seen on the subject of the student unrest.[127]

While Washington still viewed that the wave of student revolts at home and abroad as a constellation of national protest movements, by the end of 1960s, radical politics were increasingly becoming transnational. In Japan, the areas that hosted US military facilities and bases in particular became hotbeds of transpacific activism. On October 12, 1969, two members of the Black Panther Party from the United States spoke on a radio broadcast by local antiwar protesters in Asaka, Saitama, which hosted a US military hospital. Directly appealing to American GIs in the hospital, the Panthers spoke against the war and oppression.[128] Outside the hospital compound, the Panthers also distributed leaflets "Appeal to Black Soldiers" that called for American GIs to "Rise and Unite Against War Oppression & Racial Domination." As the war escalated, various transnational movements began converging. By the late 1960s, the transnational alliances of antiwar activists went beyond protesting the Vietnam War and created spaces in which various critiques of imperialism and oppression converged.

Beyond Vietnam: Trans-Pacific Convergence of Radicalism

US military bases in Japan came under fire as outposts of American imperialism, but their presence in Japan also contained the potential to facilitate transnational flows of new anti-imperialist ideas. The Vietnam Veterans Against the War/Winter Soldier Organization (VVAW/WSO), originally founded in 1967 in New York,` published the biweekly newspaper *Freedom of Press* and set up a bookstore near the Yokosuka naval base to allow American GIs to access pamphlets and films that were not made available by the military. VVAW/WSO worked closely with Japanese activists and engaged in various antiwar activities, including hosting an antiwar rock concert. There was also a GI antiwar movement by active GIs stationed in Japan. Dissenting GIs printed many underground newspapers—*Kill for Peace* and *Freedom Rings* in Tokyo, *Semper FI* in Iwakuni, *Omega Press* and *Demand for Freedom* in Okinawa to name a few.

Nancy Strohl was one of American transnational activists who engaged in anti-Vietnam War activism in Japan. In 1973, Strohl, fresh out of Claremont College, came to Japan with her then-husband Richard Engle as a full-time antiwar activist.[129] They were recruited by Pacific Counseling Service (PCS), which was founded in 1970 to support GI opposition to the Vietnam War. The PCS published and distributed antiwar newspapers and ran coffee houses which served to coordinate antiwar activities by GIs near American bases in Asia.[130] Soon after she arrived at Yokosuka, she and her husband began publishing and distributing the biweekly antiwar press, *Freedom of the Press*, which soon reached a thousand people at the Yokosuka Naval Air Station.[131] Strohl recalled, "*Freedom of the Press* was a product of the natural coalition between the resistance movement of GIs and the antiwar movement in the United States."[132] At Yokosuka, she also participated in the New People's Center, which she described as "the only place in Yokosuka where black and white GIs, Japanese peace activists, and US radicals could talk."[133] The New People's Center and other antiwar centers in Japan linked not only antiwar movements across race and the Pacific but also provided the point of radical convergence, for it provided other alternative sources of information including books on "Malcolm X, James Forman, and other civil rights leaders."[134]

The network of US military bases also allowed the circulation of ideas and voices that were critical of imperialism. The Asian edition of the antiwar GI newspaper *We Got the Brass*, originally published in the spring of 1969 in West Germany, became available in Japan in the fall. The Asian edition reprinted articles originally published in the German edition, and probably vice versa. The GI underground newspapers published abroad such as *Sea Sick* in Philippines also arrived in Japan with American soldiers. These GI underground newspapers delivered not only the voices against the war but also ideas that challenged power structures. *Semper FI*, for instance, ran a special issue on the Black Power Movement in the US in March 1971, with the picture of Angela Davis on the front cover.[135] Heuy P. Newton's article reprinted in the issue delivered the ideas of the Black Panther Party and criticized the Vietnam War by identifying the violence against the Blacks in America with that waged against the Vietnamese.[136] At the end of the issue, the newspaper called for GIs to unite against not just the war but also the system as a whole.

Undocumented personal encounters between American and Japanese activists were as important as the ideas and knowledge shared through written texts in the convergence of radical politics. One tantalizing example of the dynamics of casual meetings recounted in a personal report indicates the cross-cultural tensions that also marked transnational encounters. In 1971, the American antiwar group called Free the Army (FTA), consisting of twenty-five crew members, including Jane Fonda and actor Donald Sutherland, embarked on a thirteen-day tour to perform the FTA show for American GIs stationed in Japan. Suzuki Masaho, one of the Beheiren members who organized the FTA show in Kyoto, had recorded his conversations with the FTA crew members in his personal report. For Suzuki, the meeting resulted in the discovery of the concept of "chauvinism."[137] Before the show, the flyer made by the Japanese organizers in Kyoto for the FTA show met serious criticism by FTA crews. Suzuki wrote in his personal report, "A group of women in the FTA said that the postwar itself was indeed terribly male chauvinistic and counter-revolutionary, but the more serious underlying problem was the attitudes of the activists, especially male activists and their views of women, and that the movement allowed it. These were in fact the product of male chauvinism and fascist pigs-like ideology."[138] During the discussion with the FTA crews over the images used in the flyer, one of the Japanese organizers responded to the criticism by saying that the crews' lack of effort to speak Japanese and the fact that all the translations were done by the Japanese organizers was the product of cultural chauvinism. This experience led the Japanese activists to perceive the limits of their movement in terms of gender and probably the FTA crews in terms of culture.[139] Suzuki recalled that the antiwar movement provided him opportunities to meet various people, including American antiwar activists and GIs, an Okinawan woman whose boyfriend was African American, and deserters from the US military.[140]

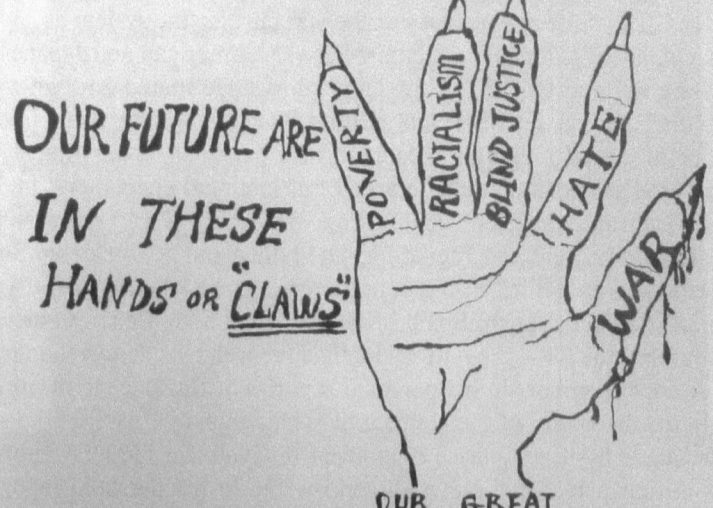

Freedom Rings newspaper, no. 3 (November 21, 1970) published by dissenting American GIs stationed in Tokyo. Endō Yōichi Papers. S3-211. Box 6. Research Center for Cooperative Civil Societies, Rikkyo University.

GI newspaper *Seasick*, vol. 1 no. 4 (November 21, 1970) published in Olongapo, Philippines. GI newspapers published in other countries also arrived in Japan. Eno Yoichi Papers. S3-211. Box 6. *Research Center for Cooperative Civil Societies, Rikkyo University*.

Members of F.T.A., including Jane Fonda at second from right and Donald Sutherland at fourth from right. They held a press conference in Tokyo on December 8, 1971 after Japanese immigration officials announced that they could not perform in Japan with their tourist visas. © *AP Photo*

During the Vietnam War, US-occupied Okinawa in particular became the juncture of complex histories and social relations, and that of diverse antagonisms. For many American and Japanese antiwar protestors, Okinawa came to symbolize imperial oppression by both Japan and the United States. On August 11 and 13, 1968, Beheiren held the International Peoples' Conference against War and for Fundamental Social Change, inviting activists overseas. Beheiren leader Oda Makoto argued at the conference that the struggle for Okinawan independence was a part of the Third World struggle; it thus had to be called the movement for "liberation" rather than "reversion."[141] At the conference, the participants declared the formation of the US-Japan United Front for the Liberation of Okinawa. A few days after the conference, some of the American and Japanese participants of the conference, including SNCC activists J. Wilson and D. Stone, traveled to Okinawa to protest against American "oppression" in Okinawa. Zengakuren called for a Japan-Okinawa proletariat united front aimed to liberate Okinawa from the double oppression of American and Japanese imperialism.

In the fall of 1968, Zengakuren, Beheiren, and other young radicals planned to launch a major campaign in Okinawa against the Vietnam War and for the liberation of Okinawa. The first direct election for Chief Executive of the Government of the Ryukyu Islands, the election for Legislature of the Government of the Ryukyu Islands, and the mayoral election for the capital city, Naha, were going to take place between November and December. The results of these "Big Three" elections were considered to have a profound influence on the terms and timing of the Okinawan reversion, including the question of the post-reversion US military bases in Okinawa. Zengakuren students thought to prevent the bourgeoisie marriage that would fail to "liberate" Okinawan people from the US and Japanese imperialism. The *Kyoto University Shimbun* claimed that the campaign in Okinawa would be a watershed in the struggle for liberation in Japan as a whole.[142]

Alarmed by the offensive planned by the Japanese radicals, USARYIS immediately completed the "Agitator Study" in October, with the assistance of USCAR and HICOM Political Advisers. The objective of the study was to safeguard US military facilities in Okinawa from a planned concerted campaign by Zengakuren, Beheiren, and other antiwar groups, whom the report collectively called "agitators." This intelligence report indicated that these "agitators" would storm into Okinawa between October 21 and December 1 during key elections in Okinawa. It warned, "Our best intelligence indicated the agitator groups would attempt to bring about a confrontation with US Forces personnel and create an international incident by causing serious injury or even death to one of their members, placing the blame on the US."[143] The report concluded that the most effective and least provocative countermeasure would be to elaborately restrict entry to Okinawa by "any Japanese national in the 17–30 age group," whose period of stay on the island included days between October 18 and 21, through elaborate immigration procedures.[144]

The US authority in Okinawa feared the development of powerful anti-American sentiments on the islands. First, it thought that the issue of Okinawa would radicalize relatively peaceful elements like Beheiren to follow Zengakuren-style radicalism.[145] More serious attention was paid to their effects on the local Okinawan population. The "Agitator Study" assumed that Zengakuren and other mainland radicals would influence "a volatile element on Okinawa which can be galvanized into aggressive, violence action."[146] It stated that "it must be remembered . . . that the Okinawans are noticeably easy to incite to the necessary pitch of emotion."[147] The prevailing assumption was that these agitators would stir up anti-American sentiments among Okinawans and would be the source of trouble on the islands.

By October 18, the US authority in Okinawa had developed a plan for the defense of Okinawa and sent it to the relevant US organizations: USCAR, USARYIS, 313th Air Division, Fleet Marine Force, Pacific, and Fleet Activities in Ryukyu Islands. The "Agitator Study" identified the following organizations as the main forces in the campaign: Antiwar Youth Committee,

"Agitator Study" The US Civil Administration of the Ryukyu islands (USCAR). *Liaison Department (HCRI-LN). RG 260. Box1. NARAII.*

Communist-affiliated Okinawa Democratic Youth League, Ryukyu University Marxist Study Club, Okinawa District Japan Socialist Youth League, and Okinawa Prefectural Council for the Prohibition of A and H Bombs, in addition to Beheiren and other Zengakuren-affiliated radicals. The probable locations of protests were Gates 1, 2, and 23 of Kadena Air Base, the Government of the Ryukyu Islands (GRI) Plaza, Naha Port, and USARYIS Headquarters. Trying to avoid a confrontation between Japanese protestors and American military forces, which would provide negative publicity, the US Occupation planned to place local GRI police of Okinawans at the forefront and prepared American forces inside the gates of military bases.

The election result in Okinawa increased pressure on the United States. The victory of Yara Chobyo, backed by the Socialist and other leftist and progressive parties, as Chief Executive of the Ryukyu Islands alarmed the United States that wished to maintain the "keystone of the Pacific." Yara stood for the immediate and unconditional reversion of Okinawa to Japan and opposed the presence of US military bases that housed nuclear weapons. The election result demonstrated the pressure for change regarding the status of Okinawa. Washington was not ready to give up its military bases in Okinawa, which it considered necessary for the defense of the rest of East Asia, and "declared 'as strongly as possible' that nuclear weapons should continue to be available at the Okinawan bases."[148] Thus it indicated that the timing of the reversion of Okinawa to Japan depended on whether the US would be allowed to "retain its bases under present operating conditions—that is, without restrictions on troop movements and with the nuclear capacity."[149] To alleviate Washington's concern, Sato and his conservative political allies had assured them that the Japanese government would make sure that the reversion of Okinawa to Japan would not bring any change to the current state of US military bases. Yet, the election result and popular outcry for Okinawa as an equally nuclear-free prefecture of Japan made it impossible for Sato government to apply exceptional status for Okinawa. In the spring of 1969, the Foreign Ministry in Tokyo agreed on the "nuclear-free, homeland-level" plan for post-reversion Okinawa.[150] The Japanese government agreed to make Okinawa free of nuclear weapons, as in mainland Japan, but the "homeland-level" meant it would be equally subject to the provision of the US-Security Treaty that agreed to host US military bases.

Given its status as the US-occupied territory governed with the Japanese "residual sovereignty," Okinawa played a unique role as the point of convergence for transnational radicalism. Some black liberation activists in the United States paid attention to the issue of Okinawa. Writing for *The Black Panther*, Diahnne Jenkins, Lieutenant of Health of the Black Panther branch in New York, characterized Okinawa as a "military colony" chained to "US imperialism" under the US-Japan Security Treaty.¹⁵¹ She praised Beheiren's actions and declared the Black Panther's support for the movement to liberate Okinawa, expressed as follows:

> Comrade Macota [sic.] Oda has extended his hand for our support and co-operation in reaching a unity of will between the peoples of Asia, fighting for liberation of the military colony, and peoples of the US, fighting for liberation from fascism.¹⁵²

Some black American GIs stationed in Okinawa also expressed feelings of solidarity with people in Okinawa, identifying with them as oppressed peoples. The first issue of *Demand for Freedom* published by GIs at Kaneda Airbase in Okinawa declared, "I identify with you. Because we are oppressed, and together with our power (unity) we will free ourselves of this oppressor, or die doing so. This is what power is."¹⁵³ In the second issue, a black GI wrote, "I am a minority, just like you, culturally. But united we are a majority, if we fight for the same goals, liberation, and the fight to determine one's own destiny . . . Help stamp out Amerika's [sic.] imperialism!"¹⁵⁴ Historian Onishi Yuichiro has also noted this affinity, arguing that, "The appeal of dissenting black GIs to Okinawans was an effort to base their own liberation struggle within the localized project of the internationalist, anti-imperialist, antiracist, and anticolonial struggle in occupied Okinawa."¹⁵⁵ Indeed, the sense of shared racial oppression expressed by African Americans in Okinawa was the projection of their radical imagination, and demonstrated the expansiveness of anti-imperialist ideas in the late 1960s, particularly as people moved and encountered new circumstances with recognizable contours.

Inspired by the black liberation movement at home, African Americans in Okinawa began revolting against racially discriminatory practices of the US military. Although probably somewhat exaggerated, Toma Kenshuke, reporting to *Beheiren*'s JATEC-run newspaper *Dassōhei Tsūshin* (Deserter Correspondence), wrote "There are about 10,000 black soldiers in Okinawa, and 6,000 of them were ardent supporters of black power and 2,000 are involved in the Black Panther Party."¹⁵⁶ On August 30, 1969, antiwar Black soldiers clashed with white Military Police (MP) and Criminal Investigation Division (CID) officers in the black community in Koza. The incident occurred when a crew of fifty to seventy black servicemen surrounded the white officers who were there for a routine check of the area.¹⁵⁷ The MPs responded by firing eight warning shots in the air and escaped from the crowd. It resulted in the injury of five white officers. The rumor that the black power movement was behind this incident germinated in Okinawa. Referring to the rumor, a black serviceman said to Toma, "It was just an accident, we did not know that they were coming," but that the most black servicemen here were aware of racial inequality in the military.¹⁵⁸ He then said, "How come we fight on the front lines while the white men sit on the chairs and type on computers?"¹⁵⁹

Expressing sympathy toward African American GIs, a group of students at Ryukyu University distributed a leaflet titled, "An Appeal from the Oppressed People of Okinawa to Those of America," to African American servicemen in the black district of Koza city known as "Four Corners."¹⁶⁰ It read:

> Two-thirds of the people in Africa, India, and America are suffering from starvation. And in Vietnam mass-killing is being done every day and a great number of people are injured and killed whether they are Vietnamese, Whites, or Blacks. Why did you come all the way from America and kill the Vietnamese who are seeking freedom? Why do you occupy Okinawa with military bases and put us under the threat of the nuclear weapons and poisonous gas? Why do you have to die in Vietnam? Don't you have to join your brothers who are fighting for their freedom in their country?¹⁶¹

The Public Safety Department of USCAR reported on November 20, 1969, that some African American servicemen who belonged to a black organization formed in Okinawa called "Bushmasters" visited student radicals in Ryukyu University after reading the leaflet.¹⁶²

On December 20, 1970, a large-scale uprising at Koza shocked the US authorities in Okinawa. The incident was initially triggered by a car accident by an American serviceman that led to the death of an Okinawan woman. Okinawans quickly mobilized against the US authority when it found him innocent and refused to turn him over to Okinawan authorities.

This was an incident that took place after the freeing of the GI who had been charged with raping an Okinawan waitress on December 2, which provoked local fury over the absence of legal protections for the Okinawan civilians. A crowd of 3,000 Okinawans stormed the base areas and attacked military police by throwing rocks and some set fire to American cars.¹⁶³ About 700 demonstrators were reported to have penetrated into the US air base, and 700 US military servicemen were soon mobilized to control the situation.¹⁶⁴ Mainstream American newspapers reported the incident, but what was missing from their news coverage was the story of American GIs that allied with Okinawans and joined their struggle against "US imperialism." According to Onishi, Black GIs who joined the Okinawans in the protest stressed their desire to be "a part of the solution, not the problem."¹⁶⁵ Linking the long liberation struggle of African Americans and that of Okinawans, the Black GIs took the incident as a protest against the power structure that oppressed them. According to Onishi, "The appeal of dissenting black GIs to Okinawans was an effort to base their own liberation struggle within the localized project of the internationalist, anti-imperialist, antiracist, and anticolonial struggle in occupied Okinawa."¹⁶⁶

As Onishi points out, race was undeniably an important category that the anti-base protestors in Okinawa used to challenge the US military presence, but one needs to carefully consider that the sharing of this kind of desire did not automatically create "anti-White" solidarity between Okinawans and African Americans. Labeling the local protests as "anti-White" oversimplifies tensions that existed on the island. For instance, there were also strong sentiments among Okinawan people against extraterritorial rights of the US military members, especially those related to the exercise of extraterritorial criminal jurisdiction. On the afternoon of May 30, 1970, a twenty-two-year-old African American serviceman named Herman Smith Jr. raped a 16-year-old high school student in Gushikawa and stabbed her several times when she screamed.[167] Having witnessed many occasions in which the extensive extraterritoriality protected the American military personnel who committed crimes in Okinawa, local communities immediately mobilized themselves to demand those criminals to be brought to justice by the Okinawan legal authority, rather than the US military, which had a significantly lower rate of arrest and conviction.[168] On June 3, five hundred high school students joined the protest organized by the High School Teacher and Staff Union in front of the US Administration building in Naha.[169] Responding to the local pressure, the US released the name of the criminal. This was the first instance in which the US military released the name of an American soldier who had committed a crime in Okinawa.[170] As this case demonstrates, the Okinawan struggles with the US military bases were multifaceted and involved resistance to various forms of oppressive power.

These personal encounters and the transnational flow of radical thoughts prompted young radicals in Japan to act on new concepts of revolutionary subjectivity. Max Elbaum has convincingly argued that radicalism of the period between 1968 and 1973 did not "stem from historical accident, individual idiosyncrasy, or collective irrationality."[171] Within the larger milieu of Japanese radicalism, the liberation movement of African Americans became a important source of inspiration. At the press conference of the Black Panthers held in Tokyo in 1969, Elbert "Big Man" Howard sent his message to the Japanese including those in the "oppressed" communities. He said, "We ask the people of Japan to stand in protest and to move against the oppression of the citizens of their own country and to understand that when their government makes pacts and agreements with the United States, it is endorcing [sic.] these foul and inhuman acts against mankind and they are in fact subject to the same atrocities themselves. If they do not move to put an end to this fascist action and the oppression that runs rampant in our communities today, the same kind of fascism will infest their communities tomorrow."[172]

In January 1971, a small number of Japanese leftist radicals formed the Japan Support Committee for the Black Panther Party and began publication of the Japanese translation of *The Black Panther: Black Community News Service* magazine in March. The magazine delivered the Japanese translation of the Black Panther Party's party newspaper as well as the works by Japanese activists. In its first issue, the Japan Supporting Committee declared, "The proletariat is in fact the exploited class. But we must remember that there is also a reserve army of the proletariats who were excluded from the classic Marxist definition of the working class."[173] It argued, "Today, it is not a coincidence that it was the Third World people who made a solid breakthrough for the liberation of the people and the creation of a new world by shaking the foundation of the imperialist military, reactionary governments, and [Communist] revisionists."[174] The African American liberation movement in the United States in particular offered the Japanese Black Panthers a model that allowed them to solve the contradiction between the self that was constructed in their everyday affluent life in the First World and the revolutionary self that was constructed through their opposition to oppression. Thus, the Japanese Panthers called for Japanese revolutionaries to suppress "the self that was constructed internally within the advanced imperialism" and act as a Third World revolutionary as the Black Panthers did in the US.[175]

The Black Panther Party was unique in respect that their ideas inspired communities of people who had not been visible within transnational activist networks that had so far dominated by young intellectuals and university students. In the letter to the Black Panther Party, the Japan Support Committee for the Black Panther Party wrote, "While Japan is an imperialist and militarist state, it is also under the imperialist control of the US. The people, especially the most oppressed people here, get affected most by this, so the people here (including minority people) are oppressed by both imperialists."[176] The Japanese Red Army also sent a letter to the Black Panthers and wrote, "We have not only been inspired by the causes and consequences of such revolutionary attempts and actions, but also learned a lot from your constantly advocated new view of the world, worldwide strategy and analysis of imperialism. We are saying all this not as lookers-on, but as fellow revolutionaries with a full conviction to fight for the liberation of all oppressed peoples of the world."[177] Huey P. Newton wrote back, celebrating what he called "the development of revolutionary intercommunalism."[178]

The idea for emulating the armed struggles of the Black Panther Party and the Third World revolutionaries began germinating among a small group of young radicals in Japan after 1968. In *The Black Panther* magazine, a labor union activist named Kinoshita Kazuo called for the formation of a "double authority" in Kamagasaki slum of Osaka, following a Black Panther model.[179]

He argued that the establishment of their own political authority and armed force as opposed to the official local government and the police department was necessary in order to defend the poor and workers in the slum, which was often targeted by government and police harassment. The Third World revolutionaries also inspired Japanese student activists. Victor Passy, reporting to *National Guardian*, observed, "Akiyama [Katsuyuki, the chairman of Triple Alliance] took me to the big Zengakuren headquarters here [in Japan]. The walls are covered with pictures of Che Guevara, Vietnam and the Student Nonviolent Coordinating Committee."[180]

The Third World revolutionaries and black radicalism in the United States played a crucial role in transforming the concept of revolutionary subjectivity among the Japanese radicals. They offered a way to deal with the limitations of classical Marxism through the employment of cultural categories such as race. Emulating the revolutionaries in the Third World, a small group of Japanese radicals even took up arms. In 1971, a group of Maoist radicals formed the Red Army, drawing members from Zengakuren, and began advocating for armed revolutionary struggles. The United Red Army (*Rengo Sekigun*) engaged in violent protests and committed terrorist activities, such as hijacking airplanes.

The transnational networks and inspiration they drew from the Third World revolutionaries provided the dynamics for the local struggles and brought about profound changes to the student movement in Japan. The pacifist internationalism that developed in the early 1960s was the basis for the anti-imperial solidarity and transnational activism of the student radicals during the Vietnam War. The Vietnam War provided urgency and an opportunity to strengthen international solidarity for the Zengakuren radicals to strike the imperial domination of the world, in particular the US-Japan imperialism, which they saw as the direct cause of counterrevolutionary violence in Vietnam. The antiwar activists, student radicals, and others such as the members of the Black Panther Party, who protested across the borders of the states, the US military bases and facilities in Japan, and the US-occupied Okinawa, challenged the structure of power and oppression, which they perceived as the direct cause of struggles they had engaged within specific local contexts.

Despite their growing militancy that raised security concerns, young radicals in Japan no longer posed serious political threat to US policy interests in Japan. By then, Japanese mainstream newspapers appeared less sympathetic to the student radicals. Some newspapers repeatedly picked up stories of local "victims" lamenting damages inflicted by Zengakuren students, such as storeowners who had to close their shops due to their demonstrations. The *Yomiuri Shimbun* made the coverage of Zengakuren "*Kōgai*," or pollution, reporting that the Zengakuren meeting held at Chuo University on July 22,

1968, troubled local residents. This kind of treatment of Zengakuren activities by the mainstream media more or less reflected the general public's view of student radicalism. By the end of 1960s, ordinary citizens had begun collecting signatures on petitions calling Zengakuren a problem in their neighborhoods. The US Embassy in Tokyo reported to State Department on the subject of "Radical Students in Japan" on April 18, 1968 and stated that as long as Zengakuren were isolated on their campuses, divided over factional strife, remain "exceptionally introspective," they would not be capable of bring about a major political change that would result in a change in the Japanese government's policy toward the US-Japan alliance.[181]

NOTES

1. "Study of European Youth," January 18, 1967, the Inter-Agency Youth Committee project. RG 353. Box 6. NARAII.
2. Ibid.
3. Carole Fink, Philipp Gassert, and Detlef Junker, "Introduction," in *1968: The World Transformed*, ed. Carole Fink, Philipp Gassert, and Detlef Junker (New York: Cambridge University Press, 1998), 3.
4. Timothy Scott Brown, *West Germany and the Global Sixties: The Antiauthoritarian Revolt, 1962–1978* (New York: Cambridge University Press, 2013), 3.
5. Representative of the Commander in Chief Pacific in the Ryukyus, "Agitator Study," October 14, 1968. USCAR Records. Records of Liaison Department (HCRI-LN). RG 260. Box 1. NARAII.
6. *Asahi Shimbun*, September 14, 1963.
7. ———, December 10, 1963.
8. Nihon Gakusei Undō Kenkyūkai, *Gakusei Undō no Kenkyū*, 148.
9. *The New York Times*, March 27, 1964; ———, March 31, 1964.
10. *Yomiuri Shimbun*, January 12, 1963.
11. ———, November 14, 1962.
12. Kil J. Yi, "In Search of a Panacea: Japan-Korea Rapprochement and America's 'Far Eastern Problems'," *Pacific Historical Review* 71, no. 4 (2002): 639.
13. Bruce Cummings, "The Origins and Development of the Northeast Asian Political Economy: Industrial Sectors, Product Cycles, and Political Consequences," *International Organization* 38, no. 1 (1984): 26–7.
14. Ibid., 28.
15. Victor D. Cha, "Bridging the Gap: The Strategic Context of the 1965 Korean-Japan Normalization Treaty," *Korean Studies* 20(1996): 124.
16. James Peck, *Washington's China: The National Security World, the Cold War and the Origins of Globalism* (Amherst: University of Massachusetts Press, 2006), 232.
17. Nihon Gakusei Undō Kenkyūkai, *Gakusei Undō no Kenkyū*, 183.

18. Tokyo Shagakudō Shokikyoku [The secretariat of the Socialist Student League in Tokyo], "Shagaku-dō Dai6-kai Taikai eno Teian [A proposal for the Socialist Student League 6th convention]," February 28, 1965. Document no. 5 in *Zengakuren Documents*, vol. 7, 1964–1967 (Tokyo: San-Ichi Shobo, 1970), 12.

19. Togakuren (Sanpa-kei) Saiken Jyunbikai [A committee to reestablish *Togakuren* of the Triple Alliance], "1.18 Nikkan Kaidan Kaishi ni Mukete Tatakai o Soshiki Seyo, Zenkoku Jichikai wa Saiken Jyunbikai ni Shūketsushi, 7-gatu Saiken o Sushinseyo [Mobilize for the January 18th struggle against the Japan-South Korea talk, self-governing associations throughout the country, come join the committee to achieve the reestablishment in July]," January 1, 1965. Document no. 1 in ibid., 5.

20. Togakuren (Snapa-kei) Saiken Jyunbikai, "Nikkan Kaidan Funsai, Betonamu Shinryaku Hantai Zenkoku Gakusei Sōkekki Taikai Kichō Houkoku [A report on the student rally against the Japan-South Korea meeting and the invasion of Vietnam], March 30, 1965. Document no. 7 in ibid., 24.

21. Ibid., 23.

22. Cha, "Bridging the Gap," 135.

23. Tae-Ryong Yoon, "Learning to Cooperate Not to Cooperate: Bargaining for the 1965 Korea-Japan Normalization," *Asian Perspective* 32, no. 2 (2008): 80.

24. Marugakudō (Chūkaku-ha) Chūō Shokikyoku [The central secretariat of the Central Core Faction of *Marugakudō* faction], *Chūkaku*, November 30, 1965 in *Zengakuren Documents*, vol. 7, 1964–1967, 168.

25. Ibid., 156–162.

26. Frank Griffiths, *Sino-Soviet conflict at the 7th IUS Congress. Report at the 7th Congress of the International Union of Students, Held in Leningrad, August 18–28, 1962* (Ottawa: National Federation of Canadian University Students). IISG 1590/48 folder. International Institute of Social History, Amsterdam.

27. Agent report, Subject: Subversive Activities of Ryukyus University Students, September 10, 1962. RG260. Box 112. NARAII.

28. Nihon Gakusei Undō Kenkyūkai, *Gakusei Undō no Kenkyū*, 148.

29. Zengakuren, *Zengakuren: Twenty Years' Struggle* (Tokyo: All Japan Federation of Student Autonomous Associations, 1967), 29.

30. Ibid.

31. Ibid., 30.

32. Ibid.

33. Ibid.

34. Ibid.

35. Ibid.

36. National Committee of Japan Revolutionary Communist League, *Zenshin*: International Edition/Organ of NC-JRCL, no. 2 (November 1963). Howard Zinn Papers. TAM 542. Box 37. Tamiment Library and Robert F. Wagner Labor Archives, New York University.

37. Ibid.

38. *Christian Science Monitor*, April 14, 1965.

39. *Yomiuri Shimbun*, April 23, 1965.

40. Ibid.; *Los Angeles Times*, April 23, 1965.

41. *Los Angeles Times*, April 23, 1965.
42. Ibid.
43. *Asahi Shimbun*, April 18, 1965.
44. ———, May 1, 1965.
45. ———, August 24, 1965.
46. "Check List of Helpful Japanese Actions: Past and Anticipated," attached to Memorandum for Mr. Walt W. Rostow from Executive Secretary Benjamin H. Read, November 8, 1967. National Security File (hereafter cited as NSF), Country File: Japan, Box 252. LBJ Library.
47. Thomas R. H. Havens, *Fire across the Sea: The Vietnam War and Japan 1965–1975* (Princeton: Princeton University Press, 1987), 43–4.
48. Memorandum for Mr. Walt W. Rostow from Benjamin H. Read, Subject: Japanese Trade with North Vietnam, May 10, 1966. NSF, Country File: Japan. Box 251. LBJ Library.
49. Memo, Subject: Economic Benefits to Japan Traceable to the Vietnam Conflict, November 9, 1967. NSF, Country File: Japan. Box 252. LBJ Library.
50. Ibid.
51. Havens, *Fire across the* Sea, 87–8.
52. Ibid.
53. Ibid.
54. Ibid., 86–7.
55. Ibid., 87.
56. Telegram, Department of State, February 14, 1966. NSF, Country File: Japan, Box 251. LBJ Library.
57. The translation of *Beheiren* used in English literature varies. My translation is based on *Beheiren*'s use of "Japan <peace for Vietnam!> committee" as its official English translation of its name.
58. Makoto Oda, *Beheiren* (Tokyo: San-Ichi Shobo, 1969), 247.
59. Yutaka Kokubun, "The University Problem," *Zengakuren: Japan's Revolutionary Students*, 116.
60. Momo Iida, "Shimin Minshu Shugi Undō no Ronri to Shinri [The logic and mentality of demicratc civil movements]," in *Shimin Undō Towa Nanika: Beheiren no Shisō*, ed. Makoto Oda (Tokyo: Tokuma Shoten, 1968).
61. An International Conference on Alternative Perspectives on Vietnam, Conference Program, Ann Arbor, Michigan, September 14–18, 1965. Carton 3, Folder 30, Social Protest Project, the Bancroft Library, the University of California, Berkeley; Iida, "Shimin Minshu Shugi Undō no Ronri to Shinri, 20.
62. Ken Ohara, "New Japanese Groups Assails US on Vietnam," *National Guardian*, January 1, 1966, 6.
63. Vietnam Day Committee, "International Days of Protest Oct. 15 & 16." Hardin B. Jones Paper. Box 60. Hoover Institution Archives, Stanford University.
64. Havens, *Fire across the Sea*, 64–5.
65. Ohara, "New Japanese groups assails US on Vietnam."
66. Ibid.

67. Oda, "The Ethics of Peace," in *Authority and the Individuals in Japan: Citizen Protest in Historical Perspective*, ed. J. Victor Koschmann (Tokyo: University of Tokyo Press, 1978), 170.

68. The Central Executive Committee of Zengakuren, "Report of the Zengakuren's Struggle Against the Vietnamese Aggressive War and the Japan-South Korea Talk," Bulletin no. 10 (November 20, 1965). Howard Zinn Papers. TAM 542. Box 37. Tamiment Library and Robert F. Wagner Labor Archives, New York University.

69. Oda, "Gimu to Shiteno Tabi kara Kaette [After returning from my obligatory trip]," *Beheiren Nyūsu*, no. 8 & 9 (May 28, 1966) in *Beheiren Nyūsu Shukusatsuban: 1965–1974, Dassōhei Tsūshin, JATEC Tsūshin*, ed. Beheiren Nyūsu Shukusatuban Kankō Iinkai (Tokyo: Kawade Shobō, 1974), 15.

70. Howard Zinn, *The Zinn Reader: Writings on Disobedience and Democracy*, 2nd ed. (New York: Seven Stories Press, 209, 2009), 301.

71. "Zenkoku Jyūdan Kōen Ryokō no Seika [What the lecture circuit throughout Japan achieved]," *Beheiren Nyūsu*, no. 10 (June 20, 1966) in *Beheiren Nyūsu Shukusatsuban*, 19.

72. Ibid.

73. Ichiyo Muto, "Beheiren no Shisō: Sengo Minshu Shugi no Yukue ni Yosete [Beheiren's philosophy: On the future of postwar democracy]," in *Shimin Undō Towa Nanika: Beheiren no Shisō*, ed. Makoto Oda (Tokyo: Tokuma Shoten, 1968), 88.

74. Ibid., 90.

75. Ibid.

76. Questionnaire to Mr. Howard Jin [*sic.*], From Zengakuren & Waseda University Newspaper. Howard Zinn Papers. TAM 542. Box 37. Tamiment Library and Robert F. Wagner Archives, New York University.

77. Ibid.

78. Ibid.

79. David McReynolds, "Notes from Japan," *Liberation: An Independent Monthly* (September 1966): 14. Tamiment Library and Robert F. Wagner Archives, New York University; "Watashi wa Heiwa no Tameni Nani o Surunoka: Betonamu ni Heiwa o! Nichibei Simin Kaigi [What can we do for peace: Peace in Vietnam! The Japan-US citizens' conference]," *Bungei* (1966): 180–81.

80. "Nichibei Shimin Kaigi Hiraku [We held a US-Japan citizens' conference]," *Beheiren Nyūsu*, no. 12 (September 1, 1966) in *Beheiren Nyūsu Shukusatsuban*, 25.

81. "Watashi wa Heiwa no Tameni Nani o Surunoka," 281.

82. Allan Greene, "SDS and the Japanese New Left: Position Paper for the SDS Convention with a Resolution on Our Relations with Japanese New Left," *New Left Notes*, vol. 1 no. 31 (August 19, 1966). Social Protest Collection, Bancroft Library, UCB.

83. Ibid.

84. Ibid.

85. Yoshihiko Ichida and Eiki Ishii, *Kikigaki "Bunto" Ichidai: Seiji to Iryō de Jidai o Kakenukeru* [Interviewing the Bunto generation:living through the period with politics and medicine] (Tokyo: Sekaishoin, 2010), 109.

86. Kohei Kudo, "Bunto Kokusaibu: 1968–69-nen no Ichi-nen [International affairs section of *Bunto*: One year from 1968 to 1969]," *Ichi Taishū Seijika no Kiseki: Matsumoto Reiji (Takahashi Yoshihiko) Ikō, Tsuitō Shū*, ed. Tsuitō Shū Henshū Iinkai Takahashi Yoshihiko Ikō (Tokyo: Sairyusha, 1988), 343–46.

87. Ibid.

88. Ibid.

89. Murauchi Mareto, "8.3 Kokusai Hansen Kaigi: Oboegaki [The August 3rd international antiwar conference: A memorandum]," *Kyoto Daigaku Shimbun*, September 2, 1968 in *Kyoto Daigaku Shimbun (Shukusatsuban)* [Kyoto University Newspaper (compact edition)], vol. 6 (Kyoto: Kyoto Daigaku Shimbunsha, 1970), 347.

90. Ken Cloke, "Japan and the Japanese left," *New Left Notes*, vol. 3 no. 28 (September 16, 1968). Social Protest Collection, Bancroft Library, UCB.

91. Ibid.

92. Murauchi, "8.3 Kokusai Hansen Kaigi."

93. Ibid.

94. *The New York Times*, October 31, 1966.

95. ———, January 29, 1967.

96. ———, January 27, 1967.

97. ———, February 9, 1966, 3.

98. ———, January 25, 1967; Young, *The Vietnam Wars, 1945–1990*, 210.

99. Kazuhiko Tamaki, "60-nen Anop Kara Beigun Saihen e: Zainichi Beigun to Anpo no Hensen [From the 1960 Anpo to the reorganization of US military: changes in US miliatry stationed in Japan and the Anpo]," *Gendai Shisō* 34, no. 10 (2006): 112.

100. Ibid.

101. *The New York Times*, December 1, 1967.

102. Representative of the Commander in Chief Pacific in the Ryukyus, "Agitator Study," October 14, 1968.

103. McReynolds, "Notes from Japan," 15.

104. *The New York Times*, December 11, 1967.

105. Ibid.

106. Ibid.

107. Masayuki Takagi, *Shin Sayoku 30-nen Shi* [A 30-year history of the New Left] (Tokyo: Doyō Bijyutsusha, 1988), 62–4.

108. Memorandum for the President, Subject: Your Question about Visit of Nuclear Carrier Enterprise to Sasebo, Japan, January 24, 1968, NSF, Country File: Japan, Box 252. LBJ Library.

109. Ibid.

110. Ibid.

111. *The New York Times*, March 14, 1968, 6.

112. Representative of the Commander in Chief Pacific in the Ryukyus, "Agitator Study," October 14, 1968.

113. Ibid.

114. Ibid.

115. Ibid.

116. *The New York Times*, June 30, 1968.
117. Kurata, *Anpo Zengakuren*, 351.
118. Ibid., 355.
119. Airgram from US Embassy in Tokyo (Ambassador Alexis Johnson) to State Department, November 22, 1968. RG 59. Box 2246. NARA II.
120. Airgram From US Embassy, Tokyo to Department of State, Subject: The Japanese Student Protest Movement, April 10, 1969. RG 59. Box 2246. NARA II.
121. From Thomas L. Hughes to Secretary of State [Dean Rusk], "Comments from the Field on Youth and Student Unrest," August 16, 1968. RG 353. Box 6. NARAII.
122. Department of State, "Generalizations on Student Unrest," attached to Airgram from Department of State to All American Diplomatic Posts, Subject: Student Unrest, September 3, 1968. RG 535. Box 9. NARAII.
123. Ibid.
124. Airgram from US Embassy in Tokyo (Ambassador Alexander Johnson) to State Department, November 22, 1968. RG 59. Box 2246. NARA II.
125. Ibid.
126. Ibid.
127. Robert W. Barnett, Deputy Assistant Secretary of East Asian and Pacific Affairs to Alexis Johnson, American Ambassador, Tokyo, Japan, December 1, 1968. RG 59. Box 2246. NARA II.
128. "Shichō-ritsu Kyūjyōshō!! Hansen Hōsō Zenkoku Netto e Kakudai Chū [The viewer ratings went up! Antiwar broadcasting networks expanding nationwide]," *Dassōhei Stūshin*, no. 5 (November 20, 1969) in *Beheiren Nyūsu Shukusatsuban: 1965–1974, Dassōhei Tsūshin, JATEC Tsūshin*, 702.
129. Nancy Strohl, "Freedom of the Press—or Subversion and Sabotage?," in *Voices from the Underground: Insider Histories of the Vietnam Era Underground Press*, ed. Ken Wachsberger (Ann Arbor, MI: Mica Press), 260.
130. Ibid.
131. Ibid., 261–2.
132. Ibid., 259.
133. Ibid., 261.
134. Ibid.
135. *Semper FI*, vol.1, no. 2 (March 26, 1971), published by GIs in the Iwakuni Marine Corps Air Station (Hiroshima). Endō Yōichi Papers. S3-225. Box 7. Research Center for Cooperative Civil Societies (hereafter cited as RCCCS), Rikkyo University, Tokyo, Japan.
136. Ibid.
137. Masaho Suzuki, *Bohemian repōto* [Bohemian report], no.3. March 15, 1973. Endō Yōichi Papers. S3-253. Box 10. RCCCS, Rikkyo University, Tokyo, Japan.
138. Ibid.
139. Ibid.
140. Author's interview with Suzuki Masaho in Kyoto, December 15, 2016.
141. Shinobu Yoshioka, "Mosaku no Naka e: Hansen to Henkaku [Groping for answers: antiwar and fundamental changes]," *Beheiren Nyūsu*, no. 36 (September

1, 1968) in *Beheiren Nyūsu Shukusatsuban: 1965–1974, Dassōhei Tsūshin, JATEC Tsūshin*, 161.

142. "11-gatsu 'Okinawa' 70-nen Anpo no Seijiteki Wa [November, 'Okinawa' the political circle of the 1970 Anpo]," *Kyoto Daigaku Shimbun*, November 4, 1968 in *Kyoto Daigaku Shimbun (Shukusatsuban)*, 378.

143. Representative of the Commander in Chief Pacific in the Ryukyus, "Agitator Study," October 14, 1968.

144. Ibid.

145. Ibid.

146. Ibid.

147. Ibid.

148. *The New York Times*, November 12, 1968.

149. Ibid.

150. Takuma Nakajima, *Okinawa Henkan to Nichibei Anpo Taisei* [The reversion of Okinawa and the US-Japan security arrangements] (Tokyo: Yuhikaku, 2012), 132.

151. Diahnne Jenkins, "International News: Security for All or Security for None," *The Black Panther* (San Francisco, CA), vol. 7, no. 15 (December 4, 1971). Black Panther Newspaper Collection, Black Thought and Culture database, Alexander Street Press; To distinguish *The Black Panther* newspaper published in the United States and *The Black Panther* newspaper published in Japan in Japanese language by the Japanese Committee to Support the Black Panther Party, the place of publication is hereafter provided in parentheses following the name of the newspaper.

152. Ibid.

153. *Demand for Freedom*, no.1 (October 7, 1970). Endo Yoichi Papers. S3-208. Box 6. RCCCS; the paper was published by American GIs in the Kaneda Air Base in Okinawa.

154. ———, no. 2 (November 16, 1970). Endō Yōichi Papers. S3-208. Box 6. RCCCS.

155. Yuichiro Onishi, "The Presence of (Black) Liberation in Okinawan Freedom: Transnational Moments, 1968–1972," in *Extending the Diaspora: New Histories of Black People*, ed. Dawne Y. Curry, Eric D. Duke, and Marshanda A. Smith (Chicago: University of Illinois Press, 2009), 189.

156. Kenshuke Toma, "Okinawa no Kuroi Chikara, burakku pawā [The Power of blacks in Okinawa, black power]," *Dassōhei Tsuushin*, no. 4 (October 15, 1969) in *Beheiren Nyūsu Shukusatsuban: 1965–1974, Dassōhei Tsūshin, JATEC Tsūshin*, 696.

157. *Afro-American*, September 6, 1969.

158. Toma, "Okinawa no Kuroi Chikara, burakku pawā."

159. Ibid.

160. Memorandum for Civil Administrator from Harriman N. Simmons, Director of Public Safety Department, subject: Efforts to Persuade Negro Servicemen to Join Radical Students," November 20, 1969. Public Safety Department (HCRI-PS). US-CAR Records. RG 260. Box 19.

161. "An Appeal from the Oppressed People of Okinawa to Those of America," attached to Memorandum for Civil Administrator from Harriman N. Simmons, Director of Public Safety Department, subject: Efforts to Persuade Negro Servicemen to

Join Radical Students," November 20, 1969. HCRI-PS. USCAR Records. RG 260. Box 19.

162. Memorandum for Civil Administrator from Harriman N. Simmons, Director of Public Safety Department, subject: Efforts to Persuade Negro Servicemen to Join Radical Students," November 20, 1969.

163. The *Washington Post*, December 21, 1970.

164. Ibid.

165. Onishi, "The Presence of (Black) Liberation in Okinawan Freedom," 188.

166. Ibid., 189.

167. *Asahi Shimbun*, June 1, 1970.

168. According to *Asahi Shimbun* on June 2, 1970, the arrest rate of American military personnel by the US military police was 30.5 percent in 1969 while that of Japan as a whole was 89 percent in 1968.

169. *Asahi Shimbun*, June 3, 1970.

170. ———, June 5, 1970.

171. Max Elbaum, *Revolution in the Air: Sixties Radicals Turn to Lenin, Mao and Che* (New York: Verso Books, 2006), 19.

172. "Press Release: Tokyo, Japan," *The Black Panther* (San Francisco, CA), vol. 3, no. 24 (October 4, 1969). Black Panther Newspaper Collection, Black thought and Culture database, Alexander Street Press.

173. Kurohyōtō Shien Nihon Iinkai [the Japan Support Committee for the Black Panther Party], "Sien Nihon Iinkai no Kangaeru Koto, Dekiru Koto? [What does the support committee think and what can it do?]," *The Black Panther: Black Community News Service* (Japan), no. 1 (March 20, 1971). Personal possession of Ryoko Kosugi.

174. Ibid.

175. Ibid.

176. A letter from the Committee to Support the Black Panther Party, Japan to the Black Panther, *The Black Panther* (San Francisco, CA), vol. 7, no. 15 (December 4, 1971). Black Panther Newspaper Collection, Black Thought and Culture database, Alexander Street Press.

177. Red Army Japan, "Letter from International Bureau, Red Army, Japan," *The Black Panther* (San Francisco, CA), vol. 5, no. 27 (January 2, 1971). Black Panther Newspaper Collection, Black Thought and Culture database, Alexander Street Press.

178. A letter from Huey P. Newton to the Committee to Support the Black Panther Party, Japan, *The Black Panther* (San Francisco, CA), vol. 7, no. 15 (December 4, 1971). Black Panther Newspaper Collection, Black Thought and Culture database, Alexander Street Press.

179. Kazuo Kinoshita, "Busō Jiei ni Mukete [Toward armed defense]," *The Black Panther: Black Community News Service* (Japan), no. 4 (October 10, 1971). Personal possession of Ryoko Kosugi.

180. Vitor Passy, "Action in Tokyo . . .," *National Guardian*, February 21, 1968.

181. Airgram from US Embassy, Tokyo to Department of State, Subject: Radical Students in Japan, April 18, 1968. RG 59. Box 3958. NARAII.

Conclusion

Between 1948 and 1973, the student movement played a vanguard role in the struggles against imperialism in Japan. Emerging in the aftermath of World War II, the nascent Zengakuren student movement amassed power and energy, benefiting from the era's popular democratization movements. Marxist-Leninist theories, which were popular among the intellectuals in Japan, sharpened Zengakuren's critique of imperialism and provided strong theoretical underpinnings to the Zengakuren movement. Over two decades, the student movement created tremendous tensions in the US-Japan Cold War alliance by challenging standard concepts of democracy, peace, and the history of imperialism that were increasingly shaped by the Cold War.

From Washington's perspective, the Japanese student movement led by "Communist" Zengakuren was a major threat to US Cold War policy with respect to China and Asia as a whole. During the 1950s, the popularity of Marxism among Japanese scholars and students and their critique of anti-Communist policy raised a serious concern about the future of Japan. The growing popular opposition to US hegemony in places including Latin America in the late 1950s and South Korea and Japan in 1960 led to a serious reassessment of America's fight against Communism. A series of setbacks that the US felt by 1960, including these "Communist mob agitations" in the places mentioned above, strengthened Kennedy's criticism of the Republican Party's failure to prevent the spread of Communism. In Japan, the Kennedy administration's anti-Communist campaign, which the Japanese leftists called the Kennedy-Reischauer offensive, proved remarkably effective in challenging the student radicals' attack on US foreign policy. Reischauer's intellectual offensive against Japanese Marxism was crucial in shifting the Japanese attitude toward the history of modern Japan and imperialism. Japan's economic boom in the 1960s further gave strength to Reischauer's modernizationist campaign to de-Marxize Japanese minds. The New Frontier and modernization theory succeeded in attracting the Japanese public and made Zengakuren defensive for the first time in dealing with US power. Washington's confidence in attracting the youth abroad, however, did not last long. The escalation of the US military intervention in Vietnam alienated the youth world that Kennedy sought to ally with.

The rapid development of radical movements in the West and elsewhere transformed the Japanese student radicals into global players in combatting the structures of oppression, which they saw as resulting from capitalist imperialism. Japan's economic growth convinced the student left that their country had once again joined the Western empires, and this view provided a new sense of anti-imperial international solidarity for the Japanese students. The Vietnam War became a focal point for radical youth protests throughout the world by the mid-1960s. In the views of many young activists, including those in Japan, the Vietnamese liberation fighters symbolized the heroic resistance against imperialism. The internationalization of the Vietnamese struggle led to significant bourgeoning of radical transnational networks and communication. By the late 1960s, anti-Vietnam War networks moved beyond Vietnam as activists increasingly broadened their focus and began attacking the system of imperialism as the main structure of oppression in the world that was epitomized by the Vietnam conflict. Within this context, local peace and leftist movements provided unique spaces that activated the global 1968 in Japan. The local-global convergence of radical activism was crucial in fashioning a new sense of power among the student radicals in Japan.

During the Vietnam War, the areas that hosted US military facilities and bases in Japan became hotbeds of daily antiwar protests. On April 10, 1969, the US Embassy in Tokyo reported to State Department:

> The Japanese student movement—urban, emotional, utopian, and violent—is today the single greatest threat to Japanese political stability and to and orderly resolution of the base, Okinawa and Security Treaty issues which together make the 1970 Problem. . . . By 1970, when the Government of Japan and the American military tie will be the chief targets of the movement, violent riots involving 25,000 student activists and an equal number of bystanders, or student street demonstrations several times that size are likely.[1]

The US-Japan Security Treaty once again became the "chief target" of the student protests. Furthermore, the US military presence in Japan provided a unique transnational radical space for Japanese and American radical movements.

The anti-imperial student movement of the long sixties seemed to reach its ending in 1973. The revision of the US-Japan Security Treaty was automatically ratified in 1970. The US Occupation of Okinawa was officially ended in

May 1972. It seemed that not much effort was required for the United States to make an adjustment for the post-Occupation US-Japan alliance. The Japanese national consensus proved strongly in favor of the US-Japan alliance and maintaining US military bases, which were predominantly in Okinawa. These two major diplomatic events resulted in the general feeling that the struggles with the alliance between the American Cold Warriors and Japanese conservative government had been finalized. The radical change in the US policy toward China, or what the Japanese termed "Nixon Shock," ended Chinese opposition to the US-Japan Security Treaty. After restoring US-China diplomatic relations in 1972, the Nixon administration promised Chinese leaders that the US would insure China against Japanese re-militarization in order to maintain the US-Japan Security Treaty. According to Go Tsuyoshi Ito, "Chinese leaders worried that the reduction of the U.S. security umbrella by the Nixon Doctrine would invoke the emergence of aggressive Japan," and the US successfully convinced China that the continuation of the US-Japan Security Treaty was in their mutual interests.[2] The North Vietnamese capture of Saigon in 1975 and the end of the anti-Vietnam War movement further deepened the feeling of an end to the tumultuous revolutionary period among the young radicals in Japan, reducing the pressure on the US-Japan Security Treaty in mainland Japan.

In the early 1970s, events involving small student extremist groups significantly contributed to the hostility of the general public toward the student movement as a whole. In the early 1970s, the terrorist activities of several violent factions drew significant media attention and eroded public sympathy for the student movement as a whole. The taking of a lodge owner as a hostage by the United Red Army radicals at a lodge on Mt. Asama between February 19 and 28, 1972, and the discovery of their comrades' dead bodies in the lodge had a profound impact on the public perception of the student radicalism. The prolonged television coverage provided throughout the event, and the scene of the final police operation and rescue of the hostage received almost 90 percent of viewer ratings.[3] While the incident was exceptional in terms of the level of violence, the scale of the police operation, and the extensive media coverage provided for it, the Mt. Asama incident reflected a general trend of a declining Japanese student movement. This violence that took place in the early 1970s and the consequent public alienation from the student movement has led many historians and veterans alike to imagine a different explanation for the end of the Japanese sixties, the one that considers a long-term transformation shaped by the international situations involving the Cold War, rather than one that solely focuses on violent and intensified factionalism of the student movement.

Conclusion

The decline of the radical movements in Japan in the 1970s indeed cannot be discussed without considering the impact of a long process that crafted a "solid consensus" among the general public in Japan. It provided ever more favorable political conditions for the US-Japan alliance envisioned by Cold Warriors in Washington and Tokyo. As many scholars have pointed out, student factionalism that resulted in the murders of over a hundred students by members of rival factions and the ongoing acts of terror committed by small groups of radicals, and the passage of laws that were aimed to control student radicalism were important factors that led to the decline of the student movement. Yet the sole focus on these short-term events has overshadowed the long-term processes that shaped the Japanese society as a whole. In the report sent to State Department on April 10, the US Embassy in Tokyo keenly observed:

> After years of confusion, the Japanese people are at last moving toward a solid consensus on the military tie with the United States. This consensus calls for an early return of Okinawa with our bases there under the same restrictions as those on the Japanese mainland, for a systematic reduction of our bases on the mainland and a limiting of the nuisances which accompany the remaining ones. The extent to which we are able to accommodate this consensus will help make our continued military presence in Japan acceptable and will reduce the ability of the student agitators to bring their peers to the barricades in 1970. The same may be said of the degree of success we may have in moving throughout Asia toward a reduction of tensions.[4]

The Japanese public had now begun moving in a direction that the US Cold Warriors and Japanese conservative leaders had hoped for ever since the reverse course.

Collaborating with US foreign policy became a major purpose of the Japanese foreign policy during and after the 1970s, not only for the conservative leaders but also for many ordinary Japanese citizens. Albert W. Noonan, the counsel who was stationed at the US Consulate in Nagoya, sent a report titled, "Brighter Outlook in 1969–1970 Student Violence" to the State Department on September 24, 1969.[5] Noonan optimistically reported that the Japanese student movement had already passed its peak as a result of factors such as the passage of the University Control Law which regulated student activities and improved the ability of policy to control mass demonstrations and violent street "guerillas."[6] More importantly, Noonan pointed out that the shrinking public sympathy for the student radicals was a major factor in their decline. Noonan cited an article published in the local edition of the business-oriented newspaper *Nihon Keizai Shimbun*, which claimed that even union workers in Nagoya "share employers' views" and concluded that with workers' support of the student radicalism in decline, "apprehensions on anti-Anpo confusion within enterprise bodies will prove to be groundless and imaginary in 1970."[7]

By 1973, the US-Japan Security Treaty had become not only accepted but also widely perceived as necessary by the majority of Japanese people. In 2013, Nozoe Fumiaki discovered documents in the Australian Archives that revealed that the Japanese government resisted the US decision to withdraw the Marine Corps from Japan.[8] According to Yara Tomohiro, the worsening fiscal situation resulting from the Vietnam War and the popular resistance in Okinawa had led Washington to conclude that it was "considerably cheaper and probably more effective" to withdraw all Marines throughout the Pacific."[9] Yet, given the Japanese government's resistance to letting the US Marines go, Yara wrote, "Thomas P. Shoesmith, chief minister at the US Embassy, reported to Washington, 'Our negotiating position is improved' because the Japanese side see the US Marine presence in Okinawa as 'most tangible evidence of US willingness to respond promptly to a direct threat against Japan'."[10] This was a clear invitation from the Japanese government to the US military. By 1973, the concepts of security and peace enshrined in the US-Japan Security Treaty were no longer subject to debate in mainland Japan. The consolidation of the public consensus on the US-Japan Security Treaty meant the end of what one historian of the global Cold War has called America's "battle of global alliances and political ideas" in Japan.[11]

Okinawa allowed the US and Japanese governments to mediate potentially conflicting national interests. Japan gained "security" without fully arming the Japanese mainland and the United States could keep its strategically crucial military facilities and bases in Okinawa while avoiding the intense "nationalistic" anti-base opposition outside the islands. This was the "mutuality" achieved by the US and Japanese governments under the Security Treaty. At an anti-Vietnam War show in Okinawa organized by the American antiwar group Free the Army (FTA) during its East Asian tour, an Okinawan folk singer, Sadoyama Yutaka sang a song called *Okinawa wa Ainoko* (Okinawa is a mixed-blood child) in front of the GI audiences in Okinawa in 1971:

> My father grew up during the war and lived through the world of pure militarism.
> The language is Japanese. The law is American.
> Okinawa is like a mixed-blood child.[12]

The reversion brought little change to life on Okinawa. Local citizens in Okinawa continued to pressure the Pentagon and the Japanese government, constantly demanding them to respond to the "Okinawa Problem." The local protests intensified after three US servicemen, Seaman Marcus Gill, Rodrico Harp and Kendrick Ledet, raped a 12-year-old Okinawa girl on September 4, 1995. In "Okinawa: State of Emergency," C. Douglas Lummis described,

"An all-Okinawa protest rally was held, which was attended by progressives and conservatives alike—some 70,000 people, which is a huge number in a population of 1,300,000."[13] Large-scale demonstrations in Okinawa following the rape incident, however, were not the "awakening" of the Okinawan local communities, which had long been aware of and struggling with injustice and the unequal burdens that had been imposed on the prefecture. On August 13, 2004, a US helicopter from US Futenma Air Base, which is located in the center of a residential area, crashed into the Okinawa International University. This incident intensified local demand for the closing of Futenma Air Base. Fearing the possible spread of anti-base protests in Japan, American and Japanese governments released the US-Japan Roadmap that promised to alleviate the burden of US military presence in Okinawa prefecture and eventually relocate 8,000 Marines and their families to Guam. They also decided to relocate the airbase from Futenma to a less populated area. Following the defeat of the LDP in the 2009 election, the new administration of Hatoyama Yukio of the opposition party, the Democratic Party of Japan (DPJ), ambitiously claimed that it would relocate the US airbase outside Okinawa prefecture altogether. The DPJ, however, failed to conclude an agreement with the US. Hatoyama also quickly withdrew his earlier pledge, which forced his eventual resignation from office. The Japanese government signed a bilateral agreement with the US, offering Henoko as a new construction site. Disillusioned with the Japanese government, Okinawan protestors continue to pressure Tokyo and the Pentagon, trying to prevent the construction of the new base in Henoko near Nago city in Okinawa.

The local protests have intensified since late 2014. The issue of the relocation of the US airbase currently entails not only local protests against discrimination against Okinawans and the unequal burden the Security Treaty imposed on the prefecture but also the destruction of the local environment due to the construction of a new base that requires the dumping of a massive amount of concrete into the sea. In the November gubernatorial election, Okinawans voted for an anti-relocation candidate Takeshi Onaga, and in the December 2014 general election, anti-relocation candidates won all the electoral districts in Okinawa. The electoral victories, however, seemed not enough to move Tokyo. Prime Minister Abe Shinzo, an ardent supporter of the US military bases in Okinawa, repeatedly announced that these electoral victories of anti-relocation candidates in Okinawa would not have a major impact on the national plan for the relocation of the US military bases. In 2015, local protestors relentlessly staged sit-in strikes and rallies against the relocation plan. The Japanese riot police dragged away sit-in protestors, young and old, women and men, trying to crack down the protestors in defense of the US military bases. According to a Welsh journalist based in Japan, Jon Mitchell,

"Between January and February, three senior USMC [US Marine Corps] officials accused anti-base campaigners of hate speech, 'mob rule' and 'faking injuries' while on February 22, base security guards seized two demonstrators—only to see them released the next day."[14] The issue of the US military bases in Okinawa is, however, not a "Okinawa Problem," rather it is the problem of the US-Japan relationship that continued to rely on the Cold War security structure while serving "mutual" national interests. This is the structure that significantly owes its continuing existence to the Japanese perception of "security" and "mutuality" in regard to the US-Japan Security Treaty.

Historians of postwar Japan have so far focused on the conservative political dominance led by the LDP, the buildup of the National Self-Defense Forces and the economic benefits as the legacies of the history of Japan's Cold War alliance with the United States. My study demonstrated that the Japanese concepts of security, democracy, modern history, and the alliance with the US which persist to this day are inheritances shaped by the Cold War. As shown earlier, after the reverse course, American and Japanese Cold Warriors found these concepts significantly diverse and malleable. Significant efforts were made by the US and Japanese policymakers to modify and homogenize the concepts in order to attain mutual conceptual coherency in prosecuting the US-Japan Security Treaty and counter global Communism over the period between the reverse course and the mid-1970s. The legacy of this long-term process, in addition to Japan's feeling of insecurity in the region in regard to China and North Korea, should be taken into account in analyzing the Japanese understanding of and support for the US-Japan Security Treaty and the ability of the United States to maintain its image as the sole hegemonic stabilizer of East Asia.

NOTES

1. Airgram From US Embassy, Tokyo to Department of State, subject: the Japanese Student Protest Movement, April 10, 1969. RG 59. Box 2246. NARA II.
2. Go Tsuyoshi Ito, Alliance in Anxiety: Detente and the Sino-American-Japanese Triangle (New York: Routledge, 2003), 50.
3. Shigematsu, *Scream from the Shadows*, 142.
4. Airgram From US Embassy, Tokyo to Department of State, subject: the Japanese Student Protest Movement, April 10, 1969. RG 59. Box 2246. NARA II.
5. Airgram from US Consulate in Nagoya (Noonan) to Department of State, subject: Brighter Outlook in 1969–1970 Student Violence, September 24, 1969. RG 59. Box 2246. NARA II.
6. Ibid.
7. Ibid.

8. Tomohiro Yara, "Withdrawal of US Marines Blocked by Japan in the 1970s," The Asia-Pacific Journal: Japan Focus 47, no. 4 (2013), http://www.japanfocus.org/-yara-tomohiro/4037. (accessed on March 7, 2015).

9. Ibid.

10. Ibid.

11. Westad, "Cold War and the International History of the Twentieth Century," 4.

12. Francine Parker, "F.A.T.," (Los Angeles, CA: Displaced Films, 1972), 18:10; Although the film provides its own English translation for the song's lyrics, the translations of the lyrics in the text are provided by the author in order to adopt a more direct translation of the original Japanese lyrics; the lyrics cited here differs from the official lyrics of Okinawa wa Ainoko; Ainoko in Japanese is a derogatory term for a Japanese child of mixed races.

13. C. Douglas Lummis, "Okinawa: State of Emergency," The Asia-Pacific Journal: Japan Focus 13, no. 8 (February 12, 2015), http://japanfocus.org/events/view/243#.VOyDqOurISE.mailto.(accessed on March 5, 2015).

14. On January 8, 2015, Robert Eldridge, Deputy Assistant Chief of Staff of Government and External Affairs for the United States Marine Corps, appeared on Sakura Channel, Japan's ultra-nationalist channel, accusing Okinawan protestors of hate speech; Jon Mitchell, "On Okinawa, US Marines Raise Tensions with Accusations and Arrests of Peace Campaigners," The Asia-Pacific Journal: Japan Focus 13, no. 9, no. 1 (March 1, 2015), http://japanfocus.org/events/view/245. (accessed on March 5, 2015).

Appendix

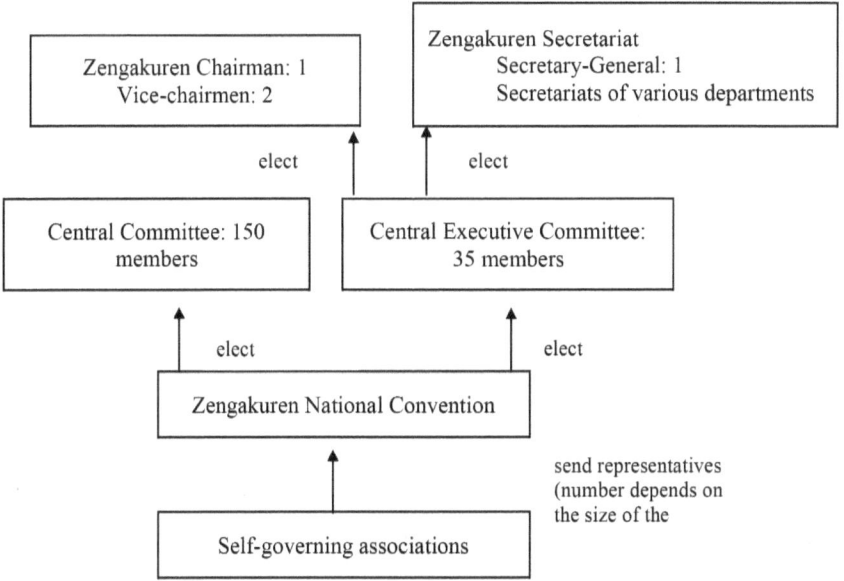

Zengakuren's Organizational Structure in 1948.

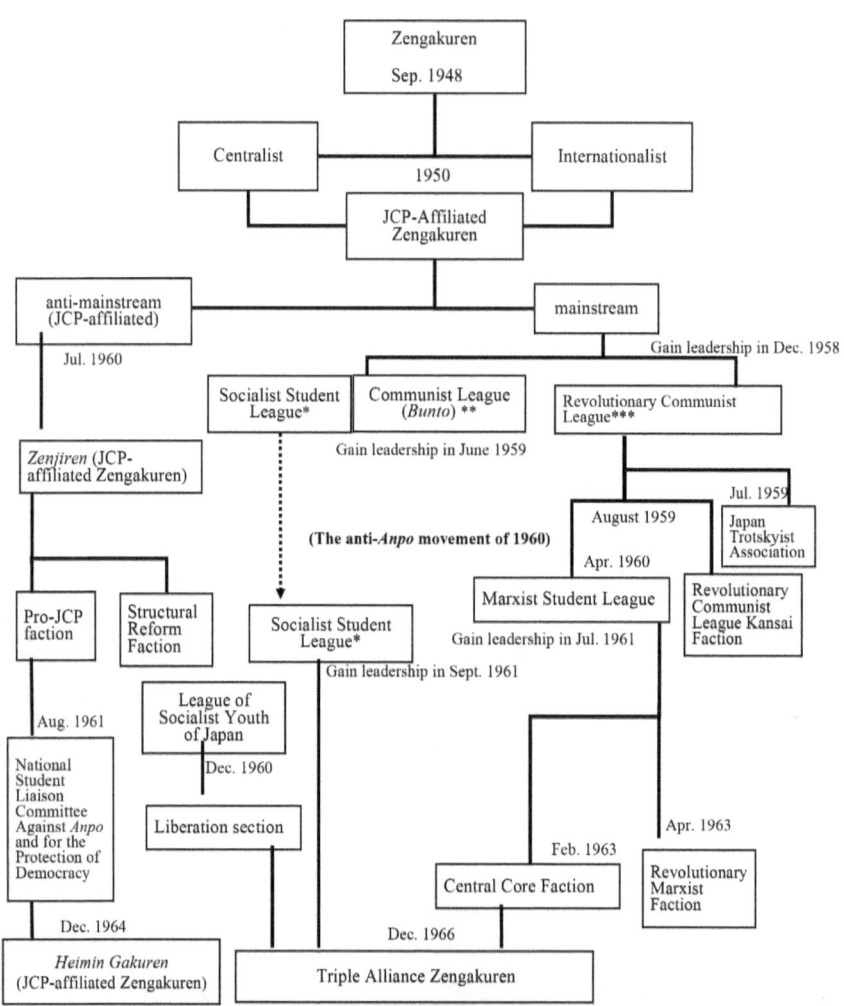

* Formally named the Japan Antiwar Student League until May 1958.
** After the anti-*Anpo* protests, *Bunto* splintered into four smaller factions.
*** Formally named the Japan Trotskyist League until December 1958.
This chart was created by the author by using information from Shakai Mondai Kenkyū Kai, *Zengakuren Kakuha: Gakusei Undō Jiten* (Tokyo: Futaba Sha, 1969).

The Genealogy of Zengakuren leadership, 1948–1963.

Selected Bibliography

Aldous, Richard. *Schlesinger: The Imperial Historian*. New York: W.W. Norton, 2017.
Amano, Kazuya. "Sunagawa no 3-Jikan: Gakusei Kara Mita 2-Ji Kara 5-Ji Made." *Bungeishunju* 34, no. 12 (December, 1956): 118–25.
"Amerika ni Okeru Akairo Kyōjyu Tuihō no Shinsō." *Gakusei Hyōron*, no. 3 (1949): 71–78.
Ando, Takemasa. *Japan's New Left Movements: Legacies for Civil Society*. New York: Routledge, 2013.
Baerwald, Hans H. *The Purge of Japanese Leaders under the Occupation*. Berkeley: University of California Press, 1959; Westport, CT: Greenwood Press, 1977.
Beheiren Nyūsu Shukusatuban Kankō Iinkai, ed. *Beheiren Nyūsu Shukusatsuban: 1965–1974, Dassōhei Tsūshin, JATEC Tsūshin*. Tokyo: Kawade Shobo, 1974.
Bōei Shisetsuchōshi Hensan Iinkai, ed. *Bōei Shisetsuchōshi: Kichimondai to Tomoni Ayunda 45-nen no Kiseki*. Tokyo: Bōei Shisetsucho, 2007.
Bromley, Simon. "The Logic of American Power in the International Capitalist Order." In *The War on Terrorism and the American Empire after the Cold War*, edited by Alejandro Coles and Richard Saull. New York: Routledge, 2006, 44–64.
Brown, Timothy Scott. *West Germany and the Global Sixties: The Antiauthoritarian Revolt, 1962–1978*. New York: Cambridge University Press, 2013.
Carlile, Lonny E. *Divisions of Labor: Globality, Ideology, and War in the Shaping of the Japanese Labor Movement*. Honolulu: University of Hawaii Press, 2004.
Cha, Victor D. "Bridging the Gap: The Strategic Context of the 1965 Korean-Japan Normalization Treaty." *Korean Studies* 20 (1996): 123–60.
Chōtatsuchō Sōmubu Sōmuka. "Hikōjyō Kakuchō ni Kansuru Shomondai ni Tsuite." *Chōtatsuchō Chōsa Jihō*, no. 15 (1957): 1–25, 83.
Chuo Daigaku Gakusei Jichikai Chōsabu. *Sunagawa-machi ni Okeru Kichi Kakuchō Hantai Tōsō o Megurite*. Tokyo: Chūō Daigaku Gakusei Jichikai, 1956.

Cummings, Bruce. "The Origins and Development of the Northeast Asian Political Economy: Industrial Sectors, Product Cycles, and Political Consequences." *International Organization* 38, no. 1 (1984): 1–40.

Dope, Stephen P. *Arthur M. Schlesinger, Jr., and the Ideological History of American Liberalism*. Tuscaloosa, AL: The University of Alabama Press, 1994.

Dower, John W. *Embracing Defeat: Japan in the Wake of World War II*. New York: W.W. Norton & Co., 1999.

———. *Empire and Aftermath: Yoshida Shigeru and the Japanese Experience, 1878–1954*. Cambridge, MA: Harvard University Press, 1988.

Dulles, John Foster. "Policy for Security and Peace." *Foreign Affairs* 32, no. 3 (1954): 355–56.

———. "The New Look: The Evolution of Foreign Policy," January 12, 1954. *US National Security Policy and Strategy: Documents and Policy Proposals*, edited by Sam C. Sarkesian and Robert A. Vitas. New York: Greenwood Press, 1988, 52–4.

Eells, Walter Crosby. *Communism in Education in Asia, Africa, and the Far Pacific*. Washington, DC: American Council on Education, 1954.

Eisenhower, Dwight D. *Public Papers of the Presidents of the United States: Dwight D. Eisenhower, 1960–1961*, edited by National Archives and Records Service Office of the Federal Register, General Services Administration. Washington DC: US Government Printing Office, 1961.

Elbaum, Max. *Revolution in the Air: Sixties Radicals Turn to Lenin, Mao and Che*. New York: Verso Books, 2006.

Emmerson, John K. *The Japanese Thread: A Life in the US Foreign Service*. New York: Holt, Rinehart and Winston, 1978.

Engerman, David C. *Modernization from the Other Shore: American Intellectuals and the Romance of Russian Development*. Cambridge, MA: Harvard University Press, 2003.

Fink, Carole, Philipp Gassert, and Detlef Junker. "Introduction." In *1968: The World Transformed*, edited by Carole Fink, Philipp Gassert, and Detlef Junker. New York: Cambridge University Press, 1998, 1–28.

Foreign Relations of the United States, 1946. Vol. VIII: The Far East. Washington, DC: US Government Printing Office, 1971.

Foreign Relations of the United States, 1947. Vol. VI: The Far East. Washington, DC: United States Government Printing Office, 1972.

Foreign Relations of the United States, 1948. Vol. VI: The Far East and Australasia. Washington, DC: United States Government Printing Office, 1974.

Foreign Relations of the United States, 1950. Vol. VI: East Asia and the Pacific. Washington, DC: United States Government Printing Office, 1976.

Foreign Relations of the United States, 1952–1954. Vol. XIV, part 2: China and Japan. Washington, DC: US Government Printing Office, 1985.

Foreign Relations of the United States, 1955–1957. Vol. XXIII, part 1: Japan. Washington, DC: United States Government Printing Office, 1991.

Foreign Relations of the United States, 1958–1960. Vol. XVIII: Japan and Korea. Washington, DC: US Government Printing Office, 1994.

Friedman, Max Paul. *Rethinking Anti-Americanism: The History of an Exceptional Concept in American Foreign Relations*. New York: Cambridge University Press, 2012.
Fukawa, Reiko, and Shōji Niihara. "The Declassified Documents of US Government Concerning the Decision of Tokyo District Court on the Sunagawa Case Judged by Akio Date." *Yamashina Gakuin Law Review* 64 (2010): 202–155.
Gardner, Lloyd C. "New Deal Diplomacy: A View from the Seventies." In *Watershed of Empire: Essays on New Deal Foreign Policy*, edited by Leonard P. Liggio and James Joseph Martin. Colorado Springs: R. Myles, 1976, 95–132.
Garon, Sheldon. "Rethinking Modernization and Modernity in Japanese History: A Focus on State-Society Relations." *The Journal of Asian Studies* 53, no. 2 (1994): 346–66.
Gayn, Mark. *Japan Diary*. New York: William Sloane Associates, 1948; Rutland, VT and Tokyo: Charles E. Tuttle Company, 1981.
Gendai Shichōsha, ed. *Sōkōsha to Seishun Zengakuren Gakusei no Shuki*. Tokyo: Gendai Shichōsha, 1960.
Grandin, Greg. "Your Americanism and Mine: Americanism and Anti-Americanism in the Americas." *The American Historical Review* 111, no. 4 (2006): 1042–66.
Guthrie-Shimizu, Sayuri. "Japan, the United States, and the Cold War, 1945–1960." In *The Cambridge History of the Cold War, Volume 1: Origin*, edited by Melvyn P. Leffler and Odd Arne Westad. New York: Cambridge University Press, 2010.
Hall, John Whitney. "Changing Conceptions of the Modernization of Japan." In *Changing Japanese Attitudes toward Modernization*, edited by Marius B. Jansen. Princeton: Princeton University Press, 1965, 7–42.
Hamanaka, Shintaro. *Asian Regionalism and Japan: The Politics of Membership in Regional Diplomatic, Financial and Trade Groups*. New York: Routledge, 2010.
Hara, Yoshihisa. *Sengo Nihon to Kokusai Seiji: Anpo Kaitei no Seiji*. Tokyo: Chūō Kōron Sha, 1988.
Harada, Hisato. "The Anti-Ampo Struggle." In *Zengakuren: Japan's Revolutionary Students*, edited by Stuart J. Dowsey. Berkeley: Ishi Press, 1970, 75–99.
Harvey, David. *The New Imperialism*. New York: Oxford University Press, 2005.
Havens, Thomas R. H. *Fire across the Sea: The Vietnam War and Japan 1965–1975*. Princeton: Princeton University Press, 1987.
Hidaka, Rokurō. *1960-nen 5-Gatu 19-Nichi*. Tokyo: Iwanami Shoten, 1960.
Hirata, Tetsuo. *Reddo Pāji no Shi-teki Kyūmei*. Tokyo: Shin Nihon Shuppansha, 2002.
Hironaka, Toshio. "Keisatsukan no Higeki." *Chūō Kōron* 71, no. 13 (December 1956): 40–48.
Höhn, Maria, and Seungsook Moon. "Introduction: The Politics of Gender, Sexuality, Race, and Class in the US Military Empire." In *Over There: Living with the U.S. Military Empire from World War Two to the Present*, edited by Maria Höhn and Seungsook Moon. Durham, NC: Duke University Press, 2010, 1–36.
Hokkaido Daigaku Shimbunkai, ed. *Hokkaido Daigaku Shimbun (Fukkoku-Ban)*. Vol. 4: Ōzorasha, 1989.

Hotta, Yoshie. "Sunagawa Kara Budapesuto Made: Rekishi ni Tsuite." *Chūō Kōron* 71, no. 13 (December 1956): 20–30.
Ichida, Yoshihiko, and Eiki Ishii. *Kikigaki "Bunto" Ichidai: Seiji to Iryō de Jidai o Kakenukeru*. Tokyo: Sekaishoin, 2010.
Iida, Momo. "Shimin Minshu Shugi Undō no Ronri to Shinri." In *Shimin Undō Towa Nanika: Beheiren no Shisō*, edited by Makoto Oda. Tokyo: Tokuma Shoten, 1968, 12–34.
Itagaki, Yoichi. "The Developmental Patterns of Political and Economic Modernization in Asia in Transitional Stage from a Point of View of Culture Contact with Special Reference to the Vestige of Colonialism." In *Report: International Conference on the Problems of Modernization in Asia, June 28–July 7, 1965*. Seoul: Korea University, 1966, 167–80.
Ito, Go Tsuyoshi. *Alliance in Anxiety: Detente and the Sino-American-Japanese Triangle*. New York: Routledge, 2003.
Kapur, Nick. *Japan at the Crossroads: Conflict and Compromise after Anpo*. Cambridge, MA: Harvard University Press, 2018.
Keisatsu Kōron Henshūbu. "Sunagawa Jiken ni Tsuite: Kichimondai no Ichi Danmen." *Keisatsu Kōron* 10, no. 11 (1955): 27–35.
Kennan, George. "Which Is the Civilized Power." *Outlook*, no. 78 (1904): 516–20.
Kennan, George F. *Memoirs*. Boston: Little, Brown, 1967.
Kersten, Rikki. *Democracy in Postwar Japan: Maruyama Masao and the Search for Autonomy*. New York: Routledge, 1996.
Kim, Charles R. "Moral Imperatives: South Korean Studenthood and April 19th." *The Journal of Asian Studies* 71 (May 2012): 399–422.
Kishi, Nobusuke. *Anpo Jyōyaku Kaitei no Ikisatsu to Sono Haikei*. Tokyo: Jiyū Minshutō Kōhō Iinkai, 1969.
Klimke, Martin. *The Other Alliance: Student Protest in West Germany and the United States in the Global Sixties*. Princeton: Princeton University Press, 2009.
Kōan Chōsachō. *Anpo Tōsō no Gaiyō: Tōsō no Keika to Bunseki*. Tokyo: Kōan Chōsachō, 1960.
Kobayashi, Yoshiaki. *Sengo Kakumei Undō Ronsōshi*. Tokyo: San-Ichi Shobo, 1971.
Kokubun, Yutaka. "The University Problem." In *Zengakuren: Japan's Revolutionary Students*, edited by Stuart J. Dowsey. Berkeley: Ishi Press, 1970, 100–35.
Kolko, Joyce. *American and the Crisis of World Capitalism*. Boston: Beacon Press, 1974.
Koschmann, J. Victor. "Intellectuals and Politics." In *Postwar Japan as History*, edited by Andrew Gordon. Berkeley: University of California Press, 1993, 395–423.
———. "Modernization and Democratic Values: The 'Japanese Model' in the 1960s." In *Staging Growth: Modernization, Development, and the Global Cold War*, edited by David Engermann, Nils Gilman, Mark Haefele and Michael E. Latham. Amherst, MA: University of Massachusetts Press, 2003, 225–49.
———. *Revolution and Subjectivity in Postwar Japan*. Chicago: University of Chicago Press, 1996.

Kudo, Kohei. "Bunto Kokusaibu: 1968–69-nen no Ichi-nen." In *Ichi Taishū Seijika no Kiseki: Matsumoto Reiji (Takahashi Yoshihiko) Ikō, Tsuitō Shū*, edited by Tsuitō Shū Henshū Iinkai Takahashi Yoshihiko Ikō. Tokyo: Sairyusha, 1988, 343–56.
Kurata, Keisei. *Anpo Zengakuren*. Tokyo: San-Ichi Shobo, 1969.
Kurlansky, Mark. *1968: The Year That Rocked the World*. New York: Ballantine Books, 2004.
Kyoto Daigaku Shimbun, ed. *Kyoto Daigaku Shimbun (Shukusatsuban)*. Vol. 6. Kyoto: Kyoto Daigaku Shimbunsha, 1970.
LaFantasie, Glenn W., ed. *Foreign Relations of the United States, 1958–1960, Vol. XVIII, Japan; Korea*. edited by Madeline Chi and Louis J. Smith. Washington DC: US Government Printing Office, 1994.
Langdon, Frank. *Japan's Foreign Policy*. Vancouver: The University of British Columbia Press, 1973.
Latham, Michael E. *Modernization as Ideology: American Social Science and "Nation Building" in the Kennedy Era*. Chapel Hill, NC: The University of North Carolina Press, 2000.
Lattimore, Owen. *The Situation in Asia*. Boston: Little, Brown and Company, 1949; New York: Greenwood Press, 1969.
Lee, Jooyoung. "Forming a Democratic Society: South Korean Responses to US Democracy Promotion, 1953–1960." *Diplomatic History* 39, no. 5 (2015): 844–75.
Lenin, Vladimir I. *"Left Wing" Communism: An Infantile Disorder*. Detroit: Marxian Educational Society, 1921.
Lichtenstein, Nelson. *State of the Union: A Century of American Labor*. Princeton: Princeton University Press, 2002.
Lummis, C. Douglas. "Okinawa: State of Emergency," *The Asia-Pacific Journal: Japan Focus* 13, no. 8 (February 12, 2015). http://japanfocus.org/events/view/243#.VOyDqOurISE.mailto.
Maruyama, Masao. "Patterns of Individuation and the Case of Japan: A Conceptual Scheme." In *Changing Japanese Attitudes toward Modernization*, edited by Marius B. Jansen. Princeton: Princeton University Press, 1965, 489–531.
Matsunami, Michihiro. "Origins of Zengakuren." In *Zengakuren: Japan's Revolutionary Students*, edited by Stuart J. Dowsey. Berkeley: Ishi Press, 1970, 42–47.
Merrill, Dennis, ed. *Documentary History of the Truman Presidency*. Vol. 5: Creating a Pluralistic Democracy in Japan: The Occupation Government, 1945–1952. Bethesda, MD: University Publications of America, 1995.
Mills, C. Wright. "Letter to the New Left." *New Left Review*, no. 5 (September–October) (1960): 18–23.
Mitchell, Jon. "On Okinawa, US Marines Raise Tensions with Accusations and Arrests of Peace Campaigners," *The Asia-Pacific Journal: Japan Focus* 13, no. 9 (March 1, 2015). http://japanfocus.org/events/view/245.
Murakami, Taro. "Arashi no Naka no Zengaukren." *Kaizo* 33, no. 6 (1952): 148–51.
Muto, Ichiyo. "Beheiren no Shisō: Sengo Minshu Shugi no Yukue ni Yosete." In *Shimin Undō Towa Nanika: Beheiren no Shisō*, edited by Makoto Oda. Tokyo: Tokuma Shoten, 1968, 82–99.

Myojin, Isao. "Īruzu Tōsō: Kenkyūsha no Tachiba Kara (a View from the Scholar of the Eells Incident)." In *Sōkū ni Kozue Tsuranete: Īruzu Tōsō 60-shūnen Anpo Tōsō 50-shūnen no Toshi ni Hokudai no Jiyū Jichi no Rekishi o Kangaeru*, edited by Hokudai 5.16 Shūkai Hōkokusho Henshū Iinkai. Sapporo: Hakurosha, 2011, 19–58.

———. "Red Purge in Universities in Occupied Japan (1): A Study on the Eells University in Hokkaidō University." *Journal of Hokkaido University of Education* 45, no. 1 (1994): 15–27.

———. "Red Purge in Universities in Occupied Japan (2): A Study on Eells's Address in Niigata University." *Journal of Hokkaido University of Education* 47, no. 1 (1966): 45–53.

———. "Red Purge in Universities in Occupied Japan (3): A Study on 'Eells Whirlwind'." *Journal of Hokkaido University of Education* 47, no. 2 (1996): 33–45.

Nakajima, Takuma. *Okinawa Henkan to Nichibei Anpo Taisei*. Tokyo: Yuhikaku, 2012.

Niebuhr, Reinhold. "The Failure of US Diplomacy." *New Leader* 43, no. 31 (August 1960): 6–7.

Nihon Gakusei Undō Kenkyūkai. *Gakusei Undō no Kenkyū*. Tokyo: Nikkan Rōdō Tsushin Sha, 1966.

Oda, Makoto. *Beheiren*. Tokyo: San-Ichi Shobo, 1969.

———. "The Ethics of Peace." In *Authority and the Individuals in Japan: Citizen Protest in Historical Perspective*, edited by J. Victor Koschmann. Tokyo: University of Tokyo Press, 1978, 154–70.

Office of the Federal Register, National Archives and Records Service, General Services Administration, ed. *Public Papers of the Presidents of the United States: Dwight D. Eisenhower, 1957* Washington, DC: US Government Printing Office, 1958.

Ogura, Jyoji, Etsuji Sumiya, and Suehide Takakuwa. *Nihon Gakusei Shakai Undō Shi: Kyoto o Chūshin ni*. Kyoto: Doshisha Daigaku Shuppanbu, 1953.

Ōhara Shakai Mondai Kenkyūjo. *Nihon Rōdō Nenkan 1949*. Vol. 22. Tokyo: Daiichi Shuppansha, 1949.

———. *Nihon Rōdō Nenkan, 1952*. Vol. 24. Tokyo: Jiji Tsūshinsha, 1951.

Oinas-Kukkonen, Henry. *Tolerance, Suspicion, and Hostility: Changing US Attitudes toward the Japanese Communist Movement, 1944–1947*. Westport, CT: Greenwood Press, 2003.

Ōkura Zaisei Chōsakai: Kyōiku Kenkyūbu, ed. *Kyōiku Gyōsei no Genjyō: Īruzu Seimei Kara Rinkyōsin*. Tokyo: Ōkura Zaisei Chōsakai, 1984.

Omori, Minoru. *Sengo Hishi, Vol. 4: Akahata to GHQ*. Tokyo: Kodansha, 1975.

Onishi, Yuichiro. "The Presence of (Black) Liberation in Okinawan Freedom: Transnational Moments, 1968–1972." In *Extending the Diaspora: New Histories of Black People*, edited by Dawne Y. Curry, Eric D. Duke and Marshanda A. Smith. Chicago: University of Illinois Press, 2009, 178–202.

Orr, Mark T. "Educational Reform in Occupied Japan, 1945–1950: A Study of Acceptance of and Resistance to Institutional Change." Ph.D. dissertation, University of Chicago, 1952.

Packard, George R. *Edwin O. Reischauer and the American Discovery of Japan.* New York: Columbia University Press, 2010.

Paget, Karen M. *Patriotic Betrayal: The Inside Story of the CIA's Secret Campaign to Enroll American Students in the Crusade against Communism.* New Haven: Yale University Press, 2015.

Parker, Francine. "F.T.A.". Los Angeles, CA: Displaced Films, 1972.

Passin, Herbert. "The Sources of Protest in Japan." *The American Political Science Review* 56, no. 2 (1962): 391–403.

Peck, James. *Ington's China: The National Security World, the Cold War, and the Origins of Globalism.* Amherst: University of Massachusetts Press, 2006.

Pons, Silvio. *The Global Revolution: A History of International Communism 1917–1991.* Oxford: Oxford University Press, 2014.

Reischauer, Edwin O. *Beyond Vietnam: The United States and Asia.* New York: Alfred A. Knopf, Inc., 1967.

———. *My Life between Japan and America.* New York: Harper & Row Publishers, 1986.

———. "Nihon no Minshu Shugi ni Tsuite: Nichi Beikan no Kōryū o Zentei ni." *Sekai* 178 (October 1960): 217–21.

———. "Our Dialogue with Japan." *Foreign Affairs* 45, no. 2 (January 1967): 215–28.

———. *Wanted: An Asian Policy.* New York: Knopf, 1955.

Reischauer, Haru Matsukata. *Samurai and Silk: A Japanese and American Heritage.* Cambridge, MA: Belknap Press of Harvard University Press, 1986.

Robin, Ron. *The Making of the Cold War Enemy: Culture and Politics in the Military-Intellectual Complex* Princeton: Princeton University Press, 2001.

Rosendorf, Neal. "John Foster Dulles' Nuclear Schizophrenia." In *Cold War Statesmen Confront the Bomb: Nuclear Diplomacy since 1945*, edited by Philip H. Gordon, John Lewis Gaddis, Earnest R. May and Jonathan Rosenberg. New York: Oxford University Press, 1999.

San-Ichi Shobo Henshūbu, ed. *Shiryō Sengo Gakusei Undō: Zengakuren Documents*, 1945–1949. Vol. 1. Tokyo: San-Ichi Shobo, 1968.

———, ed. *Shiryō Sengo Gakusei Undō: Zengakuren Documents*, 1950–1952. Vol. 2. Tokyo: San-Ichi Shobo, 1969.

———, ed. *Shiryō Sengo Gakusei Undō: Zengakuren Documents*, 1952–1955. Vol. 3. Tokyo: San-Ichi Shobo, 1969.

———, ed. *Shiryō Sengo Gakusei Undō: Zengakuren Documents*, 1956–1958. Vol. 4. Tokyo: San-Ichi Shobo, 1969.

———, ed. *Shiryō Sengo Gakusei Undō: Zengakuren Documents*, 1959–1960. Vol. 5. Tokyo: San-Ichi Shobō, 1969.

———, ed. *Shiryō Sengo Gakusei Undō: Zengakuren Documents*, 1964–1967. Vol. 7. Tokyo: San-Ichi Shobo, 1970.

Sasaki-Uemura, Wesley. *Organizing the Spontaneous: Citizen Protest in Postwar Japan.* Honolulu: University of Hawai'i Press, 2001.

Schaller, Michael. *Altered States: The United States and Japan since the Occupation.* New York: Oxford University Press, 1997.

———. *The American Occupation of Japan: The Origins of the Cold War in Asia.* New York: Oxford University Press, 1985.

Schrecker, Ellen. "McCarthyism: Political Repression and the Fear of Communism." *Social Research* 71, no. 4 (2004): 1041–86.

Senate Committee on the Judiciary. *Communist Anti-American Riots: Mob Violence as an Instrument of Red Diplomacy. Bogotá—Caracas—La Paz—Tokyo, August 26, 1960*, Congress Washington DC: United States Government Printing Office, 1960.

Shigematsu, Setsu. *Scream from the Shadows: The Women's Liberation Movement in Japan.* Minneapolis: University of Minnesota Press, 2012.

Shigeo, Shima, and Takazawa Kōji. *Bunto (Kyōsan Shugisha Dōmei) no Shisō 1*, vol. 1. Tokyo: Hihyō Sha, 1992.

Shimbori, Michiya. "Zengakuren: A Japanese Case Study of a Student Political Movement." *Sociology of Education* 37, no. 3 (1964): 229–53.

Shin Sayoku Riron Zenshi Henshū Iinkai. *Shin Sayoku Riron Zenshi.* Tokyo: Ryūdo Shuppan, 1979.

Shinseikai Henshūkyoku. "Kichi to Sunagawa Mondai Tokushū." *Shinseikai* 2, no. 13 (1956): 2–25.

"Soviet Government Statement." *Current Digest of the Soviet Press* 10, no. 48 (January 1959).

Strohl, Nancy. "Freedom of the Press—or Subversion and Sabotage?" In *Voices from the Underground: Insider Histories of the Vietnam Era Underground Press*, edited by Ken Wachsberger. Ann Arbor, MI: Mica Press, 259–68.

"Sunagawa no Shufu Nikki." *Fujin Kōron* 41, no. 12 (December 1956): 78–85.

Suzuki, Ichiro. *Shōgen: 2.1 Zenesuto.* Tokyo: Aki Shobō, 1979.

Swenson-Wright, John. *Unequal Allies?: United States Security and Alliance Policy toward Japan.* Stanford: Stanford University Press, 2005.

Takagi, Masayuki. *Shin Sayoku 30-nen Shi.* Tokyo: Doyō Bijyutsusha, 1988.

Takei, Teruo. "Nihongakusei Undō ni Okeru Hantei-teki Dentō no Kenji to Hatten no Tameni." *Gakusei Hyōron*, no. 7 (1950): 33–58.

———. *Takei Teruo Gakusei Undō Ronshū: Sō to Shiteno Gakusei Undō, Zengakuren Sōseiki no Shisō to Kōdō.* Tokyo: Supesu Kaya, 2005.

Takemae, Eiji, ed. *GHQ Shirei (SCAPIN) Sōshūsei.* Vol. 15: SCAPIN 2051–2204. Tokyo: Emutei Shuppan, 1993.

———. *Inside GHQ: The Allied Occupation of Japan and Its Legacy.* Translated by Robert Ricketts and Sebastian Swann. New York: Continuum, 2002.

———. *Sengo Rōdō Kaikaku: GHQ Rōdō Seisakushi.* Tokyo: Tokyo Daigaku Shuppankai, 1982.

Tamaki, Kazuhiko. "60-nen Anop Kara Beigun Saihen He: Zainichi Beigun to Anpo no Hensen." *Gendai Shisō* 34, no. 10 (2006): 112–21.

The Educational Policies Commission of the National Education Association of the United States and the American Association of School Administrators and the Executive Committee of the American Council on Education. *Education and National Security.* Washington, DC: American Council on Education, 1951.

Thomas, Evan. *Robert Kennedy: His Life.* New York: Simon & Schuster Paperbacks, 2000.

"Tōhoku Daigaku Jiken: Rupotājyu." *Gakusei Hyōron*, no. 6 (1950): 112–20.
Tokyo Daigaku Gakusei Undō Kenkyūkai. *Nihon no Gakusei Undō: Sono Riron to Rekishi*. Tokyo: Shinko Shuppansha, 1956.
Trachtenberg, Marc, ed. *The Development of American Strategic Thought: Basic Documents from the Eisenhower and Kennedy Periods, Including the Basic National Security Policy Papers from 1953 to 1959*. New York: Garland Publishing, Inc., 1988.
Tsurumi, Kazuko. "The Japanese Student Movement (1) Its Milieu." *Japan Quartely* 15, no. 4 (1968): 430–55.
Uemura, Shinichi. "Guromuiko Oboegaki no Nerai: Nichibei Kōshō Kara Kongo no Nisso Kankei Made." *Sekai Shūhō* 47, no. 7 (February 1960): 36–39.
United States Department of State Policy Planning Staff, ed. *The State Department Policy Planning Staff Papers*. Vol. 1. New York: Garland Publishing, Inc., 1983.
US Congress, Senate. *Congressional Record*, June 15, 1966. Congress 89, session 2. 13169–71.
US Congress, Senate, Committee on Foreign Relations. *Ambassadorial Nominations, Nomination of Edwin O. Reischauer to Be Ambassador to Japan: Hearings before the Committee on Foreign Relations United States*, March 23 and 24, 1961. Congress 87, session 1. Washington, DC: US Government Printing Office, 1961.
"Watashi wa Heiwa no Tameni Nani o Surunoka: Betonamu ni Heiwa o! Nichibei Simin Kaigi." *Bungei* (1966): 179–319.
Westad, Odd Arne. "Cold War and the International History of the Twentieth Century." In *The Cambridge History of the Cold War, Vol. 1: Origins*, edited by Melvyn P. Leffler and Odd Arne Westad. New York: Cambridge University Press, 2010, 1–19.
———. *The Global Cold War: Third World Interventions and the Making of Our Times*. New York: Cambridge University Press, 2007.
Williams, William Appleman. *The Tragedy of American Diplomacy*. Cleveland: World Publishing Company, 1959; New York: W.W. Norton & Co., 2009.
Wilson, Sandra. "Exhibiting a New Japan: The Tokyo Olympics of 1964 and Expo '70 in Osaka." 85, no. 227 (2012): 159–78.
Xing, Liu. "Rethinking Shigemitsu's Visit to US in Japan-US Security Relations." *Journal of Law and Politics (Nagoya Daigaku Hōsei Ronshū)* 207 (2005): 1–45.
Yamamoto, Kiyoshi. *Yomiuri Sōgi: 1945–1946*. Tokyo: Ochanomizu Shobō, 1978.
Yamanaka, Akira. *Sengo Gakusei Undōshi*. Tokyo: Aoki Shoten, 1961.
Yanada, Masataka. *Hokudai no Īruzu Tōsō: Sono Shinjitu o Akiraka ni Suru Tameni*. Tokyo: Kōyō Shuppan Sha, 2006.
Yara, Tomohiro. "Withdrawal of US Marines Blocked by Japan in the 1970s," *The Asia-Pacific Journal: Japan Focus* 47, no. 4 (2013). http://www.japanfocus.org/-yara-tomohiro/4037.
Yi, Kil J. "In Search of a Panacea: Japan-Korea Rapprochement and America's 'Far Eastern Problems'." *Pacific Historical Review* 71, no. 4 (2002): 633–62.
Yoneyama, Lisa. *Hiroshima Traces: Time, Space, and the Dialectics of Memory*. Berkeley: University of California Press, 1999.

Yoon, Tae-Ryong. "Learning to Cooperate Not to Cooperate: Bargaining for the 1965 Korea-Japan Normalization." *Asian Perspective* 32, no. 2 (2008): 59–91.
Yoshida, Shigeru. *The Yoshida Memoirs: The Story of Japan in Crisis*. Westport, CT: Greenwood Press, 1977.
Young, Marilyn B. *The Vietnam Wars, 1945–1990*. New York: Harper Collins, 1991.
Zengakuren. *Zengakuren: Twenty Years' Struggle*. Tokyo: All Japan Federation of Student Autonomous Associations, 1967.
Zinn, Howard. *The Zinn Reader: Writings on Disobedience and Democracy*. 2nd ed. New York: Seven Stories Press, 209, 2009.
Zinner, Paul E., ed. *Documents on American Foreign Relations, 1958*. New York: Harper and Row, 1959.
———, ed. *Documents on American Foreign Relations, 1959*. New York: Harper and Row, 1960.

Index

Page references for figures are *italicized*

Acheson, Dean, 24–25, 53, 65
AFL-CIO, 105
African Americans, 5, 10, 54, 127, 201, 209–11, 217–22
Akahata, x, 16, 38–39, 89
Algerian National Liberation Front (NLF), 87, 93
All-Japan Federation of Students' Self–Governing Associations. *See* Zengakuren
Allison, John Moore, 80
Anpo. *See* US-Japan Security Treaty
Anpo Mondai Kenkyū Kai, x, 86
anti-*Anpo* protests, 6, 8, 56, 101–2, 105, 107–9, 156–58, 165, 175, 180, 190–92, 197, 202; American perception of, 109–29, 142, 147; between May 19 and June 19, 115–24, *123*; beginning of, 65, 86, 92, 104–107; impact on the student movement, 106, 109–14, 140–42, 188; in Okinawa, 125–27; Reischauer's view of, 139, 143–44, 149–50
anti-Communism: American, 1–9, 14–15, 22–27, 30n48, 33–35, 38, 42, 47, 52–55, 65, 68–73, 77–78, 101–5, 107, 110, 112, 115, 122, 124, 128–29, 139, 142, 146–47, 149, 157, 167, 179, 193, 208, 231, 237; in education, 7, 33–36, 40–44, 46–48, 139; Japanese, 19, 25, 37–41, 48, 50, 74–77, 85, 101, 112, 115, 117, 120–21, 155, 196, 237; of GHQ/SCAP, 2, 7–8, 14, 19–20, 22, 25, 33–35, 38, 43–44, 46–47, 50, 55; of Edwin O. Reischauer, 143–44, 146, 151, 174–75; of Robert F. Kennedy, 168, 170–71, 178–79
anti–Vietnam War protests, 9–10, 181, 187, 204, 201, 222, 232–233; in Japan, 86, 156, 171, 193, 197–208, *199*, 210, 214, 219, 235; in the United States, 187, 198–200, *199*, 203, 210–11, 214, 222
Antiwar Student League. *See Hansen Gakusei Dōmei*
ANZUS. *See* Australia, New Zealand and United States Security Treaty
Article 9. *See* Constitution of Japan, Article 9 of
Asahi Shimbun, 48, 174, 176, 196
Association to Defend Democracy with Everyone. *See Minnade Minshu Shugi o Mamorukai*

251

Index

Australia, New Zealand and United States Security Treaty, *ix*, 101

Bandung Conference, 86
Beheiren, *x*, 86, 197–202, 205, 211, 214–15, 217–18, 225n57
Black Panther Party, 209, 211, 217–18, 220–22, 229n151
Bund. *See Bunto*
Bunto, *x*, 56, 64n165, 79, 90, 106, 109–11, 121, 136n154, 140–41
Burger, Vonna, 126

Central Core Faction. *See Chūkaku-ha*
Central Intelligence Agency (CIA), 1, 5, 65, 112, 178
China, 4, 10, 14, 42–43, 50, 66–67, 73–74, 108, 120, 154, 156, 176, 192, 205, 233, 237; American views of, 2, 14, 24, 52, 68, 73, 112, 122, 128–29, 144, 152, 155, 186, 190, 231; "loss" of, 2, 142, 146. *See also* Nationalists (China)
Chūkaku-ha (Central Core Faction), *x*, 188, 191, 193, *195*
CIA. *See* Central Intelligence Agency
Civil Information and Education Section (CIE), 22, 33–34, 43
Cold War, 2–10, 37–40, 42, 62n116, 81, 101–2, 107, 124, 148, 150–52; Japan's role in, 4, 7, 39–40, 75, 115, 143–45, 154–56, 177; US policies and objectives, 1, 3–4, 7, 24–26, 33–34, 39–40, 48, 53, 65–71, 103–4, 139, 142–44, 156, 165, 170–80. *See also* neutrality, in the Cold War
Cominform, 49, 63n122
communism, 118, 190; Japanese students and, 22–23, 25, 39, 51, 56, 79–80, 89, 106, 111, 125, 140, 188, 191, 231
Communism, 79–80, 108, 203, 205, 221; in Japan, 16, 36–39, 42, 48–49, 62n116, 63n122, 66–67, 78–80; Japanese students and, 16, 42–43, 48–49, 54–56, 62n116, 79–81, 89, 110, 175–76, 192
Communist bloc, 24–25, 42, 52, 65–66, 69–70, 176, 179, 191–192
Communist Party (Japan), *ix*, 14, 16, 19, 38, 40, 55–56, 143, 197; American views of, 9, 22, 38, 40, 48, 55, 77, 110, 119, 143; against the revision of the Anpo, 109, 115–16; in Sunagawa protests, 76, 84; internal conflicts of, 49, 56; "lovable" approach of, 48–49; relations with student movement, 48–50, 56, 76, 79, 81, 88–90, 106, 119, 121, 135n140, 141, 174, 188, 190–92, 194, 198, 217
Conference of Modern Japan. *See* Hakone Conference
Congress (US), 22, 80, 102, 128, 144, 147
Constitution of Japan, 8, 68,117, 142; Article 9 of, 8, 68, 90–92, 109, 117

Daigo Fukuryū Maru, 74
Date Akio, 90
democracy, 4, 7–8, 19, 22, 43, 45–47, 50, 69, 76, 89, 113, 116, 124–25, 144, 148, 151, 153, 156, 158, 167, 169–71, 173–79, 181, 194, 231, 237; American, 6–7, 15, 37, 42, 125, 128, 148–49, 166, 170, 174, 181; postwar Japanese, 7–8, 11, 16, 21, 33, 35–38, 40–42, 116, 120–21, 141, 148–49, 157, 201. *See also* democratization
Democratic Party (Japan), 67, 75, 236
Democratic Party (US), 128–129, 165
democratization, 2, 7, 13–18, 20, 27, 33–36, 48–49, 55–56, 155, 157, 231
deserters, 205, 211, 218
Diet, 22, 71, 112–13, 115–16, 119; protests at, 35, 109, 115, 118–21, *123*
Dillon, Clarence Douglas, 102–3
domino theory, 68, 71, 107, 122

Doshisha University, 84, 188
Dulles, John Foster, 67–69, 73–75, 101–4

Eastern bloc. *See* Communist bloc
economic growth, of Japan, 4, 33, 54, 67–70, 89, 102–103, 107, 141, 152, 157–58, 180, 188–90, 196, 199–200, 231–32, 237
education, 7, 22, 39, 43–44, 45, 48, 50–53, 55, 113–14, 126, 129, 143, 166; democratization of, 17, 33, 35–38, 40–41, 46–47
Eells Incident, 7, 40, 41–50, *44–45*, 50–51, 55–56, 177
Eells, Walter Crosby, 7, 33–36, 40–50, *44*, 50, 55, 177
Eisenhower, Dwight D., 51, 69, 80, 88, 93–94n23, 101, 104, 121–122, 124, 125, 142, 146; planned visit to Japan, 117–19, 121–22, 124–25, 127, 142; policies toward Japan, 69–70, 104, 112, 146
Emmerson, John K., 14, 146–47, 180
Europe, 2, 5, 10, 14, 24, 30n48, 63n122, 66, 79, 80, 86, 105, 124, 151–53, 192, 203

factionalism, 6, 165, 188, 190, 197, 233–34
FBI. *See* Federal Bureau of Investigation
February 1st general strike, 14, 20–22
Federal Bureau of Investigation (FBI), 39
Federation of National University Students' Self–Governing Associations. *See* Kokugakuren
Fonda, Jane. *See* Free the Army (FTA)
Free the Army (FTA), *ix*, 211, *214*, 235
FTA. See Free the Army
Fujiyama Aiichiro, 91, 117–19

Gakusei Hyōron (*Student Review*), 42, 47

General Council of Japanese Trade Unions. *See Sōhyō*
Gensuikyō (Japan Council Against Atomic and Hydrogen Weapons), *x*, 192, 197
Germany, *x*, 24, 66, 101, 153, 158, 174, 192–93, 200, 211
GHQ/SCAP (General Headquarters/ Supreme Commander for Allied Power), 2, 7, 13, 16–22, 25, 33–34, 36–38, 43–44, 48, 50, 71, 73. *See also* Civil Information and Education Section (CIE); Government Section, GHQ (GS)
GIs, 203, 209–11, *212–13*, 218–19
Government Section, GHQ (GS), 39
Gromyko, Andrei Andreevich, 108

Hagerty, James, 119, *123*, 124, 135n140, 177
Hakone Conference, 148–49, 161n59
Hall, John Whitney. *See* Hakone Conference
Haneda Airport, 119, 144; protests at, 110–14, 135n140, 194
Hansen Gakusei Dōmei (Antiwar Student League), x, 56, 81, 87, 89, 240
Harriman, Averell, 15, 146
Hatoyama Inchiro, 18, 28n18, 66–67, 69–70, 74–75, 77, 84
Heimin Gakuren (National Student Federation of Student Self-Governing Associations Against Anpo, Defend Peace and Democracy), *x*, 141, 159n10, 192
High Commissioner (HICOM) of Okinawa, 125–127, 215
High-speed economic growth. *See* economic growth
history, 1, 3–6, 8, 10, 34, 50, 86, 102, 106, 148, 158, 166–67, 203, 205, 231, 237; of modern Japan, 107, 140, 149–57
Hokkaido University, 46–48, 84, 121

Homecoming Movement. *See Kikyō Undō*
Hotta Yoshie, 86
House of Un-American Activities (HUAC), *ix*, 42
Hungary, 86, 129; Soviet invasion of, 79, 191
hydrogen bombs, 68, 73; tests at Bikini Atoll, 73–74

Ikeda Hayato, 114–15, 140, 158
Interagency Youth Committee (IAYC), 9, 178–81, 187, 208
International Union of Students (IUS), 47–48, 191–92

Japan Communist Party (JCP). *See* Communist Party (Japan)
Japan Communist Party Sixth National Party Congress. *See Rokuzenkyō*
Japan Council Against Atomic and Hydrogen Weapons. *See Gensuikyō*
Japan Marxist Student League. *See Marugakudō*
Japan Self-Defense Forces, 70, 237
Japan Socialist Party. *See* Socialist Party (Japan)
Japan Technical Committee to aid US Anti-War Deserters (JATEC), *x*, 205, 218
Johnson, Alexis, 207, 209
Johnson, Lyndon B., 178, 181, 204, 206

Kakukyōdō (Revolutionary Communist League), 96n94, 111, 140, 188
Kakumaru-ha (Revolutionary Marxist Faction), *xi*, 188
Kanba Michiko, 120–21, 136n154
Karoji Kentaro, 111
Kennan, George F., 13, 23–27, 142, 147, 152
"Kennedy-Reischauer Offensive," 9, 129, 155, 180, 231
Kennedy, John F., 1, 9, 129, 139, 143, 155, 165, 180–81, 187, 231–32

Kennedy, Robert F., 204; visit to Japan, 165–179, *171–72*, 181; wife of, 168, 176–77
Khrushchev, Nikita, 79, 127
Kikyō Undō (Homecoming Movement), *x*, 141.
Kishi Nobusuke, 9, 75, 91, 104, 107, 110–12, 114–117, 119–22, 124, 127, 140, 146
Koenaki Koe no Kai (Voiceless Voices), *xi*, 197
Kokugakuren (Federation of National University Students' Self–Governing Associations), *xi*, 35–36
Korea, 2, 38, 66, 156; North Korea, 128, 237; South Korea, 4, 11n11, 53, 66, 122, 124, 129, 139, 152–54, 170, 175–76, 179, 189–91, 197, 200, 231
Korean minority in Japan, 35, 38, 190
Korean War, 2, 8, 38–39, 53–54, 62n1116, 65–68, 70–71, 73, 89, 103
Koyama Kenichi, 56, 76, 97n101, 106
Kurihara Toichi. *See* Ota Ryu
Kuroda Hirokazu. *See* Kuroda Kanichi
Kuroda Kanichi, 79–80
Kyōsandō (Communist League), xi, 89, 140, 188
Kyoto University, 28n18, 36, 41, 54, 84, 154–156, 161n59, 196, 203, 215
Kyushu University, 45, 84, 207

labor and labor unions, 3, 5, 8, 13, 16–22, 34–35, 38, 53, 71, 76–78, 81, 88, 96n72, 106, 109, 112, 118–20, 127, 147, 166, 168, 175, 189, 206–7, 221
Latin America, 104–5, 122, 128, 139, 149, 175–76, 231
League of Socialist Youth of Japan. *See Shaseidō*
Liberal Democratic Party (LDP), 112–16, 121, 141, 196

MacArthur, Douglas II., 90–91, 110–11, 113–19, *123*, 128–29, 141, 146

MacArthur, Douglas, 1–2, 13–15, 19, 21–22, 35, 38, 40, 50, 129, 142, 145–46
Marshall Plan, 13, 24
Marugakudō (Japan Marxist Student League), *xi*, 141
Maruyama Masao, 116, 148, 157, 161n59
Marxism, 9, 14–16, 28n18, 46, 54–55, 127, 148–49, 154, 156–157, 179, 199, 221; Japanese students and, 15–16, 50, 54–55, 79–80, 89–90, 106, 141, 150, 158, 181, 188, 193, 198, 201–2, 217, 222, 231; Reischauer's challenge to, 139–40, 147, 149, 151, 153, 168, 231–32; RFK's challenge to, 165–68, 177
McCarthyism, 21, 146, 170
Middle East, 80–81, 124
military bases, 3–4, 8, 10, 50–52, 65–66, 68–71, 76–79, 82, 84, 86–87, 92, 103, 112, 115, 122, 125, 127, 170, 197, 204–205, 209–10, 215, 217, 219–20, 222, 232–37. *See also* Tachikawa Air Base
Mills, C. Wright, 127–28
Ministry of Education (Japan), 28n18, 33, 35–37, 50, 113–14, 126
Minnade Minshu Shugi o Mamorukai (Association to Defend Democracy with Everyone), *xi*, 141
Mitsui Miike Coal Mine, 106
modernization theory, 139–40, 148–49, 151–58, 167, 231–32
Morita Minoru, 56, 76, 81, 97n101, 106
Mountain-Village operation (JCP-directed), 56, 81

Nakasone Yasuhiro, 168
National Committee Faction of the Revolutionary Communist League. *See Kakukyōdō*

National Federation of Private University Students Self–Government Associations. *See Shigakuren*
National Liaison Council Against the Military Bases. *See Zenkoku Gunji Kichi Hantai Renraku Kaigi*
National Security Council (NSC), *ix*, 27, 65, 67–70
National Student Federation of Student Self-Governing Associations Against Anpo, Defend Peace and Democracy. *See Heimin Gakuren*
nationalism, 39, 41–42, 50, 69, 80–81, 85–87, 93–94n23, 104, 150, 152,191, 238n14
Nationalists (China), 24, 107
North Atlantic Treaty Organization (NATO), *ix*, 101
neutrality, in the Cold War, 22, 68–70, 75, 90, 107–8, 112, 115, 122, 127–29, 142, 144, 175, 191–92, *194*
New Frontier, 165–66, 168, 176
New Left, 5–6, 193, 127–28, 166, 193, 198, 201–3, 208
The New York Times, 21, 48, 78, 111–12, 121–22, 124–25, 177, 205, 207
Newton, Heuy P., 211, 221
Niigata University, 40–41, 84
Nixon, Richard, 10, 104–5, 122, 128–29, 233
normalization treaty between Japan and South Korea, 171, 188–91
Nosaka Sanzo, 14, 49
nuclear bombs and weapons, 46, 74, 88, 170, 191–92, *194*; fear of, 8, 22, 68–69, 73, 85, 88, 206; protests against 74, 170, 191–92, *194*, 201, 217, 219

occupation: of Japan, 1–2, 6–7, 13–14, 16–17, 19–24, 26, 33, 35–36, 38–42,

44, 47–49, 53, 56, 70–71, 75–76, 103, 111, 141, 145, 147; of Okinawa, 10, 26, 65–66, 75–76, 80, 104, 110, 197, 125–27, 142, 177, 197, 204, 214–15, *216*, 217, 232–33
Oda Makoto, 197–99, 202, 214, 218
Okinawa, 4, 10, 26, 66, 68, 75–76, 80, 83, 97, 104, 110, 125–27, 170, 171, 173, 192, 215, 233–37; anti–Vietnam War protests in, 200, 210, 211, 214, 219, 222, 235; black liberation movement in, 217–220; reversion of, 170, 173, 196, 215, 217, 234. *See also* occupation, of Okinawa
Operations Coordinating Board, 70
Ota Ryu, 80, 112–13

Passin, Herbert, 149–50
Peace for Vietnam! Committee. *See Beheiren*
peace treaty, 15, 26, 53, 66
People's Council to Stop the Revised Security Treaty (*Anpo Kaitei Soshi Kokumin Kaigi*), *x*, 108–9, 118
Philippines, 27, 69, 121–22, 197, 200, 211, *213*
police, 19, 26–27, 39–40, 53, 176, 230; mobilized against protestors and activists, 44, 47, 50–51, *51–52*, 76–78, 84–86, 88, 109, 111, 113–16, 118–22, *194*, 206, 209, 217–19, 222, 233, 236
Procurement Agency, 71, 73–74, 78, 83, 85–86
purge, 18, 23, 33, 39; wartime, 17, 42. *See also* red purge

Radford Plan, 103
rearmament, 7, 68, 70, 89, 146
Red Army. *See Sekigun*
red purge, 20, 22, 38–43, 45–47, 49, 54–55
Reischauer, Edwin O., 9, 129, 139–58, *145*, 205, 231; appointment of, 9, 129, 139, 142–146; as ambassador, 144–58, 179; background of, 144; during RFK's visit to Japan, 168–69, 174–75; wife of, 144–45, *145*
Republican Party (US), 22, 129, 158, 231
Revolutionary Marxist Faction. *See Kakumaru-ha*
Robertson, Walter S., 71, 75, 102, 104
Rokuzenkyō (Japan Communist Party Sixth National Party Congress) of, xi, 56, 79
Rostow, Walt, 149, 155, 167, 193–94, 196, 206
Rusk, Dean, 53, 144, 178, 208
Ryukyu University Students' Association (RUSA), *ix*, 110, 125–26
Ryukyu. *See* Okinawa

SANE Nuclear Policy (SANE), *ix*, 201
Sanpa Rengō (Triple Alliance of Zengakuren), *xi*, 141, 188, 207
SCAP. See GHQ/SCAP
Schlesinger, Arthur Jr., 166–69
SDS. *See* Socialist German Student Union for German SDS, Students for a Democratic Society for American SDS
Sebald, William J., 22, 38
Sekigun (Red Army), *xi*, 221–22, 233
Shagakudō (Socialist Student League), *xi*, 89, 141, 188, 190
Shaseidō (League of Socialist Youth of Japan), *xi*, 141, 188
Shigemitsu Mamoru, 67, 75–76, 84
Shima Shigeo, 56, 89, 97n101, 106
Shimizu Ikutaro, 81, 86, 93
SIB. *See* Special Investigation Bureau
Sino-Soviet relations, 2, 112, 192
SNCC. *See* Student Nonviolent Coordinating Committee
Socialist German Student Union (SDS), *x*, 193, 203
Socialist Party (Japan), *ix*, 20, 76–78, 82, *83*, 84, 88, 96n72, 109, 115, 168, 176

Socialist Student League. See *Shagakudō*
Sōhyō (General Council of Japanese Trade Unions), xi, 77–78, 88, 96n72, 106, 109
Southeast Asia Treaty Organization (SEATO), *x*, 101
Southeast Asia, 101, 107, 152, 154–55, 204
Soviet Union, 3, 14, 46, 48, 63n122, 73, 79, 84, 89, 102, 108, 120–21, 127–29, 153, 176; American views of, 13–15, 21, 23, 26–27, 35, 40, 52, 67, 102–3, 105, 112, 129, 178–79; nuclear testing of, 191, *194*,
Special Investigation Bureau (SIB), 39, 51
Spring Mobilization Committee to End the War in Vietnam, 203
Stalin, 79, 90, 105
Stalinism, 42, 49, 79–80, 87, 90, 111, 191, 193, *194*, 198
Student Nonviolent Coordinating Committee (SNCC), *x*, 198, 200–3, 214
Student Peace Union, *x*, 192
Student Review. See *Gakusei Hyōron*
Students for a Democratic Society (SDS), *x*, 198, 201–3
students, female, 17, 83, 85, 120, 173
Study Group of the US-Japan Security Treaty Problems. See *Anpo Mondai Kenkyū Kai*
Suez crisis, 80, 83, 129
Sunagawa, *xi*, 65, 71–73, *72*; anti-base protests in, 3–4, 8, 56, 66, 69, 73–78, 80–88, 90–92, 103, 105–6, 110, 156, 207; court case, 90–91, 108–9
Supreme Court (Japan), 22, 91–92, 108

Tachikawa Air Base, 8, 56, 66, 70, 71, *72*, 73–74, 76–78, *83*, 84–85, *86*, 88, 104, 197, 207
Taft-Hartley Act, 22
Takei Teruo, 16, 35, 37, 47, 51, 56

Takeuchi Yoshimi, 116
teachers, 16–17, 20, 29n43, 38, 220
The National Student Federation of Student Self-Governing Associations Against Anpo, Defend Peace and Democracy. See *Heimin Gakurein*
Third World, 7, 168, 187, 208, 214, 221; Japanese students and, 80–81, 88, 170, 200, 222; US policies toward, 2, 69, 93–94n23, 156
Tohoku University, 43–46, *44–45*, 46, 48–49
trade, 24–25, 33, 67, 102, 112, 141–42, 189–90, 196, 200
Triple Alliance of Zengakuren. See *Sanpa Rengō*
Truman, Harry S, 22–24, 27, 43, 53; Doctrine, 13, 19
Tsurumi Shunsuke, 116, 197
Tsurumi Yoshiyuki, 198
Turkey, 122, 124, 139, 179

University of Tokyo, 18, 41, 49, *51–52*, 54, 56, 81, *83*, 89, 109, 114, 120–21, 126, 148–49, 155–56, 161n59
US Air Force, 70, 112
US Army Ryukyu Islands (USARYIS), *x*, 110, 125–26, 215, 217
US Army, 10, 53, 103, 110, 112, 125, 197, 206–7
US Civil Administration of the Ryukyu Islands (USCAR), *x*, 10, 110, 126, 127, 215, *216*, 219
US Department of Defense, 53, 67, 75, 178
US Department of State, 14, 23–24, 34, 71, 73, 75, 102, 104, 112, 115, 117, 143–44, 146–47, 152, 166, 178–80, 193, 209; Policy Planning Staff of, 23, 26; reports to, 14, 54–55, 109, 111, 113, 168, 174, 207–8, 223, 232, 234
US-Japan Security Treaty of 1951, 52–53, 66, 70, 73, 75, 85–86, 90–92; of 1960, 115–16, 196–97, 218

revision of, 101, 103–4, 107, 114–16, 124. *See also* anti-*Anpo* protests
US Navy, 103, 112, 205–6

veterans, *x*, 35, 201, 210
Vietnam Day Committee (VDC), *x*, 198, *199*, 201
Vietnam War, 1–2, 5, 50, 66, 68, 165, 181, 187, 189–190, 193, 196–207, 232–33. *See also* anti–Vietnam War protests
Vietnam, 1–2, 4–5, 50, 66, 68, 156, 170, 181, 189–90, 193. *See also* Vietnam War
Voiceless Voices. See *Koenaki Koe no Kai*

War Resisters League (WRL), *x*, 201
Warsaw Pact, 68
Waseda Universiyty, 18, 42, 49–50, 81, 120, 201; RFK's visit to, 169–75, *171–72*
Washington Post, 85, 102
World War II, 14–17, 19, 36–37, 39, 41, 107, 143, 146, 152, 155; impacts of, 1–3, 18, 27, 35; memory of, 6, 16, 18, 43–44, 50, 68, 73, 84, 114; post–, 3–4, 7–9, 11, 15, 17,19, 22–26, 33–34, 55, 80–81, 102, 116, 124–25, 1227, 129, 141, 144, 157, 174, 201, 237

Yomiuri Shimbun, 19–20, 77–78, 82, 88, 119, 121, 157, 222
Yoshida Shigeru, 18–20, 25, 37–38, 49, 67, 71, 114–15
Yoshikawa Mitsusada. *See* SIB
Young Socialist Alliance (YSA), 122

Zainichi Koreans. *See* Korean minority in Japan
Zengakuren, *xi–xii*, 1, 4, 6, 16, 27, 66, 74, 80, 92, 125, 156, 181, 192, 198, 223, 231–32, *239–38*; against nuclear testing, 191–92, *194*; American views of, 40, 43, 109–114, 119, 122, 126, 129, 202, 209, 215, 217, 231; authorities against, 38, 40, 50–52, *51–52*, 113–14, 120; creation of, 7, 17–18; during RFK's visit to Japan, 9, 156, 169, 173–175, 177; factionalism and internal conflicts of, 56, 121, 140–41 165, 177, 188, 190–92, 209; in anti-Anpo protests, 8, 56, 101–2, 105–14, 118–22, *123*, 126, 188; in democratizing movement, 18, 27, 35–38; in protests against the normalization treaty between Japan and Korea, 188, 190–191; in protests against the red purge and the Eells Statement, 33, 40–43, 45–50, 55–56; in protests against the US occupation of Okinawa, 214–215; in protests against the Vietnam War, 198–203, 205–7, 209, 214, 222; in Sunagawa protests, 76–76, 79, 81–84, *83*, 86–88; internationalism of, 190–193, 198–202, 222; National Convention of, 36, 42–43, 50, 81, 87, 89, 106; relations with JCP, 48–50, 56, 76, 79, 88–89, 106, 141, 143, 188, 192
Zenkoku Gunji Kichi Hantai Renraku Kaigi (National Liaison Council Against the Military Bases), *xii*, 79
Zinn, Howard, 193, 200–1

About the Author

Naoko Koda is associate professor in the international studies department at Kindai University, Osaka, and a contributor to *Media and Revolt: Strategies and Performances from the 1960s to the Present* (2014) and *The Routledge Handbook of the Global Sixties: Between Protest and Nation* (2019).

www.ingramcontent.com/pod-product-compliance
Lightning Source LLC
Chambersburg PA
CBHW050901300426
44111CB00010B/1327